Enrique Granados

ENRIQUE GRANADOS

ENRIQUE GRANADOS

Poet of the Piano

WALTER AARON CLARK

OXFORD
UNIVERSITY PRESS

2006

OXFORD
UNIVERSITY PRESS

Oxford University Press, Inc., publishes works that further
Oxford University's objective of excellence
in research, scholarship, and education.

Oxford   New York
Auckland   Cape Town   Dar es Salaam   Hong Kong   Karachi
Kuala Lumpur   Madrid   Melbourne   Mexico City   Nairobi
New Delhi   Shanghai   Taipei   Toronto

With offices in
Argentina   Austria   Brazil   Chile   Czech Republic   France   Greece
Guatemala   Hungary   Italy   Japan Poland   Portugal   Singapore
South Korea   Switzerland   Thailand   Turkey   Ukraine   Vietnam

Copyright © 2006 by Oxford University Press, Inc.

Published by Oxford University Press, Inc.
198 Madison Avenue, New York, New York 10016
www.oup.com

Library of Congress Cataloging-in-Publication Data
Clark, Walter Aaron.
Enrique Granados : poet of the piano / Walter Aaron Clark ;
foreword by Alicia de Larrocha.
p.   cm.
Includes bibliographical references and indexes.
ISBN-13 978-0-19-514066-8
ISBN 0-19-514066-4
1. Granados, Enrique, 1867–1916.
2. Composers—Spain—Biography.   I. Title.
ML410.G763C53 2005
780′.92—dc22
[B]   2004063648

2   4   6   8   9   7   5   3   1

Printed in the United States of America
on acid-free paper

To Granados's daughter
Natalia Granados y Gal,
her husband,
Dr. Antoni Carreras i Verdaguer,
and their son Antoni Carreras i Granados

In gratitude for keeping the flame of Granados's music alive
and making books such as this one possible

His strangely vivid music pursues you like certain perfumes,
more persistent than strong.

Claude Debussy

FOREWORD

The first notes that I learned to play on the piano and that I presented in my first public recital were those of "The Afternoon Bell" from *Sketches*, which Enrique Granados had written for the students at his music academy and which I learned from his foremost disciple, Frank Marshall.

My musical and pianistic formation followed the pedagogic model that Granados had created and that my mother and aunt also learned as his direct disciples. It was they who introduced me to the piano and led me to maestro Marshall. As I matured musically and personally, I immersed myself in Granados's piano compositions, which form a major part of the foundation of modern Spanish music. My identification with his artistic temperament and his musical sensibility has profoundly influenced my career, and as often as I could, I have tried to familiarize the world with his music.

The spirit of Granados is inextricably bound up with European Romanticism, with an adoration of Schumann, and with the soul of Spain's immemorial folkloric traditions, which the composers of his generation discovered and which he knew how to transform with his instinctive musical genius.

The life and work of this great composer demand an exhaustive and detailed study, and I congratulate Walter Aaron Clark and Oxford University Press for making this biography a reality and thereby contributing to the preservation of Granados's music for succeeding generations.

Alicia de Larrocha
(trans. Walter Aaron Clark)

ACKNOWLEDGMENTS

Samuel Johnson once observed that "a certain degree of reputation is acquired merely by approving the works of genius, and testifying a regard to the memory of authours." Granados affords any biographer seeking "reputation" plenty of genius for this purpose. Thus, it is surprising to me that no English-speaking author has ever written a book-length account of his life and music, and that the most recent substantial biography of him in any language—by Antonio Fernández-Cid, in Spanish—is now a half century old and out of date.

No one has done more for Granados scholarship than the American piano virtuoso and musicologist Douglas Riva, through his exhaustive research, his editions, his performances, and his recordings. Yet, in 1981 he complained to *The El Paso Times* (September 19, 1-C) that there was a "desperate need" for a Granados biography. Although encouraged by musicologists to tackle the job himself, Riva explained that he was "not a writer. I am a pianist." Ten years elapsed before the appearance of Carol Hess's groundbreaking bio-bibliography of Granados for Greenwood Press. She was certainly then in a position to follow up with a full-fledged biography but instead chose to devote herself to the study of Manuel de Falla. Twenty years after Riva's complaint, at the beginning of his entry on Granados in *The New Grove Dictionary of Music and Musicians* (2d ed.), Mark Larrad lamented that *still* "no detailed study has been made of his life." Why he, a leading Granados scholar, did not undertake the task himself I do not know. Almost ninety years after the composer's death, the time has at last arrived for an in-depth examination of Granados's life and music that meets the standards of modern musicological scholarship. I could not have written this book without considerable help, however, and I gratefully recognize below the many institutions and individuals who have assisted me in my work.

Alicia de Larrocha has been a dominant figure in the piano world for over half a century, and she has dedicated her life to promoting the music of her native land, especially that of Granados. She has perhaps done more than any other pianist to bring the music of Spanish composers to the public's awareness, through her thousands of concerts and many recordings. I am deeply grateful to her for consenting to write the foreword to this book, for her family has a close connection to the composer. Her mother and aunt were students of Granados, and she herself became a pupil of Granados's successor, Frank Marshall.

It was Marshall, of Catalan birth but English ancestry, who took over the Acadèmia Granados in Barcelona after the founder's death, and whose name the Academy bears today. My research there was made pleasurable not only by the elegant surroundings but also by the friendly and expert assistance of Eva Gomà, archivist, and by the cooperation of Alicia Torra, daughter of Alicia de Larrocha. Closely associated with the Academy is the brilliant journalist and music historian Mónica Pagès, who provided invaluable guidance to me.

The most important collection of Granados materials is the Museu de la Música in Barcelona. The competence and industry of Romà Escalas and his staff, especially Judit Bombardó and Imma Cuscó, made the difference between success and failure in my research. I also extend my gratitude to Barcelona's Registro Civil and the Centre de Documentació Musical, especially director Nuria Potrell and her assistant Montserrat, for their cooperation in locating and sharing with me their materials. The Biblioteca de Catalunya, Arxiu Històric de la Ciutat (Hemeroteca), Arxiu Municipal, Arxiu Administratiu de la Ciutat, Centre de Documentació i Museu de les Arts Escèniques de L'Institut del Teatre, and Serveis Funeraris also merit thanks for their patient help. Of outstanding assistance was the Archivo del Obispado, in particular Sister Felicidad and Joaquím Mora Estrada, for service above and beyond their actual responsibilities. I am likewise indebted to the Archivo General Militar de Segovia for its assistance in finding and supplying me with records of military service for Granados's grandfather, father, and brother. I am grateful to Editorial Boileau for permission to excerpt passages from DLR.

Madrid is another important locale for Granados research. I am grateful to the Dirección General de Personal y Pensiones Públicas, in particular Rosa Verge Prades and her capable staff. Antonio Gil at the Sociedad General de Autores y Editores made documents available to me in a most friendly and collegial fashion, as did the staff of the Biblioteca Nacional. My good friend Dr. Jacinto Torres has yet again come to the rescue, this time with original research concerning the 1903 composition competition at the Conservatorio Real, which Granados won. I thank him for sharing it in advance of its publication, and for his insights into the complexities of Spanish history and culture.

In the United States, New York is a major repository of archival materials. I benefited enormously from the highly professional support of the Hispanic Society of America, the Pierpont Morgan Library, the archive of the Metropolitan Opera, and the New York Public Library. I also wish to extend thanks to Niel Shell, grandson of the noted American musician Nathanial Shilkret, for sharing with me Granados manuscripts in his family's possession. He has graciously made available for publication two compositions thought lost or incomplete. Oxford University Press merits kudos for its ongoing interest in Hispanic subjects and encouragement of books such as this. Maribeth Anderson Payne (now at Norton) contracted this biography, and her successor as senior music editor, Kim Robinson, was wonderfully patient and helpful. I also appreciate Robert Milks's fine work in the editing and production of this book.

Douglas Riva has shared with me his entire archive and library, as well as his counsel, and has been of invaluable assistance. His passionate dedication to Granados is a continuing source of inspiration to me, and I appreciate his encouragement and moral support more than mere words can convey. Besides Riva, two other Americans have provided me not only with assistance but motivation. Carol Hess's bio-bibliography has been of immense help, as have been her ideas and the example of her own work. She lent me her research notes and photocopies, which saved me untold hours of difficult labor. John Milton, my fellow Minnesotan, has done commendably detailed research on Granados and has written an engrossing novel based on the life of the Spanish composer, entitled *The Fallen Nightingale* (Swan Books). He and I have had many fruitful exchanges, and I have benefited from his impressive archive of Granados materials and openhanded sharing of information, especially concerning the sinking of the *Sussex*. All three scholars gave this manuscript a close critical reading and made excellent suggestions.

Jay Batzner at the University of Missouri, Kansas City, merits thanks for his prompt and accurate typesetting of musical examples. I am indebted to Luis Cortest at the University of Oklahoma for useful bibliographic guidance, and to John Koegel at California State University, Fullerton, for a thorough vetting of the proofs. At the University of California, Riverside, I am very grateful to Ruth Cabré Chacón for her timely assistance in translating certain difficult passages in Catalan, and to Bart Kats and Leo Schouest for help with indispensable technological hindrances such as computers and scanners.

Research support came from the National Endowment for the Humanities in the form of a summer stipend. Additional support was provided by a fellowship and travel grant from the Hall Center for the Humanities at the University of Kansas, a General Research Fund award and sabbatical leave from KU, and a grant from the Program for Cultural Cooperation between Spain's Ministry of Education, Culture, and Sports and United States' Universities. The University of California, Riverside, also provided generous research funding and release time.

As ever, I deeply appreciate the support and patience of my family, wife Nancy, son Robert, and mother-in-law Grace Golden. I am not always easy to live with when a project like this is weighing on my mind night and day, and they have contributed more than they know to its completion.

I close here with something I found among Carol Hess's research notes from 1989, an inspiring bit of marginalia that I continue to savor: "My motivation: to learn more about the creator of *Goyescas*." That, rather than "reputation," has been and continues to be my motivation as well.

CONTENTS

ABBREVIATIONS

Ag	Archivo Granados, Barcelona (most of this is now in the Mm, fons Granados; the rest remains with the family)
Agm	Archivo General Militar, Segovia
Am	Archive of the Acadèmia Marshall, Barcelona
Bc	Biblioteca de Catalunya, Barcelona
Bn	Biblioteca Nacional, Madrid
Cdm	Centre de Documentació Musical, Barcelona
DLR	De Larrocha/Riva Critical Edition of Granados's Piano Music: *Integral para piano de E. Granados*. Barcelona: Editorial Boileau, 2002.
DME	*Diccionario de la música española e hispanoamericana*. Ed. Emilio Casares. Madrid: Sociedad General de Autores y Editores, 1999–2002.
Lcw	Library of Congress, Washington, D.C.
Es	Archive of Éditions Salabert, Paris
Gs	Archive of G. Schirmer, New York
Hsa	Hispanic Society of America, New York
Mm	Museu de la Música, Barcelona
NGD (2d)	*The New Grove Dictionary of Music and Musicians*. 2d ed. Ed. Stanley Sadie. London: Macmillan, 2001.
Ns	Nathaniel Shilkret Archive, New York
Oc	Biblioteca del Orfeó Català, Barcelona
Pml	Pierpont Morgan Library, New York
Ra	Douglas Riva Archive, Albuquerque
Sa	Ernest Schelling Archive, University of Maryland, College Park
Sgae	Sociedad General de Autores y Editores, Madrid

FRANCE

Figueras
(Figueres)

VASCONGADAS

Santander

LA
CORUÑA

ASTURIAS

SANTANDER

GERONA
(GIRONA)

PONTEVEDRA

LUGO

LEÓN

NAVARRA

Olot

ORENSE

PALENCIA

BURGOS

LOGROÑO

HUESCA

LÉRIDA
(LLEIDA)

Gerona

ZAMORA

VALLADOLID

SORIA

Zaragoza

Lérida

BARCELONA

Vilafranca

Barcelona

SEGOVIA

ZARAGOZA

TARRAGONA

Sitges

PORTUGAL

SALAMANCA

ÁVILA

GUADALAJARA

MADRID

Madrid

TERUEL

CASTELLÓN

MALLORCA

Palma

CÁCERES

TOLEDO

CUENCA

VALENCIA

Valencia

d

BADAJOZ

CIUDAD REAL

ALBACETE

VALENCIA

ALICANTE

CÓRDOBA

JAÉN

Murcia

HUELVA

MURCIA

SEVILLA

GRANADA

ALMERÍA

Sanlúcar de
Barrameda

MÁLAGA

CÁDIZ

0   50   100 km

Enrique Granados

Renaissance

Song and tale is poetry.
One sings a living history,
telling its melody.

"De mi cartera"
Nuevas canciones
Antonio Machado (1875–1939)

In the Nelson-Atkins Museum of Art in Kansas City hangs a portrait by Francisco Goya of Don Ignacio O'Mulryan y Rourera, and the curatorial commentary alongside it declares with breathtaking self-assurance that between Goya and Picasso, Spanish art descended into "bourgeois mediocrity." There is a lot of ideological baggage in such a view. The automatic linking of the bourgeoisie with mediocrity strikes an especially curious note. For, were not the art, literature, and music of the nineteenth century molded by the tastes of the bourgeoisie that patronized them? In particular, are we prepared to dismiss all Spanish paintings between the royally commissioned works of Goya and the modernistic creations of Picasso as tainted by mediocrity? Obviously, some of us are.

Even around 1900, there was disdain for Spanish artists in Spain itself, particularly those who gained popularity. As one journalist noted:

> The critics in general were hard on painters who actually made money. Moreover, insofar as the only people buying pictures were from the upper middle class, successful artists were said to have "sold out" to the bourgeoisie. Be this as it may, those same patrons also bought the paintings of Picasso, who could charge whatever price he liked. Is it possible that the bourgeoisie was intelligent when it bought one kind of painting and stupid when it bought something different?[1]

Robert Hughes summed this situation up perfectly: "The idea that the *avant-garde* and the bourgeoisie were natural enemies is one of the least useful myths of modernism."[2]

And, in fact, the curator's statement is inaccurate. It is true that during the middle decades of the century, there were no Spanish artists of international stature. But then the situation began to change rather dramatically. Joaquín Sorolla was a pre-Picasso painter who was among the most eminent and celebrated artists in Europe and America around 1900. Anyone who has savored the canvases of Santiago Rusiñol or Ramon Casas (and Picasso was among their admirers) knows that they are anything but mediocre. Other names could be added to the list, including those of Ignacio Zuloaga and Darío de Regoyos, who were both influenced by Impressionism.[3]

In the latter part of the nineteenth century and the first years of the twentieth, Spaniards were busy excelling in many areas, which a simple exercise in name-dropping will demonstrate. Architects Antoni Gaudí and Lluís Domènech i Montaner; novelists Juan Valera, Vicente Blasco Ibáñez, Benito Pérez Galdós, and Pedro Antonio de Alarcón; poets Gustavo Adolfo Bécquer and Antonio Machado; philosophers José Ortega y Gasset, Miguel de Unamuno, and Marcelino Menéndez y Pelayo; and playwrights Joaquín Dicenta and José Echagaray gained considerable celebrity, in and outside of Spain. Although fragmented politically like the country itself, the press also flourished, and many leading artists and writers contributed their illustrations and essays to the newspapers and journals of Barcelona, Madrid, and other cities. In the capital city alone there were dozens of newspapers and periodicals to meet the needs of an increasingly literate and engaged populace.[4]

And in music? Many names come to mind, especially the composer, teacher, and musicologist Felip Pedrell (1841–1922), about whom more will be said later, and Francisco Asenjo Barbieri (1823–94), who advanced Spanish musicology in his seminal *Cancionero musical de los siglos XV y XVI* (1890) and promoted the revival of the zarzuela (Spanish operetta), authoring such hits as *Jugar con fuego* (1851) and *El barberillo de Lavapiés* (1874). But foremost among Spanish musicians ca. 1900 were Isaac Albéniz (1860–1909)[5] and the subject of this study, Enrique Granados (1867–1916). They were representatives in music of a larger renaissance in Spanish arts and letters during their lifetimes, a surge of creativity sustained by the patronage of the very bourgeoisie our Kansas City curator mistakenly associated with mediocrity.

Snobbery toward bourgeois taste in art and music was a byproduct of this class's increasing wealth and power in the latter part of the nineteenth century. To be sure, the bourgeoisie was not then the largest class in Spain, and neither was it monolithic.[6] In addition to entrepreneurs, among its most prominent members in Spanish society were intellectuals, civil servants, and military officers.[7] It was from this class that both Albéniz (civil service) and Granados (military) came, and into which they married, as both their wives were daughters of prosperous businessmen. It was primarily the bourgeoisie for whom they wrote and performed their music, and from which they received their support. For instance, Granados benefited throughout his career from the largesse of entrepreneurs and doctors. The royal family gave him honors, but his bourgeois patrons gave him what he needed most: money.

In truth, it was this middle class from which the vast majority of the artists, architects, and authors invoked above came. This only stands to reason. Artsy professions were *déclassé* for the progeny of the upper crust, while the very poor struggled simply to survive and rarely had access to the education or the means and time to pursue such a vocation. Granados himself said, shortly before his death, "When I travel by train, I derive the greatest satisfaction from the fact that my fellow passengers take me for a businessman."[8] How bourgeois!

Perhaps our curator simply meant "mediocre" in the sense that Spanish art (and music) was not on a par with contemporary work in France (or Germany). That may well have been true, and the explanation is not hard to divine. The nineteenth century was an epoch of disasters for Spain, and this had a pronounced impact on the country's culture.[9] The century began with the invasion of Spain by Napoleon in 1808 and the installation of his brother on the Spanish throne. Whatever sympathy Spaniards had had for the French evaporated in the heat of widespread rebellion. The nation plunged into a war that was nasty, brutish, and protracted, lasting until 1814. The French invaded again in 1823, to restore the despotic regime of Fernando VII, an anti-liberal reactionary.

After the death of Fernando VII in 1833, the country experienced an intermittent civil war that went on for decades. The so-called Carlist Wars were fought between rival parties claiming the Spanish throne, namely, those who wanted Fernando's brother Carlos to be their king, and the supporters of Fernando's wife and daughter, María Cristina and Isabel II. The fundamental conflict was not so much between personalities, however, as it was between competing visions of Spain's future, between a backward-looking, isolationist view, and a more liberal outlook receptive to progressive trends elsewhere in Europe. Carlism was an "ultra-Catholic, agrarian creed" that appealed to regionalist sensibilities in the north of Spain, especially the Basque country and Catalonia.[10] The Castilian court, naturally, sought to exert its authority and maintain national unity.

As the Carlist conflict subsided toward the end of the century, the curse of anarchism descended on the country, particularly Catalonia. In 1893, anarchist Paulina Pallás hurled two bombs under the horse of General Martínez Campos during a military parade, nearly killing him. Pallás's execution was avenged only a few weeks later, on November 7, by a bomb in the Gran Teatre del Liceu in Barcelona, during a performance of Rossini's *William Tell*. Planted by Santiago Salvador, it killed and injured scores of people; Salvador was executed the following year. In 1896, yet another bomb went off, during a Corpus Christi procession, taking a grievous toll in maimed and lifeless bodies. These attacks reached their climax when strongman Antonio Cánovas del Castillo (b. 1828), premier of the Spanish government and leader of the conservative faction, was assassinated in August 1897 by Catalan anarchists. Not yet content with this slaughter, anarchists made an attempt on Antonio Maura, a later Spanish premier, in April 1904, and on King Alfonso XIII himself, in Paris a year later. All of this mayhem exhibits a dreary similarity to the terrorist attacks and suicide bombings of our own time.

The growing prosperity of the bourgeoisie was, in fact, inextricably connected to this violence. Catalan industry, for instance, depended on cheap labor from outside the region, and immigrants streamed into Barcelona from around the country in search of work in the city's burgeoning industrial sector. But as the ranks of the urban proletariat swelled, the socialist and anarchist movements gained in strength; labor unrest increased, culminating in the riots, destruction, and bloodshed of the Setmana

Tràgica ("Tragic Week") in July 1909. This began as a protest against military conscription for the war in Morocco but was fueled by simmering labor discontent and fanned by anarchist agitators, some of whom were later executed.[11] Anti-clerical sentiment ran high among the Left, who viewed the Church as the ally of the bourgeoisie, and no fewer than seventy convents and churches were destroyed during the riots.

The center of the country was not immune to upheaval either. The Revolution of 1868, led by General Juan Prim, sent the monarchy packing and led to a short-lived Republic. The royal family eventually returned from exile in Paris, inaugurating the Bourbon Restoration that lasted from 1874 to 1931. But the very institution of the monarchy had been undermined, and the pattern of military intervention in the affairs of government would bedevil Spanish politics for decades to come.[12] At any rate, the regime of Alfonso XII and his successors, María Cristina (the Queen Regent) and Alfonso XIII, was characterized by a conservative and even oppressive political atmosphere in which Cánovas encouraged an isolationist *Weltanschauung*, exaggerated Spain's global importance, and promoted a sort of xenophobic *españolismo*. Many artists and musicians, especially Albéniz, who went into self-imposed exile in Paris, found these developments deeply disturbing. As Ann Livermore has observed, the nineteenth century in Spain exhibited "an uninspiring lack of greatness in public life."[13]

And there were other problems. Spain lost most of its empire during the 1820s in the wake of the Peninsular War against Napoleon, as the American colonies used that window of opportunity to gain their independence from the mother country. In the space of a few years, Mexico, Peru, Venezuela, and almost all of Spain's other possessions in the western hemisphere went their own way. Spain did retain its grip on the Caribbean, but the year 1898 added insult to injury as Cuba and Puerto Rico, not to mention the Philippines and Guam, departed from the Spanish sphere as a result of the Spanish-American War. All that was left of a once immense empire were some territories in Africa, which became more of a burden than a boon.

In addition to spectacular events such as coups d'état, wars, riots, invasions, and assassinations, the daily reality for many Spaniards was one of poverty, illiteracy, inefficiency, and stagnation.[14] Given the manifold political, military, economic, and social dislocations of the nineteenth and early twentieth centuries in Spain, it seems ironic that a robust revival of the country's cultural life would take place at the apparent low point of its national fortunes. However, the Industrial Revolution gradually provided Spain with the means to generate for itself the bounty it had previously been content to take by force from the New World. This accounts for the simultaneity of imperial demise and cultural florescence, the latter depending on new, internal sources of wealth other than royal or ecclesiastical patronage. However, such wealth was unevenly distributed throughout the country.[15]

The florescence was especially pronounced in Barcelona because it was an industrial and commercial powerhouse intent on establishing itself as a major cultural center.[16] In music, native musical theater experienced a comeback after over a century of living in the shadow of Italian opera, while virtuoso instrumentalists such as Albéniz, Granados, and Pablo [Pau] Casals thrilled audiences at home and abroad. In turn, concert artists from all over Europe appeared on the Barcelona stage, integrating the city into the mainstream of European musical culture.[17]

In fact, concert organizations flourished during this period. An early step forward had been taken by Josep Anselm Clavé (1824–74) in 1845, when he established the choral group L'Aurora (later called La Fraternitat, then Euterpe) to encourage public singing for the masses. Clavé promoted not only singing but also Catalan folk song, and he composed his own patriotic songs. Clavé's movement took root among Barcelona's proletariat and then spread throughout Catalonia and Spain.[18] This was followed by the establishment of the Societat Coral Catalunya Nova (1885), Orfeó Català (1891), Societat Catalana de Concerts (1892), Societat Filharmònica de Barcelona (1897), Cuarteto Belga (founded by Mathieu Crickboom), Quartet Renaixement (1912), Associació de Música da Camera (1914), and the Orquestra Simfònica de Barcelona (1910), founded by Joan Lamote de Grignon, who also conducted the Banda Municipal (1914–39).

Music schools flourished as well, with the establishment of the Conservatorio del Liceu (1838), Escola Municipal de Música (1886), and Orfeó Català (1891), in addition to private schools founded by Joan Baptista Pujol, Crickboom, and Granados. Periodicals devoted to music sprang up, the most important being *La ilustración musical* (1883), *La ilustración musical hispano-americana* (1888), *La música ilustrada* (1896), and *Revista musical catalana* (1904), which was published by the Orfeó Català.[19] These all featured articles by and about leading musicians and chronicled the musical life of the city. Other journals, such as *L'Avenç* and *Joventut*, also covered music, as did newspapers like *Diario de Barcelona*, *El correo catalán*, and *La vanguardia*. Music publishing thrived in this cultural environment, some of the major firms being Ildefons Alier, Casa Dotesio, and J. B. Pujol.

The Gran Teatre del Liceu (established 1847) was the leading venue for opera. Although it has sometimes been accused of favoring foreign composers, in fact it also premiered works by native authors such as Albéniz, Granados, Tomás Bretón, Enric Morera, and Pedrell, as well as by such lesser lights as Giró, Baratta, Gavanyach, Manén, and Lamote de Grignon. There were several other venues for musical theater, in particular the Teatre Principal, which served a growing audience for opera, zarzuela, and theatrical productions with music. Concerts of instrumental and choral music took place at the Palau de la Música Catalana, a modernist edifice completed in 1908.

All of these developments paralleled similar advances in literature and the visual arts. Civic pride grew in direct proportion to these accomplishments, and it fed an increasing sense of ethnic and cultural distinctiveness, as well as a desire for autonomy from Castile, which Catalans increasingly viewed as an incompetent manager of the nation's affairs. Indeed, the tension between Catalonia and Castile goes back centuries, and though Catalonia may remain forever a part of the Spanish republic, it will always be, in heart and mind, a land apart.[20]

This Catalan sense of separateness and uniqueness, indeed of specialness, was ultimately rooted in language. The revival of Catalan literature in the nineteenth century, the *Renaixença*, was a natural outgrowth of the Romantic preoccupation with regional language and folklore, with a nationalist political dimension. The central Castilian administration had, over the centuries, suppressed the Catalan language in order to facilitate the realm's incorporation into what was essentially a Castilian empire. This was especially pronounced in the aftermath of the Wars of the Spanish Succession in the early eighteenth century, in which Catalonia backed the losing side. There was a marked liberalization in Madrid's policies in the nineteenth century, however, and this led to a full-blown revival of Catalan literature, which had flowered during the Middle Ages but lain largely dormant since the Renaissance. The Zeitgeist was perhaps best expressed in the *Oda a Barcelona* by Jacint Verdaguer, one of the leaders of the Catalan literary renascence. Published in 1883 by the city council, it extolled the spirit of progress and expansion typical of Catalonia's industrial bourgeoisie.[21]

If the cultural revival in Barcelona had remained focused solely on Catalan culture, it would have garnered little international attention. The *Renaixença* preceded and then coexisted with a phenomenon that swept Europe and the United States: *modernisme*. In France and the United States, this is known as Art Nouveau, while the Germans call it *Jugendstil*. Whatever the label, it was the dominant artistic movement of the late nineteenth and early twentieth centuries, and Barcelona became, with Paris and Munich, one of the principal centers for it. The *Renaixença* and *modernisme*, then, made and make Barcelona unique. The *Renaixença* looked back to a haloed past in the Middle Ages, while *modernisme* represented the cutting edge of contemporary culture. Barcelona thus negotiated the terrain between past and present, embracing both and creating something new and distinctive in the process.

Barcelona's preoccupation with its Catalan identity was further mitigated by two ineluctable realities, however, which kept this resurgence from degenerating into parochialism and xenophobia: (1) the ongoing relationship with the other parts of Spain, to which the city was bound politically and economically, and (2) its status as a seaport and its close proximity to France and Italy, which insured a constant inflow of new ideas and influences from the world outside of Spain. Barcelona therefore found, and daily finds, itself in the position of attempting to maintain its "Catalanness" while mediating the twin poles between which it lies: Spain (mostly Castile) and the rest of Europe. Such a situation gives rise to special tensions but also to intense creativity.

Enrique Granados embodied this set of geo-cultural circumstances in his family history, his life, and in his music. He spent nearly his entire career in Barcelona and made significant contributions to its cultural life in several areas, including performing, composing, conducting, and teaching. But he was Catalan only by birth, not by ethnicity: his father was at least second-generation Cuban, and his mother was from Santander, in Cantabria, and also had some Mexican ancestry. Spain had been unified since the days of the Catholic kings, and Granados felt himself to be both Spanish and Catholic. Moreover, he grew up playing the music of Central European composers such as Schumann, Chopin, and Liszt, and these figures exerted a lifelong influence on his composition. In short, Granados was also a citizen of Europe and claimed its cultural legacy as his own.

Perhaps Granados's greatest achievement as a creative artist, then, was the almost quantum-like way he inhabited three realms at the same time: the Catalan, the Spanish, and the European. His ability to communicate simultaneously on several cultural "wavelengths" was the principal ingredient in his creative life, a theme that will run throughout this book. His versatility was remarkable and set him apart from most contemporary musicians in Barcelona, many of whom, like Enric Morera (1865–1942), were men of extraordinary talent and energy but who will forever remain unknown outside of Catalonia precisely because of their ideological rigidity in relation to Catalan nationalism in music. To be sure, Granados did write several stage works with Catalan texts steeped in medieval lore. But he was also an innovator in the creation of a distinctively Spanish national style drawing inspiration from Madrid and the epoch of Goya ca. 1800. And much of his piano music looks back to the Romantic tradition of the early nineteenth century. In other words, he mediated not only three cultural areas but past and present as well. So, how did he do it?

Above and beyond all other considerations, Granados had a strongly developed sense of his individual identity. As he said: "I consider myself to be as Catalan as anyone, but in my music I wish to express what I feel, what I admire and what is attractive to me, whether it be Andalusian or Chinese."[22] Antonio Fernández-Cid put it more simply when he stated that Granados was always "faithful to himself."[23] Here was a perfect summation of Ortega y Gasset's contention that the self, the *yo*, is neither a material nor spiritual essence but rather "is in each instant something that we feel 'has to be' in the next moment and beyond this in a longer temporal perspective."[24] This indefinable "something," which we recognize in the realm of intuitive feeling, is what Granados possessed and made him what he was.

Thus, Granados never wholly committed himself to any particular camp, ideology, identity, or movement. In an ongoing affirmation of his individuality, he embraced the beautiful, not the political, wherever he found it: in a Chopin mazurka, a Goya print, a *malagueña murciana*, Catalan-modernist poetry, or Wagnerian opera. Consequently, Granados's finest work is unmistakably his own. Pedrell justifiably described him as a "poet who could say, along with Rubén Darío, that his poetry was 'his own in himself,' and sustain the primary condition of his existence by living in intense love of the absolute in beauty."[25]

As for the title of this book, some explanation is in order. The literary historian Francisco Márquez Villanueva objects to synaesthetic metaphors in connection with Granados. Poets are poets and pianists are pianists, he insists, and music and literature are different. He does not believe in the "once fashionable idea of the unity of literature and the [other] arts."[26] Fairly said. I refer to Granados as a poet of the piano not out of any personal predilection for such metaphors, but because that is how he was referred to during his life, by the press, by students, by those familiar with him and his music.[27] Over and over, poetry was invoked to convey some otherwise inexplicable dimension of his art. Conxita Badia, one of his foremost disciples, said that "To hear Granados speaking in class was sheer poetry," or that his songs were characterized by "poetic lyricism."[28] The composer Lluís Millet perceived in Granados's best work "an elegiac poetic sentiment."[29] Pedrell evoked his "genial and poetic spirit,"[30] and Casals said that "Granados is our great poet."[31] His pupil and biographer Guillermo de Boladeres Ibern described him as "a poet of the heart who rhymed with chords and melodies an endless song of his artistic visions, sincerely felt and nobly expressed"; in short, he was a "true poet of the piano."[32] During Granados's lifetime, poetry occupied an exalted place among the arts, and these descriptions were the highest accolade he could have received. As Antonio Machado wrote, "Neither marble, hard and eternal, / nor painting nor music, / but the word in time."[33]

This book is about Granados, the era in which he lived, and the impression he made on others. And during his lifetime, the Wagnerian notion of the *Gesamtkunstwerk*, a "complete art work" that unites all of the arts, was at the height of fashion. Granados was closely connected with poets, playwrights, and painters, and many of the artists he knew were accomplished in more than one field of endeavor. He himself enjoyed drawing sketches and writing verse, and he composed piano works with titles such as "Poetic Scenes" and "Poetic Waltzes." In the context of the world Granados and his contemporaries inhabited, the unity of the arts was not a vague aesthetic concept—it was a reality. For the purposes of the present narrative, it remains a vital and relevant idea.

Granados's status as a poet of the piano possesses symbolic significance on another level. He was a unifying presence on the Spanish cultural landscape in general, bringing together in his music various regions, styles, and epochs. Thus, in his life and work, the unity of the arts finds a parallel in the political and cultural "unity" of the country, a unity sorely tested by the trials through which Spain passed during his life, a unity in which he firmly believed, and a conception of the nation that ultimately prevailed.

Unless otherwise noted, all translations are my own. Although modern Catalan spellings are utilized for persons, places, and institutions in that region, English spellings of common Spanish place names, such as Seville and Andalusia, are the rule. Passages from letters, diaries, and other primary documents retain their original spelling, punctuation, and orthography, unless they come from an edited source. All excerpts from Granados's piano works come from DLR.

CHAPTER 1

A Born Pianist

The medieval cathedral (Seu Vella) of Lleida, on the Segre River in Catalonia, sits high atop a hill overlooking the surrounding plain and the mountains beyond. It thus occupies a very defensible position, and the fortifications around it bear mute witness to the violent dramas that have taken place beneath their parapets. Whoever held Lleida held a large region around it. No army ever approached the town by surprise, though it has been besieged over the millennia by Romans, Goths, Moors, and French, as well as Catalans and Castilians.[1] It has suffered its fair share of destruction, but the well-preserved Romanesque and Gothic churches and buildings throughout the city give evidence of a hearty longevity.

The nineteenth century was an especially convulsive epoch in Spanish history, and a sizable military detachment maintained Lleida's security. On January 20, 1867, an officer in the Spanish army by the name of Calixto Granados y Armenteros, captain of Company 5, First Battalion, 25th Infantry Regiment of Navarra, departed from Havana aboard the steamer *Príncipe Alfonso*, bound for the peninsula.[2] He docked at Cádiz, spent some time in Seville, then moved on to his final destination, Lleida, at that time a city of about 20,000. He arrived there on June 8 and took up residence just a short distance down the hill from the Seu Vella, on the second floor of a dwelling at carrer del Marqués de Tallada, 1. He was accompanied by his wife, Enriqueta Elvira Campiña, seven months pregnant, and their young family.

Calixto and Enriqueta had married in 1853 in Havana, the same city where Calixto was born on October 14, 1824. His parents, Manuel Granados (b. 1803) and Irene Armenteros, were also from Havana, as were both their parents. In fact, Manuel had been a military man as well, and he reached the rank of captain before retiring in 1850 after thirty years of service, on account of the financial burdens imposed by a large family. The military was a profession of some prestige in Spanish society, but not remuneration. In truth, Manuel was a capable soldier but seems to have had a fairly unexceptional career, his records indicating that his industry and knowledge were merely "regular." His son and grandson would go much further in their careers. However, he instilled in Calixto, from earliest years, a love for the profession of arms and loyalty to the crown.[3] Calixto in turn passed these values on to his children.

The name Granados is Castilian and means "distinguished" or "select." It is common in the mountainous region around Santander, a seaport in the northern Spanish region of Cantabria, suggesting that our composer's paternal ancestors may have come from that area when they settled in Cuba.[4] In any event, the name is an ancient one and can be found among lists of medieval knights who participated in the *reconquista* during the reign of Alfonso el Sabio, in the thirteenth century.[5] In keeping with this tradition, Calixto was a fine officer and a brave soldier who eventually advanced to the rank of major (*comandante*) and was decorated several times.

Ten years younger than Calixto, Enriqueta was a native of Santander, which was also the city of birth of her mother, María Ramona. However, her father, Antonio, was a native of Mexico City, as was her paternal grandmother, María Migueleño. Enriqueta came from a prominent business family and apparently left Santander in 1850 bound for Cuba, possibly with her brothers who had business dealings there.[6]

At five in the morning of July 27, 1867, Calixto and Enriqueta became the proud parents of a son who would inscribe the name of Granados in the annals of music history. His baptism took place in the main cathedral of the city two days later; Marcelino Anievas, chaplain of Calixto's battalion, presided over the ritual. His godparents were *madrileños* Joaquín González Estafaní and his wife, Sofia Arambarri, represented on this occasion by Captain José Bernal (of the same company as Calixto) and his daughter Carolina.

Calixto and Enriqueta named their son Pantaleón Enrique Joaquín, but he would be known throughout life simply as Enrique, after his mother. Although born in Catalonia, there was no Catalan branch in his family tree. The Catalan version of his name is Enric (or earlier, Enrich), and that is how one reads of him in all Catalan accounts. But the baptismal certificate bears his names only in Castilian.[7] Although he was fluent in Catalan as well as Castilian and often communicated in that language, he would customarily sign his letters and otherwise identify himself as Enrique.[8]

For unknown reasons, Granados apparently thought he was born in 1868, not 1867. For instance, he took out a life-insurance policy on May 29, 1903, and when asked about his birth year, he responded that it was 1868.[9] Further evidence is at hand in a letter of May 26, 1907, that he wrote to Albéniz, informing him that he would be celebrating his thirty-ninth birthday on July 27. Of course, it would be his fortieth.[10] This explains why so many sources during his lifetime and after gave 1868 as the year of his birth. The extant birth certificate proves otherwise.

Enriqueta bore four other children, about whom we know very little: Concepción, Calixto, José, and Francisco.[11] Like his father and grandfather, Enrique's brother Calixto entered the military at an early age. Born in Havana on May 9, 1858, he became a cadet in June 1874 and ultimately attained the rank of major. He served with distinction in the Philippines in 1897, receiving the Cross of María Cristina for his heroism in fighting insurgents. Unfortunately, he contracted a fever during those operations and died the following year, leaving a wife (María Carlota Carreras y Caiguet) and children behind.[12]

Many decades later, Granados's biographer Antonio Fernández-Cid would correctly assert that "Enrique Granados felt a true admiration for everything related to the army," noting that the composer "enjoyed firing blanks with a pistol" and possessed other firearms as well.[13] Granados never entered the military, but as a bourgeois loyal to the crown, he never questioned its legitimacy, and he maintained a lifelong fascination with martial trappings and weaponry.

In his diary, Granados recalled very little about his childhood in Lleida, having spent only three years there before his father was transferred to Santa Cruz on the island of Tenerife in the Canaries, where he served as military commander for the island; the family departed from Cádiz for Tenerife on July 2, 1870. His recollections of Tenerife remained strong, especially of the lemon and orange groves in bloom, which were part of the former Franciscan convent in which they lived. The sight of the harbor also made a deep impression on him, sheltering "a multitude of sailing ships with their sails stretching towards the sun like the extended wings of doves seeking out the gentle warmth of a summer morning."[14] To him, this was a paradise.

Calixto held his post in Tenerife until January 1872, after which the family removed to Barcelona. He fought the Carlists in 1873 and was active in the area around Vilafranca del Penedés south of Barcelona and in Girona to the north. In 1875 he was forced to retire from the military on disability due to a recent aggravation of persistent back problems, caused by a riding accident that had occurred in Tenerife. His malady was diagnosed as *mielitis* (spinal inflammation), and it left him virtually paralyzed from the waist down.

The family occupied a number of residences in Barcelona during the 1870s before establishing themselves in the Passeig de Gracia, near where it intersects the Diagonal. (The building they lived in is no longer standing.) This was a rapidly developing part of the city, which was undergoing a dramatic transformation as it expanded to accommodate a growing population. Young Enrique was early on fascinated by architecture and spent many hours watching the construction of a convent near his home. "In those days, I was delirious with the desire to become an architect!" he remembered. His mother suffered some aggravation when he would bring home materials from the construction site so he could "build at least a cathedral in our apartment."[15]

In 1874, when Granados was 7, his elder brother Calixto was wounded in combat with the Carlists. He was shot through the hand and foot, wounds that were not life-threatening; however, Granados recalls that when his mother got news of this from her husband, she hastily packed their bags to head to the military hospital where her wounded son lay. An unforgettable experience of Granados's early years was witnessing the return of his father and brother's unit, accompanied by the sound of cornets and drums, as the Regimiento de Navarra came parading down the Passeig de Gracia. No doubt such memories inspired his later composition of spirited military marches for piano.

Another early musical impression was made on Granados by the family cook, Rosa, also from Lleida, who liked to sing. "What songs!" Granados recalled. "They say that music is born of the word. Very well, but from Rosa's words was born a noise that she called singing but which caused one to cover not only one's ears but also to close one's nostrils when she sang."[16]

One other formative impression on the teenage Granados came from a harpist who lived in the apartment next to his, Carmen Miralles. He recalled loving to practice when she did, imitating the sound of her harp on his piano. At other times he enjoyed putting his ear to the wall to listen to her delicate music. As we shall see, this association with Carmen would have far-reaching implications not only for his musical sensitivities but his entire career as well.

Granados received his first musical instruction from an elderly Castilian soldier in Calixto's outfit, José Junqueda. He was a flutist whose performance was impeded by missing teeth, which Granados sardonically noted "are very necessary to blow and to play, at least according to those who know about such things."[17] So, the effect of this instruction was evidently negligible, and Granados says that his first real "maestro" was Francisco Xavier Jurnet, who taught at the Escolania de la Mercè in Barcelona.[18] Granados took piano lessons with Jurnet until he was 13, from 1878 to 1882.[19]

The young Granados often entertained people at the piano in his home. One willing listener was a young man named Pico, a pianist employed at the Café de Lisboa. He was deeply impressed by Granados's talent and advised his mother: "What happens with this creature is a matter of conscience; you must take the boy to Pujol."[20] This posed a crisis of conscience for Granados, however, who could not figure out how to break the news to Jurnet. Not that he was entirely satisfied with Jurnet's instruction: he found that the works his teacher assigned him were excessively "sentimental," for example, *L'harpe d'or* by Félix Godefroid, *Las perlas* by E. Nollet, and *The Last Hope* by Louis Moreau Gottschalk. Granados called upon his former instructor Junqueda to talk to Jurnet on his behalf. Jurnet was not happy with the news and remained bitter about it for years. But "it had to be done, and it was."[21]

Joan Baptista Pujol (1835–98) had his own music academy and was the teacher of several eminent pianists, including Joaquím Malats, Ricard Viñes, and Carles Vidiella. He was also the author of an influential treatise on piano playing, and his dedication to pedagogy set an example Granados would later follow. Pujol had a direct connection to the tradition of Liszt insofar as he was a student of Pere Tintorer, a Catalan pianist who studied with Liszt in Paris and subsequently taught at the conservatory of the Liceu. Pujol himself went to Paris to finish his training, with Henri Reber at the Conservatoire, then returned to Barcelona and brought to full flower a school of Catalan piano virtuosity that played a crucial role not simply in the world of pianism but also in the course of Spanish music.

For Pujol trained many of the pianist-composers who would advance the cause of Spanish national music through performance and composition. The publishing concern he established in 1888 also made available many of the works of Granados and

Albéniz.[22] The school of piano playing he fostered in Barcelona was renowned for its attention to clarity of voicing, tone color, and especially to mastery of pedaling.[23] Years later, the American pianist Ernest Schelling would say of Granados's execution that "his ravishing results at the keyboard were all a matter of the pedal."[24]

Granados and his mother went to Pujol to ask for lessons, but Pujol said he already had too many students and could not take on more. Enriqueta persisted, however, and asked him just to listen to her son. Finally Pujol relented and sat the young man at the piano. "[From] that moment, he was a different person," said Granados, who performed Gottschalk's *The Last Hope* for him.[25] After a short period of study, Pujol felt his protégé was ready for competition and had him perform Schumann's Sonata in G Minor during the 1883 contest named after Pujol himself. Granados also executed a difficult exercise by Claudio Martínez Imbert at sight. The jury included Martínez Imbert, Pedrell, and Albéniz, who was living in Barcelona at that time.[26] They judged Granados the winner of the contest.

As Granados recalled it, the Schumann sonata was the first "decent" work he had studied, and he declared Pujol "a good professor." Still, compared to Albéniz, who first appeared in public at age 4, the teenage Granados was off to a relatively late start. But early on he showed amazing talent, and he quickly made up for any lost time. He was, as Casals later described him, "a born pianist."[27]

Granados's father never witnessed his son's early triumphs, however. Sometime in the early 1880s, Calixto decided that the family should spend a season in Olot, where Enrique's elder brother was stationed with his battalion.[28] Perhaps as a result of the exertions this visit required, shortly after their return, Calixto, *père*, succumbed to the spinal inflammation that had precipitated his early retirement and done what no enemy's bullet had been able to. Calixto died at one in the afternoon on June 24, 1882, at the age of 57.[29] The effect of his death on the entire family, particularly Enrique, was devastating, especially as it was apparently unexpected. Granados wrote that "the death of the father I loved so much was a revelation in my life. His passing produced an enormous emptiness in our home in terms of our morale, as well as material hardship. I look back now with great sadness on what must have been the martyrdom of my poor mother."[30] Calixto was buried in the Poble Nou cemetery, the only cemetery in Barcelona at the time.[31]

Although Enriqueta continued to receive her late husband's military pension, this barely supported the family. Young Enrique would have to contribute to the family larder, which he did in the only way he knew how: playing the piano. Fortunately, he was living in an epoch when opportunities for informal performance were abundant. Starting in the late eighteenth century, *cafés* sprang up in Madrid and Barcelona. These quickly insinuated themselves into Spanish culture and even became the subject for plays, the most famous being Ramón de la Cruz's light drama *El Café de Barcelona* of 1788.[32] In the nineteenth century, many more such establishments opened, and they became important locales where people exchanged ideas and discussed the latest trends in politics and the arts. Since these businesses were often connected to opera houses, such as the Café de les Delicies on the Ramblas next to the Teatre Principal in Barcelona, music was often featured along with coffee, drinks, and food.[33] In this very venue, in fact, Granados got his start as a professional musician, with the help of Vidiella, who had preceded him there.

Granados normally played from 2:00 to 4:30 in the afternoon and from 9:00 to 11:30 at night. The work was tedious, but it brought in 100 pesetas a month, a huge addition to the family coffers. This went on for a few months but did little to lift the young man's spirits after the death of his father. The work was as distasteful to him as it was necessary to his desperate family. The owner was fond of opera excerpts, which Granados did not want to play. So, the proprietor one day peremptorily announced to Granados that his services would no longer be needed. This plunged him into a new crisis. His mother tried to reassure him: "Don't worry, Enrique. God will not abandon us."[34] Apparently reluctant to rely solely on supernatural aid, Granados sought out more tangible means of support.

Through his sister, Granados became acquainted with Eduardo Conde, a wealthy merchant in Barcelona and owner of the huge El Siglo department store. Conde was a lover of music and the arts, and he took a special interest in Granados after hearing the young man play. "From that time forward, he was my protector, and I owe him everything I have become."[35] Conde employed him to teach his own children piano and matched his former salary at the café. "I was the most expensive teacher in Barcelona," Granados later exclaimed.[36] Young Enrique also found work at another café, El Filipino, but this venue posed its own set of challenges. Here he was expected to accompany musically inspired customers, who might feel the need to burst forth in song or play an instrument. For instance, a trombonist required our pianist to accompany him in a no doubt memorable rendition of the overture to *William Tell*.[37]

Granados finally appeared in his first formal public concert at the age of 18, in 1886. The program featured students of Pujol and took place on April 9 at the Ateneu Barcelonés. He performed with fellow pianist Francisco Viñas and acquitted himself admirably in the chamber works in which he participated. Together they played Gottschalk's *Tarantella* and a *Fantasía* by José García Robles.[38]

We notice that, aside from piano study, young Granados had a near-total lack of formal education. And yet, he eventually became a very refined and educated man, fluent in three languages—Castilian, Catalan, and French—and current with the latest literary developments. Those who later frequented his home commented on his large collection of books, including prose and poetry, by authors foreign and native. He especially prized the Spanish classics.[39] The composer Amadeu Vives recalled that the mature Granados's bookshelves in Barcelona were replete with poetry and novels. Especially prominent were works of Goethe, Byron, and poems of Tennyson (in Spanish translation). Many volumes were full of illustrations, which he relished.[40] And he gained from private music instruction an understanding and appreciation of music history as well as theory. Through his repeated and close associations with artists, he also expanded his awareness of culture in general. Another factor at work in Granados's self-education was his "storehouse of knowledge and ideas," acquired through his "great intelligence and an ever-alert curiosity about things."[41] Moreover, he was aware that he had much to learn and always exhibited not only a certain humility as a result, but also an openness to new knowledge.

However, like so many young Spanish musicians before and after him, Granados realized he would have to leave the country for advanced study and to gain legitimacy in the eyes of the public and critics. And the principal destination for budding Spanish musicians like himself was Paris. Conde clearly recognized this need. He also recognized that the Granados family had nowhere near the means to facilitate such studies. He would have to provide that himself. With the generous help of Conde, then, Granados was able to pursue his education in Paris. It was his desire to study at the Conservatoire, where he hoped to work with Charles de Bériot (1833–1916), one of the leading pedagogues of the era. Bériot's mother was the Spanish soprano María Malibrán, daughter of the Spanish tenor and composer Manuel García.[42]

Granados arrived in the French capital in the summer of 1887 but was prevented from auditioning for the Conservatoire by a sudden case of typhus, which might well have ended not only his studies but also his life. In fact, he was unconscious for two or three weeks.[43] He convalesced for several more weeks in a well-appointed and modern hospital, but by the time he had recuperated, the entrance exams were over; he had passed his twentieth birthday and was no longer eligible to enter the Conservatoire. However, he could still pursue private studies with Bériot, and this he wasted no time in doing.

Bériot emphasized in his teaching the development of a singing, lyrical style, which is not surprising given his mother's profession. Granados's love of the human voice readily responded to this counsel. Moreover, Bériot sought to refine a student's tone production and believed strongly in cultivating improvisational skills. He also wrote two methods on accompaniment. Finally, he laid great stress on pedaling. Granados would eventually excel in all these areas.

A vivid account of Granados's two years in Paris comes to us from his roommate and fellow student Ricard Viñes (1875–1943), also a Bériot student. Like Granados, he was from Lleida. Viñes later became famous for his interpretations of the modern French and Spanish piano repertoire.[44] In 1916, after Granados's death, he published passages from a diary he kept during the time he and Granados were there together in Paris.[45] Viñes was only 12 when he went to Paris, with his mother, to study with Bériot, on a grant from the Escola Municipal de Música in Barcelona. He arrived on October 13, 1887, and less than a month later was admitted to Bériot's class at the Conservatoire as an auditor; two years later, he gained admission as a regular student.[46]

Granados and Viñes resided at the Hôtel de Cologne et d'Espagne, in the rue de Trévise 10–12. At first, their rooms were far apart and required the "extremely irksome gymnastics" of running up and down stairs all the time to see one another. Finally, a room opened up right next to Viñes's, and this Granados occupied in the fall of 1887. "Every day I had to awaken Granados because he was always a little tardy in getting up," said Viñes. "He would pass much of the morning yawning and trying to wake up before getting out of bed. However, once he was up and working, he labored very hard and with tremendous enthusiasm."[47]

They took lessons from Bériot not only at the Conservatoire but also at his house. They "venerated" Beethoven but "preferred" Schumann and Chopin, their "idols." In fact, together they performed the Rondo in C Major, op. 73, of Chopin on May 24, 1888, at the Salle Erard in a concert of Conservatoire students. They rounded out their musical diet with helpings of contemporary works by Bizet, Grieg, and Albéniz. They also regularly attended the Concerts Lamoureux.

On Sundays, Granados visited the home of the painter Francesc Miralles (1848–1901), Carmen's brother, who had resided in Paris since the mid-1860s. There Granados also dined with the pianist Mario Calado. He preferred to arrive much earlier than dinnertime, however, in order to join Miralles in his studio and discuss art. Not content merely to observe Miralles, he actually executed a series of paintings himself. Viñes noted that water was a constant motif from one painting to the next, in the form of lakes, lagoons, rivers, and seas. Obviously Granados found large expanses of water to be a source of inspiration. They would later cause him considerable dread.

Back at the hotel, Enrique and Ricard loved to spend time throwing loose tiles off the roof, just for the fun of watching them explode in clouds of dust on the ground below. Such antics earned a rebuke from their neighbors, which failed to bring a complete halt to their rooftop high jinks. And there were other diversions. One Sunday in April 1889, the boys decided to amuse themselves by renting a "prehistoric" tricycle with two seats, "as wide as a landau and as heavy as an omnibus." They rode all over Paris seeing the sights on this improbable, and no doubt comical, conveyance.

Not all of their extra-musical pursuits were quite so frivolous. They immersed themselves in literature, novels mostly, and gave musical expression to their favorite characters, the majority of which seem to have been women, e.g., Laura, Beatrice, Ophelia, and Marguerite. Their favorite poet was the Spanish *costumbrista* (regionalist) author Gustavo Adolfo Bécquer (1836–70), whose *Rimas* were a source of inspiration to many artists and musicians in Spain during that epoch. "For months and months, [the *Rimas*] constituted our daily spiritual nourishment. We recited them together at all hours, and Granados, inspired by one of them, set it very well to music."[48] This was the very simple yet vehement quatrain:

> For a glance, a world;
> For a smile, a heaven;
> For a kiss . . . I don't know
> What I would give you for a kiss!

Granados eventually wanted a change of locale and moved to a different hotel, in the rue Fontaine, 48, on October 1, 1888. But he grew lonely there and moved back to his old residence, where Viñes had remained, on May 1, 1889. Only a short time later, on July 14, he returned to Barcelona.

For Granados, this youthful sojourn in Paris would forever remain haloed in nostalgia. Viñes saw his old friend for the last time on Granados's return visit to Paris in 1914. The composer unburdened himself to Viñes about his worries, his children, all the projects he had in mind, finally breaking down altogether and sobbing. They walked back to Granados's hotel, which by coincidence happened to be across the street from their residence of twenty-five years before. "'Do you remember those years?' we finally said to one another, practically at the same time. And that was all."[49] The old hotel was now a relic from a past of irretrievable insouciance.

In mid-September 1889, shortly after his return to Barcelona, Granados gave a recital at the home of Miguel Navas, a prominent businessman. The performance received a rapturous review in *El diario mercantil*[50] and included a concerto by Bériot as well as standard repertoire by Mendelssohn and Chopin; after "deafening applause," he threw in encores by Massenet and Saint-Saëns.

Granados's first public appearance took place at the Teatre Líric, on April 20, 1890. The press raved about the young man just back from "finishing school" in Paris. One critic noted his "fine taste" and praised him for eschewing the "*brillante* pianistic style" now in vogue, predicting instead that "Granados will be one of the good artists who always seek applause in pure art, without flashiness and cheap concessions." The critic was especially impressed by the young man's "good technical education" as well as his "delicate touch, full of delicious smoothness."[51] Total technical command, lack of ostentation, and exquisite refinement in programming and interpretation: these are the qualities that many critics lauded in reviews of his appearances at this time. *Diario de Barcelona* enthused about his performance, in which he was assisted by several other musicians playing works by Chopin, Mendelssohn, Keller, Bizet, Saint-Saëns, Espino, Albéniz, and Granados himself, for example, *Serenata española* (now lost), *Arabesca*, and some *Danzas españolas*: "As a pianist, he is a paragon of elegance and sentiment. Without the gymnastic exertions adopted by some performers who seek to attract attention to themselves, he draws from the piano the sounds that suit his fancy, aided by a mechanism that allows him to do anything."[52]

Granados made another triumphal appearance in Barcelona two years later, on April 10, 1892, again at the Líric. He performed the Grieg A-minor Piano Concerto, as well as tossing in a few *Danzas españolas*.[53] Some months after this, on July 31, he again offered some of his popular *Danzas* at the Palau de les Ciencies, in a concert of the newly formed Orfeó Català. A final performance that year took place on October 29, 1892, at the Líric, for the Societat Catalana de Concerts. Here, too, he played from the *Danzas* (No. 3). His concertizing was about to undergo a dramatic attenuation, however, due to his new status: married with children. It would be two and a half years before he gave another concert in Barcelona.

During a concert trip to Valencia, probably in 1891, Granados had stayed with friends of his father's, the Carbajosa family. They were people of status and wealth and lived in Porta-Coeli, a converted monastery surrounded by forests and gardens. The Carbajosas loved to entertain, and at these festivities Granados would play the piano. At one such party the list of invitees included a Valencian businessman by the name of Francisco Gal y Sabater; his wife, Francisca Lloveras Foix, of Catalan stock; and their daughters Amparo and Paulita. Enrique and Amparo quickly developed a mutual attraction, and though the young pianist had to return to Barcelona, he took with him the memory of her. The budding romance might have ended at this point, but a change of circumstances kept it alive.

Francisco's business fell on hard times, and he relocated with his family to Barcelona. Enrique and Amparo were reunited, and after a brief courtship, he proposed to her. The difference in their social stations might have proved an obstacle, for despite the temporary pecuniary embarrassments of Amparo's family, they were still higher in status than the Granadoses. Some maternal diplomacy smoothed the way. Being proud but nonetheless aware of life's realities, Enrique's mother wrote to Amparo's, laying her cards on the table:

> As one mother to another, I must speak with complete honesty. My son is poor, very poor. For now, he has nothing more than a good name. I have no doubt that over time he will be successful, but that will not just happen, and the struggle will be difficult.
>
> You are already aware of everything else. If this is acceptable to you, it is to me. I agree to their marriage with all my best wishes. My first embrace is for my new daughter, Amparo; those that follow are for you and Paulita and, I dare say, for your husband and your fine son. I am most grateful to you all for the affection you have shown to my Enrique.[54]

These are the only actual words we can attribute with any certainty to Granados's mother. They suggest a certain eloquence, sincerity, and dignity on her part. In a letter to Amparo, Granados expressed his own views about affairs of the heart, as well as of the wallet: "How sad that it is not possible to be at once very rich and very poor. For then I would be able to give you what you deserve and at the same time be worthy of your compassion, which matters more than life itself. Rich for your well-being; poor for your heart."[55] Like mother, like son.

The exact date of Granados's marriage has remained a mystery until recently. Family tradition holds that it took place in the summer of 1893, but newly recovered documentation compels us to move the date up six months. Amparo, which means succor or aid, was actually the nickname of Granados's young, pretty bride, María de los Desamparados Gal y Lloveras. Twenty-two years old, she was three years younger than our pianist at the time they announced their *proclamas* (banns) in November 1892, on the 6th, 13th, and 20th. The banns were drafted at the Parish Church of Santa María de Jesús de Gracia; on the 21st, their intent to marry was officially approved and formally written up.[56] The wedding took place on December 7, 1892, in the lovely Romanesque church of San Pedro de las Puellas (Sant Pere de les Puel·les).[57]

Natalia described their union in glowing terms: "[Granados] had the fortune to be assisted by a strong wife, loving, a perfect homemaker and enthusiastic companion of the artist."[58] Fernández-Cid portrayed Amparo as nothing less than the ideal spouse:

"Sweetness and femininity were the essence of her being. She was friendly, simple, organized, and completely faithful to her spouse, whom she loved and admired as the most exceptional man in the world."[59] The reality was not quite so sugarcoated, and hers would be a most difficult assignment: to raise six children under constant financial pressure, endure the frequent absences of a husband who was often in a distracted state even at home, and tolerate his roving eye and susceptibility to romantic involvement with young and nubile female students who would have loved to take her place by his side.

This gives us pause to reflect on the status of women at this time in Spain, for clearly Amparo was fulfilling in exemplary fashion the role scripted for her by the conventions of society at the end of the nineteenth century. As Mary Nash points out, "The predominant discourse on women in the late nineteenth and early twentieth century [in Spain] was based on the ideology of domesticity, evoking a female prototype of the *perfecta casada* (perfect married lady), whose primordial gender role was that of caring for home and family." This was due in part to the pervasive influence of the Catholic Church, and in part to an "elitist political structure . . . unfavorable for the development of liberal political feminism."[60]

Women enjoyed relatively little independence and rarely worked outside the home. Respectable single women were expected not even to appear in public alone. For obvious reasons, marriageable middle-class women hoping to improve their lot in life through a favorable union were keen to preserve their virginity until the nuptials were over. Pío Baroja, a leading author of the time, spoke to the uncompromising virtue of young Spanish women in this epoch: "They were like fortified positions, trenched and walled. They wore a corset as if it were the Great Wall of China or the bastion of Verdun. If a young man just happened to place his hand on her waist, he felt a kind of armor as hard as that worn by Godefroid de Bouillon to the Crusades."[61] In all the pictures of Amparo, there is an intensity and will in her flashing eyes that leads one to suspect she was one such woman.

The few extant letters from Granados to Amparo reveal an intense adoration (none of hers have survived). Granados rarely dated his letters and manuscripts precisely, but in a letter of "Friday the 26th" he addresses Amparo as "Beloved heaven of my soul" and writes, "I love you with all my soul, life of my life. . . . I love you so much! Do you remember me all the time as I remember you? Do you think about your Enrique a lot? Do you love him a lot? I think of my heaven a lot, and I think that I love you more than my own life. How delicious it is to have the affection of a Titín [his pet name for her]!" In another letter, he declares, "I am awaiting the happiness of receiving a letter from you, love! I will devour it with my eyes and with my heart. . . . I am realizing more and more how happy I am by your side."[62] Amparo was clearly the inspiration for his music now: "Do I have talent? Well, it is you. My music is nice? Well, you are making it within my soul."[63]

On July 28, 1894, one day after Enrique's birthday, the first of their six children was born, Eduardo, named after Granados's patron Eduardo Conde. He was followed in turn by Soledad (1896), Enrique (1897), Víctor (1899), Natalia (1900), and Paquito

(1902). The new family man needed a steady source of income but was unable to find a suitable teaching post in Barcelona; an audition at the Escola Municipal de Música resulted in the hiring not of Granados but another Pujol disciple, Joan Baptista Pellicer.[64] So, Granados traveled to Madrid in 1894 to try to interest publishers in his music and to audition for a position as professor of piano that had opened up at the Escuela Nacional de Música y Declamación (now the Real Conservatorio). Once again, however, sickness intervened between him and conservatory aspirations. He fell ill and could not compete; Pilar Fernández de la Mora won the job instead.

Granados's letters to Amparo from this period reflect something of the crisis of confidence and bleak prospects for the future that seemed to be haunting him at every turn.

> I die from pain when I reflect on the fact that up until now I have accomplished nothing. What is more, you torment me cruelly when you talk about what will become of us if I do not get this position, and that consumes my soul. . . . My ambition is to become to Spain what Saint-Saëns and Brahms are to their countries.[65]

However, he appeared at one of the most prestigious venues in the city, the salon of the publisher Romero.[66] The concert, on February 15, 1895, featured his *Valses poéticos* and some *Danzas españolas*, as well as a newly composed Quintet, op. 49, and Trio, op. 50. Granados's concert was a triumph and buoyed his sagging spirits. He joyously reported to Amparo that "Last night I had the greatest success of my life. It was a night of true glory. . . . It was the first time that a chamber work by a living Spanish composer was performed in the Salón Romero."[67] Still, money would continue to be a problem and a headache for most of his life. He held on to hope and persisted in the face of every obstacle. His diary makes clear an unbreakable resolve: "My only ambition is that my work will endure, though at the expense of my suffering. For it causes me great sadness . . . to live at the mercy of the pettiness and envy of losers."[68]

In 1895 Granados returned to Barcelona and participated in a major concert featuring works by Catalan composers at the Teatre Líric on November 14. He performed his own *Danzas españolas* (Nos. 5 & 7) and *Valses poéticos*, as well as Albéniz's *Rapsodia española*. The evening also featured pieces by Lluís Millet, Antoni Nicolau, and Enric Morera.[69] This appearance initiated a decade of intense concertizing, during which he gave dozens of recitals for the Societat Catalana de Concerts, Societat Filharmònica, and other organizations in Barcelona. He and Joaquím Malats appeared together in a concert in June 1899 playing music for two pianos that provoked "a noisy and well-deserved ovation."[70] Their ambitious program included works by Mozart, Saint-Saëns, Schumann, Chaminade, Chabrier, and Fischhof. In fact, Granados performed a lot of chamber music during his career, especially with the Crickboom quartet, consisting of Mathieu Crickboom, José Rocabruna, Rafael Galvez, and Pablo [Pau] Casals.

During the 1890s, Granados attained maturity as a concert artist, but what kind of pianist was he? The Cuban pianist and composer Joaquín Nin said of his performances: "He united the sensual morbidity and the most virile energy; the rapid short wrist passages were like violent apostrophes; where it needed to sing, the touch received an impulse which was invisible but surprisingly effective; he was, moreover, a very able and fine colorist; his nuances were of an inexhaustible variety."[71] Conxita Badia corroborated Nin's assessment: "He possessed a touch so delicate that he did not strike but rather stroked the note."[72]

Granados had a distinctive way of practicing before a concert, as a former student at his music academy related, having observed him many times. He rarely practiced a work in its entirety; instead, he would focus on repeating certain passages, "as if nothing existed for him except the keyboard and the sounds that he was caressing," until he was satisfied with the result.[73] He prepared very carefully for his concerts and always kept himself in pianistic trim. "The notion . . . of him as an indolent fellow who was given more to improvisation than to methodical labor is inaccurate. The truth is that he himself took pleasure in joking around and contributed greatly to the diffusion of his own legend."[74] Indeed, one of his most endearing traits was that he did not take himself too seriously.

Mental practice formed an important part of his regimen as well.[75] Despite all of this painstaking physical and psychological preparation (or perhaps because of it), Granados's nervousness tended to flare up before a concert. The following was a typical predicament, noted by all his biographers.[76] His fear was so great that,

> Almost with tears in his eyes, he appealed to all those present to allow him to go home because he was feeling ill, terribly ill. His friends, who were familiar with the artist's nerves, did not relent in the slightest. To the contrary, they pushed him forcibly, virtually throwing him on stage. Granados took note of the applause that greeted him, and after a few measures he had recovered completely, now disposed to astonish the public with his exquisite art and famous touch, which had brought him renown.[77]

As Granados himself explained, "If in an audience of a thousand spectators I know that nine hundred and ninety-nine like me but one does not, I will play poorly, because for me, that one person will be the only one out there, and I know that nothing I do will please him."[78] Such an attitude may strike us as fairly neurotic, but it did not prevent him from gaining international fame and becoming one of the finest pianists of his time.

Other tales abound of his mercurial nature and nervousness. Once the Comtessa de Castellà, a poet, intellectual, and admirer of Granados, asked him to give a concert in her salon. She invited numerous guests to the occasion, and all were eager to hear the maestro perform. When the appointed hour for the concert came, Granados was nowhere to be seen. He arrived late, apologized, and seated himself on a sofa. He made nervous conversation, and after some time, the Countess encouraged him to begin. "I don't feel well, I don't feel well," he protested. "I can't perform!" The Countess, perhaps not unfamiliar with such episodes, led him patiently by the arm to the piano and sat him down. He lifted one finger over the keyboard, the way a child would, and then, with digit poised in mid-air, pleaded, "Don't kill me, don't kill me!" By now the Countess was livid and the audience indignant. Granados rose from the piano and returned to the sofa. "It is impossible for me to play today, Countess!" he declared. Two hours passed as the guests chatted and ate. Everyone pretty much forgot about the concert. Suddenly, without prompting of any kind, Granados seated himself at the piano and began to play—and play, and play.[79]

The writer Apeles Mestres summed up the centrality of his nervous condition to his personality:

> The nervousness of Granados was always the dominant note in his character. It was an excessive nervousness, uncontrollable, in enthusiasm as well as depression, in happiness and sadness, in humor as well as the most serious actions of his life. That is, as far as I understand it, the secret of the extreme vibrancy of his music.[80]

Boladeres Ibern allowed that "Granados was perhaps a bit neurasthenic."[81] Joan Llongueras simply found him to be a person of contrasts: "He was infantile and lovesick, timid and dreamy, aristocratic and disorganized, but above all else he was an artist, passionate, sincere, and intensely personal."[82]

The critics were almost always encomiastic in their appraisal of Granados as a pianist. However, there is a significant difference between French and Spanish critics in terms of what they valued most in his playing. What were the qualities that made his performances so memorable to critics from the one country or the other? Although we jump ahead of our story a bit in the process, some highlights from press reaction to his playing over the decades shed light on this issue.

Of a March 31, 1905, recital at the Salle Pleyel in Paris, a critic commented favorably on the traits that he acquired from the "excellent tutelage" of Charles de Bériot: "the force and delicacy within the sonority, the rectitude of the measure, the confidence and breadth of style, the self-possession that confers assurance to his playing and security to the listener."[83] Along the same lines, Paul de Stoeklin wrote, "Granados is an admirable pianist who never beats the piano but who plays with sobriety, discretion, without bad taste and pointless *tours de force* but remaining always musical."[84] Jean Huré found his playing "hardy, elegant, always impeccable, sometimes wild."[85]

Clearly, the French prized good taste, delicacy, refinement, and "sobriety." Spanish critics had another set of criteria altogether, as soon becomes apparent from the following excerpts:

> In Beethoven's Piano Sonata 21 [op. 53, "Waldstein"], he was COLOSSAL. As an artist of the heart, he probes and penetrates the romantic master's secrets and mysteries, unknown even to many cognoscenti.[86]

> The young Spanish pianist interpreted Beethoven in a magisterial manner, with a passion and an emotional richness that were truly impressive.[87]

> He is the poet of the piano. His hands stroke the keys with a delicacy, with a spirituality, of extraordinary uniqueness. . . . We witnessed him absorbed, transported, electrified before the piano, whose accents vibrated with eloquence and emotion in harmony with the inspirations of the author and of the interpreter, inspirations grounded in an enchanting grandeur.[88]

In short, Spanish critics prized, not restraint, sobriety, and good taste, but rather passion and poetry, spirituality and sentiment, eloquence and emotion, intimacy and inspiration. These reviews tell us as much about the aesthetic expectations of the critics and public in both countries as they do about Granados's performances. Whatever it was he possessed, it appealed to two rather different constituencies that perceived distinct yet complementary qualities in his playing. Both, however, would have agreed with Granados's self-assessment. Once, as the Feast of Saint Cecilia was approaching, a student asked him if he would be celebrating it. "Why?" he asked. "Because she is the patron saint of musicians," the student responded, somewhat perplexed. "Of musicians?" he asked, a smile forming on lips. "Ah, well then, it would not be appropriate for me to celebrate it. I am an *artist*."[89] To Granados, who firmly believed in an underlying "unity" among all the arts, it was not enough merely to be a musician. The purpose of all music-making was to achieve something higher, namely, art itself. Music became poetry, and the pianist, a veritable poet.

However, his would not merely be an art of re-creating what others had written, but rather one of creating his own music, the works on which his legacy would securely rest. For in the same decade in which he arrived as a concert virtuoso, he also emerged as a composer of national and even international renown.

CHAPTER 2

The Emerging Composer

Granados's musical creativity was grounded in his pianism. His first works were for the piano, composed while he was still a student in Paris, and he continued throughout his life to write for that instrument. He was a gifted improviser, and improvisation remained at the heart of his compositional method.

There is abundant anecdotal evidence of the suddenness with which inspiration could come upon him, in response to some stimulus. For instance, during one of his many trips to Valencia, he was improvising at the piano in the home of a friend when someone asked what music he was playing. Gesturing toward the courtyard, he explained that he was "playing" "that garden, those flowers, the blue and orange heavens at sunset, the peace of the jasmines." [1] Beautiful women also inspired his musical outpourings. Amadeu Vives relates one particularly illustrative incident:

> At five in the afternoon, I went to the Oriental Baths in Barceloneta. There I met Granados, who was with three or four friends. We sat in cane chairs and watched the pretty girls coming and going. . . . Suddenly, a very beautiful, tall, slender, majestic girl came in. . . . Granados lost all sense of free will and began swimming in the blaze of her look and grew intoxicated with the dance of her walk. . . . We went up to the first floor and Granados improvised a romantic, passionate, tender, and inflamed melody [at the piano]. [2]

This penchant continued throughout Granados's career. In 1914, Frank Marshall had a ringside seat at one prodigious demonstration of his teacher's capacity for spontaneous creativity under pressure. Marshall was turning pages for him as he performed a recent composition, El pelele. It soon became clear to Marshall that Granados was not paying attention to the manuscript or playing what he had written there. Marshall later told Alicia de Larrocha, "That day Granados improvised a new Pelele that contained the themes and phrases of the authentic [one]. They unfolded in a form completely distinct, but with authenticity and a feeling of the original form so that this version could well have stayed as the definitive one."[3] The audience was enraptured with this "Pelele" and demanded a repetition. Granados obliged, but this time he played it strictly according to the score. Afterwards, a friend congratulated him on the performance, saying: "Yes, yes, of course it was wonderful. But why did you not repeat the piece the public and I asked for?"[4] Why? Because, as Henri Collet once observed, Granados created "without order and method, but with an infallible logic."[5]

Unfortunately, many such creations proved entirely ephemeral, and Amparo often had to prevail on him to write them down. Like Beethoven, he often carried pencil and music paper with him so that he could jot down ideas as they occurred to him, wherever he might be. Thus armed, he felt that his livelihood was secure.[6] At home, Granados often paced nervously about when composing, writing ideas down on a tall desk. On the street or in his house, Granados's absorption in the inspiration of the moment was total when creating music, and he disclosed that in the heat of melodic invention he would lose all awareness of his surroundings, even his family.[7] The conductor Eduardo Toldrà recalled a visit to Granados's house one afternoon. Granados was at the piano, jotting ideas down on the manuscript in front of him. He invited Toldrà to seat himself, and promised he would join him in a moment. That "moment" became more than an hour.[8]

As impressive as his improvisational ability was, it was connected to a certain lack of technical skill that dogged him through most of his career. In the opinion of Fernández-Cid, Granados "wrote with spontaneity, without worrying about the rigors of proportion."[9] Even Boladeres Ibern clearly recognized "the excessive liberty in the relative proportions of his phrases, themes, and sections of his works."[10] In truth, Granados struggled with the more intellectual dimension of composition, the patient and painstaking working out of ideas to spin a web of musical sound over long periods of time. Thematic development and formal coherence were aspects of the compositional art he never mastered.

Riva feels that Granados's music "resembles Spanish poetry in its penchant for repetition of ideas. . . . adding with each repetition distinctive embellishment, each time more luminous and sumptuous."[11] The same might be said of Granados's idol Chopin. This method does not work well with symphonies and concertos, though it can be quite effective in character and programmatic pieces for piano, where one can rely on simple part forms or theme and variations. Even in the soloistic medium, however, Granados confronted his own limitations. He rarely employed sonata form, perhaps because he found its complexities too much to cope with. Unlike all of the piano composers he sought to emulate—Beethoven, Schumann, Chopin, and Liszt—he never so much as attempted to compose a piano sonata.

His response to the challenge of writing an opera or extended work for piano was a kind of "miniaturism," that is, stringing together a series of shorter numbers. Even at that, none of his individual piano pieces lasts much more than about ten minutes, and his stage works are usually one-act affairs about an hour in length. What he lacked in architectonic ability he made up for as a colorist. His harmonic language is rich, and his penchant for modulations to distant keys, added-note sonorities, augmented-sixth chords, and altered dominants marks his idiom as belonging to the late nineteenth century. Many of his pieces are infused with the melos and rhythm of Spanish folk song and dance. These elements of melodic embellishment, harmonic inventiveness, and folkloric inspiration supplied him with all the expressive materials he required to create a style uniquely his own.

Why did Granados not get the training in composition he needed to master the challenges summarized above? The main reason is that there were not many opportunities for aspiring composers in Spain to study with composition teachers of the first order, or to get their large-scale instrumental works performed. Generally one had to go to France or Germany to get that kind of education. Granados, as we have seen, did study piano in Paris, but not composition. He received his only real training in composition during the mid-1880s in Barcelona, from Felip Pedrell.[12]

Pedrell was a musician whose activities were wide-ranging, if somewhat uneven in quality. His greatest ambition was to compose, and it remains one of the ironies of his career—and was a source of bitterness to him—that for as much energy and time as he poured into writing all kinds of music, especially opera, his works remained obscure. Yet he was at the forefront of Catalan opera, and his *Els Pirineus* (premiered in 1902), composed to a text by Jacint Verdaguer, was a significant achievement.[13] His contributions to musicology were considerable, and here his legacy is more secure. Pedrell was a product of the *Renaixença*, and his antiquarian interests were perfectly consistent with that movement. For example, he edited the works of the Spanish Renaissance polyphonist Tomás Luis de Victoria. Pedrell was not fixated solely on Catalonia, and he embraced the entire cultural patrimony of Spain as his own.[14]

Perhaps Pedrell's most important contribution, however, was as a teacher, and he counted Albéniz, Granados, Falla, and Roberto Gerhard (1896–1970) among his disciples. Here, though, it is often difficult to know exactly what and how much they learned from him. They all regarded him with reverence and affection, but they also departed in important ways from his own predilections. For instance, their attraction to certain vernacular styles, flamenco, for example, ran counter to his own tastes. In general terms, though, the influence was there. Pedrell firmly believed that Spanish composers should use the musical heritage of their own country—both "cultivated" music and traditional folklore—as the basis for their concert music. He was the apostle of nationalism in Spain, and his manifesto *Por nuestra música* (1891), clearly inspired by Wagner's *Oper und Drama*, had a surpassing effect on Spanish composers of that epoch. His advocacy of Wagner's teachings concerning *Gesamtkunstwerk* and use of *Leitmotiv* were central to this, though he had reservations about making the orchestra so prominent. The Mediterranean aesthetic demanded, he thought, primacy for the voice.[15] Granados shared Pedrell's devotion to Wagner.

However, we have little documentation to shed light on the nature of Pedrell's tutelage. The "lessons" Granados had with him probably took the form of conversations, and these were not pursued on a systematic or regular basis. In fact, Pedrell has been faulted for not imparting to his students greater technical command as composers. However, records, to the extent that they exist, show that he did not completely neglect their development of technique. Pedrell assigned Granados the task of arranging Clementi's Sonatinas, op. 36, for string trio (the manuscript bears the inscription "curso de composición del Sr. Pedrell"). This is precisely the kind of practical experience in orchestration we would have expected him to give Granados. In addition, Granados dedicated several early works to his teacher, which suggests that these, too, were exercises of a sort.[16]

Other evidence of Pedrell's assistance to Granados the composer is found in their correspondence. In one letter to his teacher, Granados asks a question about writing for chorus. He sketches out a series of first-inversion chords in treble clef and asks him how he should distribute the notes among the voices. He even draws in the lines on the next page where Pedrell can answer; whether he did or not, we do not know.[17] Certainly Granados revered Pedrell, and his letters to the master make this readily apparent. After a successful concert, he wrote a letter to Pedrell stating that "I prefer a single word from my maestro to all the triumphs . . . that I might gain. I owe you the major part of my artistic revelation, and to you I give the congratulations for this triumph."[18] It is not clear which triumph he means (possibly his 1898 opera María del Carmen), but his intention is perfectly clear. On other occasions, he declared himself "a su orden mi general" (at your command, my General) and "Vuestro devoto amigo" (Your devoted friend).

For his part, Pedrell declared Granados an apt pupil, saying that he made rapid progress and demonstrated an extraordinary capacity to absorb what he was learning. This proved to Pedrell that Granados possessed a "privileged" intelligence.[19] His ability to assimilate music was phenomenal:

> [Granados] . . . possessed a faculty for assimilation so impressive that he had no need of reinforcing what he had learned through the study of books and treatises or immersing himself in current systems and trends. All that was necessary was to place any kind of music before him, and he would absorb it with his extraordinary faculty. Thus were born those musical blossoms that sprouted suddenly from the ambience of any particular region of Spain, be they *Murcianas, Valencianas, Valses poéticos, Valses sentimentales*. All his assimilations became autobiographical utterances from the heart.[20]

Among Granados's earliest "utterances" are those he wrote down in a notebook labeled "Álbum: París, 1888," when he was 21 years old. Containing upwards of forty pieces, as well as drawings and caricatures, this is the first record that survives of his early attempts to develop into a serious composer.[21] The works are charming juvenilia that exhibit the features of salon music of that period, with titles such as "Melodía," "Vals," "Primavera (Romanza sin palabras)" (Spring: Romance without Words), and "Mazurka." These pithy, lyrical essays reveal the influence of Chopin and Schumann. In fact, he actually borrowed one of Schumann's titles: "Glückes genug" (Perfect Happiness). Most of the works bear dedications to young women, some of whom were probably students of his. One of the dedicatees, Pepita Conde, was the daughter of Eduardo Conde. Granados published many of his early salon works in "general-interest magazines" in Barcelona, intended for the amateur pianist.[22]

One of the works in this album has some significance, if only symbolic, relative to his future celebrity as a composer. It is a piano duet entitled *En la aldea* (In the Village), a multi-movement composition in which one movement, "La siesta," includes for the first time in his oeuvre the nightingale's song.[23] In his diary, Granados recounts an evening in Paris when he, Malats, and Albéniz (in Paris on a concert tour) stayed up one night copying out a concerto by Bériot so he could take it back to Spain with him.[24] They finally finished their labor, exhausted but exultant, at five in the morning. After a breakfast of ham, cheese, and wine, Granados began drifting off to sleep, enchanted by the song of a nightingale. The bird assumed sentimental importance to him after that, and its song would always "resonate in my soul."[25]

Danzas españolas

Granados's first important and enduring composition, however, was undoubtedly the collection of twelve piano solos entitled *Danzas españolas* (Spanish Dances). The work is divided into four books of three dances each. They were probably begun in 1888 during his Paris tenure.[26] When he finished the set is not clear, but he began to perform them in Barcelona on April 20, 1890, at the Teatre Líric; he presented them to Casa Dotesio for publication in that same year.

After the *Danzas* were published, Granados sent copies to several of the leading musicians in Europe, including Camille Saint-Saëns, Jules Massenet, Edvard Grieg, and César Cui. Cui found them "charming both in melody and harmonization" and outstanding in their "individual originality."[27] Massenet hailed him as "the Spanish Grieg," while Saint-Saëns and Bériot added their voices to the chorus of praise. Spaniards, too, found much inspiration in them. The Barcelona conductor and composer Joan Lamote de Grignon orchestrated them, as did Rafael Ferrer many years later. Alfonso Albéniz, son of the composer, claimed that Isaac always kept a copy of the *Danzas españolas* on his piano.[28] Perhaps the organization of Albéniz's *Iberia*, consisting as it does of four books of three pieces each, was inspired by Granados's *Danzas españolas* and was even intended as a gesture of admiration. Pedrell thought highly of the *Danzas* as well.[29]

Granados's *Danzas* exhibit uncomplicated directness and unaffected rhythmic and melodic appeal. They are nearly all in ternary form, and the retransitions and codas are brief and perfunctory. The harmonic language is diatonic, and chromaticism appears only as surface color. Reliance on thematic reiteration rather than development is both a weakness and a strength, and commentators have had mixed opinions about this procedure. One critic thought that,

> [The *Danzas*] are not quite free from the defect which is apparent in many of
> Granados's works: the too numerous repetitions of a theme. But in those which
> are strongly marked with emotion and melancholy, it is this very repetition, plain,
> unsophisticated, that increases tenfold the emotional effect.[30]

Another critique echoed and amplified this last observation:

By endlessly varied repetition he conveys an obsessive and static insistence on the intrinsic beauty of his conception. . . . [T]he tireless exploration of sonorities and ornaments derives from the simplest possible material, and a constant and intensifying process occurs that is entirely different [from] the dynamic structure of a classical sonata.[31]

In any case, the very first thing someone approaching this music must understand is that the subtitles can be misleading. To try to analyze the music itself as some manifestation of the subtitles placed there, not by Granados but by his publishers, may lead to a misinterpretation of its character. In truth, these dances are highly stylized renditions, filtered through Granados's own personality and background. They do not quote folk melodies per se and were in no way the product of anything like fieldwork or transcription. In their rhythms and scale types, they often exude a Spanish fragrance, sometimes of a faux-Oriental kind suggestive of Andalusia. At other times, however, they are scarcely identifiable as Spanish at all. We focus here on those numbers that best exemplify his nascent nationalist style, no doubt inspired by the teachings of Pedrell and by Albéniz's early Spanish works of the 1880s.

No. 1 ("Galante")

Fully nine of the twelve dances are in $\frac{3}{4}$ meter, starting with this one. Triple meter is highly characteristic of Spanish folk music. If we halve the rhythmic values of the two measures and view them as a single bar in $\frac{3}{4}$ time, what we have is essentially the so-called bolero rhythm, a series of six eighth notes elaborated by the substitution of a sixteenth-note triplet or two sixteenths on the first anacrusis and often others as well. This, too, is a trademark. Here, however, Granados stretches out this characteristic rhythm, long associated with *seguidillas* and *fandangos*, in a sort of bold fanfare to introduce the work as a whole (ex. 2.1).[32]

Ex. 2.1: *Danzas españolas*, No. 1, mm. 1–2

As is usually the case in Granados's approach to da capo form, the A theme is very dance-like while the B theme, in the parallel minor, is more lyrical in character.

No. 2 ("Oriental")

The "Oriental" is a specimen of the "exotic" that one encounters so frequently in nineteenth-century art, literature, and music. Spanish composers, especially, churned

out a long succession of "serenatas moriscas," "caprichos árabes," and "marchas orientales" that all rely more or less on the same codes and markers to identify them as
"other" (Moorish, Gypsy, or some conflation of the two): minor scales with chromatic
inflections and the augmented-second interval; ostinato rhythms; sinuously arabesque
melodic tracery; asymmetrical themes that are highly embellished and often synco-
pated, in imitation of florid melismas; and the simulation of Middle Eastern instruments such as cymbals and double-reed or plucked-string instruments.[33] Such pieces
are reminiscent of the poetry of Spanish Romantics like José de Zorrilla (1817–93),
whose verses, such as the epic poem *Granada*, are full of "sultans and moonstruck
Moorish princesses, of turbans and pearly *alcázars*, of geraniums and carnations and
Andalusian 'passion.'"[34] However, Granados's "Oriental" rises above the level of hackneyed clichés and exhibits compelling charm and sincerity.

The accompaniment in the left hand that introduces the piece outlines a simple
minor scale between tonic and dominant, but the omission of the fourth scale degree
results in a little gap between E-flat and G that creates a plangent effect. Its curving,
arabesque contour and flowing character may remind some of Schubert's *Gretchen
am Spinnrade*. The melody that enters soon thereafter is one of Granados's most enchanting inventions. The disarmingly simple tune is presented in thirds in the right
hand over the running eighth notes in the left. This sort of singing (and guitar playing)
in thirds is typical of Hispanic music in general and has nothing to do, of course, with
"Oriental" music as such, except insofar as that word is code for the Gypsy/Moorish
south (ex. 2.2).

Ex. 2.2: *Danzas españolas*, No. 2, mm. 3–9

Granados creates a seductively undulating effect by juxtaposing $\frac{3}{4}$ in the bass with
hemiola in the treble. The murmuring stream of the left hand contrasts effectively
with the longer note values of the melody, and some remarkably effective perform-

ances of this piece have been for guitar duet, because of the clearly delineated parts. This dance resembles a Chopin Nocturne in its stirring melody and murmuring accompaniment.[35] The B theme of this ternary form persists in the right hand against an arpeggiated accompaniment in the left. It simulates flamenco singing in its embellishments, syncopations (basically hemiola) and accents that obscure the downbeat, iterance on a single note, and descending contour within a limited range (ex. 2.3).

Ex. 2.3: *Danzas españolas*, No. 2, mm. 49–52

No. 5 ("Andaluza")

No. 5 is without doubt the most popular and well known of the numbers in this collection, even in his entire output. In no specific or meaningful sense is this an Andalusian *playera*, as one publisher's subtitle claims, but its allusion to southern folklore is clear from the outset (hence the main subtitle, "Andaluza"). Just this sort of thing antagonized many a Catalan nationalist, upset to see a compatriot descend to such depths of *andalucismo*. Granados actually received "insults and anonymous letters accusing me of writing Andalusian dances! As if that were some kind of crime."[36]

One of the reasons this work is so popular is because it is a staple in the guitar repertoire, having been transcribed numerous times by guitarists over the years. Its translation to the guitar medium is logical precisely because the very texture and figurations of the animated accompaniment are idiomatic to that instrument. Granados could not play the guitar and wrote absolutely nothing for it. But he no doubt gained familiarity with it through his acquaintance with guitarists such as Miquel Llobet (1878–1938), the Catalan virtuoso, who in turn transcribed for the guitar works by Granados and Albéniz. Because of the guitar's centrality to Spanish folk music, evocations of it occur frequently in Granados's nationalist piano pieces.

In this dance, Granados is clearly painting a scene in which a guitarist accompanies an Andalusian dancer and singer. The agitated syncopations create an atmosphere of both excitement and mystery. The melody itself exhibits the typical contour of the concertized flamenco melody. Insofar as one of the origins of flamenco singing is liturgical chant, it is not too much to suggest that what we have here is an initial ascent from the final to a reciting tone on the dominant (i.e., from E to B), embellished by a lower-neighbor tone (A), and a descent to the cadence on the final (ex. 2.4).

Ex. 2.4: *Danzas españolas*, No. 5, mm. 3–5

Granados achieves some unity between his A and B themes in that the latter, in the parallel major, begins with the same ascending motive, recitation, and neighbor tone, though from there it goes through series of sequences, to be followed by a consequent phrase moving in the opposite melodic direction (ex. 2.5). The simple symmetry and graceful lyricism of this section provide a strong contrast with the more agitated A theme.

Ex. 2.5: *Danzas españolas*, No. 5, mm. 37–41

No. 6 ("Rondalla aragonesa")

Along with evocations of the Moorish "Orient" and Gypsy flamenco, composers in and outside of Spain have been drawn to the *jota*. Originally from Aragon, there are variants of it in many regions, even Andalusia. In all its forms the *jota* is a sprightly song and dance in triple meter in which castanets figure prominently. Some of the best-known concert *jotas* are Emmanuel Chabrier's *España* and this number.

Typical of the *jota*, real and composed, is the alternation between *estribillo* and *copla* (refrain and verse), between sections in which either dance or song predominates: the dance sections are in strict rhythm, while the *coplas* tend to be freer. Just so there would be no mistaking his intentions, and perhaps to add a splash of local color to the visual appearance of the score, he actually marks the *copla* as such at m. 74 (ex. 2.6a/b).

Ex. 2.6a: *Danzas españolas*, No. 6, mm. 1–4

Ex. 2.6b: *Danzas españolas*, No. 6, mm. 74–79

Granados was often under financial pressure and would rush a piece to the publisher before it had matured. Later he might make significant changes to the published version, which he would then incorporate into his performances and convey to his students.[37] A case in point is the seventh dance, subtitled by Granados himself "Valenciana." Granados was never satisfied with the original version and made numerous adjustments over the years, which he passed on to his disciples and incorporated into his recorded performance.[38] Alicia de Larrocha has hewed to the oral tradition in her recordings of this piece, and the recent critical edition by her and Douglas Riva finally puts into print the changes Granados would himself have made had he lived long enough to do so.

To be sure, the thematic material and structure of the work remain the same, and the revision is only a single measure longer than the original, to accommodate a revised coda. Most of the alterations are minor and pertain to articulation, voicing, and accidentals. In some cases, however, an accumulation of such changes can produce quite a different effect (ex. 2.7a/b).

Ex. 2.7a: *Danzas españolas*, No. 7, original, mm. 32–35

Ex. 2.7b: *Danzas españolas*, No. 7, revision, mm. 32–35

In terms of style, the strumming and plucking of chords on the guitar are the initial point of reference in this piece, along with the sound of castanets. This is interrupted by "vocal" interjections, in octaves played between right and left hands (ex. 2.8).

Ex. 2.8: *Danzas españolas*, No. 7, mm. 9–13

This sort of alternation between instruments and voices, dancing and singing, is typical of Spanish folk music in general, and few works by Granados more effectively depict the color and clatter of a folk dance, perhaps a Valencian variant of the *jota*. The B section, marked Poco più moto, moves to the dominant key (D major) but features the same melodic ideas and rhythmic patterns of the A section. This is an instance, however, where repetition leads to intensity, not monotony.

Nos. 8 ("Sardana"), 11 ("Arabesca"), and 12 ("Bolero")

Dramatic registral contrasts distinguish No. 8, especially the resonant chords and pedal notes in the low register against the embellishments in the right hand that rise and fall in a series of dramatic arches. Such melodic gestures make one think of wind instruments of some kind, perhaps the *flabiols* and *tenoras* (flutes and double reeds) in the *cobla* (band) that accompanies a *sardana*, the Catalan circle dance (ex. 2.9). This is no doubt the reason why some editor attached the "Sardana" subtitle to this work. Orchestrations of the piece rely heavily on double reeds and reinforce this impression.

Ex. 2.9: *Danzas españolas*, No. 8, mm. 1–2

While the rhythm and timbre of the A section give it a Catalan flavor, the B section has nothing of the *sardana* about it and seems, in its minor key and ostinato rhythm in the left hand, to return to a quasi-Andalusian mood.

The same could be said of the last two dances in the collection, especially No. 11, with its Phrygian modality D. The beginning is entrancing, with a single melody line undulating around d^1 on the piano, like the plaintive cry of a solo singer to introduce the dance. The widely spaced accompaniment supports a melody that picks up the motive of the introduction; tightly woven around the persistent d^1 are its upper and lower neighbors, in a hypnotic bit of filigree.

In the final number, an ostinato in the left hand dances nimbly between the tonic and dominant in the key of A minor, decorated by whimsical appoggiaturas (ex. 2.10).

Ex. 2.10: *Danzas españolas*, No. 12, mm. 1–4

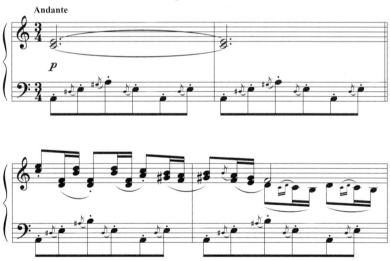

This piece is in rondo form, and its main theme alternates with contrasting ideas of a more song-like character. The dance ends as mysteriously as it began, bringing the collection to a close.

Theatrical Works

Like many Spanish composers of his generation, Granados was determined to make his mark in the theater. Indeed, in Spain that was the only venue in which he could gain any real measure of fame and fortune. He never achieved the level of either that he desired, but not for lack of effort. He might have eventually, had he lived long enough.

Granados's first literary collaborator was José Feliu y Codina (1845–97). Catalan by birth (né Josep Feliu i Codina), his initial contributions were to Catalan literature in the context of the *Renaixença*. His theatrical works, which included comedies and serious drama, exhibit a mordant social satire. He also wrote novels and worked as an editor for the Barcelona press. In 1886 he moved to Madrid and continued to work as a journalist there. He began to write plays in Castilian, in which he became remarkably fluent. He also developed a passion for regionalism in his writing, and he traveled widely throughout Spain to observe people, dialects, and customs that he could incorporate into his works. This resulted in several plays, including *Miel de la Alcarria* (1895), *María del Carmen* (1896),[39] and *Los Ovillejos* (1897).[40] Granados wrote incidental music for the first and turned the last into a zarzuela. He converted the middle one into an opera.

Miel de la Alcarria

Miel de la Alcarria is set in Alcarria, a region of Castile famous for its honey. The title drips with irony, however, in that this is a "bitter and most brutal portrait of life in the Spanish countryside."[41] The three-act drama depicts the rigors and deceits of rural life: a daughter sacrifices her love to salvage the reputation of her mother, who was wrongly accused of adultery. Other characters include a grieving grandfather, a father who leaves home forever, a sinner who admits her guilt only when her niece vows to abandon her fiancé and enter a convent, and a shepherd who knows all that has gone on and declares that if he cannot win the hand of his beloved, he will renounce earthly love.[42] In his equally dramatic score, Granados reveals a flair for orchestration in his instrumental combinations, while the opening of act 3 features a memorable setting for female chorus and muted strings. This is the first instance of Granados's employment of an offstage chorus for dramatic effect, a technique he exploited in later stage works.

Los Ovillejos

Los Ovillejos, a zarzuela in one act and three scenes, was no doubt inspired by the celebration of the sesquicentennial of Goya's birth in 1896, as its subtitle, "La gallina ciega," is the title of one of Goya's best-known cartoons, depicting a game of "blindman's bluff." The cast includes not only the Duke and Duchess of Ovillejo but also an assortment of lower-class types like servants and cooks, as well as a *majo* and a *maja*, streetwise types known for their colorful costume and uninhibited manner. The "epoch" of the innocuous little comedy is the 1790s, precisely the decade of Goya's involvement with the Duchess of Alba and most intense fascination with the figure of the *majo*. Moreover, a two-act version and Feliu y Codina's libretto identify this work as a *sainete lírico* (a musical skit), and the *sainete* was a light theatrical entertainment immensely popular in the eighteenth century. The use of the fandango is yet another signal that this was an excursion, Granados's first, into Goya's world.[43]

The extant manuscripts indicate that *Los Ovillejos* was nearly completed in 1897, but their disordered state has led scholars to differ as to whether Granados actually ever finished the zarzuela.[44] In fact, the scores are incomplete, and it would not be possible to reconstruct or revive this work in any of its four versions.[45] There is much wonderful music in them, however, which could and should be performed. Granados may have abandoned it because of the death of Feliu y Codina, though the libretto was complete and the author's collaboration was no longer absolutely necessary. Perhaps Granados had trouble securing rights to the work. Further research is necessary to clarify the reasons for its incompletion and absence from the stage. At all events, it was no doubt a valuable exercise for the aspiring composer, and Granados was able to recycle some of it in other works.[46]

María del Carmen

Granados was composing *Los Ovillejos* at the same that he was completing his first opera, *María del Carmen*. Granados retained a special fondness for *María del Carmen*, which he thought to be his finest work.[47] Musically similar to *Los Ovillejos*, the two works are otherwise quite different in character and thrust. And whereas *Los Ovillejos* remained unknown, *María del Carmen* had a brief but reasonably successful career on the stage during Granados's life; it has been revived periodically since his death.

The loss of the original manuscript orchestral score complicates any attempt to analyze this work, as the opera survives in its entirety only in a revision, probably by Granados's son Eduardo. The following discussion depends not on that extant revision, since it is impossible to know how closely it follows the original, but rather on the libretto and on press accounts of the productions during Granados's life.[48] Another useful source of information is Henri Collet's biography, which treats the opera in some detail.[49] Three numbers from the opera were published during Granados's lifetime, and these are also important sources for any discussion of musical style.[50]

The setting of the story is a village in rural Murcia. The opera deals with a struggle between two men, Javier and Pencho, for the love of the beautiful María del Carmen. An element of class conflict is involved, as Javier comes from the local elite, while Pencho is poor. Pencho wounded Javier in a fight over water rights and was forced to flee town. María del Carmen nursed the injured Javier back to health, not out of love but in order to save Pencho's life, upon his return. This is where the opera commences the action, with the return of Pencho from hiding in North Africa. The second act centers around a fiesta featuring local folk music, and this forms the backdrop for a confrontation between Javier and Pencho. The antagonists agree to fight a duel, which is the focus of the third and final act. The similarity of this story to *verismo* operas like *Cavalleria rusticana* and *I pagliacci* is obvious, though this drama has a happy ending, and it may well be that local audiences were not quite ready for a Spanish opera that dealt with the more sordid side of life in a shocking and brutal way.[51]

The libretto represented a considerable reduction in the text of the play and simplification of the plot, not only to accommodate the music but also to fit into a much shorter amount of time, about an hour and a half. Yet, additions were also made, mostly in terms of spectacle: a lavish procession at the end of the first act and a dance number in the fiesta of the second.

The opera commences with a prelude in E major of a slightly "Oriental" character, featuring augmented seconds in the melody, to evoke the drama's setting in southern Spain. One critic felt this entirely appropriate, noting that the Murcians "had much Arab in their blood."[52] The orchestration is rich and distinctive in its reliance on winds, low strings, and harp. Granados's creative exploitation of orchestral resources inspired Collet to refer to the opera as a "vast symphony in three parts."[53] A novel feature of the symphonic introduction is the deployment of chorus, in imitation of *Los auroros*, a Murcian group of singers that performed during processions to morning mass. The opera uses some other novel choral effects, including offstage chorus and choral interludes between scenes.

The first act begins with a scene infused with the popular Murcian song "El paño" (The Cloth), whose guitar accompaniment is suggested in the orchestra. Another folk-style number is Pepuso's song "Con zaragüelles vine al mundo," which evokes the *parranda*, a Murcian dance. The *parranda* appears in other contexts as well, including the "Canción de la zagalica" (ex. 2.11) in which Fuensanta's *parranda*-like phrases alternate with a group of three other characters (Don Fulgencio, Roque, and Pepuso).

Ex. 2.11: *María del Carmen,* act 1, "Canción de la zagalica"

The entrance of María del Carmen takes place in the context of a lovely sextet, while a recurring motive heralds Javier's appearance. This tendency toward leitmotif throughout the score, even if not fully worked out, reveals Wagner's influence. Especially effective is the finale to act 1, a procession to mass featuring *Los auroros*. Many commentators found the simplicity and grandeur of this scene most impressive.

Act 2 begins with a very brief prelude in D. After the initial "Romanza" sung by a heartsick María del Carmen, the drama centers around the duet between her and Pencho, which is interrupted by the arrival of Javier and mounting tension between the rival suitors. María del Carmen has agreed to marry Javier in exchange for Pencho's freedom from prosecution, but Pencho sternly rejects this arrangement. Granados makes effective use of Murcian folk song and dance in this act as well, in the context of an outdoor fiesta. In fact, one of the published numbers from the opera was the dance from scene 10 of act 2, marked "Tiempo algo movido de Malagueña murciana" (ex. 2.12). This selection is replete with characteristic Spanish rhythms in triple meter, and it presents repeated evocations of guitar playing. In fact, for this number an ensemble of mandolins and guitars provided authentic local color on stage.

Ex. 2.12: *María del Carmen*, act 2, scene 10, "Malagueña murciana"

This is followed by another fetching number, the "Canción cartagenera" (ex. 2.13), in which Pencho sings of his undying love for María del Carmen. This actual folk song contains a well-known verse, cited by several critics as one of the highlights of the opera:

> To look at you, my eyes;
> To love you, my soul;
> To lull you, my arms;
> To protect you, my sword.[54]

Ex. 2.13: *María del Carmen*, act 2, scene 11, "Canción cartagenera"

Granados's inventive orchestral accompaniment includes tremolandi strings and colorful use of clarinet and trombone.

Act 3 commences with a lugubrious prelude featuring the menacing sound of timpani and low strings, under a theme in the horns played in sixths. The woodwinds enter with phrases associated with the two antagonists, setting the stage for their confrontation in this act. Pencho and María sing a duet to the accompaniment of muted strings; both are apprehensive about the coming showdown, and it is clear that María, though loving Pencho, still feels affection for Javier and does want not to see either man hurt. Javier soon appears to face Pencho in a duel. Javier's father, Domingo, attempts to intervene and persuade Pencho to relinquish his claim; however, tragedy is only averted with the arrival of Don Fulgencio, the local doctor. He informs Domingo that Javier is already at death's door and nothing can save him. The drama now approaches its climax, or anti-climax, depending on one's point of view. For Javier finally realizes the futility of his suit and, abandoning all thoughts of a fight, helps the lovers flee to safety in a spirit of reconciliation. In this context Granados uses an offstage chorus to represent justice, "as a means of exteriorizing Pencho's guilt."[55]

Amadeu Vives, a highly successful zarzuela composer turned impresario and fellow Catalan now residing in the capital, was instrumental in securing the production of Granados's opera in Madrid. He helped coordinate preparations for the production with Manuel Figueras, director of the opera and zarzuela company at the Teatro de Parish.[56] Granados was assisted at rehearsals by Casals, who conducted a private performance of the work at the Teatro Principal in Madrid. *María del Carmen* formally premiered at the Parish on November 12, 1898.[57] It was a triumphant occasion for the composer but one unfortunately not shared by Feliu y Codina, who had passed away the previous year at age 52.[58]

Diario de Barcelona reported on the premiere and noted some grumbling in the Castilian press. "Those in the know believe that the libretto is not suitable for setting to music and that the score is lacking in traditional numbers, like duos and romanzas. Instead, Granados has abused the recitative dialogue, which is the specialty of Wagner." This same journalist recalled a conversation between one of the critics and Feliu y Codina after the premiere of the play two years earlier. At that time, the critic had adjured the author, "For God's sake, don't allow anyone to set this to music." In the opinion of the journalist writing for *Diario de Barcelona*, this play was not suitable material for musical theater; however, he thought Feliu y Codina was fortunate to have Granados do the job, whether or not the job should have been done at all.[59]

There was indeed much complaining about "Wagnerisms" in the score: continuous music with a general avoidance of separable numbers and an emphasis on the orchestra and orchestral commentary on the drama that actually competed with the voices on an equal footing. This in particular aroused the indignation of Count Guillermo Morphy (1836–99), secretary to the royal family, musicologist, and composer. He assigned *María del Carmen* to the "Modern School" and condemned its lack of traditional forms and preference for the orchestra. All this he found unsuited to "Latin" taste.[60] The feature most critics did not care for at all was the extensive use of prose recitative. This was perhaps Granados's attempt at speech-melody, but it ran counter to Spanish predilections, conditioned as they were by the zarzuela, in which musical numbers alternated with poetic spoken dialogue. Such devices led one reviewer to declare with exasperation, "All this is Wagnerian, and they should take it to the [Teatro] Real!" where Wagner's operas were in vogue and where a Wagnerian faction headed by the critic Antonio Peña y Goñi held court.[61]

To be sure, some critics valued Granados's orchestration and thought it rivaled that of "other maestros of European renown."[62] Certainly his employment of Murcian folklore, like the *parranda* and the *auroros*, was the most endearing feature of the score, "giving it brilliant local color."[63] However, if Granados's musical efforts had passed the test, the libretto had not. The general consensus was that Feliu y Codina's use of prose instead of poetry did not meet the lyrical exigencies of the opera. One reviewer thought that, in order to avoid a "disconnect" between the music and the words, the music "must always correspond, as Rossini said, to the 'emotions of those who are singing.'"[64] This appeal to Rossini speaks volumes about the expectations critics brought to a Spanish opera, namely, that it should behave like its Italian cousins.

Some thought the librettist had prepared his work rather carelessly, though this cannot have been the case. He and Granados traveled to Murcia to observe and absorb its natural and cultural ambience.[65] Perhaps they did their work too well, for *El liberal* opined that "opera is the final refuge of romanticism, and above all, it requires as a general rule the choice of a story that is truly poetic and elevated, far removed from the prosaic familiarities of ordinary life."[66] In short, the ordinary language of the lower classes was not suited to the elevated music Granados had written.

One critic—and fortunately for Granados, among the most influential in Madrid—was unstinting in his praise.[67] This was Antonio Guerra y Alarcón. He found no contradiction between Granados's "modern" approach and the provincial setting and subject matter of the drama. And, alone among reviewers, he approved the prose dialogue and use of recitative, as well as the advanced use of the orchestra to comment on and participate in the drama. Certainly he found Granados's Wagner-indebted approach to dramatic structure more satisfying than "the solution to the problem of continuity offered by Italian opera. . . . In effect, melody runs throughout the score, a modern kind of melody whose structure follows the dramatic flow and whose varied repetitions deepen the psychology of the character or comment on the action."[68] Despite any German or Italian influence on the opera, Guerra y Alarcón was certain that the play and music were both "eminently Spanish," averring that it was always more "meritorious and patriotic" to search for the story of a national opera in native literary works that deal with regional folklore than to resort to the "exotic types" one finds in foreign literature. This may well have been a jab at *Carmen*. In any case, he thought Granados had done a commendable job of fleshing out the characters and conferring on them "musical individuality."

All commentators agreed that the cast acquitted itself admirably. The sets and costumes received approbation, as did the direction of Miguel Soler. Nearly all the reviewers agreed that the audience warmed to the work, interrupting it with applause and demanding the repetition of selected numbers, especially Fuensanta's solo in the first act. Granados, who conducted, made five or six curtain calls already at the end of the first act, and repeated this at the end of the entire opera.

Yet, despite its qualified success, it did not have a long run. It appeared on November 12–25, 27, 30, December 6, 8 (a benefit for the composer and one of the singers, Puiggener), 17, 26, and finally on January 8, 1899. For unknown reasons, the management of the Teatro de Parish decided to pull the work from the theater bill, and it never again made it onto the stage in Madrid. Granados was very upset by this and sought to revive its fortunes in the capital, but to no avail. The musicologist José Subirá speculated that the early withdrawal of the opera had to do with "incomprehension, envy, and bad faith" on the part of the theater's management.[69] Whatever the case, this was but the first episode in the work's checkered career.

To put the opera in historical context, we should bear in mind the tumultuous period through which Spain was passing at this time. Its war with the United States had begun on April 25, 1898, and by July 26, Spain was suing for peace. The conflict officially ended on December 10, 1898, with the signing of the Treaty of Paris. Spain's loss of its overseas colonies coincided with increasing tension within the country. For example, two days after the opera's premiere in November, the Barcelona express train arrived in Madrid carrying commissioners from Catalonia who were intent on negotiating with Queen María Cristina concerning organizational reforms.[70] They desired direct election of governing and legislative bodies, as well as greater autonomy for the various regions, especially their own.[71]

Ultimately unsuccessful, this effort was emblematic of growing friction between Barcelona and Madrid and the increasingly restive nature of *catalanisme* (Catalanism). The loss of Cuba had serious economic repercussions in Catalonia because of a subsequent decline in trade, and this exacerbated the agitation for autonomy.[72] To the Catalanists, Madrid was mismanaging the whole national enterprise. During the elections of 1905, Catalan separatists conducted an intensive propaganda campaign in Barcelona, with cries of "Long Live Catalonia" and "Death to Spain." Newspapers such as *El poble català*, *El diluvio*, *La veu de Catalunya*, all of which ran reviews of Granados's operas, were likewise Catalanist in orientation.[73]

And yet, in Granados's first opera one perceives no hint of national catastrophe in the loss of Cuba, Puerto Rico, and the Philippines, no spirit of searing national self-examination. There is certainly no assertion of Catalan separatism in this veristic, Spanish-language opera set in Murcia and musically replete with *malagueñas murcianas*. Granados's musical drama seems disconnected from these goings-on and suggests a certain indifference to politics on his part. Those who knew Granados intimately understood him to have a blasé attitude toward political issues.

> Granados listened to political conversations with impatience, or he just did not
> listen to them at all. Toward the political press he felt a delicious indifference that
> educated people sometimes found surprising. He did not concern himself with
> "fixing" Spain or pretend to know what the Ministry of the Interior or the State
> Department, the governor or the mayor should be doing. He left all such matters

to those whose business they were, even as they left to him the job of playing the piano and composing music.[74]

It would be too cynical to portray Granados as someone willing to look with indifference upon any sordid spectacle of mismanagement, corruption, or debauchery, as long as it did not interfere with his piano playing.[75] Still, he may have been an example of the kind of person Spanish politicians had in mind when they bemoaned the political apathy of many citizens. However, those same politicians were often responsible for the apathy. One Catalan observer, a Señor Cambó, conservative banker and industrialist, complained that "During a whole century, Spain has lived under the appearance of a constitutional democratic regime, without the people having ever, directly or indirectly, had the least share in the Government. The same men who gave them their political rights took good care to prevent their ever using them."[76] One clearly sees why Gerald Brenan found it unsurprising that "the majority of Spaniards . . . preferred to keep clear of politics. It was better to put up with wrongs and injustices of every kind than to risk worse things by protesting. For the law courts gave no protection."[77]

For his part, Granados apparently felt that a true artist should be above politics. It might be well to bear in mind George Orwell's assertion that indifference to politics in the name of art is itself a political attitude. From that perspective, Granados was anything but apolitical. And there is, after all, a certain political dimension to *María del Carmen*. Regardless of what Granados's own intentions in writing it may have been, it was consistent with the ambition of many Spanish composers to establish a national operatic style on a par with French, German, and Italian opera. In this way, they could assert Spain's continuing importance in European civilization. Madrid audiences responded to the folkloric elements in *María del Carmen* as a patriotic statement and an affirmation of national renewal.[78]

María Cristina certainly appreciated Granados's operatic essay, for she rewarded him with the Cross of Carlos III on January 9, 1899. In Granados, she had an exemplary Catalan subject, one still loyal to Castile. After an earlier meeting with María Cristina, he reported back to his wife that he was thrilled to have met her. She had been positively personable, addressing him like an old friend—"¡Hola Granados! ¿Qué tal?" ("Hello, Granados! How are you?")—and inquiring about his latest musical projects.[79] That he was not merely loyal to but very much in love with Castile would eventually become apparent in ways more durable and spectacular than anyone yet imagined.

Despite all this, Barcelona audiences were generally receptive to *María del Carmen* when it appeared at the Teatro del Tívoli on May 31, 1899.[80] To be sure, some Catalanists resented this opera, and a small but disruptive claque on opening night registered its disapproval of the opera's non-Catalan subject matter and stylistic proximity to zarzuela, a despised symbol of Castilian domination.[81] The conflict between foes and friends of Castile was on display in reviews of the opera.

One the one hand, the pro-Castilian *La vanguardia* delighted in its "most honorable sincerity" and went on to declare that by enriching simple popular melody with colorful orchestration, Granados "transports us to the gardens of Murcia, presenting the freshness of the countryside, the healthful air, and the character of the local inhabitants, without deceiving us."[82] It scarcely seems possible that this author attended the same opera reviewed by the Catalanist *Lo teatro català*, which skewered the score's "monotony and diffuseness" and the composer's lack of rapport with the drama, which resulted in indifference and fatigue on the part of the audience.[83]

Some saw the work not simply as a vindication of the young composer's artistic promise but also of the dream of "ópera española." "The success of *María del Carmen* at the Tívoli is a powerful argument in defense of Spanish opera against the despair or skepticism of those who think it impossible to consolidate such an important national institution." [84] The pianist Joaquím Malats also appealed to the greater cause of national opera, exhorting other composers to follow Granados's lead.[85]

As for the performance itself, most of the cast from the Madrid premiere reprised its roles. However, one reviewer thought that "the men acquitted themselves more admirably than the women,"[86] while another thought the chorus rather out of tune and the orchestra "insecure and inadequate."[87] *María del Carmen* ran for eleven more performances in June and received brief revivals throughout the year, ending with one at the Teatre Principal on December 31 and January 1, 1900. It was apparently done in Valencia in 1899, but the run was brief.[88]

To summarize, *María del Carmen* represented an attempt by the 31-year-old Granados to create Spanish national opera through an amalgamation of three major trends in contemporary musical theater: use of regional folkloric elements, a practice borrowed from zarzuela; a *verismo*-style plot indebted to Italian opera of the 1890s; and Wagnerian musico-dramatic innovations. As we have seen, Granados steered clear of any overt political statement in this work. However, his choice of subject matter and music placed him in line with those who embraced a united Spain under Castilian administration. This antagonized the Catalan separatists. But his cosmopolitan approach to opera could not wholly satisfy the *españolista* xenophobes, either. For these reasons, *María del Carmen* was perhaps the most controversial stage work he ever wrote, and the most interesting.

In any event, *El correo español* declared that as a result of this opera, henceforth the name of Granados would appear in the "gallery of artists whose merit is recognized."[89] This reminds us that up to this time, Granados had not really made a mark as a composer. Indeed, he was not yet known for much beyond his *Spanish Dances*. *María del Carmen* was his first major work, his announcement that he had arrived. Granados had taken to heart the teachings of Pedrell and gained prominence by writing music based on Spanish folklore and by embracing the musical heritage of the entire country, rather than confining himself to one particular region.

Although his most successful compositions during the 1890s were the ones inspired by Spanish music and dance, at this same time and throughout his career he cultivated the mainstream Central European style that was the inspiration for his earliest efforts as a composer and that formed the bulk of his repertoire as a concert pianist. His non-Spanish works merit their own chapter.

CHAPTER 3

Works for Piano in a Central European Style

Granados grew up playing the music of Schumann, Chopin, and Liszt. This Central European literature was the sum and substance of his musical infancy and adolescence, and it supplied the foundation for everything he was later to do. Not only did he play this music, but he no doubt improvised many waltzes and mazurkas à la Chopin during his stints as a café entertainer. As noted earlier, Pedrell was astounded at his knowledge of repertoire and ability to acquire music. By this he meant not only Granados's facility, his capacity to get the notes "under his fingers" quickly, but also his complete assimilation of the melodic gestures, harmonic language, and rhythmic traits that distinguish a composer's style.

As a result of his talent and training, Granados was never content merely to become a noted interpreter of this Central European tradition. Rather, he strove throughout his life to contribute to it. That he did this in works that have found a permanent place in the piano repertoire is remarkable enough; however, even as he pursued this ambition, he was also helping define Spanish nationalism in opera and piano music, all the while writing several Catalan stage works. The simultaneity of these accomplishments forbids breaking his oeuvre down into "style periods," since they defy any chronological organization. Granados inhabited several musical worlds at the same time, moving among them with notable ease and skill, and we will examine these worlds separately.

There are several parallels between Schumann and Granados. For example, both were deeply inspired by literary models and sources, striving for a narrative or quasi-narrative structure in their works. And both were partial to series of short, highly descriptive vignettes that, strung together, form a larger work.

Another model for Granados's music was provided by the composer he adored most: Chopin. Readily apparent is their mutual gravitation toward character pieces such as the mazurka, berceuse, waltz, and impromptu. Each composer relied heavily on elaborated repetition as a structural mechanism and deployed a rich variety of ornaments and accompanimental patterns. Persuasive interpretation of Granados's music also depends on a mastery of *tempo rubato*, a hallmark of Chopin's style. Crucial to all these musical procedures is skillful use of the damper pedal. Granados was very concerned with pedaling and devoted considerable attention to it in performance, teaching, and composing.

One other decisive Central European influence on Granados's piano music was Liszt. The Lisztian virtuosic element in much of his music is pronounced and reminds us of Granados's prodigious technique and effortless execution. However, it is important to recall as well that Granados had profound misgivings about the overtly flashy aspect of Lisztian pyrotechnics and did not strive to write mere showpieces. Granados would have agreed with Unamuno's assessment that fame interferes with the inspiration that "comes out of our [depths] . . . that sings [the] pure song of distant childhood."[1] Rather, he responded to the world of sound that Liszt had opened up at the piano, and he used those new possibilities to serious artistic effect.

Valses poéticos

These unaffected works emanated from Granados's ongoing love affair with the waltz. Indeed, waltzes appear in his scores time and again, whether marked as such or not. For instance, the entire stage work *Gaziel* centers musically around waltz themes that recur throughout and play a crucial role in characterization and unifying the score. In the early 1890s, he dedicated a collection of piano waltzes to his future bride Amparo Gal, entitled *Cartas de amor (Valses íntimos)*; yet another collection is the *Valses sentimentales*. As with so many of his works, we cannot be sure when Granados composed his "Poetic Waltzes," but almost certainly they were of early vintage, in 1893–94.[2] In any case, these waltzes have remained popular with performers from that day to this. Granados himself continued to perform them throughout his life, even in New York shortly before his death in 1916.

Valses poéticos (Páginas íntimas), dedicated to Joaquim Malats, contains eight numbers, with an Introduction—oddly enough, in duple meter—and a reprise of the first waltz at the conclusion of the final piece. Their "poetic" character is a matter of subjective perception, but clearly Granados had a typically Romantic love of literary metaphors, and the musical character of these works more than justifies the title. For these are poetic utterances of a lyric kind, surveying a wide variety of human emotions.

The waltz had traditionally been considered a rather risqué dance because the partners danced with their bodies touching.[3] The sensuality of the waltz, then, made it the musical vehicle par excellence for exploring the "intimate" feelings that Granados discloses in this suite: the cheerful animation of the Introduction, the serene gracefulness of the "Vals melódico," the minuet-like dignity of the "Vals apasionado," the bittersweet melancholy of the "Vals lento," the jocund, robust choreography of the "Vals humorístico," the elegant poise of the "Vals brillante," the introspective lyricism of the "Vals sentimental," and the sparkling flights of fancy in the "Vals mariposa" (Butterfly Waltz). The "Vals ideal" is a musical joke, insofar as it is $\frac{6}{8}$ meter and contains only a few measures of "waltz time" $\frac{3}{4}$. The whimsy of these titles and the uncomplicated sentiment of the music itself add immeasurably to the suite's charm.[4]

The tonal scheme of the collection reveals Granados's penchant for tertian relations, proceeding through A, F, d, B-flat, f-sharp, and A. Formal procedures include variation (Nos. 1 and 2), binary (Nos. 6 and 8), and ternary (Nos. 3–5 and 7). Finally, there is a striking similarity between the "Vals melódico" and the opening of Schumann's *Papillons*, op. 2, a work with which Granados was undoubtedly familiar (ex. 3.1a/b).[5]

Ex. 3.1a: *Valses poéticos*, "Vals melódico," mm. 1–4

Ex. 3.1b: Schumann, *Papillons*, op. 2, mm. 1–4

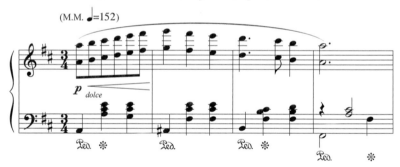

Piano Trio, op. 50

Granados began or completed several chamber works. However, considering his repeated appearances as a pianist in chamber ensembles, it is very strange that he did not write more chamber music, and that he did not promote and perform the few works that he did complete.[6] The Piano Quintet in G Minor, op. 49, and Piano Trio, op. 50, are the most important chamber works by Granados, both dating from 1895, when he premiered them at the Salón Romero in Madrid. The Quintet is a lovely work but perhaps the less remarkable of the two. The Trio exudes some of the regional flavor of the *Danzas españolas* and *María del Carmen* from this same decade, but the folkloric elements are more a matter of surface color and appear prominently and consistently only in the second movement. In any case, the Trio features keyboard writing of virtuosic brilliance, and for this reason it appears in a chapter devoted to piano music.

Opus 50 is in four movements. The first begins with a striking effect, a C pedal in the left hand of the piano and the cello while the right hand (in the middle register) arpeggiates the tonic chord (C major) and then the dominant minor (G minor). The introduction of the subtonic already in bar two creates a modal effect reminiscent of Fauré, and there seems to be more than a little French influence in this movement. All this merely sets the stage, however, for the entrance of the principal theme, in m. 10 in the first violin, as the murmuring accompaniment in the piano persists (ex. 3.2).

Ex. 3.2: Trio, op. 50, 1st mvmt., mm. 10–16

A new theme, in G major, emerges at m. 31 over a D pedal. The reliance on pedal notes in all four movements of this work is a conspicuous feature, one that allowed Granados to achieve some striking harmonic effects. Critics might find its frequent use a mark of relative immaturity, but Granados was taking a quantum leap over what his predecessors on the peninsula had essayed in the realm of chamber music.

A cadenza at m. 61 reintroduces the A theme in C, though it quickly leads to a new idea that adds a faint whiff of Hispanism. At m. 78, a C theme in B minor appears that Granados has marked "como canción popular" (like a popular song). The audience at the Romero might well have found this theme vaguely reminiscent of "El vito," a traditional tune in triple meter that Falla and other Spaniards used to good effect. This stylized "popular song" very cleverly alternates $\frac{2}{4}$ and $\frac{3}{8}$, marked *meno* and *più*, respectively. The melodic and harmonic descent through the tetrachord B–A–G–F# is a cliché of Spanish music in general (ex. 3.3).

Ex. 3.3: Trio, op. 50, 1st mvmt., mm. 78–86

Granados gets considerable mileage out of this new idea and does not return to his A theme until m. 125. A D theme at m. 142 leads us to conclude that, despite the occasional feeling of sonata form, this is basically a rondo movement. A reprise of the folk-style theme at m. 184 is scored charmingly for strings alone before the piano solo on the same tune at m. 201 leads us back to a final statement of the B and A themes and a tranquil conclusion of the piece.

Granados is developing a style uniquely his own in which folkloric elements are used in a sparing and stylized way in the context of an otherwise conventional Romantic work. But the second movement, a ternary Scherzetto in A minor, is more directly and consistently Spanish in character. Again we have the pedal note (here on the dominant), ornamented in folklike fashion with an appoggiatura. The $\frac{3}{8}$ meter recalls the C theme of the earlier movement, as does the alternation of duple and triple with actual hemiola at rehearsal 1. Arresting bits of local color show up in the evocation of the guitar, through pizzicato in the strings and rolled chords in the piano; strumming is suggested beginning in m. 10 with a trill-like flourish in the left hand of the piano. The rapid runs at rehearsal 2 further suggest a guitarist's bravura solo passages (*falsetas*).

The contrasting B section at rehearsal 10 is in A major and is marked "alla pastorale." Drone fifths in the left hand, diatonic harmony, and a flute-like stream of notes in the strings would have told us this even without the marking (ex. 3.4).

Ex. 3.4: Trio, op. 50, 2nd mvmt., rehearsal 10

Indeed, just after rehearsal 13 there is a brief recollection of the "Villanesca" from *Danzas españolas* in the migration of the tonic pedal to the right hand of the piano, if only briefly.

Just after rehearsal 15, the retransition to the A section presents a monophonic recitative (*a piacere*) in the piano that we immediately recognize as an evocation of flamenco singing, especially in its rhythmic freedom and downward melodic contour heading toward the final of the E mode, with the typical augmented second between G-sharp and F-natural (ex. 3.5).

Ex. 3.5: Trio, op. 50, 2nd mvmt., after rehearsal 15

This passage is recalled in the violin during the coda, accompanied by a grinding clash between a tonic pedal on A under a dominant-seventh chord in the piano.

The "Duetto" third movement is similarly in ABA form but sets a much different mood, akin to the lullaby or "berceuse" he returned to time and again in his piano music (it is marked "Andante con molta espessione"). Once more, he establishes the tonality (E major) through tonic and dominant pedals in the left hand, beneath a calmly rocking arpeggio in the right hand. The violin enters with the A theme after six measures of this introduction, the cello picking up the tune four measures later. The "dialogue" between the string instruments gives this movement its title, but as in the other movements, the piano remains prominent. The B section is in the relative minor (C-sharp) and introduces some stridency in its *forte* dynamics and accented syncopations. This does not interrupt the lullaby for long, however, and the coda casts an enchanting spell.

The final movement, another rondo form, is a lively evocation of Gypsy music in A minor. An A pedal persists almost until rehearsal 2, and a tonic-dominant drone in the B section (in G major) continues to suggest folk music, though not necessarily of a Spanish type (ex. 3.6).

Ex. 3.6: Trio, op. 50, 4th mvmt., opening

The most intriguing feature of this finale is the cyclic return of thematic material from the first movement, in particular the A and B themes, as well as the folk-song idea. This takes place before a brief "cadenza" in the piano and a reprise of the finale's A theme. Yet again, we are treated to the now-familiar themes of the first movement before a final statement of the finale's A and B themes and a presto coda that tests the skill of all the players.

In his liner notes for the Beaux Arts Trio's recording of this work, Luis Carlos Gago criticized Op. 50's "tiresome reiterations of passages," "uninspired" string writing, lack of "balance" in the instrumental texture, and "problems in the handling of large musical structures."[7] Despite the validity of such criticisms, this work displays conspicuous potential, and Granados's decision not to compose more chamber music is all the more regrettable in the light of this youthful yet imaginative effort.

Allegro de concierto

A work that brought Granados national attention was the *Allegro de concierto*, composed in the decade following the Piano Trio, in 1903. He submitted this bravura showpiece for solo piano to a competition sponsored by the Real Conservatorio in Madrid. The competition itself, which solicited only "concert allegros" for solo piano, was the brainchild of the Conservatory's new director, the composer Tomás Bretón (1850–1923). The contest was announced on October 1, 1903, with a deadline for submission of December 31. The winning piece would be a required selection for graduating piano students, and Granados's entry was one of twenty-four submissions. The winner would receive 500 pesetas, a considerable sum at that time, and publication of his work. Bretón presided over the jury, which consisted of the Conservatory's three piano professors and two professors of composition: Pilar Fernández de la Mora (who had gained the chair Granados coveted a decade earlier), former Albéniz student José Tragó (teacher of Joaquín Turina and Manuel de Falla), and Manuel Fernández Grajal; Grajal's brother Tomás joined Emilio Serrano as the two composition professors on the jury.

Not surprisingly, political currents swirled around the competition and Bretón's position in general. These currents revealed the existence of two primary cabals, one consisting of Bretón's followers, the other of his chief competitor, Ruperto Chapí, the immensely successful composer of such zarzuelas as *La Gran Via* and *La revoltosa*. Among Chapí's allies was Vicente Zurrón, who submitted an *Allegro* for the jury's consideration. (Although it was unsuccessful, it survived as a required work in the Conservatory's piano competitions and was actually published two years before the winning work, already in 1904.) He was perhaps the most eminent of Granados's competitors at that time. José María Guervos, pianist and composer from Granada, submitted a work as well (also published in 1904). Another submission came from a music professor in Valladolid, Jacinto Ruiz Manzanares (later professor at the conservatory in Valencia).

The most intriguing aspect of this competition is that Granados would confront a young composer from Cádiz now making his way in the Spanish capital, Manuel de Falla, who received honorable mention.[8] Granados took first prize, though his work was not published until 1906. It is not clear whether he was allied with Bretón or Chapí, or if he remained neutral. In the absence of evidence to the contrary, we can assume that he won the contest strictly on merit.

This brilliant work features Lisztian virtuosity in its rapid octaves and arpeggios spanning the entire keyboard. It also reminds us of Liszt in its chordal melodies and forceful accompaniments. The structure of this work is something of an anomaly in Granados's piano music, however, as it is in sonata form. His treatment of the form is conservative, for he adheres to the traditional tonic-dominant tonal structure in the exposition and assimilates all of the themes into the tonic during the recapitulation. Nonetheless, some modulations and key relations are typical of the late-Romantic period in which he was writing.

The work commences with a brilliant two-bar flourish, followed by the principal theme in C-sharp major. The arpeggiation of the tonic chord in this theme includes an added sixth, exuding a faint whiff of pentatonicism that may suggest to many listeners a folkloric quality, though there is nothing distinctly Spanish about it (ex. 3.7).

Ex. 3.7: *Allegro de concierto*, mm. 1–2

This is but the first of three themes in the exposition, and the second, in the dominant minor, is more lyrical in character. A brief reprise of the first theme occurs in G major, a tritone away from the home key, and leads to a third theme before the development section beginning in the same key area. The development commences at m. 80 with a new melody, marked "Andante spianato," over the arpeggiated A theme (ex. 3.8). The cadenza-like retransition leads to a recapitulation in C-sharp major at m. 127, though the second theme is in the parallel minor. Granados omits the third theme here and instead moves directly to the coda, based on the principal theme.

Ex. 3.8: *Allegro de concierto*, mm. 80–83

Escenas románticas

The *Escenas románticas* (Romantic Scenes) date from 1904 and bear a dedication to his young student María Oliveró. Apparent in these beautiful pieces is the influence of Chopin, as the key (not to mention the title) of the "Berceuse," C-sharp major, is the enharmonic equivalent of Chopin's Berceuse, op. 57.[9] Moreover, there are textural similarities, as the opening "Mazurka" in this collection exhibits a Chopinesque minor melody presented as a duet between the soprano and alto "voices."[10]

Simple part forms are typical of Chopin's character pieces, and the ABA structure of the first movement is consistent with that model. Also consistent with the mazurka is the way the melody hovers around a central note, in this case D-flat. In terms of rhythm, triple meter and the accenting of weak beats are absolutely essential to conveying the essence of the mazurka. Granados creates accentuation through means both subtle and overt: accent marks, grace notes, trills, arpeggiations, and pedal notes. Indeed, something reminiscent of a folklike drone bass is the persistence of the tonic B-flat throughout the first twenty-six measures of the piece. Also folkloric is the modal flavor Granados adds by avoiding the dominant in B-flat minor, and the opening alternation between tonic and subdominant instead.[11] The monothematic nature of the form combined with the repetition of D-flat and the drone gives this piece an obsessive character. A largely monophonic "Recitativo" connects the "Mazurka" and the "Berceuse," and it exhibits a rhapsodic quality, a rhythmic freedom reminiscent of Liszt (ex. 3.9).

Ex. 3.9: *Escenas románticas*, "Recitativo," mm. 67–76

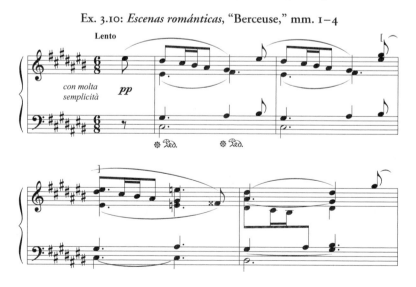

Granados introduces the "Berceuse" without pause. In addition to the key, its quiet, introspective character, compound meter, limited harmonic range (alternating between I and V), and phrase lengths certainly recall Chopin's Op. 57 (ex. 3.10).

Ex. 3.10: *Escenas románticas*, "Berceuse," mm. 1–4

1. Granados's birthplace, an apartment at Marqués de Tallada, 1, in Lleida, Catalonia. It bears two commemorative plaques to the composer.

2. Left: Granados maintained a lifelong devotion to his teacher Felip Pedrell, the patriarch of Spanish nationalism in music. Courtesy of the Museu de la Música, Barcelona.
3. Right: Charles de Bériot was professor of piano at the Paris Conservatoire when Granados studied privately with him, 1887–89. He was a grandson of Manuel García. Courtesy of the Museu de la Música, Barcelona.

4. Granados (right) with Ricard
Viñes (left) during their studies with
Bériot in Paris. Viñes was eight years
younger than Granados. Courtesy of the
Museu de la Música, Barcelona.

5. Granados in 1893, at age 26,
shortly after his marriage to
Amparo Gal. Courtesy of the
Museu de la Música, Barcelona.

6. Granados and his wife during their early years.
Courtesy of the Museu de la Música, Barcelona.

7. Granados and Amparo had six children, shown here ca. 1916.
Eduardo, Solita, Natalia (front); Víctor, Enrique, Paquito (back).
Courtesy of the Museu de la Música, Barcelona.

8. Camille Saint-Saëns (seated) and his friend Granados (standing) held one another in high regard. Courtesy of the Museu de la Música, Barcelona.

9. Program for the premiere of *María del Carmen*, Madrid, 1898. The librettist, José Feliu y Codina (right), had died the previous year.

TEATRO DE PARISH

Programa ilustrado.

VIERNES 11 DE NOVIEMBRE DE 1898

María del Carmen

Opera española

en tres actos, basada en el drama del mismo título
recientemente premiado por
la Real Academia Española.

LOS AUTORES DE LA ÓPERA

Don Enrique Granados
AUTOR DE LA MÚSICA

† Don José Feliu y Codina.
AUTOR DEL LIBRO.

10. Apeles Mestres, poet and illustrator, provided Granados with texts for his Catalan-modernist stage works and for songs. Courtesy of the Museu de la Música, Barcelona.

11. *Follet*, with a libretto by Mestres, is probably Granados's finest opera, but it was performed only once, in 1903, and has not been heard since. Courtesy of the Centre de Documentació i Museu de les Arts Escèniques de L'Institut del Teatre, Barcelona.

UN PERSONATJE DEL TEATRO

(Dibuix de APELES MESTRES)

PICAROL

Protagonista de la nova obra de Apeles Mestres, estrenada últimament al Tívoli.

LILIANA.—Poema líric en tres quadros.

(Estrenat ab extraordinari èxit, diumenge passat, a «Belles Arts».)

Alguns dels figurins de l'obra.

12. Left: *Picarol* was the most successful of all Granados's stage works, receiving about 100 performances during its five-year career. Courtesy of the Biblioteca de Catalunya.

13. Right: Mestres not only wrote the libretto for *Liliana* but also designed the costumes. Courtesy of the Biblioteca de Catalunya

14. Conxita Badia was a prize pupil of Granados and gifted both as pianist and soprano. She performed and recorded many of her maestro's works. Courtesy of the Museu de la Música, Barcelona.

15. Left: Granados had a talent for caricature, and this rendering of a *maja* includes a self-portrait revealing his sense of humor as well. From a notebook of sketches for *Los Ovillejos*, *Tonadillas*, and *Goyescas*. Courtesy of the Pierpont Morgan Library.

16. Right: In this drawing from the same book, a *majo* and *maja* converse through a *reja*, or iron grill. This is the inspiration for "Coloquio en la reja" from *Goyescas*. Courtesy of the Pierpont Morgan Library.

17. Another Granados drawing depicts a flirtatious *maja* out for a stroll, wearing a lace mantilla and holding an *abanico* (fan). Courtesy of the Pierpont Morgan Library.

18. Granados's sketch conveys the strength and self-reliance of the *majo*. Courtesy of the Pierpont Morgan Library.

19. Dr. Salvador Andreu, friend and patron of Granados, financed the construction of the Sala Granados in 1912

20. Granados exhibited just the right combination of strength and vulnerability, worldly success and poetic dreaminess, to make him exceedingly attractive to women.

21. Granados's most serious affair was with a student, the wealthy Barcelona socialite Clotilde Godó, at whose home in Tiana he composed much of *Goyescas*.

22. The cover of the first edition of *Goyescas* displays Goya's etching *Tal para cual* and is visible on the piano. Godó is attired as a *maja*, and their pose mimics that of the etching, depicting a flirtatious *maja* exercising her charms on a man.

23. The cover of the first edition of *Goyescas* featuring one of Goya's *Caprichos*, *Tal para cual*, the inspiration for the first movement, "Los requiebros."

24. Granados in his little cabin, or Tartanita, in Vilasar de Mar, working on the opera *Goyescas*, probably in 1915. Courtesy of the Metropolitan Opera Archive.

25. Fernando Periquet, journalist, poet, and devotee of Goya, wrote the lyrics for the *Tonadillas* as well the libretto for *Goyescas*.

26. Anna Fitziu and Giovanni Martinelli, in their roles as Rosario and Fernando
for the Met production of *Goyescas* in January 1916.
Courtesy of the Metropolitan Opera Archive.

27. Enrico Caruso penned this caricature of Granados in January 1916. Caruso was appearing at the Met in *I pagliacci*, which shared the marquee with *Goyescas*.

28. The sets for the *Goyescas* were among the most lavish ever for a Met production. This interior was the setting for Tableau II, in which the "Fandango de candil" took place. Courtesy of the Metropolitan Opera Archive.

BAILE DE CANDIL

29. A *baile de candil*, or dance by candlelight, as performed in the early 19th century.

30. This *Capricho* by Goya, *El amor y la muerte*, was the inspiration for the penultimate movement of the *Goyescas* suite and the closing scene of the opera, in which Rosario holds the dying Fernando, mortally wounded in his duel with Paquiro. Courtesy of the Metropolitan Opera Archive.

31. Granados composed his *Danza gitana* (Gypsy Dance) for the vivacious Spanish dancer Tórtola Valencia (1882–1955), who performed it in this costume designed by the artist Ignacio Zuloaga. Courtesy of the Metropolitan Opera Archive.

32. Granados records
his music on a piano
roll at the Aeolian Co.
in New York, 1916.
A recording technician
monitors the process.

33. Granados and Amparo in New York, shortly before
the return voyage they would not complete.

34. The *Sussex*, a cross-channel ferry, as it looked before it was torpedoed by
U-boat 29 on March 24, 1916.
Courtesy of the National Maritime Museum, London.

35. The *Sussex* in port after the attack. The explosion bent
the hull up, keeping out the sea.
Courtesy of the National Maritime Museum, London.

ESPAÑA

1916

SEMANARIO DE LA VIDA NACIONAL

Núm. 10 Cts. Núm. 10 Cts.

WAGNER A GRANADOS
—No nos culpes, que también nosotros tuvimos que sufrir y aguantar a nuestro pueblo, y eso que éramos sus hijos.

36. The cover illustration of the weekly *España*, April 6, 1916, shows Beethoven and Wagner receiving Granados into heaven, asking him not to blame them for German injustice, as they had also suffered at the hands of their own people.

37. The Granados memorial in Lleida, Catalonia, erected in 1966 with funds from a public subscription. Granados was much younger than the local boys posing here when his family left the town of his birth.

At first glance, the formal treatment is also similar. Both composers deploy variation technique, but in Chopin's case there is a conspicuous development of ideas that leads to a significant expansion of his materials. In the case of Granados, repetition with slight variation is the modus operandi, and, as is so often the case in his music, the result is a feeling of stasis rather than growth. Within this formal framework, there are four distinct sections (AA′BA), but the absence of any link between them demonstrates a certain indifference to organicism. However, this is not necessarily a flaw. Insofar as the movement is marked "con molta semplicità," one would have to say that he achieved his musical aims in every way: harmonic, melodic, and structural.

The third movement bears no title except for three asterisks and is simply marked "Lento con estasi." However, tradition holds that the composer referred to this piece as "El poeta y el ruiseñor" (The Poet and the Nightingale), one of several evocations of that musical bird in his music. The form of the piece is clear-cut: ABCAB. The A and C sections are marked "con estasi" and "appassionatamente," while the B section (marked "vivo" and "velocemente") evokes the nightingale in its athletic trills, alternating notes, and arpeggios (ex. 3.11).[12]

Ex. 3.11: *Escenas románticas*, "Lento con estasi," mm. 17–20

This cadenza-like material displays the sort of rapid, interlocking thirds typical of Liszt, especially his "Sonetto 104 del Petrarca" from the second book of *Années de Pèlerinage*. The opening of the piece exhibits a close texture and rapid harmonic rhythm indebted to Schumann.

The fourth movement is similarly untitled, but without asterisks, and marked "Allegretto"; however, its resemblance to the first piece is so pronounced that we are safe in labeling it a mazurka. In any event, it is very brief, comprising a mere nineteen measures (with repeat signs at mm. 8 and 14). Its folkloric character is established by the drone on the tonic G that persists throughout most of the movement. The piece is harmonically static and offers no real modulations. The form is equally rudimentary, a kind of rounded binary in which both the A and B sections are repeated, with a very abbreviated reprise of the A theme appearing at the end as a kind of coda (this truncated reappearance is not enough to qualify the movement as ABA[13]). Melodically, there is a great deal of repetition of motives and phrases, even in so short a piece, and there is constant hovering around b^1. The simplicity of this piece's three-voice texture as well as its limited range and minimal technical demands make it very suitable for students.

The penultimate movement, marked "Allegro appassionato," poses greater difficulties. A remarkable set of free variations on an eight-bar theme, its thickly woven interlocking accompaniment supports an arching melody in the treble, in E-flat minor, and has a Brahmsian quality. Although the piece is highly tonal, it features frequent chromatic alterations, starting already on the very first note of the theme (an A-natural leading to the dominant, B-flat, followed by a leap up to the tonic). These opening measures present chords that presage the various tonal centers Granados will explore, including G-flat major (mm. 17–23), which is followed by a dominant pedal in preparation for a return to the home key. G-flat major reappears in more extended fashion in mm. 40–64. The alternation between tonic and mediant key areas is characteristic of Granados's tonal schemes, in this case using B-flat as the pivot note. This pattern continues with an exploration of B-flat minor up to m. 72. A curious turn of tonal events occurs further on, at m. 116, as an anticipated return to the home key is thwarted by the appearance of E major, by way of a dominant-seventh sonority on B (which we hear as an enharmonically spelled augmented-sixth chord in E-flat). This aberration is only temporary, and we go out the same door we came in to modulate to E-flat minor and a final statement of the theme, in a texture more sparse than before.

"Epílogo," in E-flat major, harkens again to Chopin, particularly the Nocturnes. The marking "Andantino spianato" makes use of a term—*spianato* means smooth, even—that Granados picked up from Chopin, particularly in the *Grande Polonaise Brillante*, op. 22. To reinforce the literary allusion of the title, he adds the parenthetical indication "con exaltación poética." Here, poetic exaltation manifests in a leisurely, lyrical upper line supported by a simple arpeggiation in the accompaniment (ex. 3.12).

The formal plan is AABA´. The B section exhibits no change in texture or rhythm; though it begins in the dominant key, the melody is clearly a continuation of the A theme. A brief excursion to the mediant minor in mm. 23–30 quickly dissolves in a series of fifth-related movements to bring us again to the home key at m. 33. A coda beginning at m. 49 features an extended dominant pedal in the upper voice for the final seven measures, bringing this brief work of 61 bars to a conclusion.

Cuentos de la juventud

Cuentos de la juventud (Tales of Youth) was inspired by a tune that his son Eduardo once sang and that Granados liked and used; it appears in a musical epigram at the top of the printed score.[14] We do not know its date of composition or exactly when it was first published. Its title is reminiscent of Schumann's *Kinderscenen*, op. 15, and *Album für die Jugend*, op. 68.

Subtitled "Easy Pieces for Piano," it comprises ten short selections in different keys. The structural procedure is confined to simple part forms, for example, ABA in Nos. 1, 4, 6, 7, and 10; ABAB in Nos. 2, 3, 8, and 9; and ABABA in No. 5. The harmonic language is equally simple, with an emphasis on the keys of F and G. The textures are at times intricate, and the middle section of "Berceuse" is notable for its complex voice leading and chromaticism. Not surprisingly, word painting figures in these descriptive pieces, as suggested by their titles, for example, "The Beggar Woman," "Song of May," "Old Tale," "Coming from the Fountain," "Memories of Childhood," "The Phantom," and "March." Of poignant interest is the penultimate movement, "The Orphan," the extant manuscript for which bears a dedication "To the memory of my father."[15] As he did in *Escenas románticas*, Granados writes three asterisks in place of a title, perhaps suggesting a meaning so sublime it defies description. This use of three asterisks comes directly from Nos. 21 and 30 of Schumann's *Album für die Jugend*. Such a practice is also vaguely reminiscent of the playfully enigmatic "Sphinxes" in *Carnaval*, op. 9. These charming little "Tales" do not reveal the composer at his most distinctive, but they demonstrate his profound rapport with the Romantic style. They also reflect Granados's pedagogical concerns at this point in his career and are eminently suitable for students.

The *Escenas poéticas* were first published in 1912, though their actual date of composition may have been a few years earlier. In fact, there are two collections of "Poetic Scenes," the first comprising three, and the second, four movements (pub. 1923). The three "Scenes" of *Libro de horas* (Book of Hours), premiered in 1913, are treated together with the *Escenas poéticas* here because of their stylistic similarity.

The first movement, a Berceuse in ABA form, is disarming in its simple charm. Granados composed several such lullabies, and among the inspirations for them may be counted not only Chopin but also, one supposes, his own children. The first collection bears a dedication to Granados's eldest daughter, Soledad (known as Solita), though the second collection is without dedication. "Eva y Walter" is clearly inspired by *Die Meistersinger*, in its C-major tonality and contrapuntal texture.[16] In fact, Granados differentiates between Eva and Walter in the alternation of tenderly *piano* and stridently *forte* passages. The final movement, "Danza de la rosa" (Dance of the Rose), is a melancholy little waltz only thirty-two measures in length.

The idea of a "Book of Hours" clearly harkens back to the Middle Ages, and in this sense the *Libro de horas* resonates with the modernist movement in Barcelona, which was preoccupied with medieval art and literature.[17]

The first movement, "En el jardín" (In the Garden), is a brief vignette of only thirty-two measures. Its arching melody in F major conveys an inner response to the garden rather than a pictorial description. The curvaceous contour and connection with nature may again suggest the influence of modernism, so apparent in his Catalan operas of this period (ex. 3.13).

Ex. 3.13: *Libro de horas*, "En el jardín," mm. 1–4

In the second movement, Granados returns to a favorite subject, the nightingale. "El invierno (La muerte del ruiseñor)" (Winter: The Death of the Nightingale) is in ternary form, and the A theme in particular establishes an ominous mood with its agitated accompaniment and minor key. The expected birdcall does not make its appearance until the coda. A rapid descent through an E-minor chord, repeated three times (a fourth time in augmentation), brings the bird's life to a close. Lest there be any doubt as to the meaning of this passage, Granados marks it *pianissimo* and *morendo* (dying) and writes below the staff "muerte del ruiseñor" (ex. 3.14).

Ex. 3.14: *Libro de horas*, "El invierno (La muerte del ruiseñor)," mm. 45–49

"Al suplicio" (To the Execution) is a lugubrious lento in the simplest of forms, AA, and seems to sound the death knell for the tragic bird (ex. 3.15).

Ex. 3.15: *Libro de horas*, "Al suplicio," mm. 18–19

In terms of emotional intensity and depth, we are here far removed from the works of the early 1890s, with their juvenile buoyancy, optimism, and charm. A note of pessimism and despair has crept into Granados's art. Here is a portent of the final two movements from *Goyescas*, which though in a much different style, are infused with the same spiritual malaise.[18]

The second series of *Escenas poéticas* (not published until 1923) contains some memorable inspirations, along the same descriptive and stylistic lines as its predecessors. Here we have "Recuerdo de países lejanos" (Memory of Distant Lands), "El ángel de los claustros" (The Angel of the Cloisters), "Canción de Margarita" (Margarita's Song), and "Sueños del poeta" (The Poet's Dreams). The title of the first number recalls Schumann's "Von fremden Ländern und Menschen" (About Strange Lands and People) from *Kinderscenen*, while the second is consistent with Granados's spiritual inclinations as a devout Catholic. Its serenity is conveyed in a varied fourfold repetition of the A theme. An exquisite chorale in miniature adorns mm. 10–12 (ex. 3.16) and recurs in varied form seven measures later.

Ex. 3.16: *Escenas poéticas*, second series, "El ángel de los claustros," mm. 10–12

Margarita's ternary song reminds us of Granados's fascination with famous women in fiction, in this case, from Goethe's *Faust*, an interest already manifest during his Paris years.

The final movement's title again invokes Schumann, in the last selection from *Kinderscenen*, "Der Dichter spricht" (The Poet Speaks).[19] This piece is preceded by an unsigned poem that is probably by Granados himself. For at the time he was composing his *Poetic Scenes*, he was romantically involved with a student, Clotilde Godó, and the scene described in the poem strongly resembles the garden of her Tiana residence near Barcelona, luxuriant with cypress trees and roses.[20] Whom the "muse" represents is not difficult to gather, if indeed this is the little verse's encrypted message:

> In the garden of cypresses and roses,
> Leaning against a pedestal of white marble
> And awaiting his hour,
> The poet slumbered . . .
> At his side, caressing his brow,
> The Muse maintained her vigil.[21]

In real life, our poet was, in fact, not slumbering at all, and during the first decade of the twentieth century, he was busy on many fronts. As I noted in connection with *Cuentos de la juventud* and *Escenas románticas*, teaching was especially important to him. His contributions in this area are of genuine importance and invite detailed examination.

CHAPTER 4

Teacher, Conductor, Organizer

Had Granados devoted himself exclusively to performing and composing, his accomplishments would still merit a major biography. We can appreciate his achievements more fully, however, by surveying the many other activities that competed for his limited time and energy. Granados was very committed to teaching, and his contributions in the realm of pedagogy are of lasting significance. He was also active as a conductor and organizer of concerts. In fact, he became involved in most aspects of musical life in Barcelona. He undertook these responsibilities at least in part because he needed the income to support a growing family. We begin with his teaching.

Teaching

Granados had a solid "upbringing" at the keyboard, thorough and systematic, but he was also a natural talent. People who do something naturally often have a hard time analyzing how they do it and showing others how to do the same. This is one reason why few great performers are equally gifted as teachers. Impatience and an inability to elucidate doom their attempts at teaching. Granados, yet again, was able to mediate two realms, that of the virtuoso and of the pedagogue.

During the 1890s Granados taught individual students privately out of his home on carrer Tallers. Boladeres Ibern gives us a glimpse of what Granados was like as a teacher in those early years in Barcelona. "I really felt myself in the presence of a youth, courteous and likeable, rather than a professor. He appeared as a fellow student, who knew how to impart the secrets that he also loved."[1] Granados did not emulate his own teacher, Pujol, who had a booming, stentorian voice and was authoritarian in his pedagogical approach. Pujol encouraged his students to do as they were told and not think for themselves. Granados went so far in the opposite direction that some people "interpreted my liberal spirit in teaching as a kind of submission to the student on the part of the teacher."[2] It was never in his nature to be dictatorial, and at any rate, there were plenty of authoritarian maestros around if one did not like Granados's approach. Most, however, did.

Granados also taught at the Acadèmia de la Societat Filharmònica, which was founded by the Belgian violinist and conductor Mathieu Crickboom. As a business arrangement, this proved unsatisfactory, and giving concerts did not provide much money. So, Granados decided to establish an academy that might insure him a steadier and ampler income. He founded the Acadèmia Granados in 1901, at carrer de Fontanella, 14. After two years, it moved to new quarters at carrer de Girona, 89. Later it moved to number 20 on the same street. Here Granados not only taught but also lived with his family. Of course, the Academy needed financial support and sage business advice. To this end, it had a board of trustees, which included the mayor of Barcelona as well as Eduardo Conde and the physician August Pi i Sunyer.

The new Academy offered a complete musical education, including courses in music history, theory, solfège, harmony, composition, orchestration, violin, and piano, which ran through a full academic year (September to June). The entire curriculum in piano at the Academy, according to its "Plan de Estudios," lasted nine years. Many of his pupils were young women seeking to enhance their social graces.[3] Granados was able to attract to his faculty some of the finest musicians in Barcelona, especially Domènech Mas i Serracant, a church musician who served as assistant director and taught theory and composition.[4] Joan Llongueras taught Emile-Jacques Dalcroze's Eurythmics, which developed sensitivity to music through physical movement and which he had learned in Geneva.[5] Prices for instruction were reasonable. Private lessons with Granados cost 30 pesetas monthly, while a harmony class for the same period cost only 10. For the sake of comparison, the least expensive seats at most concerts went for a single peseta or less. For the cost of a cheap seat at the theater every day, one could study with one of the finest pianists in Europe.[6]

Moreover, Granados wanted his Academy to become a cultural hub, sponsoring conferences and symposia as well as putting on concerts. Among the most important of these was a series of lectures by Felip Pedrell in 1905–6 on the "Origin and Evolution of Musical Forms" ("Origen y evoluciones de las formas musicales"). Much later, in 1916, the Academy began publication of a journal, *Musiciana*, which ran for nine issues and featured a serialized article by Pedrell, "Origin and Transformations of Pianistic Forms" ("Origen y transformaciones de las formas pianísticas").[7] It also sponsored concerts, such as Edouard Risler's appearance at the Teatre Principal in 1907 playing the complete Beethoven Sonatas. In the early years, Academy students and teachers performed at various venues, for example, the Salle Chassaigne, where on March 22, 1902, Granados participated in a program with his foremost pupils, some of whom eventually joined the teaching staff.

In 1912, the Academy finally got its own performance space with the construction of a new building, the Sala Granados, on the Avinguda del Tibidabo. As Milton describes it, the neighborhood was one of "large villas and small palaces of three and four stories" whose affluent owners enjoyed the Tibidabo's "cleaner air and superior view of the city below."[8] The new hall included a two-story concert hall on the main level, accommodating about 200 people. The lower level of the structure was devoted to rehearsal space and classrooms, not just for piano but also for solfège and Eurhythmics.[9] The inaugural concert took place there on February 4, 1912, featuring a recital by Granados.

The Sala Granados was made possible through the financial support of Dr. Salvador Andreu i Grau (1841–1928), a renowned pharmacist and one of the pioneers of the pharmaceutical industry in Spain. He established an important laboratory and developed overseas markets for his products, which included medicines for respiratory problems. He eventually became the honorary president of all pharmaceutical colleges in Spain. Also a great supporter of urban development in Barcelona, he put his influence and money behind important projects, such as the Tibidabo where the Sala was located.[10]

Granados was close to the Andreu family because Dr. Andreu had married Carmen Miralles, whom Granados had known since his youth. Granados was also the piano instructor for Andreu's daughters Carmen and Paquita, and he passed happy months at the family's summer residence in Puigcerdà, a resort town near the French border that attracted Barcelona's social and cultural upper crust.[11]

Granados was extraordinarily concerned with a student's technical as well as artistic development, and he understood that the two were inextricably intertwined. Achieving greater physical control and deepening one's interpretative abilities go hand in hand. Thus, students had two lessons a week, one for mechanism and the other for interpretation. Granados's dedication to pedagogy manifested in several ways. Not only did he found the Academy and teach there, but he also published a treatise on pedaling, *Theoretical and Practical Method on How to Use the Pedals of a Piano* (*Método, teórico-práctico, para el uso de los pedales del piano*), the first such work published in Spain.[12]

In this *Method*, Granados sets forth his fundamental view that the pedal mechanism constitutes the piano's "lungs," allowing the performer to control the connectedness of the sounds produced. He deals with pedaling individual notes in legato playing and tone production, connecting groups of notes into consonant or dissonant sonorities, and controlling timbre in a melody. It is understood, however, that these instructions are intended only for the beginner and do not encompass all the possibilities. This is why Alicia de Larrocha has said of Granados's treatise that it represents "only the most basic—the primer level of pedal study."[13] Granados also wrote other, unpublished, treatises on technique, including *Brief Considerations Concerning Legato, Ornamentation*, and *Special Difficulties of the Piano* (*Breves consideraciones sobre el ligado, Ornamentos*, and *Dificultades especiales del piano*).[14]

Two of Granados's own lectures at the Sala Granados shed much light not only on his approach to playing the piano but to teaching as well.[15] On October 30, 1913, he gave a presentation on "The Interpretation of Works with Sentiment" ("La interpretación de las obras con sentimiento"). *Sentimiento* does not mean sentimentality per se; it does not have the same pejorative connotation in Spanish as it does in English. It means, simply, feeling and emotion, without which there would not be much music we would care to listen to.

What most impresses about this talk, however, is the quasi-scientific way he goes about his work. The precision of his reasoning is remarkable, especially considering the topic. He begins with a brief introduction to the actual mechanism of tone production on the piano, and he illustrates his point with a graph showing how the intensity of a note necessarily decreases over time, unlike that of, say, a violin or trumpet.

Having established that ineluctable reality of piano playing, he predicates a rule upon it: "Always in a melody when two notes are separated by an interval of time greater than that corresponding to two beats at an andante tempo, we should play the second note with an intensity approximately equal to that remaining from the first note."[16] He then provides another graph illustrating this point. It does not matter, now, whether or not we agree with him. What concerns us is the systematic way he presents his arguments. He recognizes, for instance, that there are potential objections to this dictum. He concedes that the composer's dynamic markings take precedence in all cases, and that in arpeggios and scales there is always a natural tendency for intensity to increase on the way up and decrease on the way down. In other words, the "rule" is a general principle to be applied with intelligence and sensitivity, not in a dogmatic way.

Granados next concerns himself with rhythmic flexibility in playing a melody, and though he does not use the word, he is referring to rubato. Again employing precisely drawn graphs, he shows how there is a natural and commendable tendency to increase velocity towards the middle of a melodic unit, be it a period or phrase. Such nearly imperceptible changes in tempo help the performer avoid "the rigidity and monotony produced by an ill-advised squareness." In summary, he believes that both principles, dealing with subtle changes in the intensity of sound production and tempo, are crucial to expression and artistry in interpretation.

The second lecture was given on November 27, 1913, in the same locale, and its theme, "The Technique of Expression" ("La técnica de expresión"), was clearly an extension of the first. Granados states at the outset:

> The interpretation of musical works is parallel to the life of the artist. If he has lived in the society and environment that were behind the composition of those works, if he knows the human emotions, expression will flow intuitively without the artist perhaps even being aware of it. However, if he does not know these things [from personal experience], it is not likely that, without preparation, he will succeed in the difficult task [of interpretation].[17]

He then establishes the rules that inform his approach to the technique of "correct" expression, which is characterized by "energy, gentleness, grace, and agility." Staccato is essential to acquiring energy, while legato and shading of sonority add the elements of gentleness and suavity. Grace and agility result from the combination of all of these.

Granados elucidates the essential tendency of rhythm to create patterns of tension and relaxation, and here his poetic instincts serve him well in the context of an otherwise scientific presentation. For he deploys several useful similes to illustrate his point, augmenting their impact with more drawings. Rhythm, he says, is like a series of arches, or a ball suspended from elastic, or even the movement of water around rocks in a stream. It is like all of these things because there are moments of maximum tension, for example, the height of the arch, the top of the ball's bounce, the water passing over the top of the rock, and those of maximum relaxation. He goes on to invoke other examples, such as the rocking of a boat in the water or the movement of a bird's wings. Rhythm is of two basic varieties, rigorous and free. In rigorous rhythm there is a definite consistency and regularity. Examples of free rhythm include Gregorian chant, which he likens to the outlines of the mountains against the sky in the unequal heights of the various peaks.

Articulation can be of three types: staccato, tenuto ("picado-ligado"), and legato. Here Granados has his listeners imagine a series of iron plates going from cool to extremely hot. Upon touching the latter, one would withdraw a finger as rapidly as possible, and this corresponds to one of two types of staccato, which he calls "staccato of recoil." *Picado-ligado* lies somewhere between extreme heat and cold, while legato is associated with the cool plates, where one's finger can rest without discomfort. It is possible to create a staccato effect at the cool end of the spectrum, and this he labels "hammer staccato." Governing all manner of articulation in the service of expression is the "law of contrast." This, he concludes, is what imparts and sustains expressivity in musical performance.

As for his commitment to developing a student's "mecanismo," he was precise and detailed in his prescriptions: (1) five-finger exercises of Bériot in all keys; (2) arpeggios, scales in thirds and sixths, chromatic scales, and octaves, checking once a week (Saturday) one's progress with a metronome; (3) slow, forceful practice of each measure, repeating each bar (or two, depending on difficulty) 15 or 20 times; (4) profound study of a passage or page of an etude, especially by Chopin, for a month; (5) repetition of all of the above faster and softer; (6) weekly monitoring by him of a student's practice (again, on Saturday) and carefully recording it in a ledger.[18]

Naturally, interpretation was of paramount importance and the goal toward which all of this digital dexterity was directed. Granados's own commentary on the first movement of Beethoven's Sonata Op. 111 is of great interest, not necessarily for its intrinsic insights but rather for the way he approached it. Although too long to quote in its entirety here, a few choice sentences will demonstrate how Granados understood such a work and the interpretive abilities he imparted to his students.

> The phrase ends with a lively crescendo that initiates a dialogue full of passion, an
> energetic passion in the lowest part, D, F, A, D; a simple and tender passion in
> the upper part, A, G, A B A, A, while the accompaniment continues on its way
> in a regular and unobtrusive manner. . . . In the paroxysm of passion the feeling
> of agitation suddenly reappears, with its rhythm altered into irregular patterns. It
> appears that the shouts have died down, and nothing remains but the beating of
> the heart. . . . Suddenly thereafter, violence and fire erupt, and this entire section
> concludes in a paroxysm of unsettled emotion as the implacable rhythm pounds

out its heavy notes (black and white), in a feverish and rabid way. Thus ends the most passionate work for piano, a work of inexplicable beauty and which, despite our best intentions, we have inexplicably neglected. It contains truly terrifying beauties, which cannot be put into words.[19]

Clearly, this "interpretation" does not conform to modern standards of theoretical analysis. It is, instead, a highly subjective, personal, and idiosyncratic reduction based on poetic, affective images and metaphors. As a former student pointed out, "In general, all the works we studied received a scenic version more or less definite. Lakes with gondolas, enchanted forests, monasteries in ruins, epic poems, funeral corteges, love duets, and a thousand other scenes or landscapes guided the student's interpretation of the works under consideration."[20] This is entirely consistent with the fanciful titles and subtitles of many of his own creations, for instance *Países soñados (El palacio encantado en el mar)* (Imaginary Lands: Enchanted Palace in the Sea).

This stark juxtaposition of scientific disquisition and romantic flights of imagination presents a curious paradox in his musical personality, another straddling of two realms. However, both approaches worked toward a single goal, which Granados made clear: "To educate my young students in the poetic sentiment that the entire work must breathe."[21] This simple sentence probably sums up his philosophy of teaching better than anything else. Poetry truly informed all his musical endeavors.

Granados advocated a very precise and disciplined approach to studying the piano. When a new student came to him, he or she would receive a sort of medical exam from the "doctor," who assessed every aspect of his or her execution and then put the student on a "diet" of prescribed exercises and repertoire.[22] "Continue working methodically, or you will get absolutely nowhere," Granados once commented to a student who was having problems with a Chopin Polonaise.[23] Nonetheless, it is true that Granados much preferred to deal with musical expression and often found mechanical remediation tiresome.

The curriculum of the Academy was rigorous. Students were regularly tested during their studies to measure their progress, and prize competitions were also part of the regimen. The didactic repertoire that Granados favored included the usual studies of Czerny and Clementi and Bach fugues, as well as the etudes of Liszt, Chopin, Schumann, and especially those of Cramer. In fact, there was a time when "it was impossible to enter the Academy without hearing, to the right or left, some passage from Cramer's etudes."[24] Such rapport did Granados himself feel with these pieces by Cramer that during one lesson he accompanied a student's execution of an etude with a spontaneous improvisation on the same work that matched the original measure for measure.[25]

A composer whose works were not usually on the students' repertoire list was Granados himself. One day, a pupil asked why they were given so much Chopin to perform and so little Granados. The teacher/composer's rueful reply displays his capacity for trenchant wit, as well as his humility: "Because you cannot do much damage to Chopin, whereas to me you would do a lot of harm!"[26] Other authors whose works could withstand inexpert handling included Mendelssohn (*Songs without Words*), Schumann (*Fantasy*, op. 17, *Carnaval*, op. 9), and Weber (Sonatas). Beethoven and Schubert occupied places of special honor. On one occasion Granados asserted that had Schubert lived to an old age, he would have become superior to Beethoven. Be that as it may, Granados revered Beethoven and thought the aforementioned Sonata Op. 111 to be nothing less than an allusion to death and the soul's journey to heaven (for once, no castles or enchanted lakes).[27] He occasionally wore on his wrist a "muñequera," a leather string bearing a metal reproduction of Beethoven's death mask.[28] This mask also served as the symbol for the Academy.

Sometimes Granados's classes went beyond what some of his students could comprehend. Conxita Badia recounted one such incident:

> [Once] a group of us were in class, and Granados was as usual explaining the nature of the work with illustrations on the piano. We all listened, spellbound by his interpretative powers, and time ran on happily. Inevitably, the lesson had to come to an end. To our astonishment a girl suddenly stood up and demanded: "Are we not having a lesson today, *Señor* Granados?" You can well imagine his utter dismay and disappointment. He quickly sat down beside the piano and resumed. "Yes, yes, of course you are right! Sit down and play." He then restricted himself to warning her not to rush the piece, to keep the tempo, not to overlook that sharp, to observe the note values, etc. She of course got the impression that she had had a marvelous lesson and seemed altogether very pleased with herself. The *Maestro* slumped back into his armchair with a heavy sigh and an expression of total disenchantment on his face.[29]

If Granados had any defect as a teacher, it was his occasional ill-humor and lack of tolerance for mediocrity. He could be curtly dismissive: "Have you looked at this passage? All right, enough. Bring it back another day!"[30] His sense of humor got him over the rough spots and perhaps made pedantry tolerable. One incident illustrates this very well:

> There was a young woman who was interpreting the Allegretto (Scherzo) from Beethoven's Sonata, op. 10, no. 2, and was playing the music at an inappropriately fast tempo, in poor taste. Granados began to encourage her, saying, "Faster, faster," in a manner that caused the poor woman to obey by continually increasing the rapidity of the notes. As soon as she reached the tempo he wanted, Granados delivered the punch line: "Very good. Now we can dance!" Everyone laughed, and the student sat there looking as embarrassed as a monkey.[31]

On another occasion, a young woman lost her way in a difficult piece and cried out, "Ay, maestro, I'm lost! I don't know where I am!" In response to which Granados sighed laconically, "Neither do I, neither do I."[32]

It is little wonder, then, that Granados did weary of the tremendous load of teaching imposed on him by financial necessity. Granados lamented the time lost in teaching that he could have devoted to developing his skills and many ideas as a composer.

He did not have unlimited amounts of time or of physical energy. He was frequently plagued by digestive problems, fevers, and migraine headaches over the years, as well as "persistent sadness and vague nostalgia."[33] And his students sometimes took advantage of his generosity. "People would take up his time for lessons, let the account run on and then plead inability to pay, and go on having lessons thanks to his good nature, whilst all the time he was struggling to bring up a family of six on straitened means."[34] As it was, one marvels that he accomplished what he did, especially in the realm of opera. This was due, at least in part, to his ability to concentrate—anywhere, under almost any circumstances—on his work. For instance, one day he was observed working on the orchestration of a piece while riding a streetcar.[35]

Being aware of these hardships also gives us insight into the observations of those who knew him over a long period. For the optimism of the composer at age 32, after the premiere of *María del Carmen*, contrasts starkly with the pessimism of much of *Goyescas*, written at age 46. Despite the laurels heaped upon him, Granados still felt that in some important respect, he had not achieved the success he craved and deserved. For popular acclaim and actual success were two different things to him: "A true artist must renounce being understood by the common people, precisely so that he does not become a common artist."[36] Such an elitist observation seems incongruent with the accessible character of so much of Granados's music and is yet another apparent contradiction in his personality. Perhaps here was the motivation for his stated desire to appear to his fellow train travelers like nothing more than an ordinary businessman. In anonymity, he could find relief from the painful alienation of the artist from society.

Of course, Granados could never melt into any crowd, no matter how much he tried. If for no other reason than sheer physical appeal and charm, he stood out. Almost any photograph of him reveals striking features: a walrus mustache (very much in vogue in Barcelona around 1900), long and supple fingers, fine facial features, an abundant mane of thick hair, slender build, and, most of all, those eyes—those liquidy dark orbs of tenderness and sorrow, twin magnets of seductive charm. One author noted that "they gazed into the distance with a distracted air, as though his imagination were in another realm altogether."[37]

Such a man, given his talent and fame as well, would have been extremely attractive to women. He exhibited just the right combination of strength and vulnerability. Conxita Badia certainly recognized his charms: "He always seemed like an overgrown child. His kindness was overwhelming and he was a great friend to his colleagues."[38] Víctor Granados confirmed the childlike nature of his father: "He used to sit on the floor playing with our toys, as if he had been six. I believe that the toys gave him more satisfaction than they did to us."[39] Even men were aware of his attractive power. Vidiella once exclaimed, "If I had been born a woman, I would be totally enamored of Granados."[40] Such a man would indeed be hard to resist, if he made himself available.

In fact, Granados had a roving eye, and we know that in at least two instances he became involved with students. Evidence is at hand in the testimony of one of Granados's leading pupils, Paquita Madriguera, who caught her maestro *in flagrante delicto* with a mistress at the Academy.[41] This woman was Clotilde Godó (1885–1988), a viva-cious and attractive socialite and the daughter of a wealthy industrialist. She married in 1903, while still in her teens, but the pope annulled the unhappy union after only three years. A prodigy, she was studying with Granados when, around 1910, she became his ardent supporter and lover. One of the pictures of them in this book emits a kind of electricity in their gazes—her "come hither" glance, his absorption in her ample bosom—that a platonic relationship does not generate. Amparo knew of this affair, and it was no secret to the composer's descendants. Naturally, they were disinclined to present Granados to the print media and public as anything but a doting father and husband, and Madriguera is the only one who ever openly treated the relationship.

This was no mere fling: Granados and Clotilde seem genuinely to have been in love. As Madriguera described it, "A great passion ignited the hearts of the maestro and his student. Their passion was worthy of inclusion in the history of famous love affairs, especially as it ended like most, with death coming between them."[42] Grana-dos apparently felt sincere regret and guilt over the pain he was causing his wife, but his love for Godó was "stronger than my will and reason."[43]

This was not his first fling, only the most passionate. A few years before, ca. 1904, Granados had become involved with another student, María Oliveró, dedicatee of the *Escenas románticas*. María wrote impassioned love letters to her teacher; unfortunately, Amparo found them and was justifiably furious. Granados ended the dalliance im-mediately. In reality, the teenage María did not pose much of a threat to Amparo; the situation with Clotilde was much more serious and might have jeopardized the mar-riage, had not death intervened.

Madriguera believed that as Amparo grew plump and less attractive over time, Granados's sexual passion for her "evolved slowly and converted into fraternal affec-tion, admiration for a strong woman, and also shame."[44] Indeed, in his last months on earth, Granados visited the Hermitage of Samalus during Holy Week in 1915 and attended service on Holy Friday. According to the parish priest, after these devotions Granados had his head in his hands and was weeping. The priest expressed compas-sionate concern for the composer's welfare and inquired after the cause of his distress. Granados answered: "My tears will remain in this church imploring God's pardon for all my sins, offenses, and transgressions."[45] It is not easy for a biographer to grasp just what terrible sins a harmless artistic genius like Granados could have committed, un-less they pertained to his marital infidelities.

Conducting and Organizing

Granados was not active solely as a teacher and "schoolmaster" but also as a conduc-tor, concert organizer, and adjudicator. He played a minor role in the founding of the Orfeó Català in 1891, the prime movers behind it having been Amadeu Vives and Lluís Millet, and he participated in its pedagogical activities on the Instruction Com-mittee (Comissió d'Ensenyança).[46] One should note, however, that Granados held the Orfeó at arm's length. True, he gave concerts and benefits for them over the years and fully approved their musical agenda. But what bothered him about this organization and its co-founders was the hard political edge they put on its purposes. This was not just about the beauties of Catalan culture, it was about chauvinism and separatism as well. As Granados himself expressed it: "They wanted to give a Catalanist political color to the Orfeó, something with which I am not in agreement. To my way of thinking, art has nothing to do with politics. Perhaps that is because I neither understand nor care about politics."[47] Still, this did not keep him from participating in Morera's musical activities, even with their blatantly Catalanist slant. For example, Morera organized a Primera Sessió Musical on January 17, 1897, featuring his Catalunya Nova and several instrumentalists, including Granados, who accompanied them and played his own *Impromptu*.[48]

His organizational activities did not end with the Orfeó but were merely beginning. Concert life blossomed around 1900 in Barcelona, and numerous symphonic and concert organizations came into existence to satisfy the public's growing appetite for classical music. Of course, these groups not only catered to but also attempted to expand this market. One such organization was launched by Granados in the spring of 1900, the Sociedad de Conciertos Clásicos (Societat de Concerts Clàssics), whose stated purpose was to begin by creating a string ensemble of high quality and later to add wind and brass instruments, as well as percussion. The critic F. Suárez Bravo addressed the reality that to some people, "to hear the word 'classical' is the same as saying 'boring': something profound and proper, but cold and heavy."[49] Granados set out to dispel such illusions. The first concert, on May 15, was a brilliant exposition of works by Bach, Handel, Grieg, Schumann, and Chopin. This met with the critic's approbation: "This means that all that is vulgar, crude, and anti-aesthetic—all that does not adhere to the rules of art—will find no place in their repertoire."[50] (What repertoire would have been "anti-aesthetic" and contrary to the "rules of art" he did not bother to specify.) Casals appeared as soloist in the second concert, performing the Saint-Saëns Cello Concerto, op. 33, and some solo works. The November 4 concert featured Granados conducting Beethoven's Fourth Symphony. A week later, on November 11 at the Teatro de Novedades, a "Gran Concierto Extraordinario" featured three pianos and orchestra, conducted not by Granados but Domingo Sánchez. Granados was joined by fellow former Pujol pupils Joaquím Malats and Carles Vidiella in a Bach concerto, while Malats soloed in the A-minor Concerto of Ignacy Paderewski; Vidiella soloed in Granados's reorchestration of the Chopin F-minor Concerto.

However, the organization had a brief life span and did not survive the year 1900, giving its final performance on December 9. The exact reasons for its premature demise are unclear, but certainly disappointing attendance and income must have played a central role.[51]

Granados soon founded another orchestra to conduct. The Orquesta de Barcelona gave three performances at the Teatre Principal under the aegis of the Circól de Belles Artes. The programs featured the standard fare of Wagner, Beethoven, Schumann, Mendelssohn, and Franck. The second concert honored the guest conductor of that program, Miguel Marqués, and featured some of his music. This venture, too, had a short life and ended in the spring of 1901. Granados did not relinquish his baton, however, and he conducted noted touring virtuosi on several occasions. For instance, in the spring of 1903, he led an orchestra in Teresa Carreño's performances of concertos by Beethoven and Grieg.[52] Three years later, on January 7, 1906, he directed an ensemble at the Teatre Principal accompanying the 14-year-old Mieczyslaw Horszowski in Mozart's D-minor Piano Concerto, K. 466, as well as the *Grande Polonaise Brillante*, op. 22, of Chopin. Granados was so impressed by the young Pole's performance that he invited him to appear at the Sala Granados on a subsequent visit.

Granados founded one other performance group. In 1910 the Acadèmia Granados organized a Societat de Concerts de Música de Cambra (Society of Chamber Music Concerts), inspired by the Filarmónica of Madrid. The Trio Granados formed the basis of the new Societat, with Perelló (violin) and Raventós (cello).[53] However, Granados did not confine himself to helping direct the affairs only of ensembles he established or conducted. He took an active interest in the musical life of the entire city and involved himself with many facets of it. For example, when a controversy arose, in the summer of 1910, about Lamote de Grignon's direction of the Banda Municipal, Granados served on the commission appointed to investigate the matter.[54]

Granados was occasionally called upon to serve as an adjudicator and was on the jury for the 1907 Festa de la Música Catalana. Other judges included Lluís Millet and Antoni Nicolau. This awarded prizes to outstanding choral works with Catalan texts, Catalan folk song arrangements, and piano music. The works were performed in an Orfeó Català concert in October 1907.[55] Two years later, on May 1–2, 1909, Granados served on the jury for the prestigious Louis Diémer Prize, awarded every three years by the Paris Conservatoire; he was the first Catalan to serve on the committee.[56] Gabriel Fauré, director of the Conservatoire, invited him to join an international panel that included Moriz Rosenthal, Arthur de Greef, and Moritz Moskowski. The musical establishment in Barcelona took special notice of this appointment, which was repeated in 1912, and held a testimonial in his honor on February 12, 1911, at the Sala de Cent. In attendance were numerous government officials not only from Barcelona but Lleida as well. Granados received a plaque bearing his likeness in relief, and he offered a few well-chosen words of gratitude, which one spectator thought he delivered with "endearing simplicity."[57] A banquet was held later at the Mundial Palace. Certainly this was one of the highlights of Granados's life.

In the decade after his rise to fame as a pianist and composer, Granados worked hard to establish his reputation in several other areas of musical endeavor. He was not equally successful in every enterprise, and clearly his teaching and the establishment of his Academy had the biggest impact. Still, he had made conspicuous contributions to the cultural life of Barcelona in many ways. And Granados's promotion of Catalan culture went far beyond his involvement with the Orfeó, despite his rejection of Catalan separatism. For during this same period, Granados composed Catalan musical theater and in the process became a leading figure in the world of Catalan modernism.

CHAPTER 5

Modernisme Catalan

In the nineteenth century, classical composers occasionally had a major impact on politics and culture. For instance, Daniel François Auber's now obscure opera *Masaniello, ou La muette de Portici* sparked a revolution in Belgium in 1830, while Verdi and his operas played a central role in the struggle for Italian independence and nationhood. When Sibelius raised his patriotic voice in *Finlandia*, the world listened. However, as composer and conductor Esa-Pekka Salonen has said in comparing classical musicians of the nineteenth century with their counterparts today, "Their voice was heard. Now we've been marginalized. . . . It's only the rock performers who seem to have clout."[1] However, few musicians, rock or otherwise, ever wielded the kind of clout that Richard Wagner did. And few areas of Europe responded more enthusiastically to or embraced the Wagnerian cult more fervently than Barcelona.

The nature of the attraction can be understood in the context of those twin pillars of the Catalan cultural revival, the *Renaixença* and *modernisme*. As mentioned before, the *Renaixença* sought to re-create the glory days of Catalan literature in the late medieval period, through promotion of the Catalan language and the region's medieval heritage. A major manifestation of this literary renascence was the *Jocs Florals*, or "Floral Games," a poetry competition intended to stimulate the creation of modern Catalan verse. Founded in 1859, the Games were named after contests formerly sponsored by King Joan I starting in 1393. Their motto—Patria, Fides, Amor (Fatherland, Loyalty, Love)—spoke volumes about the centrality of these contests to the revival not just of the Catalan language but also of a sense of national, even ethnic, identity. For as Miroslav Hroch points out, the "'memory' of former independence or statehood, even situated far in the past, could play an important role in stimulating national historical consciousness and ethnic solidarity."[2] The survival and promotion of Catalan in the *Jocs Florals* was key to this process of memory. Over the years, first-prize winners in these games included major Catalan literary figures such as Joan Maragall, Víctor Balaguer, and Jacint Verdaguer. Although they became increasingly anachronistic in the twentieth century, the modern games continued until 1936 and the outbreak of the Civil War, after which the Franco regime reverted to suppressing Catalan, as well as Basque and Galician.[3]

As Robert Hughes explains, "Barcelonans saw in Wagner their own desire to create a myth of national identity." The *Jocs Florals* were reminiscent of the "Sängerkrieg" in *Die Meistersinger*, and though Wagner had never been to Catalunya, the centrality of Montsalvat to the Parsifal story meant that "Catalunya *was* Wagnerian Spain."[4]

Modernisme was, unlike the *Renaixença*, an international movement with local inflections. Variously known as *Jugendstil, Sezessionstil*, Modern Style, or Art Nouveau, it grew out of the work of the Pre-Raphaelites and Symbolists. It is exemplified in the United States by the architecture of Louis Sullivan and the glasswork of C. L. Tiffany. In England, the artist William Morris and the illustrator Aubrey Beardsley were leading exponents. The influence of nature is apparent in lush, idealized forest settings and in curvilinear rather than rectilinear forms.[5] *Modernisme* took root in Catalonia in the 1880s in the paintings of Ramon Casas and Santiago Rusiñol, and the early architecture of Antoni Gaudí.[6]

Modernisme was not diametrically opposed to the *Renaixença* but had a different agenda. Its preoccupation with Catalonia manifested as a desire to shake off the parochialism of the *Renaixença* and to modernize the region. This progressive movement, though, had an ironically conservative bent, for it rejected much of modern society that it found dehumanizing, especially academicism and the constraints of classicism, instead looking to nature for its inspiration in form and content. Inherent in it was a pronounced nostalgia for a mythical world of long ago.

Wagner's music perfectly reflected the Catalan-modernist zeitgeist in its glorification of a haloed medieval past through the use of musical means that were revolutionary and thoroughly modern. His evocation of the sacred, the primal forces of nature, heroic figures from a primitive past, the vibrant spirituality of medieval legend, and the concomitant rejection of neoclassicism made his operas moving and relevant to modernist sensibilities.[7] It also served the greater social enterprise of creating, in Alexandre Pellicer's words, a "new aristocracy of the spirit, a self-disciplined corps of idealists at the service of common humanity, in opposition to the egotism and exploitation typical of society in that period."[8] Is this not the basic idea of the *Ring* cycle, the generation of a new world order in which greed, inequality, and injustice have been eliminated in the dawn of the Millennium? The rapid industrialization of Barcelona, the plight of the urban proletariat, and the consequent radical agitation created an environment conducive to such millenarianism. As Hughes observed, Wagner showed how "to combine the myths of a legendary past with the supreme myth of the capitalist middle class, that of progress and innovation."[9] The epic grandeur of Wagnerian opera resonated with such aspirations, and it symbolized German nationalism and industrial prowess, which Catalans admired and emulated.

The rapidly changing structure of Barcelona itself reflected this futuristic thinking rooted in the remote past. The nineteenth century witnessed a rapid expansion of the city away from its traditional center, in the Gothic Quarter near the harbor, toward the hills beyond. This was necessary to accommodate a dramatic increase in the city's population, mostly from immigration of rural poor seeking jobs in the city's thriving industrial sector and the expanding bourgeoisie. For instance, between 1872 and 1900, the population doubled, from a quarter million residents to over a half million.[10] Not only the population but also the sheer size of the city swelled during this time, with the tearing down of the old walls and the rapid development of new districts. Granados's own change of residences followed this general urban movement.

This development produced not only an excited preoccupation with the future, but a nostalgic glance toward Barcelona's glorious medieval heritage. Thus, *moderniste* art and theater were populated by castles, legends, fairies, and all sorts of recollections of a mythical medieval realm. However, this was increasingly out of step with the realities of the city as it actually was, with widespread labor unrest, political conflict, socialism, and anarchism.[11] When these realities engulfed the city in the riots, bloodshed, and destruction of the "Tragic Week" in 1909, the end of *modernisme* was in view.

To be sure, Wagner's music appeared in Barcelona fairly late, with the performance of *Lohengrin* in 1882. *Der fliegende Holländer* followed in 1885 (at the Liceu) and *Tannhäuser* in 1887.[12] In January 1899, *Die Walküre* was produced at the Liceu,[13] and the following season *Siegfried* and *Tristan und Isolde* appeared there. The early years of the twentieth century witnessed the production of *Die Gotterdämmerung* and *Die Meistersinger*. The *Ring* premiered in its entirety in 1910, and *Parsifal*, on the evening of the last day of 1913, thirty years after Wagner's death.[14] The local public preferred to hear these works in Catalan, and translations were made by, among others, Joan Maragall, who translated *Tristan und Isolde* into Catalan, as well as Schiller's *Ode to Joy* for Beethoven's Ninth Symphony. Not only opera houses but also symphonic organizations fed the growing appetite for Wagner in the Catalan capital. The Societat Catalana de Concerts (1892–97), conducted by Antoni Nicolau, was at the forefront of musical life in Barcelona, performing symphonic repertoire from Beethoven through Strauss, with generous dollops of Wagner as well. Orchestral excerpts from the *Ring*, *Tristan und Isolde*, and *Parsifal* figured prominently on the programs of the Societat and other symphonic organizations in Barcelona.[15]

The ever-increasing popularity of Wagner's music led, in 1901, to the founding of the Associació Wagneriana by journalist Joaquím Pena, Granados, and others.[16] This organization championed the music and philosophy of Wagner through conferences, publication of his works (translated into Catalan), and performances. It also promoted other composers, including Mozart, Chopin, and Schumann, celebrations in which Granados participated as a performer.[17] In 1913, Barcelona celebrated the hundredth anniversary of Wagner's birth. The German composer's influence was so pervasive that he became the standard for judging new works and for "evaluating the attitude" of conductors and orchestras in their concerts.[18]

In fact, Wagner's impact extended beyond music to *moderniste* architecture.[19] Gaudí attempted to impart to his designs the kind of primitive magic and subterranean organicism that characterize the opening of *Das Rheingold* and much of the *Ring*. Pellicer believes that his aesthetic represented a desire to "return to the primordial ideas and the spirituality of symbolic culture, combined with an obsession with the future." His schemes are nothing less than "a transposition of Wagner's symphonic forms" into architecture, "including the character of Wagner's orchestration."[20] Another example of Wagner's impact on local architecture is Lluís Domènech i Montaner's 1908 designs for the Palau de la Música Catalana, featuring the "Ride of the Valkyries" on the proscenium.[21] Not only the Palau but also the Liceu acquired Wagnerian décor. It was undergoing renovation at this same time, and a scene featuring Wotan and Brünnhilde was painted on the central and most prominent part of the proscenium.

Granados certainly came under the Wagnerian spell. Of Wagner's final opera he wrote, "*Parsifal*! Like an ideal being, created to resemble the divine! Let us study it and feel it with fervor. Let us perfect our spirits. *Parsifal* will make them forget all the human offenses and perfect our soul. Musically, I cannot, I should not. Nothing should be said about a piece of art that stopped being music to become something bigger than music itself."[22] And Granados also had a personal connection with the Wagner family. In 1910, Isolde Wagner and her husband Walther were in Barcelona, and they attended a soirée at Granados's home that included a presentation of some of his newly composed pieces for piano.[23]

Granados was deeply involved with the Catalan-modernist movement and shared its devotion to Wagner, but it is nonetheless difficult to classify Granados as a *moderniste* per se, because, as was customary for him, he was moving in several spheres at the same time. To be sure, it would be a mistake to think that the *modernistes* had some clearly defined ideology or manifesto, or even a coherent doctrine. Modernism was not so much an idea as a feeling, a kind of emotional response to the world mediated through the process of art.[24] It is in this sense that Granados comes closest to being a Catalan modernist.

Granados remained on the margins of the *moderniste* movement, particularly in respect to its Catalanist political thrust. He could never have agreed with Maragall that "love of Catalonia entails enmity towards Castile."[25] Granados would much more likely have concurred with Gerald Brenan, who from the vantage point of the post–Civil War era concluded that "Spain can only be held together by Castile," despite the Castilians' "industrial and commercial apathy," which was the principal cause of regional separatism.[26]

Given that opera became the vehicle par excellence for the expression of nationalist sentiment throughout all of Europe, it comes as no surprise that Catalan opera was the principal desideratum of the *modernistes*. And Catalan composers were industrious and prolific in their efforts to make Catalan opera a reality. Xosé Aviñoa has shown that nearly a hundred Catalan operas were composed during the period 1880–1920, roughly equivalent to the number of foreign operas produced at the Liceu. However, there is a glaring disparity in the number of performances each group received: roughly 350 for the Catalan works, and a whopping 3,192 for the Liceu's international fare. Aviñoa speculates that Barcelona opera-goers were repelled by the "aesthetic complications" of *modernisme*.[27] Be that as it may, their relative indifference to Catalan lyric theater meant that the Herculean efforts of Morera, Pedrell, Vives, Granados, and a host of obscure locals came largely to naught. Catalan musical theater, such as it was, reached the peak of its popularity in the first decade of the twentieth century, after which its limited appeal to the general public largely doomed it to irrelevance.[28]

The impulse toward Catalan musical theater gave rise to a short but inspired season of Teatre Líric Català at the Tívoli in 1901. This was the brainchild of Morera, Ignasi Iglesias, and Miquel Utrillo.[29] The company Morera brought together for this enterprise was impressive, consisting of over two score actors, an orchestra of thirty musicians, and a chorus of equal size. Performances took place throughout the week (except on Sunday) and throughout the day, in the mid-morning, mid-afternoon, and in the evening. One could enjoy a box for less than eight pesetas or stand for a mere half of a peseta. Although the Teatre Líric Català had a short life, it produced thirteen works by five composers and ten authors, and in the span of about two months gave no fewer than 200 performances.[30] This was an impressive run by any standards and a monument to the energy and devotion of Morera, two of whose operas figured prominently in the series: *Los Rosons*, with a text by Apeles Mestres, and *L'alegria que passa*, with a libretto by Rusiñol. Understandably, the quality of the many productions was uneven, given such a killing pace, and this contributed to the rapid downfall of the project.

The Teatre Líric Català and Catalan musical theater in general existed not simply to promote one thing but to oppose another: the *género chico*, or light zarzuela, which was everywhere popular in Spain at this time and was closely associated with Madrid, Castile, and everything that the Catalan *modernistes* found oppressive. Maragall published an article in *Diario de Barcelona* entitled "La sardana y el género chico" in which he brought this conflict into clear, and passionate, focus:

> In the evening I went to the theater: *género chico*. It had been a long time since I had seen one, and the blood rose to my cheeks—from shame. What actions, what passions, what characters, what words! . . . and inevitably, the knife, supreme arbiter of the action. And that heartbreaking love, cruel and without illusion, which only knows possession or death. And that song of pleasure that is like a death rattle, and that dance that crudely conveys animal movements without joy. *Género chico, género grande de muerte* [of death].[31]

In the view of the *modernistes*, the best way to fight the zarzuela was to beat it at its own game, by offering short dramas in Catalan based on local folklore, interspersed with musical numbers of a Catalan flavor. This would not be an easy task, for the *género chico* had made deep inroads into Barcelona's cultural life, and at least four theaters presented them. Of course, there had to be reasons for the light zarzuela's popularity, and we can summarize these as follows.[32]

The zarzuela dealt with scenes from everyday life as people lived it in Spain. Replete with urban folklore, for example, *pasodobles*, habaneras, waltzes, and polkas, it was a welcome diversion for the masses. And it was predictable and consistent from one show to the next, regardless of title or author. The actors were not always skilled vocalists, so both plot and music were generally simple. Choruses, such as they were, were often sung in unison.

This says nothing of the quality of the productions, which in terms of staging, acting, singing, and overall performance was occasionally quite high. And some of Spain's most talented composers devoted themselves to composing zarzuelas. Still, there was something democratic about it, precisely because it had no snob appeal, did not require erudition or knowledge of "high culture," and because the subjects and music were imbued with popular appeal. Moreover, the public could dress more casually than for the opera. As one journalist observed, "The *género chico* was a valve for letting off the people's steam, a humorous escape that sometimes had an element of sociopolitical satire."[33] For a few pesetas, a middle-class family could get an hour's worth of entertainment and be home in time to put the kids to bed.[34]

Despite all this, the *modernistes* were convinced that, if given a compelling alternative rooted in their own culture, Barcelona audiences would turn toward Catalan musical theater. Somewhat ironically, Granados's first attempt to prove this came hard on the heels of his zarzuela-inspired regionalist opera *María del Carmen*. Titled *Blancaflor*, it employed a text by Adrià Gual i Queralt (1872–1943), a Catalan who, like so many of the *modernistes*, was gifted in several areas, including painting, writing, and theatrical direction. In fact, he studied direction in Paris, and after returning to Barcelona, he founded the Teatre Íntim in the late 1890s, an alternative to purely commercial theater that he hoped would bring high art to the masses through the production in Catalan of plays by Goethe, Shakespeare, Molière, Ibsen, as well as Catalan playwrights like Maragall, Rusiñol, and Gual himself.[35]

The Teatre Íntim represented a collaboration of several *modernistes*, including painter Jose Maria Sert, writer Oriol Marti, critic Joaquím Pena, businessmen Claudio Sabadell and Francisco Soler, and playwright T. Caballé y Clos, whose play *Silenci* was the inaugural production (Teatre Líric, 1898). In this first show, which attracted a small audience of about sixty, each of them invested fifty pesetas (600 total).[36] Granados improvised music for Gual's production of *Ifigènia a Tauris* by Goethe on January 23, 1899.[37] These musical offerings were, unfortunately, entirely emphemeral.[38] Joan Llongueras, however, recalls that Granados's improvisations for the "sublime" drama were nothing short of "delicious."[39]

Blancaflor premiered on January 30, 1899, at the Teatre Líric, as the final presentation of the Teatre Íntim.[40] Granados provided incidental music consisting of a prelude and three numbers, meant as melodramatic backdrop; he also conducted the orchestra. The little drama shared the evening with *Interior* by the Belgian Symbolist Maurice Maeterlinck. The story, derived from Catalan folklore, concerns a princess who remains seven years under a mint tree waiting for her seafaring husband to return from a war. He arrives incognito in order to test her fidelity, and in the end they are blissfully reunited. The Indo-European patrilineage of such a tale is traceable to Homer's *Odyssey*; some elements of the story recall Wagner's *Flying Dutchman* as well. Granados introduces the Catalan folk song "Blancaflor," based on this legend, at the beginning and end of the play. Interestingly, Granados alters the rhythm and melodic contour so much that the melody resembles a *jota* or *malagueña* more than the original (ex. 5.1a/b).[41] Perhaps he was still composing under the spell of *María del Carmen*.

Ex. 5.1a: Original *Blancaflor* melody

Es - ta - ra la Blan - ca - flor

Ex. 5.1b: Granados's transformation

Diario de Barcelona thought that Granados's score highlighted the text "with great sobriety and art." But it speculated that the work may not have won over the audience, which was not capable of surrendering to the almost hypnotic suggestion of the drama or of savoring its "delicacy."[42] *La veu de Catalunya* did not find that the music of *Blancaflor* was of "considerable importance," but its relative simplicity was entirely appropriate: "It is a thing I have always noticed. No matter how good the music is that you invent using an old and pretty popular song as a basis, always, always when you offer it to the public in its simplest and purest form, it produces the best effect."[43]

La vanguardia, ever unsympathetic to Catalanism, offered a brief and stinging appraisal of both *Blancaflor* and *Interior*: "Suffice it to say that the greater part of the audience neither completely understood nor felt either of the works presented. . . . May they continue on with this noble enterprise, . . . perhaps someday they will gain the victory that eluded them last night."[44] Gual himself admitted that the audience was not ready for *Interior*, and he and his company approached *Blancaflor* with "a certain anxious distrust," made all the worse by the fact that three members of the orchestra failed to show up. All of this unease was communicated to the audience and, in addition to lengthy scene changes, exacerbated their incomprehension of the drama.[45] In fact, the audience responded with outbursts of ridicule and scorn. *Blancaflor* never returned to the stage.[46]

One other collaboration between Granados and Gual was the author's *Última primavera*, a scenic representation of Edvard Grieg's *Letzter Frühling* (Last Spring). This was produced on June 6, 1904, at the Granados Academy, with Granados conducting a string orchestra.[47] Also on the program was *La nuit d'octubre*, based on a text by Alfred de Musset with "scenic dialogue" by Marie Monros and Pierre Rettmeyer. The music consisted of improvisations at the piano by Granados.

The most important and enduring operatic association that Granados formed was not with Gual, however, but with another *moderniste*, Apeles (or Apel·les) Mestres i Óños (1854–1936). Mestres supplied him not only with librettos but also with song texts and inspiration for various instrumental works. The son of a famous architect, Mestres grew up in an atmosphere redolent of Barcelona's ancient and medieval past. Thirteen years Granados's senior, he outlived him by a good twenty years; despite this, they were kindred spirits and felt, already in Granados's youth, a profound rapport. Both men were deeply romantic and prone to nostalgia. Yet, they possessed the ability to work very fast in the heat of inspiration.

Mestres vividly recalled their first meeting. He had been invited to the Granados home, and Granados played some of his pieces for him, which were "extremely melodic" and "sensual," revealing the "great influence" of Chopin. Mestres learned from Enriqueta that some of his own drawings and poems inspired the young pianist's improvisations. Moved by this, Mestres conveyed to him another of his poems, *El cavaller se'n va a la guerra*, and Granados set it to music. This was his first song, though as far as Mestres knew, it was never published or performed.[48]

Mestres was a truly renaissance man, equally gifted as a poet, artist, dramatist, and folklorist. In his spare time, he pursued gardening and published 200 songs he himself composed.[49] He contributed illustrations to the periodical *L'Esquella de la Torratxa* and wrote narrative poems of an epic character, accompanied by his own illustrations, which achieved considerable popularity among the Catalan-reading public. Several of these formed the basis for operatic collaborations with Granados and other composers in Barcelona, most notably Amadeu Vives and Enric Morera.[50] Mestres's dramas exhibit very simple plot lines, and as Curet notes, "[They are] always clear and understandable. There are no deceptions, ambiguous feelings, or half tones in his productions."[51]

Regardless of the intrinsic dramatic merits of the works Granados and Mestres produced, they form a significant part of the composer's oeuvre, and he invested a great deal of time and energy in them. Larrad is convinced that "Granados's Catalan theatre works reveal a level of compositional ingenuity and inspiration which is at least equal to his greatest piano works, and they present us with a more rounded picture of the composer than has hitherto been accepted."[52] The next chapter will survey this important collaboration.

CHAPTER 6

Catalan Works with Texts by Apeles Mestres

Granados wrote music for a total of five stage works with texts by Mestres: *Petrarca*, *Picarol*, *Follet*, *Gaziel*, and *Liliana*.[1] Of these, only *Follet* and *Petrarca* are true operas; the others alternate various kinds of musical numbers with spoken dialogue. The emphasis in all of their theatrical collaborations is not on dramatic interaction between the characters but rather on the characters themselves, fleshing out their individuality through musical means. In the opinion of Mas-López, "[h]is theater is predominantly picturesque; conflicts and/or psychological analyses are not treated."[2]

The *moderniste* elements in these works are (1) the emphasis on nature, (2) an idealized medieval setting, and (3) a Central European musical style that, despite its occasional debt to Catalan folk song, is non-Hispanic and very much in the late Romantic tradition of Wagner and Liszt. One thing they do not do is promote Catalan nationalism. One finds no references at all to actual historical events or persons in Catalonia's history, or any tales that are distinctively Catalan. Indeed, the only opera that has any basis in actual history is *Petrarca*, dealing with the Italian poet, not a local figure. The one aspect that unites all of the librettos Mestres wrote for Granados is that "the central characters experience an unyielding affection for a beautiful woman, [which] leads to unhappiness rather than emotional fulfillment."[3]

Petrarca

Granados and Mestres began their collaboration with a work that never made it to the stage, *Petrarca*. This was Granados's second real opera, and his first substantial work with a Catalan text. None of the manuscripts for the opera are dated, but it is clear that Granados began composing it shortly after Mestres completed the book in May

1899, because his composition of a "Catalan opera in one act" was reported in the press the following month.[4] He may have stopped working on it before moving on to his next venture with Mestres, but whatever the case, the surviving manuscripts are incomplete and would not permit a production today.[5] Granados did get close to completing the work and went to the expense of having a professional copyist prepare the score, but even that is lacking important material, and no combination of the extent sources would yield a finished *Petrarca*.[6] Still, the work contains some fine music and merits consideration.

Consisting of a prelude and one act in five scenes, *Petrarca* resembles a series of *tableaux vivants* loosely based on the life of the Tuscan poet, his obsessive love for Laura, and his death. (Laura has never been positively identified, but she was the inspiration of much of Petrarch's work.) The authors place great emphasis on extended soliloquies for Petrarch and Boccaccio in scenes 1 and 4, and there is little action. The drama, such as it is, takes place in Petrarch's villa in Arquà, near Padua. The date is July 18, 1374, it is evening, and Petrarch is sitting at his desk in a pensive mood, ruminating on the nature of humanity and the state of his own country. Certainly such a theme held meaning for Catalan audiences around 1900, as any story set in the late Middle Ages/early Renaissance recalled the epoch of Catalonia's greatness before it was absorbed into the Castilian sphere. However, Mestres's story pays little heed to historical accuracy, and Petrarch's friendship with Boccaccio is misrepresented. For example, Boccaccio was not present at Petrarch's death in Arquà (their last meeting there was in 1368), and neither was Boccaccio the libertine Mestres would have us believe. But such license is not a significant departure from what is common in theatrical works dealing with historical figures. The most serious problem, in Mas-López's view, is the "tenuous and almost ephemeral" nature of the play and its "scarcity of plot and the extreme sentimentality of its diction."[7]

The first scene is brief, and Petrarch's introspective reverie is followed by an offstage chorus of girls chanting the "Angelus" to orchestral accompaniment. With this devotional music as a backdrop, Petrarca stands before an effigy of Laura and confesses his undying love for her. This moment, touching and passionate, effectively contrasts the sacred and the profane in a manner reminiscent of other operas of the time, especially Massenet's *Manon* or even Albéniz's *Pepita Jiménez*. Although Petrarca is outwardly a man of God, inwardly he clearly worships Laura.

The second scene is dominated by a conversation among some girls that, through a series of questions and answers, serves to shed more light on the relationship between Petrarch and Laura. The vocal writing adds little to the overall musical effect, which is instead sustained by the scherzo-like orchestral accompaniment. Indeed, scene 3 introduces a lighthearted and jocular Boccaccio. This scene concludes with Boccaccio singing a simple strophic song to the accompaniment of his lute, which Granados simulates in the orchestra with pizzicato strings. In a serious mood, conveyed by the key of C minor, Boccaccio declares the superiority of love to erudition, the central message of the opera (ex. 6.1).

Ex. 6.1: *Petrarca*, scene 3, Boccaccio's song

Petrarch returns in scene 4, but Boccaccio's ruminations on the horrors of the plague and on the "grim reaper" who reaps "without pity" dominate the scene. Granados's capacity for word painting is on display in a repeated two-note figure that conveys the swinging back and forth of the reaper's dreadful scythe. This moment is preceded by a strident declaration in the trumpet, an instrument associated in Christian mythology with the Final Judgment.

The final scene of the opera involves a dream sequence in which Petrarca, in a final delirium of love and impending death, imagines that he sees his beloved Laura. The sparse scoring suggests the desolation of death, and here Granados reveals the master's touch as an orchestrator. However, there is a thickening of the orchestral material as Petrarch imagines he is drawing closer to the heavenly paradise toward which Laura is summoning him. She proclaims, "This is the eternity, the reward which God gives to Love, his best work." Petrarca holds Laura in passionate embrace now as she urges him to "cherish and adore me" (ex. 6.2).

Ex. 6.2: *Petrarca*, scene 5, duet, Petrarch and Laura

For the first time, they sing together, and Granados wrote on the score that they "embrace in a paroxysm of passion" as Petrarch kisses Laura. At this moment of supreme bliss, the consummation of decades of desire, the vision vanishes and the rapture ends. And not only the vision, but the score as well. Granados may have set the concluding scene of Mestres's drama, but we do not have it. In scene 6, Boccaccio discovers the lifeless body of Petrarch the next morning. Perhaps Granados intended to terminate the opera with Petrarch slumped over on his desk in a kind of stupor. That ending is not entirely satisfactory.

The music is of considerable interest.[8] Although Mestres portrays Petrarch as an embittered old man, Granados's music endows him with considerable heroism. This is accomplished in part through the orchestration, which is rich in scope and detail and calls for a large brass section and three harps. Granados eschews a prominent role for the chorus, however, and this may have prejudiced the management of the Liceu against the work, as the audiences there had a fondness for such devices. Still, Granados employs a female chorus, both on- and offstage, very effectively in the first three scenes. The solo parts are daunting in their difficulty, especially the lead role. The solo-vocal writing relies heavily on expressive recitative (there is no spoken dialogue), breaking only occasionally into actual song at crucial moments of emotional intensity.

Most interesting is Granados's use of themes with clear dramatic associations and their subsequent transformation, reflecting the influence of both Wagner and Liszt on his compositional method. The three most important such themes first appear in the prelude and recur throughout the opera. Larrad has labeled these the "Hero," "Death," and "Love" themes (ex. 6.3a/b/c).

Ex. 6.3a: *Petrarca*, "Hero" theme

Ex. 6.3b: *Petrarca*, "Death" theme

Ex. 6.3c: *Petrarca*, "Love" theme

The hero is, of course, Petrarch himself, and his theme has a predictably upward-thrusting contour. By contrast, the "Death" theme descends downward into the abyss and represents Laura's demise from the plague in 1348. The Love theme has two motivic sections, one a downward scalar descent in quarter notes, while the other leaps up boldly by a fifth, from D to A, in quarter notes and concludes with a double-neighbor-tone flourish in sixteenths around A. Clearly these highly contrasting subdivisions of the Love theme are meant to portray both Petrarch and his beloved Laura, as he reflects on his memories of her.

Granados's sense of harmonic organization is short-winded, so to speak, and he occupies himself with formulaic harmonic progressions; the score gives no evidence of long-range tonal planning. Despite its shortcomings, this is a work that gives off flashes of brilliance, making its incompletion all the more regrettable.

Picarol

Picarol remains the most successful of all Granados's Catalan theater works, if only by virtue of the sheer number of times it was produced. It premiered on February 23, 1901, in the next-to-last week of the Teatre Líric Català, on a double-bill with the highly successful *L'alegria que passa* of Rusiñol and Morera. *Picarol* received thirty performances during this run and enjoyed revivals. It was done in Sitges in the summer of 1901, with the company of Celestí Sadurní. On July 14, 1904, it was performed as part of the series Vetllades Artistiques, organized by the Circle de Propietaris at their theater.[9] *Picarol* saw new life at the Teatre Principal during twenty-seven performances from February through April of 1906, and twenty-nine more during December of that year. The production was of the highest quality, and the singers were hailed in the press for their excellence.

Its total of nearly one hundred performances over five years is easily greater than all the other Catalan works treated here combined, though this feat pales in comparison to the popularity of Morera's stage works. Yet, the world remembers Granados today, not so much Morera, as Granados had a much wider range of interests and never placed all his eggs in the basket of Catalanism and *modernisme*.

Picarol is not a full-length opera but rather a play with musical numbers, much in the manner of a zarzuela. Its plot will seem familiar to anyone who knows Hugo's *Notre-Dame de Paris* or *Le roi s'amuse*, made popular in film as *The Hunchback of Notre Dame* and in opera as Verdi's *Rigoletto*, respectively. In fact, *Picarol* represents a hybrid of the two. As is the case in so many of Mestres's plots, we have a sensitive, marginalized figure, misunderstood, rejected, and unfulfilled in love—in other words, an artist. Picarol is a court jester, a misshapen and piteous figure whose comic barbs do not win him much sympathy. He is in love with an unattainable woman whom he must watch marry another man. The action takes place in a castle of an unnamed kingdom in the fifteenth century. Details of time and place are hardly important insofar as this tale has a universal quality. Still, the medieval setting is consistent with Mestres's tastes. The proximate inspiration for this work, however, was neither Hugo nor Verdi but rather a poem Mestres had written years earlier entitled "El cuc i la estrella" (The Worm and the Star), which is recycled in the drama as the text for a song sung by Picarol. Mestres himself had set the verse to music, but Granados did not use this as a point of departure in writing his own song.

Only Picarol and his lady love, Regina, sing in this drama; all the other roles are spoken. There are also several non-speaking roles (courtiers and servants).[10] Other music is provided by the chorus in several numbers. The drama is divided into five scenes, and there are six musical numbers in all, three before Picarol's lengthy monologue in scene 3 and three after it. As in all of Mestres's librettos, there is little in the way of real drama. Picarol is a tragicomic figure whose passion for Regina is, as Petrarca's was for Laura, unrecognized and unreciprocated.

In the tradition of the "Yo soy" (I am) number in the *género chico*, Picarol's first song, in scene 2, is essentially a nametag establishing his identity, "Jo sóch un boig" (I Am a Lunatic), "I've always been crazy in mind and body." Of course, his unconventionality and ability to mock himself make him a sympathetic character, one at odds with the deadening norms of polite society (ex. 6.4).

Ex. 6.4: *Picarol*, scene 2, "Jo sóch un boig"

Like the majority of the numbers in these Catalan works, the form of this song is strophic, reinforcing the folklike simplicity and directness of his character. At points in his number (e.g., mm. 15–20), the flat melodic contour reinforces the dim view he takes of pretensions to wisdom, valor, virtue, and nobility. For Picarol is something of a cynic, but underneath that cynical exterior lurks an extreme sensitivity that he will almost but never quite reveal to Regina. Granados brilliantly exploits the chorus of noblewomen here to highlight Picarol's alienation from the society in which he finds himself, for they only see his sardonic side and never the tender human within.

Picarol has been assigned the task of informing his beloved Regina that the preparations for her wedding are almost complete. When all is finally in readiness, a cannon will be fired to signal that the procession into the chapel should begin. Regina sings the hymnlike "Acompanyeume al oratori, amigues" (Accompany Me to the Oratory, Friends), which establishes the simple, obedient, yet somewhat melancholy character of the princess. For it is clear in the ensuing conversation with Picarol that she, too, stands to lose something in the nuptials, that is, the enchantment of childhood. She asks Picarol to entertain her with a song, and here Granados supplies one of his most memorable numbers, "Cançó del cuch" (Song of the Earthworm), utilizing the aforementioned poetic text that formed the basis for the entire drama (ex. 6.5).

Ex. 6.5: *Picarol*, scene 4, "Cançó del cuch"

In this piece, Picarol sings of the love of a lowly earthworm for a shining star up above, clearly symbolizing his love for Regina (Regina coelis, or "Queen of Heaven"). Granados music expresses a poignant melancholy and bittersweet longing that made this by far and away the most popular number of the work. He accomplishes this by means of contrary-motion counterpoint that clearly constitutes a bit of word-painting: an ascending vocal line, in a sense reaching for the stars, is juxtaposed against a descending bass line, in the realm of the worm. There is an analogous tonal fluctuation between D major and B minor, finally resolved in favor of the latter. It is at this point of resolution that Picarol and Regina sing together, one bittersweet moment of union before their irrevocable separation.

At the end of his song, Picarol is overcome with emotion and confesses to Regina that she is the star in the song; sadly, before he can reveal his identity as the earthworm, a cannon shot summons the wedding procession to the chapel. Picarol's last opportunity to unburden himself of his secret feelings is lost forever. In the fifth and final scene, the wedding party processes into the chapel to the accompaniment of a lengthy celebratory chorus, whose verses are separated by expansive orchestral interludes. This is one of the boldest conceptions in all of Granados's stage works, one that posed considerable technical challenges for the strings in particular, challenges that may not have been fully met, considering the limited time for rehearsal. In a moment of startlingly intense sincerity, Picarol adjures the Duke to treat Regina well, threatening to kill him if he does not. The drama concludes with Picarol singing bits of his "earthworm" song interspersed with reprises of the wedding music. This ending was Granados's invention, and a fortunate one. Mestres's original idea, to have Picarol sing his song alone on stage, would have been anti-climactic in the extreme.

The press was generally supportive of *Picarol* upon its 1901 premiere. In a brief review, *La Esquella de la Torratxa* included Mestres's text for the "Cançó del Picarol," commenting that "Granados knew how to embellish it with a burst of the most inspired music." The critic especially appreciated the prelude, women's chorus, the Queen's aria, and the wedding march. In all of these, the composer had given "a new proof of his talent for the cultivation of lyric theater." [11] Other reviewers found that the numbers Granados composed for the work combined text and music in a dramatically effective way, and that his score bore "the stamp of distinction and of melodic elegance" that characterize his music.[12]

Joventut offered a split decision of the work in the two reviews it published. One found the only defect to be that the performers apparently had not mastered their lines, and the singers were not very good. Other than that, *Picarol* had a "great theatrical effect."[13] In the following review, however, the music struck the critic as too Wagnerian, and the march was "trivial" and lacking in spontaneity. His conclusion was that the ovation accorded the opera was among the "least justified of the season."[14] This dim view did not prevail among the majority of concert-goers, however, as the work's repeated success attests.

Follet

The opera *Follet* is based on a Breton folktale about a young man whose doomed love compels him to destroy himself by jumping off a cliff (shades of *Tosca*, or even *Flying Dutchman*). Granados began composing the work in July 1901, and it was to have been part of a Catalan Lyric Theater season being hatched by him in collaboration with Albéniz and Morera, at the Novedades.[15] This never happened, however, and the process of composition lasted until early 1903, when he played through the score in a private audition at Mestres's home.[16] The drama itself was published in March 1903 (Barcelona: Salvat y Cía), but the opera score has remained in manuscript since its birth.[17]

The high quality of *Follet* probably owes to the intimate rapport Granados felt with the text he himself had solicited from Mestres, who informed the press that "one afternoon Granados appeared in his garden to request a libretto for an opera, a lyric drama 'of few characters, with hardly any action . . . an idyll . . . a duet, all passion and nature!'"[18] Mestres was immediately captivated by the idea and began to fashion a story from an old Breton legend he recalled, about a poor troubadour who was given the name of Follet (Goblin) by the people because he did not have a name.

There seems to be no concern in *Follet* for large-scale design; rather, in a sort of through-composed manner, Granados's score responds to the changing nature and necessities of the drama itself. Like *Petrarca* and unlike his other Catalan theater works, lyrical numbers are separated by arioso and recitative and not by spoken dialogue. There are fourteen numbers in all, half of them strophic, half through-composed. They are suffused with references to Catalan folklore in a general sense, though actual attribution of this or that theme to a specific preexisting folk song has thus far proved impossible.

The tonal plan of the work may not reflect a premeditated design, but it is of some interest. The keys of F major and minor are predominant in act 1, with considerable emphasis on third-related keys in A and C (again, major and minor). The second act opens and concludes in E major, and it figures prominently in act 3 as well, though the opera finishes in B minor. The overall *Ursatz*, then, is a tritone relationship, from F to B. There is a certain dramatic logic in this, as this most unstable and dissonant of intervals perfectly reflects the nature of Follet's doomed attraction to his beloved.

In terms of dramaturgy, *Follet* reflects a post-*Tristan* preoccupation with drama that is more symbolic or psychological than active. This would be fine if that were Mestres's strong suit, but it was not. Still, insofar as the opera lasts about an hour and a half (total performance time), that is not a serious liability. Most of the action, such as it is, transpires in the outer acts (each about twenty minutes in length), while the middle act is devoted to an exposition of feeling (lasting a little over half an hour). There are also orchestral preludes before the final two acts.

Five leading motives woven into the musical fabric impart unity to the score. Larrad has labeled these motives "Folk," "Recognition," "Nadala," "Love," and "Departure/Fate." Only the Recognition motive occurs in all three acts, and it is one of two themes Granados actually referred to and explained on a piece of paper that he titled "Themes on which the prelude is based" ("Temas sobre los cuales esta basado este preludio" [to act 3]).[19] Of the Recognition motive, the composer wrote that "it denotes the profound sadness of Follet for not believing himself to be worthy of Nadala."[20] The other motive, Departure/Fate, "indicates Nadala's weakness for abandoning her happiness or the sadness which she feels on abandoning her lover."[21] Descending chromatic scales occur throughout the opera and portend Follet's eventual fate. Both Nadala's motive and Departure/Fate are linked to this idea in their descending melodic contour. The Love motive also has a certain symbolic character, as it represents the physical union of Follet and Nadala at the end of act 2 (ex. 6.6a/b/c).

Ex. 6.6a: *Follet,* "Recognition" motive

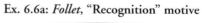

Ex. 6.6b: *Follet,* "Departure/Fate" motive

Ex. 6.6c: *Follet,* "Love" motive

The story of *Follet* is a timeless one and certainly bears more than a passing resemblance to many another illicit-love-dooming-lover-to-death tale, in particular *Tristan und Isolde*. Follet is a troubadour who falls in love with Nadala, who to his immense discomfiture is betrothed to Count Martí. In a manner reminiscent of *Pelléas et Mélisande*, Nadala and Follet meet in the forest and declare their mutual love, which must naturally remain a secret. Arnau stumbles upon the secret and threatens to reveal it. In the ensuing struggle between Follet and Arnau, both plunge over a precipice to their deaths.

It is clear that Granados's deployment of musical materials reminiscent of Catalan folklore and Mestres's commitment to sentimentality and simplicity in his story were intended to appeal to the general public, habituated as it was to the banalities of the *género chico*. Moreover, even as Granados traveled to Murcia to research *María del Carmen*, he may well have done something similar to prepare for *Follet*, as he refers in a letter to Pedrell to having taken a trip to the Pyrenees, "for the purpose of searching for folksongs and a story for a Catalan opera."[22]

The first act is rich in songs and choral music. Outside the castle of Count Guillem, festivities celebrate the upcoming marriage of Nadala to Count Martí. Granados makes effective use of reeds and brass to suggest folk music and dance, particularly during Arnau's ballad "Què'n voldrás d'una balada?" (Do You Want Me to Sing a Ballad?). This is in keeping with Mestres's reference in his text to the sound of bagpipes, shawms, and tambourines (ex. 6.7).

Ex. 6.7: *Follet*, act 1, "Què'n voldrás d'una balada?"

In contrast to the highly rhythmic and extroverted character of Arnau and his ballad, Follet's music is gentle and introverted, as befits the sensitive and lovelorn troubadour. His character emerges in a lengthy conversation between himself and Nadala, consisting of three songs connected by recitative and arioso. In these numbers Follet expresses his admiration for her beauty, tells her something about his home deep in the forest, and discloses that he has a secret love whose name he can only reveal to her there, in the Devil's Cove. The first song, "Senyora jo voldría donarte en semblant dia" (Señora, I Would Like to Give You on a Day Such As This), is in modified strophic form and may be based in part on a folk song. In any event, the harp simulates Follet's strumming of his lute, while woodwinds emphasize his rusticity. The harmony is appropriately simple, persisting on the tonic chord with occasional interruption by ii7, over a tonic drone (ex. 6.8).

Ex. 6.8: *Follet*, act 1, "Senyora jo voldría donarte en semblant dia"

In the arioso passage in mm. 385–98, Nadala asks Follet his name, to which the troubadour responds, "Ask the nightingale." At this point, Granados ingeniously mimics the song of his beloved bird in the woodwinds.

Act 2 commences with a primordial sort of prelude over an E pedal in the bass. This harkens to *Das Rheingold*, though the setting, in the Devil's Cove, reminds one of the Wolf's Glen scene in *Der Freischütz*. The Nadala and Love motives dominate here, and their musical connection, through an initial descent of a sixth, also says something of their dramatic interconnection. Their connection becomes textural as well, for Granados weaves a tightly woven contrapuntal fabric in the prelude that seems to portend the dramatic complications about to ensue.

Follet awaits the arrival of Nadala so that he can reveal to her his love. During Follet's "Els remors de la nit" (The Murmurs of the Night), Granados demonstrates his mastery of orchestral color in a delightful evocation of nighttime in the forest, with the various sounds of wildlife and wind (ex. 6.9).

Ex. 6.9: *Follet*, act 2, "Els remors de la nit"

In the duet that follows, between Follet and Nadala, Granados made substantial alterations to Mestres's text in order to convey better his dramatic purposes. So, though the libretto has three stanzas, he rearranges the verses to create a fourth, in which Follet and Nadala now sing together of the "the sun and the sunflower," symbolic of their rapturous union. Criticisms of Mestres's librettos cannot overlook the fact that Granados was an active participant in their creation and had considerable artistic license from his friend to make changes as he saw fit. Although Larrad finds in this number "an almost cloying sweetness which is French in origin," it brought the house down at the Liceu.[23]

This scene may remind one of act 2 of *Tristan*, but the similarity is superficial. The second half of the act is expressed through an extended arioso. As dawn approaches, the lovers must part, and here one recalls the troubadour tradition of the "alba," or dawn song, dealing with the parting of lovers with the rising sun, with their need to conceal their love from the light of day, lest they be caught. Here the Departure motive is introduced, which begins in the vocal part rather than orchestra and thus takes on a special significance. In the love duet that closes this act, Nadala and Follet sing the Love motive in unison for the first time, though this is their final meeting before the tragic end of the troubadour's life (anticipated by the arrival of B minor at m. 535).

The prelude to act 3, were it better known, would constitute one of the most remarkable examples of operatic "storm" music in the repertoire. The inclement first half of the prelude effectively presages Follet's doom. Granados's colorful orchestral palette calls for two harps as well as a sarrusophone, a keyed double-reed instrument that had been used by several French composers of his time, including Massenet. Granados himself averred, however, that this was an inner storm of the heart, not merely a meteorological phenomenon. One thinks, then, more readily of the first act of *Tristan*, rather than the famous "blood and thunder" of *Rigoletto*. In the second half of the prelude, calm returns, and the Recognition motive is prominent. For indeed, it is the recognition of Follet's true love by Arnau that will doom him. The close of the prelude reveals to us Granados's remarkable ability as a contrapuntalist, consisting as it does of a brief canon based on the Folk motive, followed by sustained chords articulated by arpeggios in the harp. It is no wonder that this highly effective piece found a life of its own beyond the opera.

Act 3 centers around the disclosure of Follet's secret to Arnau and the death of the two of them. The Nadala theme persists in the score as a reminder of her centrality to the coming conflict, even though she has now left the drama for good. In "Vosaltres, roures velles" (You, Ancient Oaks), Follet sings of his beloved to an old oak tree. Arnau then enters, singing a song in a contrasting style, its rhythms and tonal inflections suggesting Andalusia, not Catalonia. Arnau tricks Follet into telling the name of his lover and in his jealousy calls to a nearby group of girls, threatening to reveal Follet's secret to them. The girls repeatedly call out Follet's name, and the Recognition motive suffuses the orchestral commentary. Follet struggles with Arnau to the accompaniment of the storm music from the prelude; soon, a cymbal crash tells us that Follet and Arnau have tumbled over a cliff to their deaths. The Departure/Fate motive appears, appropriately enough, in the low strings and brass. Although Mestres had called for a closing lamentation sung by the girls, Granados deleted this and chose to conclude his opera with a chillingly discordant orchestral passage in B minor.

The opera was done at the Liceu on April 6, 1903, in a concert version performed by students, whose singing apparently left much to be desired. The session was organized by the Círcol del Liceu, a group of businessmen and prominent citizens, who footed the bill for the production and invited the audience. This was the first Liceu production in Catalan, as Catalan operas produced there were usually translated into Italian. It still attracted a good crowd, and the work itself received high praise. Few commentators had encomiums for the performance itself.

Especially attractive to reviewers were Follet's song in act 1, the prelude to and duo of act 2, and the prelude to act 3. In short, Granados's score revealed "sentiment, distinction, and elegance."[24] Several reviewers commented favorably on his deployment of Catalan folk music in the score; however, as mentioned, we have yet to identify a single melody he quoted, though it is likely that in some cases he did.[25]

F. Suárez Bravo felt that *Follet* was, in reality, not an opera but rather a dramatized poem in which the lyric element is prominent. He thought Granados handled the orchestra with genuine aplomb. "Great composers have had to wait many more years [than Granados] before giving proof of having an independent personality."[26] Indeed, Granados had not yet reached his thirty-sixth birthday. *Pèl & Ploma* described the work as "nothing more than a delicate dramatic idyll, full of tender poetry," which nonetheless constituted "one of the pillars now supporting the edifice of Catalan opera."[27] Unfortunately, the edifice needed a bit more support than this, and the work has not seen the light of day since its "premiere."

J. Roca y Roca was convinced of the work's merits but had serious reservations about the local audiences:

Our public, especially those who attend the Liceu, is not accustomed to this class of rehearsals [which is what this was, essentially], in which much of the work is left to the imagination, without scenery or movement, in the manner of a concert. The parts were entrusted not to professionals but rather to inexperienced students, which could only lead to a disaster or at least general incomprehension and dismissal of the work.

He wondered whether it might be better to present this work in the intimacy of Mestres's salon rather than in the Liceu, though he went on to say that the Círcol del Liceu merited sincere applause for assuming the costs for the work's performance, given the Liceu's proclivity for promoting "any pastiche promoted in the mercantile interests of Italian publishers [who had a controlling interest in the Liceu]," at the expense of local composers who "are locked out and are made victims of mistrust and disdain."[28] This view of the Liceu may have been somewhat unbalanced and unfair, but it was widely shared. And it is important to note that some reviewers found the student performances at least adequate.[29]

None of this withstanding, the work sank like a rock into the pond of ignominy, where it has stayed. The Teatre del Bosch announced plans for rehearsals and a full-blown production in 1906, but its season ended without the promised premiere.[30] Crickboom did conduct a performance of the prelude to act 3 at a concert of the Filharmònica in the Teatre Principal, February 29, 1904; Granados himself conducted this piece in a concert of the Orquesta de Barcelona, Palma de Mallorca, May 1905. Even years after Granados's death, the Orquestra Pau Casals occasionally performed it. But that was all that ever really came of this, Granados's finest Catalan effort on the stage.

Gaziel

Granados and Mestres may have felt discouraged about the fate of *Follet*, but they forged ahead with yet another project in the hopes of striking some kind of spark with the public. *Gaziel* premiered at the Teatre Principal on October 27, 1906, and ran for forty performances. Respectable, but not a record, at least not compared with *El comte Arnau*, an opera by Morera that ran 200 times and whose libretto (by Josep Carner) sold an amazing 10,000 copies.[31] Still, he and Mestres would have had every reason to feel good about forty, which was thirty-nine more than *Petrarca* and *Follet* together had garnered.

Gaziel was written for the second (and final) season of the Espectacles-Audicions Graner, a creation of the artist and impresario Lluís Graner. This enterprise represented yet another attempt to promote Catalan musical theater, and like all the others, it had a brief, if brilliant, life (1905–07). Cooperating with Graner was Adrià Gual, although Gual left at the end of 1906 and was succeeded by the painter Modest Urgell. Graner's series offered concerts, even cinema, as well as plays and operas; in addition, Granados gave recitals during both seasons.[32] Graner had at his disposal over thirty actors and an equal number of orchestral musicians. Moreover, his productions were noted for their "unusual splendour and prodigious magnificence."[33] Works by Mestres and Morera figured prominently in the series: the former's works provided the basis for seven dramas, while the latter contributed no fewer than twelve works. The series' appetite for works new and old was enormous, as it kept up an incredibly grueling schedule. There were as many as nine shows daily—one particular work might appear four times in a single day—six days a week.[34]

Gaziel is a retelling of the Faust legend, which inspired many composers in the nineteenth century, including Berlioz, Schumann, Liszt, Wagner, Gounod, and Boito. Mestres seems to have used Goethe's version of the legend as his point of departure; however, as was the case with *Picarol*, Mestres makes the story his own by altering important details. For in this work, there is no Mephistopheles; instead, temptation is offered by Gaziel, a fiery female genie. Significantly, though Mestres clearly identified with the Poet in this story, he named the work after the wily fairy who tempts him. Gaziel is, perhaps, the most interesting character in this drama, and Granados fleshes her out with some of his finest inspirations. The alienated relationship of the artist to society, their mutual incomprehension, is a subject Mestres returned to again and again in his writings, and *Gaziel* is no exception.

The substitution of a female genie for the devil is consistent with the fairy tales Mestres loved and knew so well; such stories are common in the folk literature of Spain as well as of northern Europe. Moreover, there is an element here of the trickster deity one frequently encounters in world mythology, as Gaziel definitely has a sense of humor, if twisted at times.[35] Of course, the whole notion of the temptress can be traced back to Eve in Judeo-Christian mythology.

Mestres wrote the libretto for *Gaziel* in the first week of November 1899, shortly after finishing *Picarol*. Like the libretto for that work, *Gaziel* was based on a previous literary effort, of 1891, and as with *Picarol*, this earliest version was "cannibalized" for song texts in the musical drama. Nearly all of the dialogue was newly written for the stage version. Mestres intended *Gaziel* for the Teatre Líric Català, but Granados did not set it to music until 1906 (the year in which the libretto was published), in his customary haste finishing the score only three weeks before the premiere in late October.[36] By that time, the Teatre Líric Català was history.

Granados may have written *Gaziel* quickly, but the eight separate numbers he composed, including a prelude and finale, as well as scene-change music, represent far more than a scatter-shot of disparate pieces. Unlike most of his other stage works, the tonal organization of the score reveals an overarching conception of the drama's musical structure. The work begins and ends in the key of D-flat major, but the key of A major is prominent throughout the play and is clearly associated with Gaziel. The key of D-flat major is associated with the Poet, and its enharmonic spelling (C-sharp) places it in the tonal orbit of A major. Another way to look at this, however, is to view A in the context of D-flat major, as a non-harmonic tone symbolic of Gaziel's location outside the dimension of ordinary human experience the Poet normally inhabits.

Thematic connections throughout the score provide an element of unity as well. The prelude presents a couple of waltz themes, each beginning with the interval of a fourth. This motive will recur throughout the drama and seems to be associated with Gaziel; the waltzes return in the central trio and in the finale, while the interval of a fourth informs Nos. 2 and 7.

The drama opens with the Poet seated at his desk (this is reminiscent of *Petrarca*), applying the finishes touches to his latest creation. He kisses the completed manuscript but soon experiences doubts about the ultimate purpose of art. In a moment of reflection reminiscent of the prelude to Goethe's *Faust*, the Poet asks of his new poem, "Why did I create you if you will never flourish in those serene regions where Poetry herself flowers eternally?" Mestres must have had in mind Goethe's words, uttered by the Stage Poet, "Nay, bring me rather to that brink of heaven, Where flowers the poet's joy, serene and still." Mestres's Poet soon falls into a slumber, and Gaziel appears in the fireplace, amidst the flames, sitting on a log. This apparition also resembles Faust's conjuring up of the earth spirit.[37]

In her first song, Gaziel reveals a playful, boastful nature, presenting herself as the genie of "hidden secrets and countless treasures" concealed in the earth. Her music has an appropriately vivacious, earthy quality, full of rhythmic verve that imbues her with an "almost pagan intensity as she boasts of her considerable powers."[38] A descending chromatic bass line, shifting between A major and minor, contrasts with the clear-cut diatonicism of her melody, suggesting her slippery, changeable, and slightly threatening nature (ex. 6.10).

Ex. 6.10: *Gaziel*, no. 2, "Só Gaziel"

Though not at all Spanish, the song possesses a directness that would have appealed to audiences accustomed to the *género chico*, despite the subject matter's being as far removed from that dramatic domain as possible. Once again, in zarzuela fashion, Gaziel's text begins with the standard "Yo soy" calling card, "I am Gaziel, I am the legendary genie of great secrets and of countless treasures that are guarded in the mysterious bowels of the earth." Granados's knack for colorful orchestration is on display as Gaziel brags that she has mastery over the wind. At this point the "wind" music in the orchestra is reinforced by an actual wind machine. The faux-Oriental sequence of open fifths between her line and the cornets suggests that Gaziel is a strange sort of "other."

In the dialogue that follows, Gaziel explains that she is drawn to poets because of their childlike innocence. She now proposes to grant the Poet three wishes, in a manner obviously indebted not only to *Faust* but also to *A Thousand and One Arabian Nights*, and ultimately to Satan's temptation of Jesus. In this case, however, the dire consequences of the Poet's acquiescence are not immediately clear. His first request, uttered without hesitation, is for glory. Gaziel immediately conjures up a fire that expunges every flaw from the poem the Poet has just completed. His second wish is for love, and this leads to their duet "Hi ha una dona en aquest mon" (There Is a Woman in This World), in which he reveals to Gaziel that there is a special woman to whom he is drawn who has not reciprocated his affections. Like the Poet himself, her name is not mentioned, and she remains known to us solely as She. The Poet's melancholy lament in A-flat major effectively distinguishes his personality from Gaziel's, and his unrequited passion reminds us of Petrarca, Picarol, and Follet. Gaziel mocks the Poet's moonstruck infatuation, but finally declares that She will be his. The Poet has no further wish, but Gaziel reminds him of the importance of riches and then leads him into a lighted garden that provides the setting for the following scene.

A festive ball is taking place, and several brutish Gomós (Louts) are making drunken advances toward the maids who wait on them. Hearing that the Poet has arrived at the party, they ridicule him in a drinking song that portrays them not just as an isolated group of brutes but rather as representatives of society in general and its contemptuous attitude toward the artist. They are the Philistines of Schumann's fantasy world. Their rhythmic *brindisi*, "Perquè no basta viure el principal es riure" (Living Is Not Enough, It is More Important to Laugh), relies heavily on winds and brass and is supported by a crude drone in the bass instruments. They deride the Poet's seriousness and dedication to art, preferring instead a life of superficiality and mirth (ex. 6.11).

Ex. 6.11: *Gaziel*, no. 5 (*brindisi*), "Perquè no basta viure el principal es riure"

In scene 4, the Poet enters the hall with She on his arm. In the ensuing trio, "Voldría decantar mon cap sobre ta espatlla" (I Would Like to Rest My Head on Your Shoulder), they express their immortal love for one another accompanied by a waltz that harkens back to the prelude and, of course, to Gaziel, who has made all this possible. In fact, Granados makes actual use of a piano in the orchestral score at this point, a singular moment in his dramatic output. This was one of the most popular numbers of the entire production (ex. 6.12).

Ex. 6.12: *Gaziel*, No. 6, "Voldría decantar mon cap
sobre ta espatlla," mm. 288–93

As the Poet and She fall ever deeper in love, Gaziel hovers on the periphery of their rapture, expressing sardonic contempt. The lovers sing in unisons and thirds, and they are joined only at the end of the trio by Gaziel herself. In Mestres's drama, Gaziel plays no role in this section at all; the addition of Gaziel was Granados's idea and a clever one that throws into satirical relief the love between the Poet and She.

In the final scene, the Poet is once again in his study. He is extremely grateful to Gaziel for the experiences he has had and, understanding how these things usually work, offers to sign the pact with his own blood. Gaziel refuses, saying she is not interested in his soul. The seventh number, a duo, is a complexly woven *scena* alternating recitative with lyrical sections. Gaziel taunts the Poet but soon confesses that all was an illusion, a dream, and that none of it really happened. The Poet is incredulous and deeply disappointed. It soon becomes clear that Gaziel was not so much interested in the Poet's soul as in seeing if she could distract him from his art. "Now you see how I have fulfilled your dreams. Now you have tasted happiness and have put your lips on the holy cup. Henceforth you will have to thirst even more." The Poet's dismayed reaction is portrayed in the score through one of the most densely chromatic passages in all of Granados's oeuvre. [39]

However, the Poet has not been defeated by Gaziel's cunning. From the experiences he has had, even in a dream, he draws renewed inspiration and commitment to his art. Crestfallen, Gaziel disappears in a burst of flame as magically as she materialized. The light of dawn pours through the window as the Poet awakens to the realization that he dreamed the entire drama, that his rendezvous with She was nothing more than a dream within a dream. But his recently finished opus is not a dream, and he holds it to his breast exclaiming the hope that even as he gave it life, perhaps it will grant him some measure of immortality.

This was more than *Gaziel* was able to grant Granados. Its final performance took place on December 5, 1906, and it has not seen the light of day since. In the end, audiences of the time were not ready for such a story, which strove for popularity and profundity at the same time. [40] *El poble català* accused the authors of having committed a faux pas, insofar as the slender, atmospheric drama was "contrary to the nature and exigencies of scenic art," which demands "action, sentiments, poetry."[41] Although the approach of Mestres and Granados might have been suitable for a drama by Ibsen, it was not appropriate for an opera, which required singing of "glory and love."[42]

However, most critics were supportive, showing that the public was not in agreement with the majority of commentators. In reviewing *Gaziel, El correo catalán* praised the "delicate and intense poetry, which satisfies the exigencies of good taste." Granados had "identified with the poem, penetrating its refinements one by one."[43] *Diario de Barcelona* thought that the poem itself was not "eminently theatrical" but nonetheless singled out "la canción de Gaziel" in the first scene as "a pleasant melody," as was the *brindisi* in the second scene.[44]

Noticiero universal thought Granados's music perfectly suited to the poem, and pointed to the duo in act 2 as proof of his ability to develop "simple and pleasing" musical ideas.[45] *La vanguardia* was in complete agreement on the suitability of Granados's music to the poem,[46] while *El diluvio* referred to the work as "a delicate filigree," though averring that it would never attract a large public. It found the orchestration especially commendable, even if the performance itself was uneven; in the reviewer's opinion, Josep Santpere was completely unsuited temperamentally for the role of Gaziel.[47] Nonetheless, Granados was warmly applauded after the performance, as were the soloists, set designers, director, and conductor.[48] This recognition must have brought some satisfaction to the composer, who would soon turn 40 years old.

Liliana

Mestres published his dramatic poem *Liliana* in 1907, replete with his own illustrations. In Curet's words, it is a "very inspired song to Mother Nature in which abound a multitude of fairies, sylphs, gnomes, and spirits in an enchanted forest."[49] Mestres later adapted *Liliana* for the theater, and Granados provided the music. It was produced at the Palau de Belles Arts on July 9, 1911, as part of the sixth International Exhibition of Art in Barcelona. The concert also included works by Weber, Richard Strauss, and Jaume Pahissa, who conducted.

If *Faust* was the font of Mestres's inspiration for *Gaziel*, Undine provided the model for this final theatrical collaboration with Granados. There were certainly operatic precedents for the work, especially E. T. A. Hoffmann's *Undine* (1816) and Dvořák's *Rusalka* (1901). Undine, of course, is a water sprite who embodies the Romantic fascination with fairies and their numinous presence in the natural world. Yet Mestres's story is not derivative but rather highly original. It deals with a beautiful water nymph, Liliana, and the three gnomes who vie for her love, and it is populated by an imaginative assortment of fairy-tale creatures, including a chorus of frogs. In the 1907 version of *Liliana*, Mestres described the gnomes thus:

> They were small of body with short legs and bearded; as light as squirrels, as intrepid as weasels, as prudent as genets and as astute as martens. . . . They were compelled by instinct to live secret lives, searching for refuge and making their palaces in rabbit warrens and ferret holes, and in the endless tunnels of shrews and voles.[50]

The gnomes are named Puk, Mik, and Flok. The first two names, Puck and Mick, will be familiar to English-speakers; Flok was Mestres's invention, however. According to Granados, "Flock [*sic*] represents the animals, Mick [*sic*] is wealth, and Puck [*sic*] is poetry."[51] Another principal character is Flor-de-Lli, who is a hybrid of an ancient Greek sylph with the fleur-de-lis of French heraldry. Sylphs were spirits of the air, and at the end of the drama, Liliana departs from the forest and the gnomes to live with Flor-de-Lli and the sylphs on the plains, thus uniting the two crucial elements of air and water. In this allegorical tale, love triumphs over the earthly concerns represented by the gnomes.

Alexandre Plana saw a direct link between Mestres's poem and the German Romantic tradition, with "that lyric pantheism of Tieck, Uhland, and Heine that spiritualizes nature and humanizes animals," a tradition that lived in the collective imagination and that Mestres captured with his pen.[52] Mestres could read and translate German and was no doubt well versed in the German Romantics, as was Granados from a musical standpoint.

Mestres worked feverishly to adapt his poem to the stage, completing the libretto on May 30, 1911, after three days of labor. Since this was to be a short entertainment as part of a larger and varied program, the original two hundred pages of poetry were reduced to a mere fifteen, the shortest text of all his ventures with Granados. As was earlier the case, the spoken dialogue is new, while the poetry of the original reincarnates in the song texts. And Granados obviously rushed to finish work on the score, judging from the numerous cuts and changes marked in the music.[53] A striking feature of this little drama is that it presents very little in the way of conversation. Instead, the text is poetic from start to finish, and the static character we have noted in Mestres's dramas is even more pronounced.

There are three scenes in this play, the first and last by the fairies' pool, and the middle one in the forest. Liliana and the gnomes (along with the chorus of frogs) dominate the first scene, while the second features the gnomes alone. All the characters appear in the closing scene, including Flor-de-Lli. Granados's music features choral and dance numbers, and the formal structures are predictable enough: the choral numbers are in refrain form, and the songs, in strophic.

Aside from the charming male chorus of "frogs," who offer up in unison a rhythmic paean of praise entitled "Salve Liliana," the finest numbers in this little stage work are the songs that Liliana herself sings.[54] The first is a hymn to the glories of the sun, which kisses the very mountaintops. The lengthy swelling prelude to her invocation suggests the growing light of dawn. Although I have noted that there is little of actual Hispanism in the musical style of the Catalan stage pieces, still, in this song one perceives in its florid line, descending melodic contour, and use of triplet figures something of the Spanish style Granados was also cultivating in *Goyescas* at this time, especially the first book, which he premiered this same year.

The sixteenth-note quintuplet motive in her second song, "Aquestes flors esplèndides" (These Splendid Flowers), suggests not only sylvan luxuriance but also a similar motive of pervasive significance in *Goyescas*. The evident love of embellishment here is attributable not only to folk influence but to the music of Scarlatti as well. Something of the linear, contrapuntal texture of *Goyescas* is also on display here in the interplay between the orchestral parts (ex. 6.13a/b).

Ex. 6.13a: *Liliana,* "Aquestes flors esplèndides"

Ex. 6.13b: *Goyescas,* "Los requiebros," mm. 73–75

Liliana's third song, "Filla de l'aigua, flor bosquetana" (Daughter of the Water, Forest Flower), is in a reflective mood, eschewing the exuberance of her earlier songs. Its simple modality, alternating between F-major and E-flat-major chords, has a folk-like quality that conforms to Liliana's vocal line, limited in range to a perfect fifth as it revolves around E-flat (ex. 6.14).

Ex. 6.14: *Liliana,* No. 5, "Filla de l'aigua, flor bosquetana"

bos - que - ta - - - na   jo no sa - ví - a

Consistent with this folk quality is the closing number, for a chorus of sylphs. This is cast as a farandole, a dance of southern France made famous in Bizet's incidental music for Daudet's play *L'Arlesienne* of 1872. We get some idea of the impact of this number from the *Diario de Barcelona* critic, who enthused that "the procession of sylphs, butterflies with translucent wings, and insects with dazzling shells is one of the most colorful to be seen on the stage."[55]

The lavish production featured an unusually large orchestra of eighty musicians as well as a corps de ballet outfitted in costumes of insects and flowers designed by Mestres himself. Unfortunately, the highly reverberant acoustics of the large exhibition hall were not suited to this kind of presentation, and the audience could not understand or even hear the spoken dialogue. The music also became muddled at times.

Critics heaped praise on Granados, one of them enthusing that his music was both "grand and tender," and that the entire production was "magnificent."[56] Another described his work simply as "elegant and distinguished."[57] *Diario de Barcelona* had nothing but encomiums for both Mestres and Granados, lauding the poet's "harmonious verses" and the "sweetness and elegance" of the composer's score. The sets for the forest, painted by Vilomara, Moragas, and Alarma, were warmly applauded, and the costumes were especially delightful, especially those for the sylphs, butterflies, and insects in the final scene.

In addition to the poor acoustics of the hall, *La vanguardia* lamented the fact that many in the audience were not well behaved and continued talking throughout.[58] The July heat made the Palau de Belles Arts uncomfortably warm, which only made matters worse. None of this was the fault of the performers, however, and by all accounts they acquitted themselves admirably. Absent to receive the audience's applause was Mestres, who had not felt well enough to appear on stage.[59]

Despite this, the production was not a success, and the work was quickly shelved, except for its revival as a symphonic suite in four movements arranged by Casals and programmed by him as director of the Orquestra Pau Casals in Barcelona during the years after Granados's death. The first such presentation took place on April 30, 1921, at the Palau de la Música Catalana.[60]

Elisenda and *Elegia eterna*

Another collaboration was a charming little suite for chamber orchestra called *Elisenda*, based on a poem by Mestres, with four movements entitled "El jardi d'Elisenda," "Trova," "Elisenda," and "La tournada o Final." The final movement included a part for soprano with a text by Mestres, but this is now lost. Dated June 8, 1912, the original manuscript bears a dedication to Casals and his sister Guillermina. The work is scored for two flutes, oboe, B-flat clarinet, two violins and solo violin, cello, bass, harp, and piano, and it premiered at the Sala Granados on January 26, 1913, featuring performers from the Academy as well as Granados himself.

One critic found the work "exquisite" and full of "profound sentiment."[61] Fernando Periquet described *Elisenda* as "a lovely bucolic poem" that evoked the beauties of nature: the opening of the flowers to the morning sun and the perfumed forest, which served as emblems of Elisenda's growing love. He affirmed that his enchantment was shared by the audience, which applauded, not out of courtesy, but out of spontaneous emotion, their hands moved by a "sincere impulse." In response, Granados exhibited his customary modesty and merely inclined his head and extended his "leonine" hands.[62]

In addition to the stage works and *Elisenda*, Granados wrote several songs with texts by Mestres.[63] Outstanding among these is the *Elegia eterna* (Eternal Elegy) for solo voice and piano. It bears a dedication to María Barrientos, who performed it in London on June 20, 1914. This short, eloquent piece is among the composer's most moving testaments. The text tells of a moth's unrequited passion for a rose, which idolizes the morning breeze, which yearns for the fog, which adores the river. Abandoned by the breeze—which is chasing the fog that is chasing the river—the rose expires: "and on the top of that stem without corolla, the moth stops, closes its wings and dies." [64] The theme of unrequited love is reminiscent of all the opera librettos Mestres wrote for Granados, and it may be this aspect of the song that inspired one English critic to remark that the Spanish people "are among the most unhappy" in Europe. Still, the Catalan works on the program were proof that "Catalan composers possess a great knowledge of choral technique." Mostly, however, reviewers focused on the golden voice of Barrientos, for which the *Elegia* was basically a vehicle.[65]

It is somewhat difficult to know how to assess the Catalan stage works today. They represented an enormous investment of time and energy on Granados's part, and it seems something of a waste considering that all of the operas are now perhaps hopelessly obscure. Márquez Villanueva thought that these ventures "had kept his talent at a standstill, limiting his potential as well as his audience."[66] This may be too harsh an assessment. Certainly *Follet* deserves its day on the stage. In any case, as a result of these unsuccessful efforts, he gradually came back to his artistic center, which was also the center of the nation, that is, Castile. What is also clear is that by the time of *Liliana*, the mood and atmosphere in Barcelona had changed. Márquez Villanueva correctly asserts that, in the wake of the Tragic Week, "[t]he Catalonian *belle époque* had been shattered forever, and Mestres's fairy-tale post-Romanticism now started looking like a toy from the distant past."[67] *Modernisme* had reached a dead end.

Spain's diminished stature as a result of its war with the United States, the loss of its American and Asian colonies, and the internal tensions between regions and social classes threatening to tear the country apart required some countervailing response, a reaffirmation of the nation's past glories and overarching unity in a shared history and common identity. This is the context in which to place Granados's next retreat into the past, not into the Middle Ages, but into the world of Goya.

CHAPTER 7

La Maja de Goya

A great debate raged in Spain in the 1890s and early 1900s, centering around the nation's place in the world, its identity and future. In the latter part of the nineteenth century, conservative politicians like Antonio Cánovas promoted xenophobia and fueled distrust of foreign influence, at the same time asserting the view that Spain was a major power and had an important role to play in the world. Spain's defeat in its war with the United States in 1898 made it more difficult to embrace such a fantasy. Illusions of national grandeur proved unsustainable in the aftermath of such humiliation and the loss of the remnants of a once-vast empire.

In response to this crisis, the fundamental question arose, "Should Spain recast herself, importing from [northern] Europe all the trappings of ideology and material progress, or should Spain retrench to her traditional self, casting aside liberalism, as well as economic and technological values?"[1] In more simplistic terms, this was a choice between conservative and liberal politics, between religion and science, between the *Siglo de Oro* and the Enlightenment, between apparently irreconcilable opposites that had clashed before in Spanish history and would culminate in a ruinous civil war and decades of right-wing dictatorship later in the twentieth century. These were the issues that preoccupied a number of writers collectively known as the Generation of '98.

Then again, maybe this was an artificial dichotomy. Perhaps there was a third way. In his 1895 essay *En torno al casticismo* ("On 'Casticism'"), Miguel de Unamuno, one of the leading writers of the Generation of '98, found a solution that came to exercise a profound influence on artists and intellectuals in the wake of the Spanish-American War. *Casticismo* means "genuine Spanishness," the pure spirit of the nation, implying a reverence for tradition. Such a term, of course, is slippery enough to be capable of almost any definition, and some used it as a shibboleth in denouncing foreign ideas and trends. That was not Unamuno's approach. He rejuvenated the notion of *casticismo*, and from his point of view, "Spain remains still undiscovered, and only will be discovered by Europeanized Spaniards."[2]

Unamuno believed that Spain could, in a sense, have its cake and eat it too, that it could Europeanize without abandoning its unique identity. Of course, Spain was already a European nation, but by "Europe" '98 writers in general were referring only to the most advanced and powerful countries, namely, France, Germany, and Britain, whence came the most influential trends in science and the arts.[3] Spain was perhaps a decade or two behind them in terms of its overall development. In *En torno al casticismo*, Unamuno declared with justification that "Only by opening the windows to European winds, drenching ourselves with European ambience, having faith that we will not lose our personality in so doing, Europeanizing ourselves to create Spain and immersing ourselves in our people, will we regenerate this treeless plain."[4]

France served as something of a model for the Generation of '98, because it, too, had undergone a crisis of national humiliation in the Franco-Prussian War of 1870–71, which had shattered its illusions of military and cultural superiority. The defeat led to an interest in monuments and museums as emblems of the nation's former glory. And the center of the country, the Île-de-France and Paris, held the key to national renewal; it was the hub around which revived greatness must revolve.[5]

Unamuno focused on Castile and Madrid as the center from which national regeneration would come. Another '98 exponent of this view was the Valencian author José Martínez Ruiz, known as "Azorín." For him, the most important cultural currents in the Spanish revival were the Generation of '98, Wagnerism, and landscape painting, which captured the essence not only of the distinctive Spanish (largely Castilian) countryside, its mountains, plains, rivers, light, and air, but also of the "soul" of the country and its people, which was inseparable from the earth they inhabited. Azorín and Unamuno promoted Castile as the region in which the pure and authentic spirit of the country resided.

Azorín was one of the leading polemicists in search of the national quintessence, and he wrote numerous articles that appeared in the periodicals *Diario de Barcelona* and *La vanguardia* on the subject of Castile and national identity. Certainly Granados read these and internalized their message.[6] Granados's deeply Romantic attraction to Castile and Madrid finds a literary equivalent in Azorín's *Castilla*, a series of short stories evoking his beloved adopted city. In the chapter "La flauta en la noche," the author describes "a flute sounding in the night: graceful, undulating, and melancholy,"[7] a wistful strain that persists through the decades, from 1820 to 1900. The melody stretches across the years, connecting Goya's epoch with his own. This quote gives us an indication of what Azorín sought to know about the past: "how one sensed the light, shadow, color, silence, solitude, the whiteness of a wall or the black or golden hue of a few earthy stones, the sun in the remote countryside, the murmuring of a fountain in a secluded garden, a white or ashen cloud that passes, and the distance, the remote distance."[8] To know these things of any time in Castile's history, he says, one would have to consult the canvases of an El Greco or the poetry of a Luis de Góngora. It was precisely this preoccupation with sensory impressions and this sort of dreamy romanticism that characterized Granados's attraction to the Castilian past and was the wellspring for so much of his music.[9]

It is ironic that Granados, Azorín, Unamuno, and other proponents of Castilian-ism were not themselves from Castile. Nonetheless, they and like-minded spirits "de-fined the nation in terms of Castile, the 'mother lode' of Spain from which the mod-ern Spanish State was to emerge: its spiritual core, center of past imperial glories, and cultural home of renowned classical poets, painters, and statesmen."[10] It was, as Azorín put it, "that most glorious part of Spain to which we owe our soul."[11]

The role music played in this reinvention of national identity is central to under-standing the significance of Granados. For his nostalgic attraction to Castile and Madrid ca. 1800 would find expression in a musical language that was thoroughly modern and thoroughly Spanish, European and *casticista* at the same time, thus bridging the gap between liberal and conservative even as Unamuno had prescribed. As he had done in so many other areas, Granados synthesized two opposites.

Granados's attraction to the life and art of Francisco Goya y Lucientes (1746–1828) in particular came to flower at a time when Spain was searching its past for great fig-ures, especially in painting, who (it was thought) had delved so deeply into the Spanish "soul" that they had found something of universal appeal.[12] Here, Unamuno's con-ception of history is relevant, for he distinguished between major events, dates, and figures, on the one hand, and the unsung, unrecorded history of the people them-selves, which he called "intrahistory." This intrahistory "consists of continuous perma-nent conditions which make up the eternal tradition [that] seems both to emerge from and to give shape to the collective unconscious of a group of people."[13] Goya's depiction of the everyday life and people of Spain, its intrahistory, resonated with Granados's desire to capture the "essential spirit" of his country, through evocation of its folk and popular music, especially that of Goya's time.

The appearance of biographies of Velázquez by Jacinto Octavio Picón (1899) and Benigno Pallol (1914) and of El Greco by Manuel Bartolomé Cossío (1908) was symp-tomatic of this quest for past greatness, but Goya most captured the imagination of writers and musicians ca. 1900. Conde de Viñaza's biography of Goya and catalogue of his works (1887) was an important landmark. It may also have been the first to em-ploy the adjective "goyesco" in relation to the artist's style.[14] This was followed thirty years later by Aureliano de Beruete y Moret's *Goya*, a three-volume magnum opus that set a new standard in Goya scholarship. In part, the disaster of 1898 seemed reminis-cent of that of 1808, when Napoleon invaded Spain, and people now looked to Goya as a symbol of Spanish resilience in the face of defeat.[15]

In particular, the bohemian character of the *majo* and *maja* captivated Goya and his admirers, and dominated the highly romanticized image of old Madrid embraced by Granados and his contemporaries, a fascination known as *majismo*. The real-life *majo* cut a dashing figure, with his large wig, lace-trimmed cape, velvet vest, silk stockings, hat, and sash in which he carried a knife.[16] The *maja*, his female counter-point, was brazen and streetwise. She worked at lower-class jobs, as a servant, perhaps, or a vendor.[17] She also carried a knife, hidden under her skirt. Lengthy courtships be-tween *majo* and *maja* were the norm, and he took her to the theatre, the park, and to the *botilleria*, a café that served light refreshments. The influence of the very word *majo/a* endures in the Spanish language, as a way of saying something is attractive or desirable.

Although in Goya's day the *Ilustrados* (upper-class adherents of the Enlightenment) looked down their noses at *majismo*, lower-class taste in fashion and pastimes became all the rage in the circles of the nobility, who were otherwise bored with the formalities and routine of court life. Many members of the upper class sought to emulate the dress and mannerisms of the free-spirited *majos* and *majas*. Among the most famous epigones of the *majas* was the thirteenth Duchess of Alba, Teresa Cayetana (1776–1802), who was the subject of several paintings and drawings by Goya.

With the renaissance of *majismo* ca. 1900, authors and writers focused on the *majo/a* as an embodiment of *casticismo*. Vicente Blasco Ibáñez wrote a novel entitled *La maja desnuda* (1906), while Blanca de los Ríos de Lamperez contributed *Madrid Goyesco (Novelas)* (1908). In 1909, Zacharia Astruc wrote a series of five sonnets inspired by Goya's *La maja desnuda*, entitled *La femme couchée de Goya*. The following year, Francisco Villaspesa presented his verse-play *La maja de Goya*. The composer Emilio Serrano collaborated with Carlos Fernández Shaw on an opera entitled *La maja de rumbo* (The Magnificent Maja), which premiered in Buenos Aires in 1910.[18] It became fashionable as well to reproduce Goya's paintings as *tableaux vivants*. One such event in Madrid in 1900 simulated four of the master's works as a benefit for the needy and was attended by the royal family and other nobility.[19]

Interestingly, Granados was most attracted to the pre-Napoleonic works of Goya, those that constitute insights into Spanish life that are at once colorful, intimate, and penetrating. The ironic, satirical, violent dimension of Goya's art seems not to have engaged him at all. When Granados visited the Prado Museum in the late 1890s, several score paintings by Goya were on display, including almost forty of the celebrated cartoons.[20] Only five of the fourteen Black Paintings were on view, however.[21] Still, even if all of them had been available to Granados, it is hard to imagine they would have exerted much more influence. He simply was not drawn to that aspect of Goya. Only the Goya of *majos* and *majas* fired his imagination and gave rise to the Goya-esque works under consideration. Especially appealing to him were the portraits of the Duchess of Alba, thought by some to be the subject in *La maja desnuda* and *La maja vestida* (the nude and clothed *majas*) and Goya's mistress, though that is not the case at all.[22]

Not only the paintings and cartoons of Goya influenced Granados but also the writings of Ramón de la Cruz (1731–94), the leader of literary *majismo* during Goya's lifetime. His more than 400 one-act comedies, or *sainetes*, portray in delightful detail everyday life in the Madrid of that epoch.[23] His stage works were highlighted by the music of Blas de Laserna (1751–1816) and Pablo Esteve (b. ca. 1730). Laserna, director of the Teatro de la Cruz, composed about a hundred *sainetes*, as well as zarzuelas and incidental music. As Ortega y Gasset pointed out about Cruz and his collaborators, "his famous *sainetes* are, literally, little more than nothing, and what is more, *they did not pretend to be poetic works of quality*" [emphasis added].[24]

Azorín, however, put *majismo* in a somewhat different light by emphasizing the importance not only of the *majo/a* but also of the Frenchified dandy called the *peti-*

metre (from the French *petit-maître*), who figures even more prominently in Cruz's *sainetes* than the *majo/a*. The pretensions of the *petimetre* were the stuff of satire, a typical example being the musical skit *La maja bailarina (El Francés y la Maja)* by Josef Castel (fl. 1761–81). In this amusing little drama, a *petimetre* attempts to seduce a *maja* by giving her dancing lessons, only to become the student rather than the teacher. For Azorín, such characters represented a nascent middle class and were as much a part of the "national reality" then as they were in the early twentieth century. From this he extrapolated that "the nation is one whole and indivisible." All classes—upper, middle, and lower—were part of the national fabric he envisioned. The refinement of the *petimetre*, superficial though it may have been, was in Azorín's view a necessary counterbalance to the coarseness of the *majo/a* and should not be neglected by contemporary proponents of *majismo*.[25] Although Granados never evoked the *petimetre* in his works, he was in accord with Azorín's view of the Spanish nation and the importance of the middle class.

Both Goya and Cruz, then, served as models for composers around 1900 seeking to infuse their stage works with the spirit of *majismo*. Barbieri's zarzuela *Pan y toros* (Bread and Bulls) of 1864 had been a big hit and was just the beginning of a major eruption of musical theater replete with *majos* and *majas*. Albéniz's zarzuela *San Antonio de la Florida* made a deep impression on the young Granados at its 1894 Madrid premiere. In fact, shortly after the premiere, Granados wrote a musical dedication to his friend expressing his support, which was no doubt welcome given the harsh reaction of the critics.[26] Albéniz's zarzuela may have provided the impetus for Granados's own *majo*-inspired zarzuela, *Los Ovillejos*, a few years later.

For a partial listing of musico-theatrical works of the time dedicated to the themes of Goya and his epoch, see table 7.1.[27]

In addition to Goya and Cruz, another eighteenth-century figure who exercised a profound influence on Granados was Domenico Scarlatti (1685–1757).[28] The Italian harpsichord virtuoso and prolific composer of keyboard works spent the final twenty-eight years of his life in Madrid and became enamored of Castilian folk music and dance, which he evoked in many of his 555 sonatas.[29] In fact, Granados made a transcription of twenty-six Scarlatti sonatas he found in a manuscript in Barcelona.[30] The origins of the manuscript are uncertain, but it was probably copied around 1800 somewhere in Catalonia. There is no way that these are autograph copies, and nearly all of them can be found in other sources. Two sonatas in the collection are not found elsewhere, however, and though Granados included them in his transcriptions, we now know that they are not by Scarlatti.[31] Granados's edition was published in 1905 (Barcelona: Vidal Llimona y Boceta) with an "Estudio biográfico-bibliográfico-crítico" by Pedrell, who naturally took a keen interest in this music. Granados gave the French premiere of some of these works at the Salle Pleyel in Paris on March 31, 1905. He was joined on this occasion by Crickboom playing violin.[32] Of Granados's performance the pianist Edouard Risler wrote, "Finally, an *artist*, after so many pinheads and nonentities."[33] He performed several of them again at two concerts he gave the following year, on March 1 and 3, at the Teatre Principal.[34]

Table 7.1. Musico-theatrical Works 1870–1920 Dedicated to the Themes of Goya and His Epoch

TITLE	TYPE	AUTHOR (Composer/Librettist)	YEAR
La gallina ciega	zarzuela	Caballero/Carrión	1873
Las majas	opera	Mateo/unknown	1889
Majos y estudiantes, o el rosario de la aurora	sainete	López Juarranz/Montesinos López	1892
San Antonio de la Florida	zarzuela	Albéniz/Sierra	1894
La maja	zarzuela	Nieto/Perrin Vico and Palacios	1895
La maja de Goya	zarzuela	Navarro Tadeo/Falcón Segura de Mateo	1908
Los majos de plante	sainete	Chapí/Dicenta and Repide y Gallego	1908
La maja desnuda	sainete	López Torregrosa/Custodio Fernández-Pintado	1909
La maja de rumbo	opera	Serrano/Fernández Shaw	1910
La maja de los claveles	sainete	Lleo/González del Castillo and Jover	1912
La maja de los madriles	humorada	Calleja/Plañiol Bonels and Fernández Lepina	1915
La maja del Rastro	sainete	Aroca/Enderiz Olaverri and Gómez	1917
San Antonio de la Florida	comedia lírica	Lleo/González Pastor	1919
La maja de los lunares	opereta	Obradors/Giralt Bullich and Capdevila Villalonga	1920
La maja celosa	zarzuela	Aroca/Gómez	unknown

These works were a revelation to most audiences at the time and enthusiastically received. F. Suárez Bravo reminded his readers that music of Scarlatti's era bore little indication as to tempo and other performance parameters. He praised Granados for having gone about his editorial work with considerable "tact," that is, he had not "falsified the style" of the music but rather displayed considerable knowledge of its structure and ornamentation.[35]

Tonadillas

Granados's first completed vocal work embodying *majismo* was not an opera or zarzuela but rather a collection of songs for voice and piano: the *Tonadillas*. Granados composed these ravishing miniatures during the period 1912–13, and they were subsequently published by Casa Dotesio.[36] To be sure, these were intimations, not historically accurate re-creations, of the eighteenth-century *tonadilla*, of which there were two kinds. The dramatic *tonadilla*, or *tonadilla escénica*, resembled the Italian intermezzo and served as light diversion between acts of a larger theatrical work. It was thoroughly imbued with Iberian musical style and employed *seguidillas*, boleros, and "other typical Spanish dances, accompanied by harps . . . guitars and castanets."[37] The composers of these charming creations, such as Antonio Rodríguez de Hita, Pablo Esteve, and Luis Misón, were famous in their day but are less well known today. The stories dealt with everyday life and characters, particularly the *majos* and *majas* of Madrid. These works were simple entertainments that were nonetheless often laced with social satire.

Granados, however, evokes the second kind of *tonadilla*, which was simply a song in a popular and accessible style. Thousands of these were written and many survive. Although Granados claimed he had written his *Tonadillas* "in the old style" ("en estilo antiguo"), in fact he has captured more the spirit rather than the musical essence of that earlier repertoire. Still, the *Tonadillas* represented a genuine innovation in Spanish music, the creation of a distinctively Spanish "Lied."

To be sure, circumspection is necessary when comparing the German Lied with the *Tonadillas*, whose verses are frothy and lighthearted evocations of *majo/a* joys and sorrows, avoiding anything psycho-metaphysical. Even the three songs entitled "La maja dolorosa" (The Sorrowful Maja), dealing with the grief of a *maja* over the death of her *majo*, make no real attempt to probe the mysteries of human mortality. These songs live purely and simply in the moment, in the moment in which Granados wrote them, and in the moment whose color and emotion they encapsulate.

The texts for Granados's *Tonadillas* were written by Fernando Periquet Zuaznábar (1873–1946), a native of Valencia. Although Periquet was, as Márquez Villanueva described him, "a mediocre novelist and playwright," [38] he became director of the newspaper *El liberal* and a freelance journalist for several others. He was also an ardent devotee of Goya and promoted himself as a leading authority on everything having to do with the great artist and his works.[39] According to Periquet, he first met Granados in Madrid in 1894, at a gathering held at the hotel room of Albéniz, who was in town that fall directing *San Antonio de la Florida*.[40] Their friendship deepened during the period of *María del Carmen* in Madrid, and it was evidently then that Granados came more deeply under the spell of Goya through Periquet's influence. Periquet may have been a mediocrity, but he nonetheless achieved a sort of immortality through his association with our composer.

As Periquet pointed out, the eighteenth-century *tonadilla*'s texts were of several kinds: patriotic, amatory, picaresque, or satirical.[41] Moreover, "pure Spanish culture, hunted by the oppressive talons of foreign taste, found refuge in the patriotic sentiment of the lower classes, in which this fragrance concentrated, according to the phrase of Feliu y Codina, waiting for time to clear the air in our land so it could diffuse itself with more intensity than ever throughout the entire nation."[42] Despite the flowery nationalistic veneer he spreads over the actual history, Periquet's essential point is well taken: under the onslaught of Italian influence in art music, autochthonous Spanish idioms survived in the vernacular arena of the lower classes.

On another occasion, Periquet had this to say about the allure of Goya's era: "Moreover, the word Goya . . . is not just a name but also an epoch. The epoch of Goya means loves and passions in relation to emotions; socially, it is an odd mixture of all classes, something like a dawn of democracy that placed bullfighters next to duchesses, and princes close to *tonadilla* singers."[43] In other words, Periquet's romantic vision of that period imputed to it some of the preoccupations of his own time, especially democratization.[44] But there was, in reality, nothing democratic about Goya's Spain, which was run by the aristocracy and Church in the manner of the *ancien régime*, despite some liberalizing tendencies of Carlos III. Still, one of the traits of Spanish society in the time of Goya was the absence of a large middle class, and this brought the extremes of society into close proximity with one another and provided the basis for a fruitful subcultural exchange. To his credit, Periquet was under no illusions about the times in which Goya lived, and he acknowledged that it was a period of widespread hunger, oppression, illiteracy, and violence.[45]

Everything in the text and music serves to create the effect of unpremeditated spontaneity. As Ramón Barce points out, the irregular character of Periquet's verses is not only characteristic of the song verse of Goya's time but also favorable to Granados's music itself. It helps to avoid a strictly symmetrical phrase structure and formal layout.[46] In "Amor y odio" (Love and Hate), for instance, the lines are of variable length, from six to nine syllables, while the three stanzas exhibit an irregular rhyme scheme: aabbbbb / cbc / adaaaaa. This irregular verse structure gives rise to freedom and variety in the structure of each song.

Consequently, most of the twelve published *Tonadillas* do not exhibit any predictable structure, though Nos. 3 and 9 are in ternary form.[47] They are like perfunctory outbursts of song and usually consist of a succession of melodies presented without repetition or development of any kind. The length of each *Tonadilla*, then, depends on the number of melodies it contains. Framing almost always consists of a simple piano introduction often echoed at the conclusion. This "form" best describes Nos. 2, 4–7, and 11.

To convey something of the plebian pedigree of the *tonadilla*, there is a relative absence of tonal contrast in these songs, and most of the internal sections cadence on the tonic. To provide some relief, Granados resorts to modal mixture, alternating between parallel major and minor keys. For instance, in "El tralalá y el punteado," the form is ABA, with the B section in the parallel minor key. "Amor y odio" follows a similar pattern, starting in G minor and moving to G major.

"Las currutacas modestas" (The Modest Belles) uses two voices to enact the dialogue between the *currutacas*. However, the voices move together in sixths, parallel movement in thirds and sixths being characteristic of Spanish folk music. "El majo tímido" (The Timid Majo) and "El majo discreto" (The Discreet Majo) make good use of guitaristic effects in the accompaniments and interludes.[48] In "El mirar de la maja" (The Maja's Gaze), the arpeggios, rolled chords, and staccato markings in the piano accompaniment clearly imitate guitar *punteo* (plucking), as do the runs in "El tralalá y el punteado" (ex. 7.1).

Ex. 7.1: *Tonadillas*, "El tralalá y el punteado," mm. 1–4

"El tralalá y el punteado" is a mere 34 measures in length, but it is one of his most arresting conceptions. Although the verses that Granados originally wrote for this were replaced by Periquet's, his sketch material reveals that the music he used for both texts is virtually identical. Clearly, Granados wrote texts that would fire his musical imagination; however, once they had served their purpose, he was not reluctant to substitute another text.[49] The lyrics are, then, subordinate to the score. In a short song, this strategy can produce highly satisfactory effects, but in an opera, no.

Indeed, it is the music and not so much the verses that make these songs so deliciously memorable. The piano part in particular is exquisitely crafted and plays a crucial yet unobtrusive role in supporting the voice and establishing *ambiente* (ambience). Never virtuosic, it nonetheless reflects Granados consummate mastery of the instrument. For instance, in "El majo discreto," the extremely simple, sparse accompaniment suggests something of the *majo's* discretion, which his lover appreciates; the rather tentative, wispy piano part of "El majo tímido" is consistent with the shy *majo* who satisfies himself with glimpses of his beloved, lacking the courage to confront her. The paradox between simplicity of means and sophistication of conception in these and the other *Tonadillas* is striking.

"La maja de Goya" is one of the best known of the collection and has been transcribed for guitar solo and for guitar accompaniment. Again, this is eminently logical insofar as the piano part clearly mimics the *punteo* of the guitar. The unusually lengthy introduction sets a mood of subdued yet alluring sensuality. Another feature that sets this song apart is the indication in the published version, "Hablado," to speak nearly the entire text, except for the last two verses. Here the tonality shifts from G minor to major, as the singer reflects on the story narrated in the spoken section. This has an entrancing effect, but has Riva points out, "even Conchita Badia, the only singer to record the *Tonadillas* who studied with Granados, does not speak this text."[50] There remains some uncertainty as to Granados's intentions, though the most recent recording hews to the published version.[51]

Granados probably wrote this song with a particular performer in mind. Aurora Mañanos Jauffret (1895–1950) had recently begun to make her way in Madrid theaters as a self-styled *tonadillera*, under the stage name of "La Goya." She specialized in solo skits, singing and dancing in eighteenth-century garb. "La maja de Goya" was likely inspired by her so-called *canciones escenificadas*, or "staged songs."[52]

The ballad relates an apocryphal episode in the life of Goya that is very witty and entertaining, concerning his dalliance with a young model posing for one of the voluptuous *maja* portraits. The young woman has nothing on and is conversing with Goya when suddenly her husband appears at the door. The woman only has time to cover her head, and the quick-thinking artist challenges the husband to identify her by examining the features of her unclothed body. He passes around the model and, not recognizing her physical attributes, apologizes and leaves the two in peace. The moral of the story is clear: any husband that oblivious to the physical charms of his wife is bound to lose her affections to another man. It is only when the singer reflects on the story that she breaks into song: "Never in my life will I forget that dear and dashing image of Goya! There is no woman . . . who does not miss Goya now!" In the final stanza, the identity of the singer becomes clear: "If I found someone to love me like he loved me, I would not envy or yearn for more happiness or joy" (ex. 7.2).

Ex. 7.2: *Tonadillas*, "La maja de Goya," mm. 77–84

Not everyone finds Granados's fusion of high and low art convincing in these songs, and some commentators believe that the art-song element often dominates that of the folk song.[53] But this is a mere quibble. Granados's aim was never to compose folklore but only to use it as a point of departure in creating something new and original, something distinctly his own. It is against that standard that we should judge the *Tonadillas*, and in so doing, we must conclude that Granados was successful in achieving his aim.

Juan José Mantecón recalled hearing an early rendition of the *Tonadillas* in a concert sponsored by the Círculo de Bellas Artes at the Ateneo in Madrid on May 26, 1913, during which Granados accompanied soprano Lola Membrives. "The memory of that evening, in which Granados revealed his songs to us, tells us that our movement is not dead, that the fecund pollen of our patriotic feeling grows in the spirit of the artist."[54] As we have seen, Granados usually distanced himself from political movements, and his inspiration was chiefly aesthetic, not ideological. But there is little doubt that he shared Mantecon's patriotic sentiments. In any event, with his *Tonadillas*, Granados claimed ground only tentatively surveyed by Albéniz and others, creating, along with Falla's *Siete canciones populares españolas*, one of the most enduring Spanish contributions to the solo-vocal repertoire.

However, the *Tonadillas* were ancillary to a much grander manifestation of *majismo*, the *Goyescas* suite for solo piano and the opera derived from it. Granados began this enormous undertaking before the *Tonadillas* but did not finish it until almost three years after the songs premiered. It is a monument in Spanish nationalist music and the focus of the next chapter.

CHAPTER 8

Goyescas

The most famous and enduring of Granados's *majismo* creations is the piano suite in two "books" entitled *Goyescas: Los majos enamorados* (Goyescas: The Majos in Love). The individual numbers of book 1 are "Los requiebros" (The Flirtations), "El coloquio en la reja" (Dialogue at the Window), "El fandango de candil" (The Fandango by Candlelight), and "Quejas o La maja y el ruiseñor" (Complaints, or The Maja and the Nightingale); of book 2, "El amor y la muerte" (Love and Death) and "Epílogo: Serenata del espectro" (Epilogue: The Ghost's Serenade). Work on this suite began in 1909 and continued into the summer of 1910, often at the home of his mistress Clotilde Godó, in Tiana outside Barcelona. By August 31, 1910, he was sufficiently satisfied with the fruit of his labors to be able to write to Joaquím Malats: "This summer I have finished a collection of *Goyescas*, works of great flights of imagination and difficulty."[1]

Constructing a precise chronology of composition is difficult because Granados usually did not date his manuscripts; nonetheless, we have a reasonably good idea of how *Goyescas* evolved. The order of composition is not the same as that one finds in the published work. A sketch of "Coloquio en la reja" dated simply "Monday, December 1909" tells us that Granados was working on the suite in that year and that this was apparently the first piece he tackled. He began work on "Los requiebros" in April of the following year and finished it on July 23, 1910. "Quejas o La maja y el ruiseñor" was completed over a month earlier, on June 16, 1910, while "Epílogo: Serenata del espectro" is dated December 28, 1911. "El fandango de candil" and "El amor y la muerte" are undated, but it is certain that the former was completed before "El amor y la muerte" and "Epílogo" because both of those works contain motives from it that Granados even labels in the score.[2] Granados himself issued a facsimile of book 1 in 1911; it was published by Casa Dotesio in Barcelona in 1912. Book 2 was published in 1914 by Unión Musical Española, which had by then acquired Casa Dotesio.

El pelele, subtitled "Escena goyesca," is usually considered part of the *Goyescas* suite; Granados premiered it at a concert in Terrassa on March 29, 1914. In fact, we should recall that the term "Goyescas" encompasses all of Granados's piano works inspired by the artist, not only the suite. Other "Goyescas" include *Jácara (Danza para cantar y bailar)*,[3] *Serenata goyesca*, *Crepúsculo*,[4] *Reverie-Improvisation* (a recording he made for Duo-Art in New York shortly before his death),[5] and the opera *Goyescas*.

We can trace the development of Granados's *majismo* through a most interesting little book, a collection of musical and artistic sketches that Granados penned during this period of the early 1900s and which record his seminal ideas for *Los Ovillejos*, the *Tonadillas*, and *Goyescas*.[6] Entitled *Apuntes y temas para mis obras* (Notes and Themes for My Works), it shows us Granados's method of composing, as well as the sources of his inspiration.

In addition to musical themes, Granados illustrates his text with occasional drawings, and he reveals his thinking in portions of the text. For instance, of the *Tonadillas* he writes: "These *Tonadillas* are original and not those known and harmonized before. I have intended this collection to serve as a document for *Goyescas*. And it should be understood that, with the exception of *Los requiebros* and *Las quejas*, in no other passages in *Goyescas* will one encounter popular melodies. Yes, they are in a popular style, but they are original."[7] Granados does not make it clear how the *Tonadillas* served him as a "document" for *Goyescas*, since the piano work was apparently completed before the songs (unless he was referring to the opera). In any event, not only the texts but also the drawings he made in this book reveal the source of his muse, namely, Goya. Prominent among these nine sketches (in pencil, ink, and pastel) are fetching *maja*s in flirtatious poses, with such fanciful titles as *La maja de paseo* (The Strolling Maja), *La maja en el balcón* (The Maja on the Balcony). *Coloquio en la reja* served as the inspiration for the second movement of the piano suite.

It is possible that *majismo* was not the only stimulus that prodded Granados to compose this suite when he did. Two unsettling events in 1909 may have persuaded him to put to good use whatever time was remaining to him on earth and get on with the job. One was the Tragic Week in July, with all its death and destruction. The other was the passing of his friend Isaac Albéniz in May. It would be difficult to put into words the depth of Granados's affection for Albéniz, who was like an older brother to him, one he had depended on for support, assistance, and inspiration.

Granados had stopped in the French Pyrenees resort town of Cambo les Bains on his return from Paris in the spring of 1909 to visit Albéniz, who was on his deathbed there. Shortly thereafter, on May 18, 1909, Albéniz died. Granados, now in Girona in Catalonia, took time to write a letter to his friend; the note is written on the stationery of the Gran Hotel del Comercio in Girona, but it is undated. This is perhaps the oddest and most moving letter in his entire extant correspondence, because the reader only gradually becomes aware that Granados is writing to someone who is no longer alive. In his grief, Granados invokes Albéniz's final masterpiece, "Iberia! Iberia!" Granados continued writing the letter a few days later in Barcelona, stating his desire that all his students at the Academy play *Iberia*. After expressing once again his respect for Albéniz and anguish over his death, he bids him farewell: "Goodbye, my beloved one . . . nothing remains for you, except to see, with time and patience, how much I admire and love you."[8]

Whatever the stimulus to composition was, Granados made clear his intentions in writing *Goyescas*:

> I should like to give a personal note in *Goyescas*, a mixture of bitterness and grace, and I desire that neither of these two phases should predominate over the other in an atmosphere of delicate poetry. Great melodic value and such a rhythm that it often completely absorbs the music. Rhythm, color, and life distinctly Spanish; the note of sentiment as suddenly amorous and passionate as it is dramatic and tragic, as it appears in all of Goya's work.[9]

And Granados clearly understood the importance of his new creation, and in a letter of October 8, 1911, he declared, "Goyescas is a work for the ages. I am convinced of that."[10]

Goyescas for Piano

Granados memorably expressed his feelings about Goya in a letter to Malats:

> I have concentrated my entire personality in *Goyescas*. I fell in love with the psychology of Goya and his palette; with his lady-like *Maja*; his aristocratic *Majo*; with him and the Duchess of Alba, his quarrels, his loves and flatteries. That rosy whiteness of the cheeks contrasted with lace and black velvet with jet, those supple-waisted figures with mother-of-pearl and jasmine-like hands resting on black tissue have dazzled me.[11]

On the basis of this revelation alone, we must question Ernest Newman's assertion that Granados was "an observer of emotions rather than of physical characteristics."[12] Indeed, Granados's chief concern was with people, how they looked, thought, and acted. It was precisely the physical characteristics of Goya's subjects that aroused within him the intense emotion he felt compelled to express through music.

The extent of his identification with Goya, with Goya's world, is remarkable. Granados was not merely depicting something of passing interest, participating in a fashion or fad. He had completely internalized these stimuli and become the subject of his creation, through the force of his romantic imagination. What one notices as well is not any interest in proto-democracy and egalitarianism in the Madrid of that epoch but rather a preoccupation with the psycho-sensual dimension of the art itself: the texture and color of the clothing, the inner being of the artist's subjects.

This gives us a vital clue as to just what it is that makes these works so appealing: one is seduced by the almost tactile quality his musical textures achieve. Granados's fixation on the rich visual detail of Goya's paintings results in a music of surpassing sensuality, through melodic lines encrusted with glistening ornaments and harmonies studded with added tones, like thick daubs of impasto applied to the canvas with a palette knife. Intricacies in rhythm, texture, and harmony even suggest the tracery of latticework and lace. And, in fact, the chromaticism, ornamentation, and sequencing in *Goyescas* harken back to the rococo style that prevailed for so long in Spain, and particularly to Scarlatti.[13]

This historicism is not altogether incongruous with the folkloric dimension, because so many of the elements of Spanish folklore as they coalesced in the early nineteenth century were indebted to the Baroque, especially the techniques of strumming and plucking developed on the Baroque guitar and the associated chordal patterns and techniques of variation, to name a few. Anyone who has played an early *chacona* is struck by the similarity of this type of music and its improvisatory realization to flamenco-guitar performance. And, of course, Scarlatti was himself deeply enamored of and influenced by Spanish folk song and dance as he encountered them in Madrid, so that we could say that much of what Granados understood to be Spanish music of the eighteenth century was mediated through the Italian eyes and ears of Scarlatti.[14] In other words, Granados's musical language is highly sophisticated, deeply connected to Spain's musical heritage even as it employs a complex late-Romantic harmonic idiom, and its matrix of referents and symbols operates on several levels at the same time.

Another influence on his style was Albéniz. The connection seems obvious the more one listens to both *Iberia* (1905–08) and *Goyescas*. Granados's thorough familiarity with Albéniz's late style exercised a deep influence on his approach to *Goyescas*. True, the French-Impressionist element is almost entirely lacking, and neither does Granados resort to sonata form as did Albéniz in most of his late-style Spanish works. Another crucial distinction is that *Iberia* displays Albeniz's love of Andalusia and flamenco, something irrelevant to the setting and style of *Goyescas*. Finally, as Linton Powell aptly points out, "While . . . *Iberia* is a series of separate pieces that can be played in any order . . . *Goyescas* is a cyclical suite, bound together by poetic and thematic unity."[15]

But the similarities are conspicuous. Granados's complex textures, at times calling for three staves, harken to *Iberia*, as does his occasional superimposition of meters.[16] So, too, does his elaborate harmonic palette, replete with many added-note sonorities (especially sixths and major sevenths to both major and minor chords) and a search for striking harmonic effects through the use of extended pedals in the bass. Abundant score markings in Italian, French, and Spanish, many of them highly unusual, are found in both *Iberia* and *Goyescas*.[17] The proliferation of accidentals across the score, even double-flats, is also familiar. The opening of "El fandango de candil" recalls the beginning of "Fête-Dieu à Seville" from *Iberia*, with its dryly insistent rhythmic stokes. The rapturous, dreamlike atmosphere of "Coloquio en la reja" is reminiscent in many places of "Evocación," with its hazy nostalgia. The secondary theme of that work, in the style of a *copla* from the *jota navarra*, bears a striking resemblance in its contour and rhythm to one of the principal themes of "Coloquio."

However, Granados was no mere imitator of Albéniz. *Goyescas* is a distinct and highly original achievement that forbids any suggestion of epigonism. As Riva has summarized this issue: "[*Iberia*] represented a new direction in Spanish music, and demanded of pianists an entirely new type of pianistic technique. *Goyescas*, on the other hand, brought Romanticism to a close. Its jewel-toned harmonies, violent mood swings, highly ornamented melodic invention, rich texture and post-Romantic fervor, had more in common with Granados's predecessors than with future composers."[18]

Granados's actual technique evokes a wide variety of responses. Some commentators feel that in these pieces he is overly repetitive and that his formal structures are ambiguous. We must always examine, however, the preconceptions we bring to a work and ask if our expectations are valid and relevant. Granados's obsessive repetition of certain themes in *Goyescas* does not emanate from a lack of compositional skill but from expressive need. The apparently rambling structure is dictated by his poetico-narrative instinct, which usually serves him very well. And close examination reveals a tonal and thematic structure of considerable logic, especially when viewed in the context of the folk and popular repertoire that informs it.

"Los requiebros" (Dedicated to Emil Sauer)

"Los requiebros" was inspired by the fifth of Goya's *Caprichos*, *Tal para cual* (Two of a Kind). Goya sketched this while visiting the Andalusian estate of the thirteenth Duchess of Alba, in Sanlúcar de Barrameda, sometime during 1796–97. It portrays a *maja* flirting with an impecunious but sword-bearing man.[19] So much importance did Granados attach to this etching that it was used as the cover illustration for the first edition of *Goyescas*. The flirtations in this piece are expressed, among other ways, through "its playful mood, its starts and stops and continually changing tempos."[20]

Granados uses a marking taken from one of his poems in the *Apuntes*, "con garbo y donaire," meaning gracefully and with spirit.[21] After a brief introduction in imitation of the guitar, Granados presents his main theme in the upper voice, which exhibits the octosyllabic rhythm so typical of the *jota* and other Spanish verse and song. The abundant ornamentation suggests something of the flirtation this movement is about.

Granados performs an interesting mutation by quoting the song "Tirana del Trípili," a *tonadilla* perhaps by Blas de Laserna that was immensely popular in the eighteenth and nineteenth centuries and figured prominently in Mercadante's opera *I due Figaro* (1835).[22] The *tirana* is an Andalusian song and dance in triple meter at a moderate tempo. The charming lyric of Laserna's tune in English is as follows (consult ex. 8.1a for the original melody and text):

> With the trípili, trípili, trápala
> One sings and dances the tirana.
> Go ahead, girl!
> I graciously concede
> That you are stealing my spirit.[23]

Here Granados recasts this *tonadilla* as a *jota*, complete with the alternation of two distinct *copla* (verse) melodies from the original and an *estribillo* (refrain) (*copla* 1, mm.

7–20; *copla* 2, mm. 57–64; *estribillo*, mm. 112–117) (ex. 8.1b/c/d). The first *copla* corresponds to the text beginning "Con el trípili, trípili, trápala"; the second, to "Dale con gracia." The *estribillo* is Granados's own invention.

Ex. 8.1a: Laserna's *tonadilla* "Con el trípili, trípili, trápala" (excerpt)

Ex. 8.1b: *Goyescas*, "Los requiebros," *copla* 1, mm. 7–11

Ex. 8.1c: *Goyescas*, "Los requiebros," *copla* 2, mm. 57–64

Ex. 8.1d: *Goyescas,* "Los requiebros," *estribillo,* mm. 112–17

"Guitar" interludes enliven the setting, as do the shifting rhythm patterns, that is, the displacement of phrases so that they sometimes end on beat three, at other times on beat two (e.g., mm. 24–32). Like the real *jota*, "Los requiebros" presents inexhaustible variations and ornamentation of its thematic material. In fact, the only literal statement of the original melody comes at m. 297. Self-borrowing is also in evidence, as the theme in mm. 217–91 ("Variante de la Tonadilla") is very reminiscent of mm. 43–48 of "El majo olvidado" from the *Tonadillas* in its harmony and melodic figurations.[24] Moreover, there is a fleeting reference to theme C from "Coloquio," in mm. 96–97; the recurring quintuplet turn establishes a motivic connection between the two movements.

Although it does not conform to any set structure, the form of "Los requiebros" is delineated by double bars that mark the various sections. Granados subjects his *copla* melodies to considerable development and modulation, and they only reappear together in the home key just before the coda. Curiously, the "refrain" occurs but once. However, this loosely arranged alternation of *copla* and *estribillo* gives him maximum room for improvisatory maneuver. It also conveys something of the insouciant gaiety of the folklore on which the piece is based.

"Coloquio en la reja" (Dedicated to Edouard Risler)

"Coloquio en la reja" was apparently the first of the *Goyescas* that Granados composed; as mentioned above, we retain a sketch dated December 1909 that antedates any other documentation. Though not the first work in the published suite, it occupies by virtue of this chronology a central place in the entire cycle, insofar as every other movement of *Goyescas* that Granados composed, except for "Quejas o La maja y el ruiseñor," utilizes thematic material from it.[25] *Goyescas* is a cyclic work that Granados clearly conceived of as an integrated whole meant to be played in a particular sequence.

Granados's self-quotation in connection with "Coloquio" has another dimension, however. In the *Apuntes* is the sketch for a *Tonadilla* he never completed, entitled "El amor del majo" (The Majo's Love). Granados incorporated the music from this incomplete song into "Coloquio" (it is quoted in full in mm. 41–48 and mm. 167–74) (ex. 8.2).[26] The ascending four-note motive he extracts from the theme of this *Tonadilla* informs the movement and provides structural unity.

Ex. 8.2: *Goyescas*, "El coloquio en la reja," mm. 41–48

There are four themes in this work (including the *Tonadilla* theme), and these are laid out in three basic sections. Section one, mm. 1–62, features the A and B themes; after a brief transition, the second section features B and C. A third section presents a D theme and variations on it. A transition dominated by elements of the B theme leads to a coda based on the A theme. The overall thematic organization, ABCDBA, has an archlike quality to it. The tonal organization, in the key of B-flat major, reflects this as well: section one, I-iv; section two, v-I; section three and transition, I-iv; coda, I. This palindromic arrangement of tonal centers reveals a good deal more sense of harmonic organization than Granados is usually given credit for.

The modal use of minor subdominant and dominant exudes a folkloric character and is also consistent with harmonic practice in his late-Romantic style, especially among French composers like Fauré. We should also note that the themes B, C, and D are related in their initial harmonic gesture (V7-I or i); moreover, B and C exhibit a similar melodic contour. Granados's intertwining of thematic material creates an effect resembling the screen (*reja*) through which the lovers converse (ornamented iron grills were placed in doors or walls, and it was through these that *majos* carried on their courtship with the *majas*).

Musical self-quotation is again at work in this movement, as the second half of the *copla* (mm. 113–17) is derived from his work for solo piano *Jácara (Danza para cantar y bailar)* (mm. 49–53) (ex. 8.3a/b).[27]

Ex. 8.3a: *Goyescas*, "El coloquio en la reja," mm. 113–17

Ex. 8.3b: *Goyescas*, "Jácara (Danza para cantar y bailar)," mm. 49–53

The *jácara* was a song and dance done with guitar accompaniment, often by an actor in a *tonadilla escénica* or *sainete*. In fact, "Coloquio" is one of two movements (the other being "Epílogo") in which Granados makes explicit written reference to the guitar: at the very opening of this piece he indicates that "all the basses imitate the guitar" ("Tout les basses imitant la guitare"). What is striking about this *Jácara* quotation, however, is the contrapuntal complexity of it, something completely uncharacteristic of any *jácaras* Goya ever heard. So dense does the writing become that Granados inserts an extra staff (in the manner of organ notation) to contain the wealth of ideas. Granados had little use for key signatures, and the notes swim in a sea of accidentals that make reading the score even more challenging.

The distinctive five-note turn Granados utilizes in this movement suggests several things: the arabesque filigree typical of Spanish folk song, the ornamentation of a Scarlatti sonata, and perhaps even the geometric pattern of a *reja*. One could add to this list something the Italian madrigalists understood very well: circling around a note in that fashion symbolizes the passionate entwining of lovers. Granados intensifies its effect by repeating it at ever-higher pitch levels. Indeed, this motive possesses such significance in *Goyescas* that it migrates to other movements; in "El amor y la muerte" it recurs so obsessively that finally Granados stops writing it out and simply places a "turn" sign above the staff. Another rhythmic element of significance is his use of hemiola. Not only does he alternate $\frac{3}{4}$ and $\frac{6}{8}$ but he also superimposes them at times, for example, mm. 134–35, where $\frac{6}{8}$ is indicated in the right hand and $\frac{3}{4}$ in the left.

It would be difficult to understand this movement without making reference to Granados's own drawing of the subject in the *Apuntes*. The conversation between the *majo* and his *maja* lover takes place through the screen, which barely separates them. This slight partition intensifies their passion (in the opera, this scene is retitled "Dúo de amor en la reja"). Significantly, however, the *majo*'s back is facing us, the viewer. This conversation is very private, and we can only "hear" the murmurings and whisperings of endearment passing between the two. This explains the intimate and withdrawn character of the opening. As the movement develops, it becomes more passionate.

In m. 187 (ex. 8.4) an important moment occurs that most commentators have viewed as an allusion to *cante jondo*, the only one found in the entire suite.

Ex. 8.4: *Goyescas*, "El coloquio en la reja," mm. 187

It bears repetition that *jondo* singing has little to do with Castile and is instead indigenous to Andalusia. There are many instances in Albéniz's works where evocations of *jondo* singing appear, often in just this way, monophonically and doubled at the octave. This passage, however, does not seem very *jondo*-like. Insufficiently florid, it lacks the augmented second interval and is not forceful enough. The fact that it is marked "Recitative" should also give us pause. It can and should be viewed, however, as a very significant moment, clearly grounded in folklore. Such an outpouring would be perfectly consistent with Castilian song, and it possesses significance in that it represents a musical joining, so to speak, of the two lovers, who sing the same melody an octave apart. How better to express their amorous coupling?

"El fandango de candil" (Dedicated to Ricard Viñes)

The title of this work has provoked some discussion over the years. The general interpretation is that this is a fandango done by candlelight, and when the candle goes out, the dance continues by other means. Interestingly, there is no portrayal in any of Goya's works of such an event, as attractive as it may be. However, a *sainete* by Ramón de la Cruz had exactly that title, and it served as the proximate inspiration for Granados's movement. Moreover, another Spanish man of letters, Ramón de Mesonero Romanos, published in 1833 a work entitled *La capa vieja y el baile de candil*, containing an illustration and description of pairs of lower-class young people dancing by candlelight to the strains of the fandango.[28]

In an early sketch for the opera, Granados shed light on the second tableau, which centers around "El fandango de candil": "Reunion of *majos*, *chisperos*, etc., in a small theater or room of the classic style, as already described by Ramón de la Cruz."[29] What Cruz was conjuring up in his *sainete* was a popular custom known as a "baile de candil," a celebration held at someone's home in which dancing by candlelight was accompanied by guitars and other string instruments. In fact, Cruz's little drama has no real plot but simply presents a charming scene replete with delicious dancing and music. The *baile* brings together people of different classes, the *majas* and *majos*, on the one hand, and their imitators in the nobility, on the other. The interaction between them gives rise to farcical comedy.

Granados's "baile" of choice here is the fandango. Granados integrates one characteristic feature of the fandango: a major-third relationship between the cadence of the first and second phrases.[30] Tertian modulations are common in the real fandango, between the instrumental interlude in A minor (or E mode, depending on how you choose to see it), on the one hand, and the *copla* in C. However, in other ways he diverges from the fandango, both in his structure and harmony.

Granados substitutes a ternary structure for the verse-and-refrain typical of the fandango. The "bookends" of this form, sections A and C, present the same sequence of three distinct themes, and related transitional material. The "da capo," however, includes a degree of rhythmic elaboration that seems to increase the movement's momentum toward its climax. Moreover, these themes are unified by the persistence of a common rhythmic motive of four sixteenths followed by a quarter. The middle section is contrasting in character and features the A motive from "Coloquio."

The tonal scheme of this movement piques our interest. The home key is D minor, though in the outer sections there is a strong emphasis on the relative major, F. In fact, the first section concludes in this key, followed by a tonally unstable reference to "Coloquio" and a subsequent passage in E-flat. The third section lurches abruptly back into D minor and finally concludes in A major, the dominant, forming the half cadence so typical of Castilian songs in particular.

The suggestion of the guitar is prominent in this movement, and Granados glories in eliciting the *rasgueo* and *punteo* of the instrument. The persistent triplet rhythms of the fandango, sometimes referred to as a "bolero" rhythm, animate Granados's musical canvas and generate a kind of tension that finds release only at the end of the movement, "on a 'fortissimo' unison on the off-beat, simulating a climactic cheer of 'olé.'"[31] The opening rhythmic pattern informs and unifies the entire movement; it was also prominent in the *Tonadilla* "Callejo" (ex. 8.5).

Ex. 8.5: *Goyescas*, "El fandango de candil," mm. 1–4

"Quejas o La maja y el ruiseñor"
(Dedicated to Amparo Granados)

Among the most celebrated of all Granados's musical utterances, this is a fanciful dialogue between a heartsick *maja* and a nightingale, which sings a virtuosic "cadenza ad libitum" at the end of the movement. In the words of Alicia de Larrocha, here is "the most tender . . . and at the same time the most intensely passionate" music Granados ever wrote.[32] "Quejas o La maja y el ruiseñor" is unique in the suite because it does not quote or utilize material from any other movement, although its invocation of the nightingale's song ties it to several earlier works by Granados.

The principal theme of this movement is a Valencian folk melody Granados evidently heard sung by a young girl in the countryside during one of his trips to that province, and which he employed to poignant effect in this movement (ex. 8.6a). In the song's lyrics, a girl tells of hearing the sorrowful song of a little bird in her garden. Granados's setting in F-sharp minor intensifies the emotion of the original (ex. 8.6b).

Ex. 8.6a: Valencian folk song, mm. 1–6

U - na tar - de que me ha - lla - ba

En mi jar - dín di - ver - ti - da

Ex. 8.6b: *Goyescas,* "Quejas o La maja y el ruiseñor," mm. 1–4

Granados sets this haunting folk tune in a skillfully contrapuntal fashion, weaving a four-voice texture with ninth chords, non-harmonic tones, and deceptive cadences. A wonderful moment in his setting is reached at the high point in the melody at the beginning of m. 2, with a B-minor ninth chord in first inversion. The tenor reaches the root, B, however, only on the upbeat, via A-sharp, creating an exquisite D-augmented sonority with an added seventh on the downbeat. At mm. 41–45, the melody migrates to the tenor line as the thick texture again calls for three staves.

Granados employs a "changing background" technique in this piece, in which each repetition of the song features a variation of the accompaniment. The overall effect is almost hypnotic and creates a mood of forlorn reverie. The song dominates the entire movement, and the ensuing three sections uncover myriad possibilities for variation of it. F-sharp minor prevails throughout most of the piece, though the third section is in the subdominant minor, while the fourth section, with its explosive bird song, explores F-sharp major briefly. The sole appearance of the dominant tonality comes at the conclusion of the work, yet another example of Granados's folk-inspired love of the half cadence. Reinforcing this effect is a downward sequence that may suggest the "cry" emitted by Castilian folksingers at the end of a *pasacalle*.[33]

Granados instructs the performer to play this piece "with the jealousy of a wife and not the sadness of a widow." His dedication of the movement to Amparo takes on significance in light of the affair he was carrying on with Clotilde Godó at the time he wrote this. No doubt Amparo complained bitterly about his infidelities. The nightingale is an enduring symbol of romantic love and has figured prominently in European literature since the Middle Ages.[34] It may evoke happy or unhappy love, ecstasy or agony, or it may sing either a lament or a song of rapturous love. Its florid outpouring at the end of this movement seems, however, to fulfill another of its functions, celebrated in the Minnesinger literature: that of counselor.

"El amor y la muerte" (Dedicated to Harold Bauer)

"El amor y la muerte" (Love and Death) was inspired by the tenth of Goya's *Caprichos*, of the same title. The etching depicts a young woman holding in her arms her dying lover, a look of terror and dismay on her face as he breathes his last.

The two movements of book 2 form a colossal recapitulation of themes previously presented. A cynic might suspect that Granados had begun to run out of ideas and was now reduced to recycling earlier inspirations. Nothing could be further from the truth. In fact, his continued reworking of these ideas is evidence of an imagination so fertile that it could always find more possibilities for variation and development in this thematic material. In any case, Granados makes no secret of this reuse and actually marks the earlier themes as they appear.

The very opening of this movement presents the quintuplet turn from "Coloquio," now in ominous octaves as the lover collapses, mortally wounded, into the woman's arms. The ensuing delirious succession of dominant-seventh chords suggests his fatal swoon. A reminiscence of the folk-song theme from "Quejas" occurs at m. 12 (marked "malinconico ricordanza"), as the woman experiences the pangs of love and death. Another such juxtaposition occurs in mm. 64–66, where the "El amor" theme appears in the bass against a recollection of the "Fandango." The "Fandango" theme itself is transfigured in mm. 81–84, appearing in the upper register, as Granados put it, "enveloped in a poetic atmosphere, as a remembrance of past happiness."[35]

The structure of the piece is a simple sectional form. A brief introduction is followed by a first section that presents two themes, A and B. The A theme is in G-flat major, while B is in the third-related key of B-flat minor. Measures 58–72 constitute a kind of development section, leading to a third section in which the themes are presented in reverse order, creating a palindrome effect, except for the insertion of a poignant adagio section, based on "Quejas," between the two themes. The progression of keys in this third section is unusual and harkens to the opening's tonal ambiguity. We emerge from the development into B minor, followed by B-flat minor, and then G major, which persists into the coda until supplanted by the concluding tonality of G minor. The descending order of the keys suggests, perhaps, a descent into the grave. In addition to third-related modulations, Granados also had a fondness for modal mixture, alternating between parallel major and minor (further suggested by the succession of B–B-flat–G).

He achieves unity in his design through a clever repetition of some part of the C theme from "Coloquio" in each section of this movement; lest the performer overlook the fact, the score at m. 22 is actually marked "El coloquio." A passage recalling material from "Requiebros" is similarly marked in m. 38, in the B theme of the first section, which also contains a marked reference to the "Fandango" in m. 45; as mentioned, another reference to "Fandango" occurs in the second section, m. 64. The adagio inserted between the B and A themes in section 3 is actually a variation on a melody in "Quejas." The end of this section and the beginning of the coda also draw on melodic materials from that movement.

A "recitativo dramático" at m. 178 heralds the death of the *majo* (marked "muerte del majo"). An E-flat German-sixth chord "resolves" in a most unsettling way to a C-sharp diminished chord, imparting to us a profound sense of the *maja*'s distress. Following this is a deafening silence suggestive of the grave. According to Granados, "The final chords are struck in short bass notes that represent the renunciation of happiness" (ex. 8.7).[36]

Ex. 8.7: *Goyescas*, "El amor y la muerte," mm. 178–85

This is an intensely emotional piece, "savage [and] mysterious."[37] Indeed, though Granados may have remained indifferent to the social satire of Goya's works, he readily responded to the note of tragedy and loss sounded in so many of his paintings and drawings. For death had visited Granados's home more than once, and there persisted within him throughout his life a despondent morbidity that found full expression in this movement. As Granados wrote of this piece in the notes he himself provided for his performance at the Acadèmia on May 30, 1915, "Three great emotions appear in this work: intense sorrow, amorous longing, and final tragedy."[38] Less than a year after writing those words, "El amor y la muerte" would become not just a set of emotions, but a terrible reality for Enrique Granados and his wife.

"Epílogo: Serenata del espectro" (Dedicated to Alfred Cortot)

In this concluding movement, the specter of the departed *majo* appears in a macabre vision, serenading his beloved with his ghostly guitar. The surreal atmosphere of the piece is established at the very outset, in that the initial series of chords virtually defies traditional harmonic analysis, at least in any functional sense.[39]

The simplicity and austerity of "Epílogo," especially in its guitar-style accompaniments, resemble the *Tonadillas* perhaps more than any of the other *Goyescas*. In mm. 87–101, the dryly staccato arpeggios suggest the *punteo* of the guitar, while throughout mm. 107–16 the strumming of the instrument is conveyed through rapidly arpeggiated ornaments before each beat. There is also a direct parallel between "Epílogo" and *Jácara* in the use of rolled chords to suggest *rasgueo*, and in the folklike melody above it.[40]

Once again, the form is based on the alternation of verse and refrain, but in a more direct and less abstracted way than in the other movements. There are three verses preceded by refrains, and each refrain introduces new themes as well as shared references to "Coloquio." The refrains are all in E major, consistent with the normal tuning of the guitar, while the verses explore third-related keys. One curious exception is an excursion to F minor and then B-flat minor in the second verse, at the point where he introduces the Dies Irae melody. Here the busy right hand cleverly accompanies the chant melody embedded in the tenor register. One is reminded at this point of Liszt's *Totentanz*, with its ghoulish pyrotechnics. The ascending line at mm. 59–62 is shrouded in furtive ornamental figures that suggest the flitting presence of a ghost (ex. 8.8).

Ex. 8.8: *Goyescas*, "Epílogo," mm. 59–62

This first section is atypical of Granados because of the angular and unmelodic character of the theme. However, this meshes perfectly with the sparse texture and conveys the lifelessness of the specter. The "love theme" from "Coloquio" makes a final, plangent appearance in the coda, at mm. 241–43. The tolling of church bells is indicated by "Campana" in the score at m. 250, and by the "high register and dissonant nature of these sonorities," which create a ringing quality.[41] At the conclusion of this fascinating piece, Granados makes explicit this reference in the score: "The ghost disappears plucking the strings of his guitar."[42] Here he presents the open strings of the instrument, symbolizing the idea that the work is over and there are no more chords to play, except the final E-major chord (ex. 8.9).

Ex. 8.9: *Goyescas*, "Epílogo," conclusion

The juxtaposition of the macabre and the sublime in this work is strongly reminiscent of Goya's later art, starting in the *Caprichos*, and is the only such instance in Granados's works inspired by him. One finds in this piece "a tinge of unutterable terror, a terror of the supernatural, . . . of a soul which departs this world without knowing where it is heading."[43] But "Epílogo" is simply the exception that proves the rule: Granados's focus always remained, in Douglas Riva's words, on the "elegance, delicacy and aristocracy" of Goya's Spain, not the grotesque or macabre.[44] This may explain why of all the piano music, only this movement was left out of the opera.

In any case, Granados could write of his *Goyescas* for piano that "Finally I have had the good fortune to write something important—Las Goyescas."[45] Granados had indeed sealed his reputation and his legacy with this defining triumph. As he later exclaimed, "They mark the payment of my efforts to arrive. They say that I have arrived."[46]

El pelele (Escena goyesca)

As mentioned above, other "Goyescas" do not appear in the set of pieces so entitled but nonetheless owe their inspiration to the same source. Foremost among these is *El pelele*. The buoyant rhythms of this piece create an exuberant feeling of "optimism, color, brilliance, and abundance."[47] The influence of Scarlatti is more marked here than in any of the other works in the sheer delight it takes in sensual virtuosity and irrepressible bonhomie.

The *pelele* was a life-size straw man that young women enjoyed tossing up in the air, using a blanket that they held at the corners as a kind of trampoline. Goya portrayed the scene unforgettably in one of his tapestry cartoons, and this inspired Granados to capture the spirit of the game in his music.[48] In fact, the rhythmic gesture of a broad trill on beat three in tandem with the ascending melodic contour at the beginning of the piece evokes the physical act of hurling the comically helpless *pelele* aloft (ex. 8.10).

Ex. 8.10: *El pelele*, mm. 3–6

There is a strong suggestion of the rhythm of the bolero or fandango in *El pelele*, and its brio is infectious. Granados spins the entire work out of an insistent four-note motive consisting of a sixteenth note, sixteenth rest, two sixteenths, and an eighth. The almost giddy exuberance the repetition of this motive produces makes *El pelele* one of Granados's most memorable compositions. The form is somewhat unusual in his output, A'A''BA''' coda; however, it appears essentially as a kind of rounded binary and hence thoroughly consistent with Scarlatti and the eighteenth-century harpsichord sonatas Granados knew so intimately. As Alicia de Larrocha has pointed out: "Inspired motivation, wide, rolling phrases embroidered with arabesques and ornaments, the evident consequence of dedication as reviewer and interpreter of the work of Scarlatti, enrich these pages in which he describes the underworld of *majas* and *chisperos* of Madrid."[49]

For many listeners at the time, in his *Goyescas* Granados had captured the elusive "essence" of Spain, for which critics and aestheticians were always on the lookout. Divorced from mere historical events and facts, this essence was immutable and perennial. "Eternal truths of eternal essence" were, Unamuno wrote in *En torno al casti-*

cismo, independent of history, even as the immortal soul was independent of the vicissitudes of corporeal existence.[50] In such a statement one detects strains of both perennialism and primordialism, evocations of a long and distinguished national history, rooted in a racial essence that was immutable.[51] These two historical paradigms inform much of the critical reception of *Goyescas*.

Thus, a contemporary journalist was moved to note that "No one has made me feel the musical soul of Spain like Granados. [*Goyescas* is] like a mixture of the three arts of painting, music, and poetry, confronting the same model: Spain, the eternal 'maja.'"[52] The arts as well as the nation itself were unified in the image of the *maja*; it had taken the place of the Virgin Mary as the appropriate icon for modern Spain. Granados had captured precisely this in his music, which led Luis Villalba to a flight of poetic fancy that nonetheless encapsulates a profoundly nationalistic sentiment:

> And above the fabric of melodies and harmonies floats a supplication, like a very pure song, in which the sexuality of the fiesta and the love of color with music unite with the black eyes of the Maja-Nation, of the priests in black in darkened side streets, and of secret tribunals and *autos de fe* in plazas shaded by convents, and of Holy Week processions and convulsive insane asylums and nocturnal witches.[53]

Villalba summons up a whole assortment of images from Goya's paintings here to make his point: Goya and now *Goyescas* captured the national essence, in both time and place, like nothing else.

Granados first performed book 1 of *Goyescas* in August 1910 for a private audience. He gave the public premiere at the Palau de la Música Catalana on March 11, 1911, beginning at what seems to us the late hour of 9:30 p.m., though this was typical at the time. The best seats were thirty pesetas, while general admission cost a single peseta. In addition to *Goyescas*, for this one peseta one could also hear Granados's *Cant de les estrelles* (with the Orfeó Català), *Valses poéticos*, his transcription of a Scarlatti sonata in B-flat, and the *Allegro de concierto*.[54] Also on the program was the premiere of *Azulejos* (Tiles) by Albéniz, posthumously completed by Granados.[55] Granados tossed in the *Danza española no. 7* for an encore.

He premiered book 2 at the Salle Pleyel in Paris on April 2, 1914, presenting the public and critics there with a bouquet of his latest compositions, including not only *Goyescas* but also the *Tonadillas*, sung by Matilde Polak. The concert was sponsored by the Société Musicale Independent, and afterwards, the Société Internationale de Musique put on a banquet in his honor.[56]

Interviewed at this time by the Société Internationale de Musique, the composer shed light on the nature of his Goyaesque inspiration. For Granados, "Goya is the representative genius of Spain," and he himself was deeply moved by Goya's statue in the vestibule of the Prado. It inspired him to emulate Goya's example by contributing to the "grandeur of our country. Goya's greatest works immortalize and exalt our national life. I subordinate my inspiration to that of the man who has so perfectly conveyed the characteristic actions and history of the Spanish people."[57]

Granados's patriotic fervor was no doubt rooted in his family's history of military service, but it also has to be understood in the post-1898 context. Granados was clearly trying to define Spanishness by tapping not only into the psychology of Goya but also, in his view, the underlying psyche of the whole nation of Spain. Moreover, his quest for the Holy Grail of *hispanidad* ran exactly counter to vague *catalanisme*. Like Unamuno and Azorín, Granados considered Castile to be the heart and soul of Spain itself, and *Goyescas* encapsulated his feelings and attitudes about the nation and its identity.

The Parisian press and public were ecstatic over these latest jewels of Spanish musical art. Commentators were quick to seize on whatever evidence the works presented of the Spanish essence and soul. One anonymous critic expatiated on the importance of Granados's Castilian orientation with a breathtakingly pithy overview of regional aesthetics,

> Asturias, Galicia, the Basque country, and Catalonia exhibit different aesthetic currents, coming generally from outside Spain; Andalusia, Murcia, and Valencia are impregnated with the Hispano-Moorish tradition; only the heart of Spain, Castile and Aragon, are free of any foreign intervention. It is that Spain that has produced the art of Granados; it is that national spirit, in all its purity and integrity, which animates his work and gives it that inimitable color, that special color.[58]

So, there it was. The peripheral regions of Spain had been corrupted by contact with the outside world. Castile and Aragon, nestled safely in the interior of the peninsula, had been spared such contamination and preserved the "essential" Spain.[59] Of course, this was not true, as the interior of the country had been overrun and occupied by various invaders over the centuries, including Moors and the French. The influence of Italian culture had been immense in the eighteenth century.[60] But despite historical realities, these notions enjoyed enormous currency at the time, and few critics seem to have questioned them seriously. Spaniards themselves left no doubt about Granados's status: "He is the singer of the spirit of our race, and the voice of our land," exclaimed the pianist and critic Montoriol-Tarrés.[61]

These fevered attempts to affirm racial, ethnic, and national identity were driven, in part, by a Darwinian conviction that modern Europe was in the grips of creeping decadence through a dilution of racial heritage. In the words of Lily Litvak, the general fear was that "the European peoples, descendants of a lengthy evolution, were threatened by an inevitable decrepitude and condemned to an approaching demise by the rise of more barbaric and vigorous peoples."[62] One way to stem this tide was through an equally vigorous reaffirmation of cultural identity and racial roots, particularly in music. Regression to the pure ethnicity of the nation's or region's origins was seen as a precondition for national renascence.[63] This, says E. Inman Fox, accounts for the "preoccupation with popular culture and is inseparable from a faith in native virility and morality, which contrast with the corruption of foreign influence and cosmopolitan decadence."[64]

The Parisian reception of *Goyescas*, however, has to be placed in the context of the nearly century-long French fascination with Goya's art. Already in the early nineteenth century, Delacroix and other French artists had become familiar with Goya's prints and developed a profound reverence for his technique and humanity. Goya had exerted a marked influence on Manet: Goya's *The Third of May 1808* provided a model for *The Execution of Emperor Maximilian*, as did *La maja desnuda* for his *Olympia*. By the early twentieth century, then, Goya's reputation was firmly established.

Goya, rivaled only by Velázquez, came to symbolize to the French what Spain was, what it meant to be Spanish. Thus, they were highly receptive to Granados's musical evocations of an artist whom they had come to admire so much.[65] Goya and Granados were together credited with having revealed the truth about Spain and its people. The Parisian musical establishment was so deeply impressed by Granados's achievements that they nominated him for the Legion of Honor, which he received upon his return to Paris in conjunction with an Orfeó Català concert on June 14.[66]

Goyescas the Opera

The impetus to compose an opera based on *Goyescas* came from Ernest Schelling shortly after the premiere of the piano suite. Schelling (1876–1939) had Swiss ancestry and was a child prodigy who began music studies in Philadelphia at age 4; he was one of the leading North American pianists of his time. He first met Granados in Barcelona while giving four concerts there in 1912. Granados attended his performances and was very impressed, inviting the American to his home. Schelling became acquainted with Granados's music at that time and resolved to champion it wherever possible. He premiered *Goyescas* in New York (Carnegie Hall, March 26, 1913) and London (Queen's Hall, December 12, 1913), and he later transformed *Goyescas* into a ballet entitled *Del amor y de la muerte*.[67] He introduced Granados's music to the New York publisher Rudolph Schirmer, and on September 1, 1913, Granados signed a two-year contract worth 6,000 French francs annually as an advance on royalties for all works composed during that time.[68] Granados was understandably grateful to his American friend for the assistance he had received and wrote to him on May 29, 1914, that "I am so glad to have a great friend like you, and you will find in me what is not very easy to find: the deep gratitude of a heart that will never deceive you."[69]

Periquet also encouraged Granados to write an operatic *Goyescas*, as he was eager to provide the libretto. The piano pieces already exhibited a quasi-programmatic framework, and all that seemed necessary was to apply an appropriately dramatic overlay. That Granados soon attached enormous importance to this project is clear in a letter he wrote to Schelling on June 10, 1912, in which he said he was putting "all my soul and all my life" into the opera, and was now able to do so because his perennial financial worries were a thing of the past.

Certainly the genesis of *Goyescas* is among the most unusual in opera history. From his earliest sketches for the work, the title page tells us that "Los majos enamorados" is a *drama lírico* in one act and four scenes, with music by Enrique Granados.[70] Granados had not yet decided on a librettist, as the author of the "libro" (book) is merely indicated by a couple of dashes. It is clear from this that his extensive notes for the work pre-date collaboration with Periquet. As Periquet described it, Granados "wrote his enchanting score, without words, in absolute liberty, visualizing in his mind's eye the entire cavalcade of Goya-esque characters, majas, duchesses, royal guards, witches and witches' Sabbaths."[71]

Granados soon brought Periquet on board, and the author supplied him with a story line in the form of a narrative poem utilizing the meters of the *romance* and *seguidilla*. This was not a libretto but merely a guide for Granados as he worked on the transformation of the suite into an opera. Once he had written the opera, vocal parts and all, it was then Periquet's unenviable task to try to put words to the music, syllable by syllable, note by note. Periquet relates that at one point, the two male antagonists had to agree to a duel in the space of four notes. Periquet pleaded with Granados to give him a little more musical room for maneuver, but the composer would not budge. Four syllables were all Periquet could have. At last he decided on "¿Hora?" "Las diez." ("What time?" "At ten."). Periquet claimed, however, that this solution was perfectly satisfactory and that Granados had been right all along.

Critics who later lambasted the libretto as weak and inadequate, then, may not have fully realized the extent to which Periquet was working in a straitjacket placed on him by the composer. They were also not familiar with the simple, unpretentious *sainetes* of Cruz that served his models. Nonetheless, Periquet's notions about the ideal libretto may give us pause: "But, as I also hold that the plot of an opera should be as simple as to be even within a child's grasp, I made of my libretto the simplest story that I have ever written."[72] One gives him credit for having accomplished what he set out to achieve.

The work is in a single act divided into three "tableaux" (*cuadros*), without intermissions and separated by *intermedios*. The four principal roles are for soprano, mezzo-soprano, tenor, and baritone. In addition, a large chorus plays a central role in the drama, which is a model of the simplicity Periquet valued so highly: The bullfighter Paquiro woos the beautiful Rosario who is also courted by the captain Fernando. At a dance party Paquiro and Fernando clash and agree to fight a duel. Just before the duel, Rosario and Fernando have an impassioned love scene in her garden as the nightingale sings. When Fernando is mortally wounded in the duel, Rosario falls prostrate on the dead body of her lover, a scene clearly inspired by Goya's tenth *Capricho* mentioned above.

Granados utilized almost the entire piano suite in his opera. The sole exception was *Epílogo: Serenata del espectro*, because he thought it inconsistent with the drama.[73] The piano music was not always suitable for the voice, and as one commentator has pointed out, "Rosario's last cry is only one example of the wide and unvocal intervals the singers are expected to negotiate when the original piano melodies are transcribed literally."[74] He also composed new music, including the two *intermedios* between the three tableaux. He borrowed from *El pelele*, the *Tonadillas*, and he cannibalized his unfinished opera *Los Ovillejos* for ideas as well. The musical structure of the opera can be diagrammed as follows:

Tableau 1:   *El pelele*
                "La calesa" from *Los Ovillejos*
Tableau 2:   "El fandango de candil"
                Tonadillas: "Amor y odio," "El mirar de la maja"
                "El fandango de candil"
Tableau 3:   "Quejas o La maja y el ruiseñor"
                "Coloquio en la reja"
                "El amor y la muerte"

Perhaps because he was working in a hurry, Granados made surprisingly few changes to his piano music in transcribing it to the operatic genre. Commonly he transcribed the piano music for voices, doubling them in the orchestra, a technique called *violinata* and much favored by Puccini. Indeed, the piano part of the vocal score bears an astonishing resemblance to the piano original itself, though he deleted repetitious development and simplified some overly complex textures. As some have noted, the principal difference between the piano and opera versions lies in numerous discrepancies in the accidentals, again the result of Granados's working in characteristic haste.[75]

Pepa arrives in her calash or chaise (*calesa*), a scene perhaps inspired by Goya's paintings of *La manola* and *La maja y los embozados*. A sedan chair (*litera*) soon appears bearing Rosario, her upper-class rival in love. All this throws some light on the additional subtitle of the opera, "Literas y calesas."[76] According to Granados, in his own imagination Fernando was actually Goya, while Rosario was the Duchess of Alba.[77] Paquiro was inspired by Goya's portrait of Martincho the bullfighter (*Retrato del Torero Martincho*), while the Captain of the Royal Guard is based on the male figure in *Tal para cual*. Pepa seems to have inspired him the least, and in fact it is Rosario who gets the best *coplas* to sing.

In any event, the idea of class conflict suggested in the subtitle is not developed in the drama at all. Perhaps it might have been, but that would have violated Periquet's dictum that an opera libretto should be so simple, even a child could understand it. However, the over-simplicity of the story is exacerbated by the lack of interaction between the characters, except in the third tableau. Rather, as Larrad notes, "the dialogue consists of the exteriorised thoughts of the characters on stage . . . [which], thanks to Granados's preference for ensembles, is often incomprehensible."[78] Still, the inherent musical appeal of the ensembles, even if we cannot understand the text, is in the choral and solo vocal writing, especially in the second tableau.

As mentioned, the opera opens with the music from *El pelele*. This game of tossing the straw doll of a man into the air suggests that a man enamored of a woman is little more than a *pelele*.[79] Such a playful, comic metaphor is in stark contrast to (and seems incongruent with) the bloody fate awaiting the "pelele" Fernando. Among Granados's most inspired creations is Rosario's aria "¿Porqué entre sombras el ruiseñor?" (Why

Is There a Nightingale in the Shadows?) in tableau three. Here, Granados successfully translates his pianistic thoughts to the vocal medium, and the voice is integrated into the orchestral writing. The same could not be said, however, of the closing scene, "El amor y la muerte"; as mentioned above, the voice part is full of awkward leaps and gets lost in the dense accompaniment. Perhaps Granados did not have time to polish the conclusion sufficiently. Still, he was convinced of the merit of this part of the opera, and when he donated the autograph of the vocal score to the Hispanic Society of America in New York, it was the opening of "El amor y la muerte" he requested be displayed (the manuscript is now kept in the archive, not out in the open).

Goyescas the opera was to have premiered in Barcelona during the 1914–15 season. But various obstacles made this impossible, and in fact the opera only made it to the Liceu long after Granados's death. The inability of Barcelona to manage a premiere led Granados to look abroad for a theater. Schelling introduced Granados to Emilio de Gogorza, the Spanish-American baritone, who in turn presented him to Jacques Rouché, director of the Paris Opéra. In June 1914, an audition for Granados to play through his music took place at the Paris apartment of Gogorza and his wife, soprano Emma Eames, with a representative of Rouché in attendance. On June 15, Rouché himself met with Granados and accepted the opera for production at the Opéra, gaining exclusive rights to its premiere by the Académie Nationale de Musique et de Danse.[80] However, the First World War broke only a few weeks later, delaying indefinitely a Paris production; fortunately, another possibility now presented itself.

Granados retired to Schelling's villa at Celigny (near Geneva) in Switzerland to work some more on the score.[81] At this same time, however, Schelling persuaded Schirmer to talk to Giulio Gatti-Casazza, general manager of the New York Metropolitan Opera, about producing the work. These efforts bore fruit, and Gatti-Casazza wrote to Granados in early 1915 requesting designs for the sets and costumes, as well as the score, of course, and informing him that he had secured the rights from Schirmer. Finally, he assured Granados that "I will do everything possible to make sure that your opera is produced in the most perfect manner."[82] Granados remained philosophical about the opera's prospects throughout all of these negotiations, and he promised that if the opera were a success overseas, he would donate a large part of the money to helping needy musicians; if not, he would go back to giving lessons.

On June 26, 1915, Granados wrote to Rouché requesting release from his contractual obligations so that *Goyescas* could be produced in New York. He cited the fact that Jean Marliave, who was to have translated the libretto from Spanish into French, had died in combat. Still, he promised that Rouché would retain the right to premiere the work in Europe. In a response dated July 3, 1915, Rouché graciously released Granados from his obligation and affirmed that he still wanted to give the European premiere of the work, "after our country's triumph."[83] No obstacles now remained to a New York premiere, an event that would represent the climax and conclusion of Granados's career.

CHAPTER 9

A World of Ideas

With the advent of *Goyescas*, Granados had arrived as a composer of transatlantic reputation. However, the last two years of his life found him at work on many projects that enhanced his stature in Spain and abroad, pointing toward an ever-brighter future.

In 1914 Granados developed a friendship with Gabriel Miró, one of the leading authors in Barcelona. Born in Alicante in 1879, Miró achieved notoriety in 1908 for his novel *Nómada*; in fact, writing novels was his stock-in-trade, and he never ventured into poetry or the theater. In 1914 he moved to Barcelona, where he soon became acquainted with Granados. The two were very similar: quiet family men, solidly bourgeois, apolitical and sympathetic to the Church, devoted to technical perfection in their respective arts, and possessing a rich interior life. Miró was as seriously interested in music as Granados was in literature.

Their bond deepened when Granados's children and Miró's daughter Clemencita came down with typhus during an outbreak in the fall of 1914. Also afflicted were the children of August Pi i Sunyer, a leading scientist and physician in Barcelona, who was also a great lover of music and patron of the arts.[1] He assumed responsibility for caring for the sick children, all of whom eventually recovered.

Miró wrote a theater piece entitled *La cieguecita de Betania (El portalico de Belén)* (The Little Blind Girl of Bethany: The Nativity in Bethlehem) for the children to perform, and Granados supplied some music for it.[2] Intended as a play of thanksgiving for their recovery, it was "produced" at a house in Vallcarca that Granados had rented outside the city, to promote the children's recuperation in more salubrious surroundings. Scored for solo voice, oboe, two clarinets, and bassoon, it consisted of five movements: "Danza-Intermedio (Gallardo, Allegretto pastoral)"; "Pantomima-Danza (Andantino piacevole)"; "Adoración"; "Tocata del pastor (Allegretto)"; and "Villancico." Solita and Víctor played the roles of Mary and Joseph, while the angel was sung by Conxita Badia. Badia, in fact, later recalled this happy moment by reciting some of the "tender" poem: "Heavenly Portals, how beautiful you look guarding the little

Child. Chosen by the Most High for your simplicity, the Saviour is born and this shall be the sign—a cavern and a swaddling band."[3]

It remains a question just what Granados and Miró might have accomplished had they been able to collaborate further, but Granados's absorption in *Goyescas* and untimely death consign such musings to the realm of pure speculation.[4] Márquez Villanueva is of the opinion that Miró was Granados's "soul-mate" in literature and that he, not Gual, Mestres, or Periquet, was the ideal person to provide him with librettos, despite Miró's inexperience and evident disinclination toward drama and verse.[5]

The little collaboration with Miró is evidence of Granados's devotional temperament. In fact, the work that bears the (no doubt spurious) designation of Op. 1, no. 1, is a Salve Regina for four-part chorus and organ.[6] Granados was a devout Catholic, and he wrote a number of religiously inspired compositions.[7] In addition to the Salve, his *L'herba de amor (Pregària en estil gregoriá)* (The Herb of Love: Prayer in Gregorian Style) for three-voice chorus and organ was composed at the Montserrat monastery, where he went on retreat in March 1914.[8] It bears a dedication to the Virgin of Montserrat and utilizes a Catalan text. The preoccupation with "Gregorian" style clearly reflects the influence of the Cecilian movement that sought to reinvigorate church music in the nineteenth century. Finally, there is an unpublished *Escena religiosa* for violin, organ, piano. A short dialogue is inscribed above the first page, between the soul (El Alma) and an angel (El Ángel).[9]

> The Angel: Come, Soul, my God calls you to reward your martyrdom.
> The Soul: I will live in the bosom of the Lord and pray for my own.

"El Ángel" is written into the violin part in a few places, indicating that it represented the heavenly emissary.

Other positive developments of this period included the premiere of Granados's *Canciones amatorias* (Love Songs) by Conxita Badia at the Sala Granados on April 5, 1915. Two of them, "Gracia mía" and "Llorad corazón," were dedicated to her.[10] The press received these new works with enthusiasm and approbation.

As Riva points out, these are not so much "songs" as chamber music, "in which the voice and piano are equal in importance."[11] Although the piano accompaniments are more complex, these ravishing songs nonetheless reflect the style of the *Tonadillas* in their suggestion of Spanish folk rhythms, modality, and the guitar, in combination with a late-Romantic harmonic idiom. Granados's choice of texts is also significant in this context, for instead of using contemporary lyrics as he had previously, he reaches back to the *Siglo de Oro* for inspiration. All of the texts are Castilian *romances* from before 1700, taken from the *Romancero general* compiled by Agustín Durán and published in Madrid in 1851. Of the seven songs, four have anonymous texts. Two have lyrics by Luis de Góngora, and one, by Lope de Vega. All of them express sentiments of an amorous/erotic nature.[12]

Granados's celebration of Castilian poetry from a bygone era of imperial glory is consistent with his fixation on Castile and Madrid as the spiritual and cultural fulcra of the nation.

Dante

The performance of his symphonic poem *Dante* by the Orquesta Sinfónica de Madrid, conducted by Enrique Fernández Arbós, must have brought Granados considerable satisfaction. The Orquesta gave a series of concerts in Barcelona in May 1915, its first appearances in the Catalan capital in two years. *Dante* was presented on the third program, along with works by Percy Grainger. *Dante* had premiered in June 1908 at the then-new Palau de la Música Catalana, for a private audience. Granados revised the work before its public premiere in the spring of 1910 in Barcelona, with the dedicatee of the work, Franz Beidler, conducting from the manuscript. Sir Henry J. Wood led the Queen's Hall Orchestra in a London performance of it on September 9, 1914. Granados revised the work some more before its definitive version was performed by the Orquesta in 1915. It was finally published that same year, by Schirmer in New York. With the work available in print from a major publisher, the Chicago Symphony Orchestra decided to program it on November 5–6, 1915. More than eight years later, on February 8–9, 1924, the CSO performed it again; Frederick Stock conducted on both occasions.[13]

Although Granados initially conceived of the work in four movements, he completed only the first two: "Dante e Virgilio" and "Paolo e Francesca." The third, "La laguna estigia," languished in the sketch stage, while he never even got started on the fourth movement, "Dante e Beatrice." Nonetheless, his thoughts about this last movement shed light on the work as a whole and reveal his sources of inspiration. In particular, his *moderniste* affinity for the Pre-Raphaelites resembles his intensely sensual attraction to Goya's portraits of the thirteenth Duchess of Alba. This also makes it clear that his own artistic inclinations were finding an outlet in orchestral composition.

> I derive my inspiration from the famous painting of G. Rossetti of the same subject.
>
> My idea while writing *Dante* has not been to follow step by step the *Divine Comedy,* but to give my own impression of a life and work. Dante–Beatrice and the *Divine Comedy* are for me the same thing; even more, I wish to enrich my work with something of the *Vita Nuova* [New life]. Cannot they all be condensed into a single one?
>
> For the pathetic painting of Beatrice's death, I want a very special color in the orchestra. In some passages I wish to produce sonorities that will resemble color more than sounds, i.e., I want to paint with the orchestra. Those violet, carmine, and green hues of Rossetti's painting have impressed my eyes so immensely, that my ears will settle for nothing less. I want to feel music of that color. I want to find that kiss that Dante gives to Beatrice by means of the angel of love.[14]

"Dante e Virgilio" commences with the descent into the Inferno. The apparent formlessness of the movement creates a sense of mystery, suspense, and even apprehension. The opening measures present a chromaticism at the very verge of atonality. Above tremolandi strings on D, the tonal center of the work, the winds present a series of lugubrious sonorities clearly derived from contemporary French music in their augmented triads (with clear implications of whole-tone scales) and unresolved dominant-sevenths (ex. 9.1).

Ex. 9.1: *Dante*, "Dante e Virgilio," mm. 3–6

In fact, the harmonic idiom and atmospheric effect of this movement are utterly *au courant* and compel us to qualify any characterization of Granados as "conservative."

There is apparently no specific program to this movement, but it does present an entrancing sequence of moods in a freely evolving manner. After the introduction, which is completely dominated by winds and brass, the violins present the principal theme. Long-winded lyricism and lushly chromatic harmonies create an almost vertiginous feeling, at times expressionistic in character. Indeed, one thinks of Schoenberg's *Verklärte Nacht* or the first movement of his D-minor String Quartet.

Two things do contribute to a sense of structural cohesion in "Dante and Virgil." One is the reappearance of the principal theme, in varied form, in the last third of the piece, lending a vaguely ABA feeling to the work, though its precise structure defies the usual theoretical taxonomies. This weak architectural sense has been considered by most commentators to be Granados's chief shortcoming as a composer. [15] In this instance, I think his structural procedure suits his aesthetic purposes aptly. However, in the common-practice tradition of the eighteenth and nineteenth centuries, tonality articulated structure. If Granados's structure appears weak, perhaps it is not because of the sort of stream-of-consciousness quality of the succession of themes but rather because of his meandering modulations, by step and third rather than by fifth. In any event, something else shines through on closer examination: his use of a basic rhythmic archetype, dactylic (long-short-short). Nearly all the themes feature this motive in some way or another, lending a subtle but important sense of connectedness—organicism, if you will—to the music, despite its otherwise rambling nature.

The second movement, "Paolo e Francesca," is a setting for mezzo-soprano of canto 5 of *The Divine Comedy*, verses 91–106 and 121–23.[16] This movement is a third again longer than the first. Here we learn of the tragic love of Paolo Vecchio and Francesca da Rimini. Francesca was married to one of Paolo's brothers but hopelessly in love with Paolo, who was much the handsomer. Upon discovering their adultery, Paolo's brother attempted to stab him with a dagger, but Francesca interposed herself and took the thrust for him, dying. Enraged, he next struck at Paolo and killed him, leaving the two lovers lifeless on the floor. They were buried in a single grave. The theme of infidelity, of true love in conflict with marital obligations, is one that had significance for Granados in the context of his personal life at the time he wrote this music.

In his composition, however, Granados dwells at greatest length on their love, not their death, choosing especially poignant verses. Francesca reflects that there is "No greater grief than to remember days / Of joy, when misery is at hand." One joyous day, she relates, Paolo and she were alone reading of Lancelot (of course) when they discovered their love for one another and gave themselves over to their passion. "The book and writer both / Were love's purveyors. / In its leaves that day / We read no more."[17]

The opening again emphasizes D as a tonal center in the tremolandi low strings, but it takes only a few measures of mounting chromaticism to blur the tonality. A vaulting theme in the strings exhibits the mark of Richard Strauss (ex. 9.2).[18]

Also reminiscent of Strauss is Granados's skillful handling of a large orchestra: a full complement of winds including three flutes, English horn, bass clarinet, three bassoons, contrabassoon, four horns, three trumpets, four trombones, and tuba, as well as timpani, strings, and harp.

The menacing, marchlike opening seems to portend the violent fate of the lovers. The dactylic motive migrates from the first movement to reappear already just after m. 30. D persists as the tonal center through m. 70 until the new theme in $\frac{12}{8}$ appears, shifting us into G minor and soon B-flat major, which continues past m. 110 in preparation for the entrance of the singer, whose initial recitative is marked "Lento con molta espressione." The harmony meanders back to D (major) after m. 150, and then to F minor around m. 190. A *Tristan*-esque atmosphere prevails throughout much of the work in its chromatic ambiguity and restless syncopations, with arching melodies that ache with longing. The vocal part, however, hews to a very dramatic kind of Wagnerian speech-melody and never breaks into arioso. Granados resorts to a through-composed setting of the text, his music conforming to its every sinuous curve of meaning.

At m. 220 occurs a reprise of the opening theme, which erupts in a spasm of Straussian orchestral turbulence, representing the struggle between the star-crossed lovers and a jealous husband. The writing for brass, especially trombones, is remarkable for its strident color and emotional intensity. The spasm reaches a climax and sudden caesura just after m. 280. A languorous chromatic line ascends slowly skyward in a clear reminiscence of the *Liebestod*, as the souls of the lovers depart this world.

Ex. 9.2: *Dante*, "Paolo e Francesca," mm. 12–15

The movement dissipates in a supernal mist of resignation, on a *pianissimo* D-major chord in the strings.

F. Suárez Bravo reviewed the 1915 performance for *Diario de Barcelona* and had mixed reactions to the work. He thought that there was insufficient contrast between the themes in the first part of the tone poem. He found its proportions too large, and its prevailing mood "somber and abstruse." The second part met with his approval, as he found Francesca to be a "ray of light that illuminates those caverns" of the first. The audience seems to have been somewhat perplexed by the work as a whole, but Suárez Bravo concluded that "it is a lofty composition; the maestro is very ambitious, because he can be."[19] Others reported that it merited the applause it received.[20]

Whatever critics of *Dante* thought at the time, we marvel today that Granados had the range to compose such a work, so different from his Goyaesque essays or his Catalan theater works of the same period. Few listeners today would attach his name to it, if they did not know in advance who wrote it. As Manuel Valls has asserted, this is a work that "requires us to heighten the regard in which we hold that great composer."[21] For it demonstrated to Valls as it does to us a mastery of Wagnerian chromatic harmony and the programmatic style of Strauss. Granados also stands out as a very skillful orchestrator.

Granados gave his last concert in Barcelona on November 14, 1915, for the Associació de Música da Camera. He also traveled to Madrid in that month to perform the Beethoven violin sonatas with Juan Manén for the Filarmónica. His final pilgrimage to Lleida took place in November as well, to give a farewell concert. Even though Granados's family had left Lleida when he was still an infant, he maintained a sentimental attachment to the town of his birth, and he visited it regularly over the years: in 1901, 1903, 1911, 1912, and 1913.[22] No one could guess that the 1915 trip would be his last. Granados had returned one more time to where his life had begun, and in a sense all had come full circle—except that the circle should have been much larger than it was to be.

The Metropolitan Opera premiere of the opera *Goyescas* was slated for January 1916, and Granados prepared to set out for New York in late November. He would not be alone in the New World, however. Casals was active giving concerts in New York, and María Barrientos, the Spanish soprano, was delighting New York audiences with her performances at the Met (she appeared as Lucia in *Lucia di Lammermoor* on January 30, 1916); "La Argentina" (Antonia Mercé) would soon enchant them with her Spanish dancing.[23] Baritone Emilio de Gogorza also had a fine reputation in the United States and, in conjunction with mezzo-soprano Rosa Culmell (wife of Joaquín Nin and mother of composer Joaquín Nin-Culmell), performed some of the *Tonadillas*. Granados's student Paquita Madriguera and her mother would be in New York, staying with Culmell. Also active in the United States at this time was mezzo-soprano Conchita Supervía, who sang several roles in Chicago during the 1915–16 season.

New York's Spanish-language newspaper *Las novedades* devoted enthusiastic and detailed attention to the *Goyescas* premiere.[24] Although many commentators at the time pointed out that this was to be the first-ever Spanish-language production at the

Met, New York was no stranger to musical theater in Spanish.[25] There was a large Hispanic community (especially Cuban) in New York that regularly patronized zarzuela productions in the city.[26] Beyond that, of course, Spain had long since put down roots in the American imagination, arts, and letters. *Don Quixote* was one of Thomas Jefferson's favorite books, while a host of nineteenth-century authors explored Spanish history and culture, including William Hickling Prescott, Washington Irving, and Henry Wadsworth Longfellow. Artists taken with Spain included Thomas Eakins, John Singer Sargent, and James McNeil Whistler. The pianist and composer Louis Moreau Gottschalk visited Spain in 1852 and absorbed its musical *ambiente* into several works.[27] Finally, around 1915 there was a "surge in U.S. interest" in learning Spanish.[28]

Before Granados could capitalize on this Hispanophilia in New York, however, he would have to get there. Traveling was never his favorite activity, and ocean voyages filled him with dread.[29] His natural aversion to traveling on water was probably heightened by the sinking of *Lusitania* that same year, on May 7, 1915. Much has been made over the years of the premonitions he and his wife had about dying during this journey. They were apparently convinced they would never return to Spain alive. In fact, he "sadly murmured" to Mestres that "This voyage will cost me my hide."[30] He wrote to his friend the composer Óscar Esplà predicting that "on this voyage I will leave my bones."[31] Such "premonitions" usually accompany feelings of acute fear and anxiety, and they can become self-fulfilling; one hesitates to ascribe actual clairvoyance to them.

A select group of friends and admirers accompanied the Granadoses to the dock to bid them adieu before they set sail aboard the *Montevideo*. Among these were his Academy associates Frank Marshall and Joan Llongueras. Granados embraced everyone before boarding the ship. He appeared very sad and apprehensive, exclaiming, "We will never see one another again!"[32] Why would Granados and Amparo board a ship convinced they were going to perish? No premiere would be worth such a sacrifice. Granados suffered from nervousness throughout most of his life, particularly in regards to performing. Yet this did not stop him from giving concerts. It may be that he had acquired the ability to forge ahead in spite of his apprehensions, which at some level he understood to be irrational. The fact that Periquet and the guitarist Miquel Llobet were traveling with them was perhaps reassuring.

In the event, the voyage *was* harrowing. The weather was inclement almost the whole way over, and on November 30, the *Montevideo* was stopped and searched for seven hours on the high seas by the French cruiser *Cassard*, apparently looking for German spies. Granados confided to a fellow passenger that if they were forced to head back to Gibraltar, he would return to Barcelona rather than continue the journey. Neither the reassurances of the captain nor anything anyone else said could calm his nerves.[33] A short time later, they were stopped by the English warship *Essex* and inspected by a boarding party, which took five hours to discover nothing amiss.[34] Once in New York, they recounted the terrifying adventure to their children: "After our departure from Cádiz, it was only supposed to take 10 days to reach New York. Instead, it took 15. We had only a few hours of smooth sailing; the rest of the time it was stormy. Your mother and I believed we would never see you again. . . . It was terrible."[35] None of this had left Granados so upset that he was unable to perform; he and Llobet appeared in an impromptu concert on the *Montevideo* during the passage, gales and heaving seas notwithstanding.[36]

They arrived in New York on December 15, 1915. Granados and his party were met at the pier, near the Battery, by a representative of the Met and taken away in a car to their rooms at the Hotel Claridge on Broadway and 44th. However, the car was so uncomfortably cold that after a short while the party switched to the subway. Granados was intrigued by these "infernal caverns" but found the noise oppressive, stopping his ears with his fingers.[37] According to *Las novedades*, "Granados condensed his opinion of New York into two impressions, which are readily apparent: huge buildings and beautiful women."[38] Granados himself was in turn something of a phenomenon. The Australian-born pianist Ernest Hutcheson said of him: "Those of us who had the good fortune to meet Granados during his stay in America were charmed by his courtesy and polished conversation no less than by the inimitable though entirely unpretentious manner of his playing."[39]

One commentator, however, extrapolated from this that "As a man Granados appears to have had a placidity of temperament unusual for a Latin." Such ethnic stereotyping plagued many a Spanish artist or musician who ventured abroad,[40] but it was never a matter of one prevailing stereotype but rather of multiple and mutually contradictory images. A critic described Granados's playing as characterized by "the languor, the smoldering fire, the tenderness and passion which belong in this music" by virtue of its Spanish heredity.[41] On the other hand, the *Kansas City Times* heard in *Goyescas* for piano "all the magic, the tenderness, the tragedy of old Spain."[42] The British Hispanist J. B. Trend perceived no such thing: "What Granados introduced into the music of northern Europe might be described as a gesture. 'Stately Spanish grace' is the first thing that strikes one in such a piece as '*Los Requiebros*' in the first book of the *Goyescas*."[43] Another British critic admitted that "the average Briton's notions of Spain are hazy, and may be represented by the words superstition, decadence, laziness, Inquisition, bull-fighting." Yet, a few paragraphs later, we learn that "Travellers tell us that every Spanish peasant has the manners of a gentleman."[44] Over and over in critical reaction to Hispanic music and musicians, one finds this polarizing tendency: they are either dignified or hysterical, languid or enraged, St. Teresa of Avila or Carmen.[45] However, even Periquet could not resist perpetuating hackneyed stereotypes about his countrymen. He assured his American readers that Goya exemplified the Spanish character, for "we either hate or love intensely. . . . The work of Granados and myself is full of the joy of Spanish life, of the sadness of our untamable passions."[46]

It is perfectly clear from reading Spanish accounts at the time that Granados's mission to the New World was a source of national pride, and regardless of how the Americans actually reacted to him and his music, the Spanish press would remain convinced that this was a great victory for the name of Granados and for the country. *Musical Emporium* crowed triumphantly that "Granados, as did Albéniz before him, has carried to foreign lands the characteristic airs of Spain, that inexhaustible fount of inspiration, in order to popularize and glorify them."[47] *Goyescas* itself represented nothing less than "A history of grandeur: a grandeur lost, and a grandeur recovered," in the arts if not in war. The heroes of peace, then, would henceforth carry the Spanish flag of "blood and gold ever farther," even as the bold conquistadors had done in an earlier epoch.[48]

In the battles waged by artists, however, there would be no losers, only winners. *Las novedades* declared New York "proud to open its arms to Spain, which arrives in fraternal fashion, covered in august splendors." This was post-colonial Spain, not the "old" one of Cortés and Pizarro, but a "new and improved" one of Cervantes, Calderón, Velázquez, Sorolla, and yes, Granados.[49] Of course, such reports were gross exaggerations, and we shall see that the opera received at best a mixed reception. Why all the jingoistic chest-thumping? Clearly, recognition by the United States meant a very great deal to Spain at this difficult time in its history, when its national self-esteem was wobbly and in need of propping up. The disastrous war with the very same United States had been the chief catalyst for this crisis of self-confidence, yet nowhere in any of this reportage is there the slightest hint of recrimination or bitterness, or even recollection of that event only eighteen years earlier.[50]

For his part, Granados *was* on a mission. He informed the U.S. press upon his arrival (in a way that struck many as rather haughty) that Americans were entirely misinformed about the music of his country, and he was here to set them straight: "For you, like so many other people, . . . know nothing of the real musical contributions of Spain. The musical interpretation of Spain is not to be found in tawdry *boleros* and *habaneras*, in Moszkowski, in *Carmen*, in anything that has sharp dance rhythms accompanied by tambourines or castanets. The music of my nation is far more complex, more poetic and subtle."[51] He was expressing justifiable national pride and understandable national exasperation at the persistent stereotyping of Spanish culture by foreigners.[52] There was much truth to what he said. But the United States had a chip on its own shoulder: it was used to being looked down upon by Europeans as a land that could scarcely be called civilized, a realm of cowboys, Indians, and buffaloes on the outermost periphery of high culture. Granados touched a nerve, which he did not intend to do, by suggesting he had come to educate the heathen. Savaging *Carmen*, one of the most popular operas ever, did not help his cause at all. He would pay dearly for this.[53]

Despite this initial faux pas, Granados enjoyed an enthusiastic reception in most quarters, partly because he was already well known to musicians in the United States through his sheet music.[54] Anticipation of the opera was keen indeed; the public turnout for the dress rehearsal was larger "than has been seen at any Metropolitan Opera House dress rehearsal in several years."[55] Among the upper-crust notables in attendance was Mrs. Vincent Astor. And on January 19, 1916, Granados received an honorary membership in the Hispanic Society of America and was presented by its founder and president, Archer Huntington, with the Silver Medal of Arts and Letters. He thus joined the ranks of other illustrious Spaniards so honored, including Zuloaga, Echegaray, Blasco Ibáñez, and Sorolla. The composer gave something in return: he inscribed a musical phrase on one of the columns in the central hall of the society's building.

As mentioned, he also gave them the original manuscript of the vocal score of *Goyescas*, and it remains there to this day.[56]

The rehearsals provoked a certain dread in Granados, however, and Casals came to the rescue by assisting with them, even as he had over seventeen years earlier with *María del Carmen* in Madrid.[57] According to the famous cellist, "Granados was there, sitting in a corner, like a frightened child who does not dare say anything."[58] What was worse, Granados was having to make last-minute changes to the score. The director insisted that more music was needed between the first and second tableaux, and in one evening he wrote a new, longer "Intermezzo" to replace the earlier *intermedio*. Shortly thereafter, however, he felt the little work to be a failure. He confided to Casals that he had made a big mistake, for what he had created was essentially a *jota*, a genre from Aragon and not at all native to the setting of the story. But the quick-thinking Casals allayed his concerns: "Was not Goya Aragonese?" Granados was relieved and exclaimed, "You're right! What a coincidence!" [59]

Granados's inspiration under pressure produced one of the best-loved numbers from the opera. The opening melody, presented forcefully in a monophonic texture in the strings, evokes Spanish folk song in its interance on B-flat and concluding triplet. The simple accompaniment suggests guitar *punteo* (ex. 9.3).

Ex. 9.3: *Goyescas*, Intermezzo, mm. 14–17

The B theme of this ABACcoda structure is a kind of *jota copla*, the very thing Granados had thought better of the next morning because it seemed inappropriate (ex. 9.4).

Ex. 9.4: *Goyescas*, Intermezzo, mm. 62–66

Still, even as he was adding new music, the director was making cuts elsewhere, especially in the second and third tableaux.[60] This made the normally nervous Granados even more anxious. Added to these worries were physical ailments involving his teeth and intestines.[61]

The cast featured the American soprano Anna Fitziu in the role of Rosario. Granados had wanted the Spaniard Lucrezia Bori to create that role, but she was unavailable due to throat surgery. Fitziu was no stranger to Spanish music, though, as she had studied Spanish in Madrid and performed at the Teatro Real there and at the Liceu in Barcelona, during the 1913–14 season. Fernando's role was interpreted by Giovanni Martinelli, while Pepa and Paquiro were played by Flora Perini and Giuseppe de Luca, respectively. Granados had hoped that La Argentina would be able to dance in it, but other engagements prevented this.[62] Rosina Galli took her place and created a sensation in her "Fandango de candil," which she danced with Giuseppe Bonafiglio. Gaetano Bavagnoli conducted. Ironically, not a single Spaniard appeared among the cast of this the first Spanish opera at the Met.

The premiere took place on January 28, 1916. Since its duration was only about an hour, it was paired with another opera: Leoncavallo's *I pagliacci*, starring Enrico Caruso, who penned an impromptu caricature of Granados. At subsequent performances, *Goyescas* shared the stage with Mascagni's *Cavalleria rusticana* or Humperdinck's *Hänsel und Gretel*. Many of New York's elite were in attendance, including the Kahns, Vanderbilts, Mackays, and Whitneys, as well as the Spanish ambassador, Juan Riaño Gayangos, the wife of New York's governor, and a large group from the local Spanish community. Appropriately, Amparo donned the garb of the *maja*, replete with black lace and green velvet. There was standing room only, and "ecstatic bravos" erupted when Granados appeared on stage, clad in a "biscuit-colored waist coat." After the show, Gustav White of Schirmer hosted a dinner at Sherry's, a famous restaurant in New York, to honor the Spanish composer.[63]

The sets were among the most beautiful ever placed on the Metropolitan stage. Designer Antonio Rovescalli had gone to Madrid to view Goya's paintings for inspiration, while the costumes were the result of Periquet's study of fashion plates at the National Archeological Museum in Madrid.[64] Granados himself was ecstatic about the entire affair. He had written to Miró on January 9 that "I have landed on my feet here. There is a magnificent atmosphere."[65] Now he breathlessly declared to the local press: "I had been told the American public is cold, but its enthusiasm tonight has overwhelmed me. This is a serious work and not written to coax applause, but the listeners took every occasion to express their approval. The performance was wonderful. There is not an opera house in all Europe that could equal to-night's presentation."[66] Years later Casals recalled that "I have never witnessed such an explosion of enthusiasm in the theatre. The audience not only applauded like mad but were crying at the same time. This audience was mostly composed of the Spanish and South American colony in New York, and they were therefore able to understand the real character of the work."[67]

So, why did *Goyescas* run for only five performances? Rumors circulated that Gatti-Casazza "was not at all in sympathy with [the] work" and deprecated Granados's presumptuous comparison of his opera with Bizet's. Another factor contributing to the opera's early demise on the Met's stage was the fact that the fifth and final performance, on March 6, was wholly unsatisfactory, due largely to Bavagnoli's inappropriate tempos. He seems simply not to have understood the work, but he was also an ineffective conductor, and the 1915–16 season was his first and last at the Met. Granados had invited Paderewski, Schelling, and critic Henry Finck to the performance, hoping that it would be the best of the five. Instead, as Finck remembered, Granados spent one of the longest hours of his life, "with a look of annoyance and . . . anguish in his face whenever the conductor made a blunder in the choice of his tempo. [Granados's] hands nervously indicated the right tempo, but I was the only person who could see those distressed hands."[68]

However, a survey of the press reaction makes it clear that the libretto's transparent lack of dramatic quality was primarily at fault. One reviewer said that "*Goyescas* is an infantile production compared with *Carmen* . . . *Goyescas* would benefit from a few of the shortcomings which he seems to have detected in *Carmen*."[69] In fact, nearly all commentators have blamed Periquet—who returned to Spain after the second performance—for the opera's early exit, because he had written such an inferior book. But it is only fair to remember that the tyranny that Granados's score held over the text itself virtually guaranteed the failure of this work as an opera. In fact, regardless of the librettist Granados was working with, what he produced in nearly all of his operas was a series of pictures—charming, colorful, evocative, and seductive, but dramatically static. Periquet was not solely to blame.

It is also important to bear in mind that the New York critics had little or no knowledge of the dramatic model for Periquet's little play, which was not really Goya at all but rather Cruz. As Jones puts it, "The reviewers' descriptions of *Goyescas*—both bad and good—might apply with few changes to Ramón de la Cruz's *sainetes*, which have inconsequential plots because their dramatic impact depends not on character development but on the fast-paced interaction of types and groups."[70] Another obstacle was that the title of the opera really made no sense, because the term *Goyesca* was a neologism for which there is no adequate English translation. And Schirmer's adaptation of the Spanish title, converting *Goyesca: Literas y calesas, o Los majos enamorados* into *Goyescas, or The Rival Lovers*, made for a colossal non sequitur. Not only was the term "Goyescas" mysterious, but what rival lovers had to do with it was anybody's guess.

For many reasons, then, the New York critics were downright scathing, even sarcastic, in their assessment of the work. In regard to the considerable effort required to mount a Spanish opera, the *New York Herald* asked rhetorically, "Was it worth all that? Hardly." It found fault with the opera's proportions—the third tableau was longer than the other two combined, and without any good reason, as the outcome is a foregone conclusion—and in general the authors "seem to have little sense of the values of dramatic action, little idea of proportion of various incidents," all of which pointed to "little real experience in the theatre."[71] *The Opera News* said that "in *Goyescas*, the composer is everything, the poet little else than a running commentary on the music."[72] Another title put it more simply: "Opera in Spanish, First Sung Here, Fails to Impress: 'Goyescas' a Series of Tapestry Pictures, Lacking in True Character and Without Real Consistency."[73]

The most acerbic critique came from another reviewer, who thought it "incredible that any composer should delude himself at this date with so hypothetical a notion as that a series of pictures strung together on the slenderest thread of a story would suffice to sustain interest or compel sympathy." Although Goya was potentially a very engaging and dramatic subject for an opera, the "dramatic technique displayed [in *Goyescas*] is puerile." Recollecting Periquet's theory that a libretto should be so simple a child could understand it, we see the upshot of such dramaturgical reductionism. And again we recall that Periquet's mediocrity was exacerbated by the strictures placed upon him by Granados. The very scene in which the antagonists agree to a duel in the course of four notes and syllables was singled out by this author for its "surprisingly maladroit under-emphasis."[74] The *New York Tribune* cut to the heart of the matter: Periquet was "led more by his intention to supply a word for each note than by the dramatic demand to express the meaning of the music in appropriate language. By this crowding of words to short notes the vocal parts become instrumental."[75]

In fact, American critics never really warmed up to it. Decades later, in 1969, Herbert Weinstock dismissed the opera as a "protracted Spanish bore. . . . I shall feel no sense of deprivation if forced to wait [many] more years before hearing *Goyescas* again."[76] *New York Times* critic Harold Schonberg felt the conclusion was especially ineffective: "The whole thing is clumsily done."[77] Ellen Pfeifer said of the Boston revival in 1982, "Unfortunately . . . there appears to be good reason for the opera's obscurity. . . . this work is full of hot air, of musical wool-gathering."[78] Periquet's dictum about the ideal libretto never gained any credibility either: "The story, a model of simplicity in the worst sense, lends itself to many awkwardnesses."[79] The opera continues to be performed in the United States, but not frequently.

The Spanish press was willfully blind to this negative reaction. *La esfera*, for example, marveled that "The most authoritative critics have devoted encomiastic articles to Granados's opera in which they acknowledge the outstanding qualities of the music of *Goyescas*." True, the *music* of the opera had received praise. Perhaps *La esfera* was not indulging in hyperbole when it claimed that "the triumph of Granados in New York is of capital importance for Spanish music."[80] But this was still a fallacious argument, as it focused only on the good and ignored the bad. Other journalists adopted the same technique. The editors at *Revista musical catalana* enumerated all the positive things North American critics said and bowdlerized the press reports of anything negative.[81] This sort of whitewash continued for decades after the premiere. In 1966 one authority offered up the tired canard that in America, *Goyescas* had achieved "an absolute unanimity among the critics."[82]

To be sure, some Spanish commentators were only too aware of the tepid response to *Goyescas* on the part of most New York critics; but their response was still defensive and evasive of the actual cause of the problems. Adolfo Salazar expatiated on one critique in particular, a January 29, 1916, review in the *New York Glass*. As Salazar relates it, the North American critic professed a familiarity with Spanish music not through direct experience but rather through the works of Chabrier, Debussy, Laparra, and Zandonai. He found that *Goyescas*, by contrast, exuded insufficient "local color," and was hence something of a disappointment. Of course, Granados had striven mightily to create a convincing ambience precisely through the use of local color, but as Salazar pointed out, "the foreign conception of *españolismo* is something indistinguishable from a watered-down *andalucismo*," which finds a ready audience outside Spain.[83]

For foreigners, the conflation of Spain and Andalusia was routine, and musically the entire country and all its regional folkloric traditions were collapsed to flamenco and the *jota*. Salazar believed that any work presenting other regional styles, either Castilian or Basque or Valencian, would run the risk of boring the foreign listener through his "incapacity to perceive in them the various gradations of 'local color.'" He concluded in Granados's defense that the composer, as a "true artist," had been "above banal conventions, altogether too accommodating to a superficial critique and poor taste."[84] Rogelio Villar ascribed some of the blame, however, to native composers themselves: "When Spanish composers propose to create a national art, they feel and express a conventional Andalusianism or erroneous Arabism or Orientalism. Granados . . . does not need to resort to Andalusian music, though at times he employs its phrases and rhythms." As a result, Villar thought Granados "the most original of present-day Spanish composers."[85]

In this commentary we get downwind of a disdain toward the Andalusian manner that lurks in Spanish (often Catalonian) attempts to define or refine national identity. A Granados pupil wrote years after the master's death that Granados's nationalist essays walked a fine line, that too much folklorism posed the real danger of "lapsing into vulgarity . . . a bit too much emphasis on a particular effect, a bit more symmetry in a given phrase, a bit too obvious an evocation of the accordion or the guitar, and the work would be converted into a zarzuela number."[86] Heaven forbid! Frank Marshall made such apprehensions more pointed, rooting them in class and ethnicity: "[Granados's] Spanishness is far removed from that of Andalusia: this Spanishness is devoid of coarseness, of violent expressions, of exultation and drama. Instead, Granados manages to capture all the elegance, subtlety, and aristocracy of eighteenth-century Spain. . . . He stylized, transformed, and polished the folklore of his music."[87]

Such opinions about Andalusia were no doubt affected by the mass migration of poor Andalusians into Barcelona in the twentieth century. Though Catalans were fascinated with certain aspects of Andalusian culture, the increasing presence of Andalusians themselves in Barcelona colored the view of local upper bourgeoisie toward the entire region. Naturally, the issue of race lurked in the background. Andalusians represented a suspect and bastardized mélange of Gypsy, Moorish, Jewish, and European bloodlines that many associated with racial decadence. Whatever the case, Andalusian music was viewed as coarse, violent, and dramatic in an undesirable way. It required transformation and refinement before being acceptable in polite company. Above and beyond that, of course, is the fact that "Andalusian" music means specifically flamenco, the art of Gypsies and other lower-class, marginalized communities. Social attitudes about these groups are ultimately inseparable from the kind of nationalist discourse Marshall presents here. For Marshall and many others, Spain is a land of aristocratic refinement and grace, not of coarseness and violence. That it embraced and embraces both was apparently not a comforting thought. And yet Goya, whom all reverenced as the oracular voice of *casticismo*, fully understood the stark contrasts and contradictions in Spanish culture and history. How could they have idolized Goya and denied the very things Goya had to say about the enduring realities of Spain, its life and its people?

All of this reflects the continuing uncertainty and uneasiness about Spain's identity that forms much of the overall context in which we must place Granados's music. It also reflects the social realities of traditional Spanish society. For middle-class types like Granados and Marshall, upward mobility was the name of the game, to put distance between oneself and the lower classes and strive toward a greater emulation of the elite. In the view of some, the *majas* were very much in need of the sublimation Granados provided:

> The *maja* of Granados was not the sexy and brazen woman of the slums, whose physical appeal could suffer greatly from her insolent manner of speaking and her crude gestures. Rather, his was an aristocratic *maja* [thinking, no doubt, of the Duchess of Alba] who, though dressed in a popular style, knew how to refine that which was plebeian, elevating it to the category of the exquisite.[88]

Granados echoed these sentiments in an interview with the *Christian Science Monitor*: "It is possible for a musician to take what is insignificant in the way of melody and to organize it until it becomes poetic and distinguished. He can keep the original rhythm, but can endow it with thought."[89] In other words, popular rhythms, though otherwise "undistinguished," could be sublimated through the intellect and transformed into suitable concert material. As one New York reviewer observed, Granados was "a man of extreme gentleness and modesty, but his music pulsates with wild emotions, fantastic rhythms and daring harmonies." There was a discomfiting contradiction here that the reviewer had somehow to reconcile: "It is built on Spanish dance instinct but with the skill of a highly trained musician."[90] His "instinct" was tamed by intellectual skill and disciplined training; it had become "upwardly mobile" and risen from the lower to upper classes. There is something Freudian in such commentary, as if the proletarian id required sublimation by the bourgeois superego.

Regardless of the critical reaction to his opera, both pro and con, *Goyescas* was the highlight of Granados's trip to the New World. But it was not the only thing he accomplished abroad. Although he had not planned to give concerts during his stay in New York, he was prevailed upon to do so, twice. In the first instance, he performed with Casals for the Friends of Music at the Hotel Ritz-Carlton on January 23, 1916. Granados presented a large audience with selections from *Goyescas*, but what attracted conspicuous attention from the critics were his *Valses poéticos*, among his earliest works. One reviewer thought they were "[c]harmingly Spanish in rhythm and in meter,"[91] though they are not "Spanish" at all. Another critic, however, sniffed at them as "mere salon pieces of no particular distinction or originality."[92] Again, this misses the mark by a wide margin. Both reviewers seemed to have reservations about him as a pianist, the first concluding that "While not a great piano virtuoso, Mr. Granados is an able player" and the second comparing him to Percy Grainger (then active on the concert circuit and an avid promoter of Spanish music) in the way that "he impresses more by the individuality of his work than by a conventionally finished pianism."

Granados himself acknowledged that his compositions were not without short-comings. He humbly admitted to J.L. from *Las novedades*: "I know the weak points of my music: but although most listeners take pleasure in it, often the critics content themselves with pointing out its flaws."[93] And yet, he held his head high in the knowl-edge that though "I am not a rich man . . . I can say that I have written no cheap music, no commercial music, no light opera [i.e., *género chico*]. I would be rich today if I had wished to be known as a composer of light opera. Spain has many men who have made their fortunes in that way. But have you in America ever heard of them? No; I have wanted to be known for serious work or not at all."[94]

The second occasion was an all-Granados program on February 22 at Aeolian Hall, which featured the vocal talents of *Goyescas* star Anna Fitziu. *Las novedades* reported that though Granados's first concert was an affair reserved for the upper crust of New York society, this one was his first truly public performance.[95] *Musical America* claimed that the only genuinely enthusiastic members of the audience were the Spaniards, who appeared to the critic to be straight out of paintings by Velázquez, Murillo, and Goya. "Those who were not Spanish seemed to be less easily roused by their fairly good, but not extraordinary music."[96]

The day after the concert, Granados stopped by the Schirmer firm to say goodbye. Sad and apprehensive, he did not feel well; no doubt, dread of another ocean voyage was getting the best of him. An employee requested that he play something at the piano, as a souvenir in sound. Granados thoughtfully obliged. After he was finished improvising, he declared: "That is my Spain, my home, my very life."[97] Although they implored him to write out the piece to preserve it, he declined, saying it was nothing but an improvisation on the spur of the moment and should not be repeated.

Although scheduled to leave New York and return directly to Barcelona on a Span-ish liner (the *Antonio López*) on March 8, events intervened to delay Granados's de-parture. President and Mrs. Wilson invited him to perform at the White House, and he could hardly refuse the honor. He rescheduled his departure on a Dutch liner, the *Rotterdam*, which would dock at Falmouth, England. He would spend a few days in London, then cross the Channel to France and take a train south to Spain.

Granados traveled to the capital on the morning of the 7th and performed that evening. The gala event at the White House was a brilliant success. The Wilsons hosted this as the first of a series of "musicales" they had planned. There were about 300 guests, whom the president and First Lady received in the Green Room before all passed into the East Room, adorned for the occasion with American Beauty roses, where the concert was given. The list of invitees included numerous diplomatic dignitaries, among them ambassadors from Britain, Japan, Chile, and France, as well as ministers from Norway, Belgium, El Salvador, and Siam. Granados and the Dutch soprano Julia Culp were the featured performers and presented a recital of songs and solos. The program was selected and arranged by the president's daughter Margaret and included the *Allegro de concierto, Spanish Dance No. 7 (Valenciana), El pelele*, a Scarlatti transcription, and a Chopin Nocturne. A buffet dinner was served afterward.[98] This was Granados's last major performance, and one of his most memorable.

The next day Granados was feted at the residence of the Spanish ambassador, Riaño, who could not make it to the White House concert and prevailed on Granados to perform again at his residence as part of the luncheon. Riaño was incredulous that Granados was not going to take a Spanish vessel on his return voyage. Although the Germans had suspended unrestricted submarine warfare after the *Lusitania* sinking, sailing into British waters still seemed too risky, even on a neutral ship. Granados respected the ambassador's opinion but could not change his reservations because the Dutch line would not refund his money.

After the reception, Granados returned hastily to New York to rejoin Amparo and embark for home. Upon his actual departure on the 11th, the Schellings, Paderewskis, Kreislers, and other admirers presented Granados with a loving cup containing a check in the amount of $4,100. A few days earlier, Schelling, Casals, Paderewski, and Fritz Kreisler had given him a velvet sack with $1,000 in gold coins. These were material expressions of their affection and admiration for him, and he cherished both gifts.

Granados had every reason to feel good about his success in New York, despite obvious disappointments. He had made, for him, a small fortune, in the neighborhood of $4,000 from the Met production, and several thousand more from the recordings he made for the Aeolian Co. The publication of his music and his public recitals also netted him substantial amounts. In addition to the $5,100 he had received as a gift from his friends, this represented a dramatic shift in his finances. It truly seemed that he had turned an important corner in his career, that the years of penury and struggle, difficult though they had been, had paid off and were now a thing of the past. During his weeks in New York, he wrote to his friend Amadeu Vives in Barcelona expressing new-found optimism about the future:

> At last I have seen my dreams realized. It is true that my hair is full of white, and it can be said that I am only now beginning my work, but I am full of confidence and enthusiasm about working more and more. . . . I am a survivor of the fruitless struggle to which the ignorance and indifference of our country subject us. All my present happiness is more for what is to come than for what I have done up to now. I am dreaming of Paris, and I have a world of ideas.[99]

We know that his "ideas" included works he was already sketching, for instance, a sequel to *Goyescas* for piano, *Librito de caprichos* (1. "Arlequín y los consejos del hombre serio"; 2. "El hablador y el confiado"), and a series of songs with texts by Mestres.[100]

He also planned to publish revised versions of the *Danzas españolas* and *Goyescas*, and to complete a Symphony in E Minor (see the *Epílogo*) and a Cello Concerto.[101] In addition, he and Miró were apparently planning an opera entitled *Jerusalén*.[102]

On the evening before their departure on the *Rotterdam*, Granados and his wife were again plagued by dire forebodings, and he unburdened himself to his friend Malvina Hoffman, an accomplished sculptor and one-time student of Rodin. He told her in a nervous voice on the telephone that Amparo was nearly hysterical with apprehension: "Never again will I see my children!" she would cry. When Malvina tried to reassure him, he said: "No, Malvina, this is the end. You will see that I am not mistaken."[103] However, the crossing was uneventful and took only eight days. Nonetheless, Mildred Bliss, wife of the first secretary at the American Embassy in Paris, who also traveled on the *Rotterdam*, recalled that Granados came to her stateroom two days before arriving in England to recite (yet again) his premonition of death.[104]

The Granadoses stayed in London for a few days, sightseeing and visiting friends. Among these was the Catalan sculptor Ismael Smith, who made a clay impression for a life mask of Granados and later designed an "Ex Libris" featuring a guitar-playing *majo* and a *maja*; he also fashioned a small sculpture of Granados playing the piano.[105] Granados hoped to interest either Sir Thomas Beecham or Sir Henry Wood in a London production of *Goyescas*, but nothing came of this.

On March 24 they boarded the *Sussex* at Folkestone, destination Dieppe. U-boats had never molested shipping on that route; thus, it would have no escort.[106] To sail from Folkestone to Dieppe would take four hours, two more than traveling from Dover to Calais, but it seemed the safer alternative, because the shorter route was known to be infested with submarines. Ironically, military transports plying the Channel along that route suffered little harm in the war because they were heavily guarded.

The ship left harbor about 1:30 p.m., and the nearly 400 passengers enjoyed a pleasant spring day. Granados discovered a piano in the smoking room and improvised something.[107] Throughout the voyage, the sky was clear and the sea, calm. Perhaps Enrique and Amparo thought the fair weather a hopeful portent and entertained thoughts that their premonitions were baseless—they would arrive home safely after all.

The relatively calm seas, however, allowed the skipper of the *Sussex* to perceive a menacing disturbance in the water at 2:55 p.m. Captain Henri Mouffet saw a torpedo approaching to port at a distance of about 100 yards.[108] No warning had been given, and no assistance was offered by the U-boat. Seemingly unarmed British ships (the so-called Q-ships) had a way of opening fire on U-boats that surfaced, so German submariners stayed submerged as much as possible when attacking. Mouffat immediately gave the order to change course hard to starboard. Had he had only a few seconds more warning, the torpedo would have missed the *Sussex* entirely; as it was, it struck just ahead of the forward bulkhead and destroyed the bow of the ship. However, the *Sussex* remained afloat because the explosion bent the hull inwards, thus forming a barrier that prevented a catastrophic inflow of water. Hundreds of mailbags stored there also helped keep out the sea.

Had he taken no evasive action, the torpedo would have struck directly amidships, and no doubt the *Sussex* would have sunk quickly and with much greater loss of life. This is especially true because no other ships were in the vicinity, and the *Sussex* would not have been able to call for help. There would have been little time to find refuge in lifeboats and rafts, and those in the water would have died from exposure and drowning long before assistance could arrive, if indeed it ever would have arrived. The loss might well have been total. Still, the *Sussex* was ill prepared to deal with such a crisis, and there were few serviceable life belts available for the passengers who did not make it into lifeboats or rafts.[109] Such was the complacency induced by the German submariners' previous indifference to Channel shipping in this area.

One survivor, an American professor by the name of James Baldwin, wrote a chilling account of the attack. We get some idea from this what the Granadoses experienced, and why they reacted the way they apparently did, which is to say, they panicked:

> A short time before the explosion came, I noticed an erect pole-like object in the water three or four hundred yards from the boat. The thought of a submarine conning tower came to mind, but . . . I dismissed the thought as we passed the object. . . . The explosion came without warning or presage. A dull sudden shock, not too loud nor too sharp. It seemed to be double; a shock first, then some seconds afterwards, the explosion proper, followed by a wave of debris and water thrown up and over, from the fore to the aft of the ship. A moment of silence, then hell let loose. My first word to my wife was, "We're struck, we're going down!" I set out to find life-belts as others were doing and finally found one that held—after several rotten ones. I then aided her, among the hundreds doing the same thing in much confusion, to a life-boat, but it was already overcrowded with women and children. . . . The scenes around us were harrowing. The water was full of men and women, swimming, sinking, drowning, clinging to spars, boards and other bits of wreckage, crying out in the agony of the last hold on life.[110]

The young German U-boat captain, Oberleutnant-zur-See Herbert Ernst Otto "Harry" Pustkuchen,[111] in command of UB-29, may have mistaken the *Sussex* for a minelayer because of its wide stern.[112] He apparently thought the passengers on deck were troops. The ship was painted black all over and bore no markings. Moreover, he was new to this area and was not familiar with the *Sussex*. So, why did not Pustkuchen finish the job? There would seem to have been little risk in attacking again. Pustkuchen may well have thought that the *Sussex* was mortally wounded and would soon go down; why waste a valuable torpedo? According to Baldwin's account, the submarine did linger in the vicinity, hoping to snare any vessels coming to assist the *Sussex*. In fact, "the British Admiralty issued a statement on March 30, saying that the destroyer that picked up the survivors was twice fired on by the submarine."[113] In any event, Pustkuchen thought he had struck a military vessel and not a passenger ship. He had made a terrible mistake, but it was that—a mistake, not a calculated act of cold-blooded murder.[114] Or so the Germans wanted people to believe.

The explosion disabled the *Sussex*'s wireless antenna, which took a couple of hours to be repaired. The telegrapher, however, was apparently so discomposed by the attack that he sent off the wrong location of the *Sussex*, and French destroyers searched in vain over twenty miles away from the actual location of the vessel, now dead in the water despite the fact that its engines were still in working order. Finally, the French destroyer *Marie Thérèse* decided to ignore the location broadcast by the *Sussex* and instead sail in the direction in which its signal was the strongest. Thus, it was the first ship to reach the *Sussex*, but only around midnight. Eventually it was joined by many other ships, military and commercial, which ferried passengers and wounded either to Dover or to Boulogne; the ship itself actually made it to Boulogne. Many people were injured in the attack, and fifty lost their lives (twenty-five of whom were Americans).

Among the fatalities were the Granadoses, but that was not definitely known for days afterward. The press and public on both sides of the Atlantic continued to hope that maybe the two would still turn up among the survivors. Josep Maria Sert, the Catalan artist, went to Boulogne to search for their corpses in a makeshift morgue there. He found nothing, though he did recover their personal effects, which included nearly all the items from their journey and the score to the opera *María del Carmen*. He found the loving cup, which is in the Museu de la Música today, but the $4,100 was gone. Schelling wired another $4,100 to the Granados children; however, the sack with $1,000 in gold coins had also disappeared and was never replaced.

Eyewitness accounts from some of the survivors who were with Granados at the time of the disaster told the story that no one really wanted to know but strained to hear. Mario Serra, son of the Catalan painter Enrique Serra and friend of the Granadoses, related his experience on the *Sussex* and the final minutes of the composer's life. Many of the passengers were in the dining area at the time of the attack. The concussive explosion created widespread alarm, especially when a geyser of water spouted in the area.[115] People scrambled to escape, and on deck, lifeboats and rafts were filling with those seeking safety. The captain implored them not to panic, but to no avail. Serra tried to persuade the Granadoses to stay put on the ship, but they were convinced that their survival depended on leaving it. Reports differ as to what happened next, but they all agree on one point: the two were separated in the water, and Enrique tried to reach Amparo.[116] Ironically, Amparo *was* a good swimmer, but he was not. He embraced his wife, and they disappeared forever beneath the waves. In the panic and confusion, no one thought to or was able to help them.[117]

Granados's death provoked genuine pathos, as well as moral outrage. *La vanguardia* expressed the perplexity of the multitudes over such a stunning loss: "Who could have suspected such a tragic end to so glorious a career?"[118] By an eerie coincidence, on the evening of the 24th, the day Granados died, Arthur Rubinstein was giving a concert at the Palau de la Música Catalana in Barcelona, during which he played "La maja y el ruiseñor" from *Goyescas*. Unknowingly, he was offering a homage to the fallen nightingale.[119]

The German government initially denied culpability, claiming the *Sussex* had struck a mine, but fragments of a torpedo were found in one of the lifeboats, and Germany agreed to make amends. Already in May 1916, reports surfaced in the press that the Germans not only regretted the incident but blamed it on the errant judgment of Pustkuchen. In April, the *New York Times* reported that the German foreign minister, Gottlieb von Jagow, had met with a Spanish journalist and said, "If they prove an error on the part of the commander of a submarine in the *Sussex*, I will regret, as all German people will regret, that such an error caused the death of your compatriot, the composer Granados."[120] Moreover, they were amenable to paying an indemnity to the orphans. This was certainly a positive development, but it did little to mitigate what quickly became an international *cause célèbre*.

The Germans were not the only ones to bear the blame. Suspicions have persisted over the intervening decades that perhaps the British had somehow engineered the debacle in order to draw the United States into the war.[121] The ship was on a course that it had not followed before, as it bore more to the west, hugging the English shore, before heading for France. Shortly before the attack, the French flag had been lowered so that the ship's nationality was no longer obvious.[122] This is an intriguing conspiracy theory, but there is not a shred of evidence to support it. In the event, on April 20 President Wilson did lodge a strenuous protest with the German government, insofar as many of the victims of the attack had been Americans. He threatened to sever diplomatic relations if Germany did not alter its conduct of submarine warfare, but it would be over a year before the United States declared war.

The spectacular nature of Granados's demise brought him and his family a degree of international celebrity and attention they probably would not have received had he died in bed. Certainly the grief expressed by admirers in France, Britain, and the Low Countries was genuine, but it was inseparable from the conflict raging in Europe, which had been the cause of Granados's premature death. The Allies used the tragedy to portray their adversaries as nothing but ruthless barbarians. At least one respected observer thought that the brouhaha threatened Granados's legacy: "[T]he homage paid to Granados since he died ran the risk of injuring his reputation, and of begetting disappointment where we should have the right to expect a durable sympathy."[123] Such reservations cast no shadow over the memorials that ensued.

Sir Thomas Beecham organized a benefit in London that brought forth eulogies and money from leading citizens and organizations. In the Museu de la Música in Barcelona is an entire book full of condolences: *Telegrams and Messages of Sympathy Received on the Occasion of the Special Representation Given in Honour of the Great Spanish Composer Senor Granados at the Aldwych Theatre London July 24th 1916*. The concert featured Beecham conducting Mozart's *Abduction from the Seraglio*, with the patronage of various Allied diplomats, English nobility, and prominent musicians such as Sir Hubert Parry and Sir Charles Stanford. It was attended by Prince Henry of Battenberg, the lord mayor of London, and the ambassadors of Japan, Italy, and Spain. The program hailed Granados as "the greatest of [modern] Spanish composers" and said that the proceeds would go to the Granados orphans. Additional donations were welcome.

The book very much resembles a photo album, with cards and telegrams pasted inside. One came from Leo Delibes: "The hands of the author of *Lakmé* salute the memory of Granados on this day of reparation for the crime of the *Sussex*."[124] The Automobile Club of France, the Lisbon Commercial Association, and even the Royal Society of Painters in Watercolours sent condolences, as did the London Chamber of Commerce and the London Stock Exchange. Hubert Parry, of the Royal College of Music, wrote: "I gratefully take the opportunity of expressing my sympathy with Spain and the family of their famous composer senor Granados." Sir Granville Bantock also expressed his sympathy. Most of these inscriptions bitterly denounce Germany's methods of warfare, one calling them appropriate for Attila the Hun and others invoking the enemy's "savageness," "promiscuous barbarity," "scientific barbarism," "foulest of outrages," and "Teutonic barbarities." Communiqués from individuals and organizations in Spain expressed gratitude to Britain and the British people for their generosity and support.

France honored the late composer at a memorial concert on April 29 at the Salle Rameau in Lyons. In addition to selections by Granados, the program began with the *Hymne à la Justice* of Magnard and concluded with the *Hymne espagnol* and *La Marsellaise* played side by side, in a musical expression of solidarity between the two countries. Another French homage took place at the Comédie Française in Paris on June 30, 1916.

In the United States, a benefit concert was presented at the Metropolitan Opera House in New York on Sunday evening, May 7, 1916, to raise money for the Granados orphans. It featured not only compatriots Barrientos and Casals but also Kreisler and Paderewski. The concert offered several works by Granados, of course, along with selections by Beethoven, Schumann, Schubert, Chopin, Bach, Haydn, and Kreisler himself. The printed program informed the audience that "Mme. Paderewski has contributed one hundred of her Polish refugee Dolls which will be sold, after the concert, for the Benefit of the Granados Children."[125] At the end of the concert, the lights were extinguished save for a single candle flickering on the piano, at which Paderewski played Chopin's Funeral March while the audience stood in respectful silence.[126]

Naturally, many commemorative events took place in Spain itself. On April 15 a memorial concert was held at Madrid's Palace Hotel and attended by the Infanta doña Isabel. The program featured Granados's best-loved Spanish works, the *Danzas españolas*, *Tonadillas*, and *Goyescas*. It concluded, appropriately enough, with two Central European masterpieces by composers who had long influenced Granados: Liszt and Wagner. Shortly thereafter, on May 31, La Sociedad Nacional de Música presented *Goyescas*, *Elisenda*, the *Navidad Suite*, and the *Tonadillas* with Badia.[127] The Orquesta Sinfónica de Madrid, under Arbós, traveled to Barcelona in November to pay its respects. The group performed at the Palau de Belles Arts on the first of the month, presenting the now-popular Intermezzo from *Goyescas*. This benefit, a "festival" organized in conjunction with the Orfeó Català, raised 3,569.20 pesetas for the orphans. Barcelona felt the loss of the composer more keenly than any other place. A memorial service for the Granadoses was held on May 2 at the Iglesia de la Casa Provincial de Caridad. Two masses were performed, at 10 and 12 noon. On May 16 a memorial concert took place at the Palau de la Música Catalana that featured several of his students, including Badia singing the *Tonadillas*.[128]

The six Granados orphans garnered as much sympathy as the attack had stirred outrage, and money poured in from European benefits and subscriptions.[129] There was considerable concern throughout the United States for the plight of the children, and no doubt the incident persuaded many in this country that if the nation did enter the conflict, it would have a moral responsibility to side with the Allies. In view of this, it is ironic that by far the largest donation to the orphans came not from the Allies and its neutral sympathizers but—from Germany itself. It expressed its sincere regret for the incident, reprimanded Pustkuchen, and eventually provided 666,000 pesetas as compensation to the Granados orphans (111,000 each). Since they were mostly still far too young to manage such sums of money, their finances as well as their education were placed in the hands of a three-member committee. This included Miró and one Rafael Rodríguez; Dr. Andreu chaired. Pi i Sunyer agreed to serve as their guardian, and Luis Carrera, as their tutor.[130]

In addition to all this activity, much ink was devoted in the press to the incident. The French periodicals were understandably vehement. *Le Figaro* lamented the disappearance of a musician who was "so vibrant and harmonious," while *L'Echo de Paris* wrote that his demise "will be felt bitterly by artists around the world." *L'Homme enchaîné* summed it up best: "Granados was one of the purest glories of his country."[131] Debussy, Fauré, Saint-Saëns, and d'Indy published letters in the Spanish press expressing their grief and outrage; all of them recalled Granados's humanity, pianistic brilliance, and distinctive qualities as a composer.[132]

The sinking provoked understandable outrage throughout Spain, especially Barcelona. *El correo catalan*'s April 10, 1916, issue predicted that public sentiment would sway further now toward the Allies, perhaps altering Spain's neutral stance by inspiring hatred toward Germany.[133] *La esfera* went beyond mere outrage and suggested an alliance of the neutral nations, especially Latin America, Spain, and the United States, insofar as most of the *Sussex*'s passengers were from the latter two countries. It decried what it perceived as the Spanish government's turning a blind eye to the incident, which in fact it was not going to do, for this was nothing less than a matter of "national dignity."[134]

Other alliances were invoked that had less to do with politics and more to do with "race," variously understood. Some Spanish writers saw the incident as evidence that Spain was naturally allied, through its "Latinity," with France and against things Teutonic. Francophile Joaquín Nin did not mince his words: "To the shock of anguish and the contractions of pain of our Latin brothers, the French, we instinctively add a secret hope of conserving intact the vital forces of our race and our intellect for a future resurrection, necessary, soon, and undoubted."[135]

Granados's "murder" was serving as a catalyst to vault the war, in the minds of many Spaniards, to a new and higher level of ideological conflict, between the racial sensibilities of two mutually inimical groups. However, the "Latin" tent was big enough to include those fighting Germany in Eastern Europe. As Nin went on to say, "Granados possessed, as did Chopin, the richness, variety, and spontaneous rhythm that so enhance a musical work; that is the vital element of Spanish music, as it is of Slavic music."[136] Earlier commentators had drawn parallels between Chopin and Granados, but now such comparisons were meant to demonstrate an underlying racial harmony among those countries (races) fighting the Germans, whether they were Latin or Slav. *El teatre català* devoted most of its April 15 number to the tragedy, and vehemently protested that this outrage was unworthy of the country of Schiller and Heine, Bach, Beethoven, and Wagner, thereby demonstrating at least residual sympathy with "Teutonic" culture.[137]

No polemics would bring Granados back to life, but *Goyescas* lived on in spite of war and controversy. The Chicago Grand Opera Co. presented a couple of scenes from it in May 1916. One review concluded that the score was "[n]ot great, epochmaking music but music of spontaneous charm, the expression of a man who believed something and had both the courage and the skill to set it down."[138] In fulfillment of one of Granados's final dreams, *Goyescas* did eventually make it to the Paris Opéra, in 1919. The gala event, however, took place in the shadow of the recent war. The press did not need to remind readers that, but for a German U-boat's attack, the composer himself would have conducted the performance.

Numerous dignitaries attended the production, including the French president, Jules-Henri Poincaré, and the Spanish queen, Victoria Eugenia. Also present were Marshals Ferdinand Foch and Philippe Pétain.[139] Ignacio Zuloaga designed the sets, and Eduardo Granados made a cameo appearance conducting the Intermezzo between the first and second tableaux. In the second tableau, Amalia Molina treated the audience to her Spanish dancing. According to Corpus Barga, "the success of the evening has been for the Queen, for Amalia Molina, for Zuloaga, and for the son of Granados."[140]

L'Opinion could not fully endorse the work, however, despite its obvious sympathy for the composer, finding the first two scenes full of "picturesque music" but the "ensemble" otherwise "static." However, the third tableau struck the reviewer as, finally, dramatic, aided by the beautiful sets representing a garden by night, enclosed in a fence with a street behind it. Henri Collet praised Granados's nuanced use of local color, avoiding the obvious Gypsyesque clichés of *Carmen*. He regretted that Eduardo did not conduct the entire performance. In his opinion, *Goyescas* was a product of the "Spanish race," and it required a Spaniard to interpret it correctly.[141]

Goyescas was supposed to have been done in Buenos Aires in July and August 1916, but that never happened, partly because of Eduardo's foot-dragging.[142] It was finally produced there in August 1929. Los Angeles was also interested in the opera, as was Boston, which would have to wait until 1982 to see it.[143]

None of these successes would Granados experience or enjoy, for his life had ended in a cruel and tragic fashion, leaving pain and disbelief in its wake. Among the most moving testaments to Granados, the meaning of his life and death, came from the heart of Apeles Mestres, who wrote the following poetic eulogy.

ON THE DEATH OF ENRIQUE GRANADOS
Apeles Mestres

To save everything along with your remains,
Your inspiration, your ideals, your glory,
Required an ample grave;
And that grave, the monster of war
—justly, in spite of himself—gave to you.
Sleep in peace there, in the deep, undisturbed
By homicidal battles,
In the sacred peace of the dead.
The grave is deep
And is wide and is sacred;
The swelling wave opens the grave,
And the next is the gravestone that closes it.
When at night, the stars,
Emerging out of the sea like luminous notes of music,
Spread themselves throughout the heavens and magnify
The immensity of the firmament, then
They will seem like melodies
That, buried with you, you are sending to the sky.
And above the passing tumult
Of that great crime they call "the war,"
Your latest songs, made into stars,
Will resound eternally more beautiful,
In the concert of eternal beauty.[144]

The Legacy of Granados

All things die and all things live forever;
but our task is to die,
to die making roads,
roads over the sea.

Proverbios y cantares, no. 11
Antonio Machado

Posterity's assessment of Granados will never place him alongside the composers he admired most: Beethoven, Schumann, Chopin, and Wagner. He was not in their class; he knew it, and so do we. There is no doubt, however, that he does enjoy a permanent place in the pantheon of European composers, if only as a minor deity. Certain of his works have attained those twin peaks of popularity and critical respect that assure some measure of immortality to a creative artist.

The relegation of Granados to secondary status is due in part to his lack of symphonic output, though he was more productive than one might suppose. The loss of the orchestral work *Romeo y Julieta* and the incompletion of *Dante* make it difficult for us to assess fully his stature in the realm of orchestral composition. Orchestral works that have not remained in the repertoire include *Suite sobre cantos gallegos* (Suite on Galician Songs) and *Marcha de los vencidos* (March of the Conquered), both of which premiered at a concert of the Societat Musical de Barcelona on October 31, 1899, with Joan Lamote de Grignon conducting. Also worthy of consideration would be his *Danza gitana* (Gypsy Dance), composed for the vivacious Spanish dancer Tórtola Valencia (1882–1955).[1] Greater familiarity with this work might cause us to reevaluate not only his status as a composer for orchestra, but also his relationship to Andalusia, which was clearly more compelling than his obsession with Castile has led many to believe.

Still, it is safe to say that Granados was not a symphonist, though he was a confident orchestrator. Inattention to the symphony by Spanish composers in general during his lifetime had four basic causes: (1) there had never been a strong symphonic tradition in Spain due to the relative absence of first-rate orchestras until the latter part of the nineteenth century, (2) the public was less interested in purely symphonic works than it was in zarzuelas, operas, and orchestral works inspired by them, (3) composers and public alike tended to view the symphony as something German, maybe French, but not Spanish, and (4) many viewed the symphony as a genre that was on its way out. As Xosé Aviñoa has described it, even as late as the early 1890s in Barcelona, "The concept of 'symphonism' was totally innovative."[2] However, Barcelona eventually developed a hearty appetite for symphonic fare, and "the modernists and the academicians concurred in adopting a certain messianic attitude that focused on the symphonist par excellence, Beethoven."[3] Brahms, Strauss, and even Mahler had all gained a permanent position in the repertoire of local orchestras by 1910. Under this inspiration, orchestral works by Spanish composers flowered in the early 1900s, especially in Barcelona, which by that time boasted professional ensembles willing to feature works by local composers. However, these symphonic works were usually tone poems of some kind, like *Dante*.

To be sure, Granados did attempt to write an actual symphony. In 1955, the conductor Rafael Ferrer and the composer Xavier Montsalvatge discovered and examined his sketches for a Symphony No. 1 in E Minor.[4] Ferrer proposed at that time to try to orchestrate them, but there remains no completed First Symphony by Granados, partly because he had only sketched out the first movement. The importance of these sketches lies in their intent and the compositional method they reveal, not their final product.[5] As Montsalvatge observes: "For good reason it has been said that many of his piano works seem extracted from symphonic ideas, reductions of authentic symphonic structures." Years earlier, Boladeres Ibern had confirmed that in many of his piano compositions Granados "perceived passages of a certain structure in an orchestral way."[6] He did develop an extraordinary ability to control dynamics and timbre at the keyboard, especially through his skillful use of the pedals. In this way, he was able to impart an almost orchestral palette of color to his piano playing. How he conceived of these colors becomes clear in his orchestration of the opera *Goyescas*. In the case of his symphony, however, the actual style of the music is indebted, not surprisingly, to Schumann.[7]

In my biography of Albéniz, I quoted a famous saying of the composer Joaquín Turina to the effect that "Albéniz showed us the road we had to follow."[8] But I did not cite the rest of his observation, which pertains directly to Granados: "[He] understood that his hour had arrived and he set out on that road, although adapting it to his musical temperament, which was at home in the early nineteenth century."[9]

The opinion of musicological posterity has not only to do with the perceived intrinsic value of a body of work but also with its extrinsic importance, the degree to which it challenged and channeled the flow of music history. Some writers have praised Granados for resisting the influence of French Impressionism, thereby keeping his style "purely" Spanish. For instance, Pedrell approvingly remarked that his former pupil "never got caught up in the caprice of exoticism, or experimented with the tempting but corrupting French manner, which has ruined so many."[10] Others, however, view Granados as more conservative and less innovative, and hence less significant, than Albéniz and Falla, who did succumb to the "corrupting French manner." Not surprisingly, the former view is usually favored by Spaniards and sometimes Americans, while the latter is common among French and English writers.

G. Jean-Aubry, who knew Granados personally, had this to say: "Within the Spanish musical renaissance, the role of Granados is not as considerable as that of Albéniz or Pedrell. Granados did not possess the intellectual patience, the technical curiosity, or the spiritual avidity that is necessary for one to become the leader of a generation." It is doubtful that either Pedrell or Albéniz possessed these qualities to a conspicuously greater degree than Granados. The interest of such commentary lies more in the point of view it reveals, that Albéniz's Parisian orientation had placed him on the right side of history. For, Jean-Aubry continues, "[Granados] was profoundly attached to a traditional aesthetic, to the style of Liszt and Chopin. Neither the innovations of Debussy nor of Richard Strauss made a great impression on him."[11] This blithely overlooks *Dante* as well as his contributions to Catalan musical theater, certainly an innovative aspect of his oeuvre. And his *Goyescas* and *Tonadillas* were hailed as fresh and new when they appeared. However, his disconnection from Debussy reduced his stature among Spanish nationalists, in the opinion of Jean-Aubry.

The centrality of Debussy in the aesthetics of modernism can scarcely be overstated. Take, for example, the opening of a classic text on twentieth-century music by William Austin: "Of all the composers who ever lived, Claude Debussy was one of the most original and most adventurous."[12] The perception has lingered over the decades that music of the modern era began with Debussy, and to that extent, Granados seemed to many to have missed the boat. However, as Celsa Alonso has pointed out, Impressionism appeared to many Spaniards as a "symbol of a conception of musical art that was essentially French." [13] Perhaps this persuaded Granados that it was not suitable for his musical purposes, as it may have seemed incompatible with the *majismo* he cultivated so assiduously in the final decade of his life.

Even though Granados was never influenced by Debussy or Stravinsky, it would be incorrect to say that Granados was necessarily hostile to trends in Paris and elsewhere. He may have had little use for them, but he was no reactionary. For instance, Granados and Joaquín Nin attended a performance of Stravinsky's *Le sacre du printemps* at the Casino de Paris on April 5, 1914, conducted by Pierre Monteux. Granados's assessment of the work was nothing if not liberal, even enthusiastic. Nin reported that he was "tremendously interested in the ballet score," especially its rhythms.[14] During an interview in 1914, Granados himself recalled this performance and again cited its "prodigious rhythm." He then went to the piano and pounded out some excerpts from memory.[15] In any case, the dialectics of Romanticism and Modernism are less relevant to us now than they were to critics a century ago, and we must view them with some detachment if we are to assay Granados's music fairly and accurately.

Granados was progressive and did pave the way for future Spanish composers in two important respects. First, his fascination with the eighteenth century and utilization of musical elements from that period prefigured the neoclassicism of Manuel de Falla (see the final note in this chapter for corroboration of this view). Though his musical language was rooted in late-Romantic practice, the *Goyescas* works form a proto-neoclassical literature that provided inspiration for Spanish neoclassicists after his death. Second, his fixation on Castile as the artistic and spiritual hub of the nation anticipated the dominant aesthetic of the Franco era and the music of the composers who flourished during it, particularly Federico Moreno Torroba (1891–1982). Many of Moreno Torroba's guitar works, such as *Aires de La Mancha* and *Suite castellana*, celebrate the riches of Castilian culture and represent a significant departure from the Frenchified *andalucismo* of Albéniz, Turina, and early Falla.

As a teacher and as the founder of a successful music academy, Granados's legacy rests on a secure foundation, namely, the numerous prominent musicians who benefited from his instruction or that of his leading disciples. Among the most distinguished of his students were Conxita Badia, the great soprano who began as a piano student at the Academy and was then "discovered" by Granados during a solfège exam; Roberto Gerhard, a composer and follower of Schoenberg who studied piano for two years with Granados at the Academy; Paquita Madriguera, a virtuosa pianist who later married Andrés Segovia; José Iturbi, an eminent pianist who was later active in Hollywood; Xavier Montsalvatge, one of the leading Catalan composers of the twentieth century; and last but by no means least, Frank Marshall, who coped with a tragic and nearly impossible situation in 1916 and somehow found the strength not simply to soldier on but to take the Academy to new heights after becoming the director in 1920. For purely legal purposes, he changed the Academy's name to the Acadèmia Marshall, and under his leadership, the Academy played an increasingly prominent and important role in the musical life of Barcelona, sponsoring concerts by such artists as Victoria de los Angeles [Victòria dels Angels], Casals, and Segovia. Marshall and the Academy were also active in promoting modern music in Barcelona. In all these ways, he brought to fulfillment the lofty aims his mentor had had for the school.

The most notable of Marshall's disciples is Alicia de Larrocha (1923–). Both her mother and her aunt studied with Granados and taught at the Academy, and she was an astounding prodigy. She began her studies with Marshall at age 4, at which time she learned her first piece by Granados ("La campana de la tarde" from *Bocetos*). She is one of the premier pianists of the last half century, with an international concert and recording career. She has been chiefly responsible for promoting the works of Granados and establishing them firmly in the canon. She also took over the directorship of the Academy for several years after Marshall's death and carried on a proud tradition; the Academy continues to play a prominent role in Barcelona's musical life.

A crucial aspect of Granados's legacy as a performer is the recordings he himself made. The height of his career as a pianist coincided with the introduction of various recording technologies, which, though they may seem primitive to us now, represented the cutting edge of technological innovation in the late 1800s. One such device was the Pianola, or mechanical piano, invented by the American firm Aeolian in the late 1800s. This produced piano rolls, that is, perforated rolls of paper that formed a recording of a performance. Aeolian later introduced the Duo-Art Reproducing Piano (1913), which was more sensitive to nuances in execution.[16] Granados took advantage of these developments and made piano-roll recordings for Aeolian during his stay in New York in 1916.

However, the sessions in New York were not his first in a recording studio. In 1912 he had made some acoustic recordings on double-sided ten-inch discs for Odeon in Barcelona. Since these could hold only a few minutes of music, longer works could not be recorded, and the repertoire on these recordings includes some of the *Danzas españolas*, a Scarlatti transcription, and an improvisation. Longer works could be transferred to piano rolls, and the Duo-Art recordings as well as rolls produced by Welte-Mignon in Paris (ca. 1912) include selections from *Goyescas*, the complete *Valses poéticos*, and more *Danzas españolas*. In fact, Nos. 7 and 10 from that collection appear on the recordings made by all three companies and give us an opportunity to compare Granados's renditions over a period of time and in different places. What we notice is an impressive consistency from one to the next.[17] His recordings do present us with notable inconsistencies, but these are between the recorded and printed versions. As Lionel Salter notes, "his performances frequently depart, sometimes seriously, from what he had written." Salter's inevitable conclusion from these discrepancies is that "Granados's performances, often arresting and exciting, were highly individual and cannot be given a blanket endorsement as guides to follow."[18]

It is something of a mystery why Aeolian did not also use the more advanced technology of discs, to which they had access and which they used with other artists.[19] One explanation is that Pianolas were very popular throughout the United States, and there was a much larger market for piano rolls than for discs. Pianolas became fixtures in many households and places of entertainment, so that Granados was among the first classical musicians ever to reach a large audience outside the confines of a concert hall.[20]

Despite Granados's enduring contributions as a teacher and performer, clearly his reputation rests chiefly on his compositions. But this aspect of his legacy is problematic because so much of his music remained in manuscript after his death, in many cases unperformed and unknown. For instance, fully 104 out of a total of 250 piano pieces remained unpublished until the recent edition by Larrocha and Riva (DLR). This is because Eduardo, the eldest son and family head, ordered Schelling to withdraw all of Granados's unpublished manuscripts from Schirmer due to a controversy over royalty payments.[21] Consequently, all these manuscripts were under Eduardo's control and remained unpublished. The operas suffered even more grievously. After having broken off relations with Schirmer, Eduardo sold five of the Mestres operas to Salabert in Paris, where they have languished ever since.[22]

After Eduardo died of typhoid fever in 1928, Natalia's husband, Dr. Antoni Carreras i Verdaguer, was appointed by the other family members as the new keeper of the Granados archive.[23] Fortunately, he was superbly equipped to tackle the job. He was an outstanding dermatologist, a member of the Spanish Royal Academy of Medicine, and honorary president of the Spanish Academy of Dermatology. A man of keen intelligence and great energy, he preserved, protected, and promoted the legacy of his father-in-law with admirable dedication. As one journalist wrote, his whole house was "a temple consecrated to the memory of the author of *Goyescas*. With indefatigable love and patience, that gentleman has been recovering everything he could of Granados."[24]

The task was time-consuming and difficult. For instance, whenever someone wanted to use Granados's music in a film, they wrote to Dr. Carreras (or his agent at the Sociedad General de Autores de España); the work to which rights were most often requested was *Spanish Dance No. 5*. The Greek pop singer Nana Moscouri requested permission to use it as the basis for her song "La Andaluza," with lyrics by José María Purón. Other pop songs based on that number were "Out of Sight Out of Mind" and "Siete Noches sin Ti" (the latter with text by Luis Gomes Escolar; I do not know who sang them). Granados's music was also used on Spanish national television and radio.

In fact, Granados made it on to the big screen in more ways than just musical. In the early 1940s the film *Goyescas* appeared, based very loosely on the opera. It used *Spanish Dance No. 5* as a kind of leitmotif throughout the score, performed by the Madrid Symphony Orchestra and guitarist Regino Sainz de la Maza.[25] The film was directed by Benito Perojo, and the ballet sequences were choreographed by Vicente Escudero. Headlining the cast was the popular actress Imperio Argentina playing the parts of both female leads, renamed Petrilla and Countess de Gualda. Other characters were renamed as well, and the plot made explicit the identities of Manuel Godoy and Queen María Luisa, who, tradition holds, were lovers. Distributed in the United States by RKO, the picture premiered at New York's World Theatre on May 27, 1944; it also ran in Mexico City, Havana, and Buenos Aires.[26]

Correspondence from the summer of 1953 reveals that Columbus Films in Madrid intended to make a movie based on Granados's life and music entitled *Danza Quinta de Granados*, with a screenplay by José María Pemán. The director, Francisco Hormaechea, assured Dr. Carreras on July 10 that "It is our intention to make a great film with utmost devotion and enthusiasm. I would greatly appreciate your support, collaboration, and assistance, so that this film can be made in an elevated manner."[27] One of their agents was already trying to line up distribution in the United States. What became of this project is still a mystery.

Another project of interest that never materialized was an Argentine film on the life of Granados. Víctor Granados was the point man on this, though the pianist José Iturbi was also involved. On June 5, 1948, Víctor wrote to Dr. Carreras urgently requesting all possible biographical material on Granados for the making of the movie by Guaranteed Pictures de la Argentina. This project held out the prospect of big profits for the family, upwards of 100,000 pesetas, or so he claimed. On August 1 of that year, he even mentioned the possibility of *María del Carmen* being turned into a movie. However, by December 20, 1948, the project had fallen through, partly because of difficulty in securing permission to use the music, but mostly because of financing.

In fact, Víctor's penchant for making deals usually made nothing but trouble for Dr. Carreras. A decade earlier, in the late 1930s, Víctor had fled the Spanish Civil War and traveled to the United States. He was touted by the American press as an "official representative of the Loyalist regime in Spain," who had come here to organize support among Loyalist sympathizers.[28] He also brought along some of Granados's manuscripts. We do not know if he did this with permission from his brother-in-law. The family was in dire financial straits during the Civil War, and they may have hoped he could make some money by selling them. The manuscripts he removed were *María del Carmen* (orchestral score), *Cant de les estrelles* (piano part), *Romeo y Julieta*, and *Torrijos*. He offered these to Nathanial Shilkret, head of Shilkret Publishing in New York. Shilkret was an outstanding musician, conductor, composer, and arranger, and he knew a good deal when he saw it. He offered Víctor $300 as an advance against the royalties from publication and also helped him find work as a cellist.[29]

When it became clear to Dr. Carreras that Víctor was going to keep the money for himself, he set about trying to get the manuscripts back. Legal wrangling went on for decades between the family and the firm, but in the end, the music was never returned to the Granados family. Shilkret wanted complete rights to the work, though he was willing to sell it back for the original $300. No deal was ever struck. In fact, the Shilkret firm eventually reported that the valuable works were damaged or destroyed in a fire at one of the company's stores.

Nathanial Shilkret did put his acquisition to some good use on August 29, 1954, when NBC Radio broadcast a performance by the NBC Concert Orchestra under Roy Shield of the Prelude to act 1 of *María del Carmen*. Shilkret spent about $1,000 to have a vocal score of the opera made for the Met's consideration, and he negotiated with both RCA Victor and Columbia to record the Prelude. Toscanini considered programming it on his Latin American Hour. And there was a real prospect for a U.S. performance of the whole opera, based on the original manuscript in Shilkret's possession. When the Granados descendants in Spain found out, however, that the sponsor was to be Scott Toilet Paper, they demurred. They did not want Granados's music associated with such a product. In the end, all these plans came to naught. Shilkret laid the blame squarely on Víctor, who had "made our firm look ridiculous."[30]

Some light has recently been shed on the state of these manuscripts, as I was able to meet with Nathanial Shilkret's grandson, Niel Shell, in New York and examine what is left of them; follow-up meetings between Douglas Riva and Shell produced further discoveries. *Torrijos* survived the fire intact, but it is a bit of a mystery. It is clearly incidental music to a play, but the only work I could find with that title is a short drama in one act and two scenes by Narciso Díaz de Escovar and Ramón A. Urbano Carrere, published in 1886 (Madrid: Administración Lírico-Dramática). The undated score calls for chorus and orchestra and consists of various introductory numbers (preludes and choruses) for three scenes, not two. None of the text in the play appears in what the chorus sings, though the choral lyrics deal with the same historical episode as the drama: General José María Torrijos arrives by boat on the Andalusian coast in 1831 to lead a heroic but doomed uprising against the despotic regime of Fernando VII. *Torrijos* is not a major work in Granados's oeuvre, but it is an intriguing one and will require more research. In any case, Granados's attraction to this subject matter may give us a clue to his closely guarded political leanings, as the work clearly celebrates a heroic Spanish officer who was also a liberal reformer.

More good news is the survival of the missing piano part for *Cant de les estrelles* (Song of the Stars), one of Granados's most important choral pieces. The piano part is highly virtuosic and constitutes by itself a significant addition to the composer's keyboard works. In addition to piano, *Cant de les estrelles* is scored for choruses and organ. The manuscript clearly indicates that Granados was striving for a polychoral spatial effect, insofar as the score specifies the placement of three choirs.[31] The work employs a Catalan text inspired by a poem of the German Romantic poet Heinrich Heine;[32] however, who wrote this text remains a mystery. The leading suspect would seem to be Mestres, but in every other case where Granados set a Mestres text to music, he freely gave credit to the author. The metaphysical tenor of these stanzas does not resonate with Mestres's customary theme: unrequited love and the alienation of the artist from society. The preoccupation with death expressed in the final strophe is eerily portentous of the fate soon to visit the other possible author of these lines: Granados himself.

> Weakness invades the heart.
> Eternal rest approaches!
> We wish to know of the death of our worlds!
> The charms of love are broken
> but we can't break the shackles
> of the eternal immensity!
> Ah![33]

After its 1911 premiere, one Barcelona critic praised the "great delicacy," "novelty," and "noble inspiration" of *Cant de les estrelles*.[34] Another reviewer went much further and declared it a "triumph" of Catalan art; Granados himself was not merely a "new" musician but rather a musician "for all time."[35] What a shame that the work has lain in near-total obscurity for almost a century after its first performance. At long last we will have a chance to enjoy this "celestial" music from Granados's mature period.

Riva was able to negotiate the purchase of *Cant de les estrelles* and *Torrijos* from the Shilkret family, and his editions of them will soon be published. Unfortunately, not all the news from the Shilkret archive was this good. No trace of *Romeo y Julieta* has surfaced, but it may turn up eventually. Only part of the first act of *María del Carmen* has been recovered, and it suffered water and fire damage; it may be some time before a proper inventory of the Shilkret archive will tell us whether any more of the score survives. The vocal score Shilkret had made of it is incomplete, lacks any text underlay, and deviates significantly from the original orchestral score. It is useless.

Another *María del Carmen* exists in Madrid, however, in the archive of the Sociedad General de Autores y Editores.[36] This is possibly a revision made by the composer's son Eduardo and the Catalan composer Francesc Montserrat i Ayarbe, who perhaps felt that the work required reorchestration and other revisions to enhance its dramatic impact and color. This is the version that was performed after Granados's passing. It was revived by the Wexford Opera in 2003, the first-ever performance outside Spain of this crucial work, and has since been recorded.[37] It may be that, in time, Granados's operas will enhance his reputation and compensate somewhat for his lack of symphonic output. But they will need modern editions and more frequent performance.

The relative absence of Granados's operas from the stage since his death has led to a certain touchiness among aficionados, that somehow the great composer was not receiving his due. As the above history demonstrates, there are reasons why these works have not been heard that have nothing to do with their inherent value. At the very least, Schirmer has made *Goyescas* available, and that does enjoy a continued place on the stage throughout the world.[38] Yet, even here one can occasionally be misled. In a 1966 interview with Miquel Utrillo, *Solidaridad nacional* claimed that the Liceu had never staged a work by Granados. Juan A. Pamias, director of the Liceu, wrote not only to the periodical but also to Dr. Carreras to protest this unjust assertion.[39] Indeed, he declared, the Liceu had produced *Goyescas* during the 1939–40 season, for a total of three performances, and again three times in 1956–57. What is more, *María del Carmen* had been produced there for a total of eleven performances. For instance, it was staged at the Liceu on December 28, 1933, and again on November 28, 1935, in anticipation of the twentieth anniversary of Granados's death.[40] It was again produced on December 1, 1938, the fortieth anniversary of the Madrid premiere. The final performance of this opera in Spain was on January 28, 1967.

Political controversy surrounded some of these performances. In announcing the 1938 production of *María del Carmen* at the Liceu, Rafael Moragas reminded his readers that Granados had been a victim of a "totalitarian Germany," even as the besieged Spanish government was then. A few months earlier, on the twenty-second anniversary of Granados's death, Moragas had drawn a parallel between the "crime" of the submariners in the First World War and the ravages now being inflicted by German bombers on Barcelona and other Spanish cities.[41] It is easy to see why *María del Carmen* appealed to the Leftists, dealing as it does with class struggle and the plight of Spain's rural poor.

The fascists preferred *Goyescas*, which recalled the glory days of absolutism and sentimentalized class distinctions. Its exaltation of Castile also accorded with right-wing ideology. This was mounted at the Liceu in late 1939 at the insistence of Francisco Franco after the recent triumph of his forces over the Loyalists. Franco's stated purpose was to cleanse the opera house itself of "Red contamination," as a sort of operatic fumigant. *Goyescas* was preceded and concluded by the National Hymn, during which the audience performed the fascist salute with ardent patriotism.[42]

Just as repugnant was the German premiere that occurred in Berlin the following year. The October production took place at the Berliner Theater, under the direction of Dr. Niedecken-Gebhardt of the German Dance Theater. The anonymous critic who wrote of this event for *Destino* was certain that the German public was anticipating the production with keen interest, "taking into account the sympathy with which our artistic manifestations are received." Unable to restrain himself any longer, the author felt compelled to note the autochthonous nature of the music: "Even if interpreted by dancers who are not Spanish, the music of Granados will infuse them with the fire of our racial spirit, which is latent in every note of the score of *Goyescas*."[43] Perhaps the soul of the composer himself would arrive from Valhalla on winged horseback and inspire them on the spot. Another production of *Goyescas* took place in Milan, on December 28, 1943, while northern Italy was still under Nazi control.

Two decades later, after the fires of partisan rancor had subsided somewhat and the apolitical poet of the piano was no longer a bone of contention between the Left and the Right, Granados again became a unifying presence on the cultural landscape. In 1965, the Amigos de Granados association was formed in Barcelona, with its head-quarters in the "Camarote Granados" at the Hotel Manila. In anticipation of the centenary of his birth and the fiftieth anniversaries of *Goyescas* and the *Sussex* attack, this group sought to preserve and promote the memory of Granados and his music through conferences, concerts, and publications. It counted among its members Alicia de Larrocha, Xavier Montsalvatge, and the Infante don Luis Alfonso de Baviera y de Borbón. On March 24, 1966, on the fiftieth anniversary of the composer's death, the Amigos de Granados celebrated a mass for the composer, at one in the afternoon at the Cristo de Lepanto chapel in Barcelona Cathedral, followed by a memorial ceremony in its meeting hall.[44] In 1967 the Spanish postal service issued a stamp bearing Granados's likeness to commemorate the centenary.

Such events have fixed Granados in the region's consciousness. My experience has been that, even to this day, people in Barcelona who apparently have no other involvement with classical music know of Granados, "the one who went down with the— *Lusitania?*" Well, the collective memory is not always perfect, but the loss of so great a talent wounded the Catalan psyche very deeply, and the scars are still palpable.

Nonetheless, one feels that Barcelona and Spain could and should do much more to honor Granados than hold periodic commemorations and issue stamps. There are no statues of or memorials to him in Barcelona or Madrid. In 1957, at a colloquium sponsored by the Escuela de Periodistas at the Barcelona Athenaeum, there was much discussion of erecting a monument to Granados in the Catalan capital. One notes now with sadness that, almost fifty years later, no such monument exists or is likely to exist in the near future, even though a model was built for one.[45]

The same neglect applies to Albéniz.[46] The reason may be that Spain does not place its musical heritage on the same level as its contributions to literature and painting. Miguel Unamuno conceded as much in *En torno al casticismo* when he declared that "Music, the most algebraic art, is German, French, or Italian."[47] Even if we were to accept his premise that music is "algebraic," Albéniz and Granados, and an army of other composers including Victoria and Falla, proved that music is decidedly a Spanish art as well. After all, Spaniards can do algebra as well as anyone else. Viewed from another perspective: one of the greatest mathematicians in history was Sir Isaac Newton, yet Unamuno does not suggest that music is an English art. Even if Granados and Albéniz are in the second rank of European composers, even if Spain has never produced a composer to rival Cervantes in literature or Goya in painting, still, these and other Spanish composers deserve at least as much honor as the Czechs have given to Smetana or the Norwegians to Grieg, who occupy the same second rank.

To be fair, Lleida has done better in honoring Granados. The city held a Granados festival in 1956–57 on the fortieth and ninetieth anniversaries of his death and birth, respectively, and the events included a production of *Goyescas* on February 6,

1957. Another commemoration featuring recitals and the opera took place a decade later, and in October 1966, for the fiftieth anniversary of his death, the city erected a lovely monument to Granados, designed by an architect from Lleida, Mariano Gomá Pujadas, and funded by a public subscription. It stands near the Seu Vella, just up the street from the birthplace, which building bears two commemorative plaques: one from the city itself, and one from the Republic of Paraguay, dated 1962.

The United States has not forgotten Granados either. In January 1982, the Boston Concert Opera sponsored a Granados Celebration to commemorate the American premiere of *Goyescas* and present a revival of the opera. There were lectures and recitals in conjunction with this celebration. Other productions of *Goyescas*, however, have been less respectful of the composer. In 1986, the Opera Royal de Wallonie revived it on a double bill with Falla's *La vida breve*. Critic Robert Boas gives us some idea of the event:

> The result was an evening of depressingly familiar anti-Romantic clichés: derelict permanent sets littered with cranes and wrecked cars; hairless, pseudo-naked supernumeraries; unscripted assassinations; humdrum modern costumes; and perpetual, soul-afflicting darkness. That most of these features were common to both works argues a paucity of ideas as well as a musical insensibility on the part of those responsible.

Why such a wretched perversion of an unabashedly Romantic work? Boas concludes that its "sensuous, atmospheric music and picturesque settings accord ill with today's cult of squalor and singularity."[48]

Or perhaps it simply had to do with the fact that the music of Granados is often incomprehensible to a contemporary world habituated to the garish crassness of so much popular culture, on the one hand, and the occasionally sterile intellectuality of modernism, on the other. In general I would say that Granados was not an anti-intellectual composer but rather a non-intellectual one. This is not to say that his music does not reveal great intelligence, for certainly it does; nor could we assert that it merits no serious analysis, for certainly it does. But we must bear in mind that his music arose from, and changed in response to, inner intuitive forces aroused by external stimuli, rather than premeditated designs or some preoccupation with forms and formulas, with innovation and "progress" for their own sake. As Jean-Aubry pointed out, "Feeling was for Granados the very reason and end of music. Neither musical science nor constructive care was ever a goal for him."[49]

So much of twentieth-century music flaunts arid complexity for its own sake, with such abstruse titles as "Structures," "Forms," and "Sequences." By contrast, the music of Granados reassures us that there is no shame in charm, grace, honest emotion—and, yes, in beauty. Long after the aforementioned Structures, Forms, and Sequences have been forgotten—have they not already?—Granados's music will still have an audience. For our relationship to him is somewhat analogous to his with Goya and the eighteenth century. In him we find a refuge, something authentic to hold on to, something that in its particularity gains universal appeal. It resonates with something basic within us, that is, a longing for color, nuance, feeling, sensuality, genuineness, and immediacy.

Perhaps Manuel de Falla offered the best testament to Granados's music. He conducted a concert in Buenos Aires featuring works by various composers, mostly his own and also Granados's "La maja y el ruiseñor," sung by Conxita Badia. Afterwards, a woman approached Falla with tears in her eyes saying: "Maestro, your music is so beautiful! However, what most touched my soul was your 'Maja y el ruiseñor.'" To this Falla dryly but sympathetically responded: "You are quite right, madam. It was the best work on the program."[50]

It is impossible for me now to look out over the sea and not think of the final resting place of one who touched the lives of so many different people so profoundly. In the vast ocean of existence itself, his was an exceptional human life. Others have felt this way before:

> Eleven years after his death, as a tribute to the artist lost to the world, his family, together with a few friends, including Frank Marshall, Manuel de Falla, and [Conxita Badia], went down to the quayside of Barcelona port. There, Frank Marshall threw a sealed bottle into the sea as a posthumous offering to a cherished friend. The bottle contained excerpts from Beethoven's Third Piano Sonata, *Goyescas*, and fragments of Falla's *Retablo de Maese Pedro*. The endless ocean engulfed a boundless source of poetry and inspiration. The world of music had lost one of its greatest and most lyrical devotees.[51]

Granados was indeed gone forever, but his memory and his music remain, and we are the grateful beneficiaries of his imperishable legacy, his road over the sea.

Genealogy

Paternal Ancestry of Granados

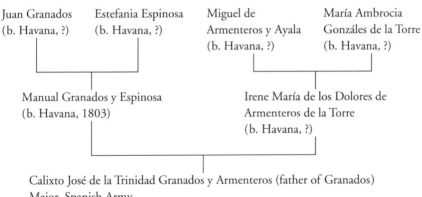

Juan Granados
(b. Havana, ?)

Estefania Espinosa
(b. Havana, ?)

Miguel de
Armenteros y Ayala
(b. Havana, ?)

María Ambrocia
Gonzáles de la Torre
(b. Havana, ?)

Manual Granados y Espinosa
(b. Havana, 1803)

Irene María de los Dolores de
Armenteros de la Torre
(b. Havana, ?)

Calixto José de la Trinidad Granados y Armenteros (father of Granados)
Major, Spanish Army
(b. Havana, October 14, 1824; d. Barcelona, June 24, 1882)

Maternal Ancestry of Granados

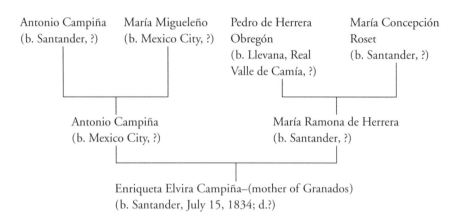

Antonio Campiña
(b. Santander, ?)

María Migueleño
(b. Mexico City, ?)

Pedro de Herrera
Obregón
(b. Llevana, Real
Valle de Camía, ?)

María Concepción
Roset
(b. Santander, ?)

Antonio Campiña
(b. Mexico City, ?)

María Ramona de Herrera
(b. Santander, ?)

Enriqueta Elvira Campiña–(mother of Granados)
(b. Santander, July 15, 1834; d.?)

Immediate Family of Granados

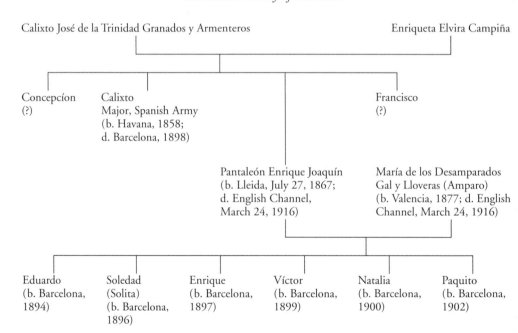

Calixto José de la Trinidad Granados y Armenteros

Enriqueta Elvira Campiña

Concepcíon
(?)

Calixto
Major, Spanish Army
(b. Havana, 1858;
d. Barcelona, 1898)

Francisco
(?)

Pantaleón Enrique Joaquín
(b. Lleida, July 27, 1867;
d. English Channel,
March 24, 1916)

María de los Desamparados
Gal y Lloveras (Amparo)
(b. Valencia, 1877; d. English
Channel, March 24, 1916)

Eduardo
(b. Barcelona,
1894)

Soledad
(Solita)
(b. Barcelona,
1896)

Enrique
(b. Barcelona,
1897)

Víctor
(b. Barcelona,
1899)

Natalia
(b. Barcelona,
1900)

Paquito
(b. Barcelona,
1902)

List of Works

This catalogue is an updated version of previous works lists, principally in *DME, NGD* (2d), and the Hess bio-bibliography. With Douglas Riva's assistance, the list below incorporates important revisions and additions, necessitated by recent discoveries as well as the publication of DLR and the impending publication of various orchestral and choral works, edited by Riva. Granados's oeuvre includes a considerable number of unpublished works and incomplete compositions. All works listed here as unpublished (unpub) are complete. Pieces catalogued as incomplete (inc) vary a great deal. While many of them lack only a few measures, others are sketches, consisting of only a few measures of music. Works of this latter type are listed separately under "Fragments." (Granados often supplied such sketches with complete titles, even sub-titles, occasionally including opus numbers and dedications.) Granados's use of opus numbers is inconsistent, and they do not tell us the order of composition or publication. Their only function is for identification. Each entry provides the title, information about the work (genre, structure, medium, text author), premiere, publication, and manuscript sources.

PUBLISHER ABBREVIATIONS

(archive abbreviations appear on p. xvii)

CD	Casa Dotesio (Barcelona)
CEM	Catalana d' Edicions Musicals (Barcelona)
DLR	De Larrocha/Riva edition (Barcelona: Editorial Boileau, 2002)
EB	Editorial Boileau (Barcelona)
EM	Éditions Mutuelle (Paris)
EMEC	Editorial de Música Española Contemporánea (Barcelona)
ES	Édicions Salabert (Paris)
GM	García Morante edition (Barcelona: Tritó, 1996)
GS	G. Schirmer (New York)
ICCMU	Instituto Complutense de Ciencias Musicales (Madrid)
JA	Juan Ayné (Barcelona)

JBP   J. B. Pujol (Barcelona)
LM   Llobet y Mas (Barcelona)
RG   R. Guardia (Barcelona)
RL   Rouart Lerolle (Paris)
UME   Unión Musical Española (Madrid)
VLB   Vidal Llimona y Boceta (Barcelona)

THEATRICAL

Blancaflor, incidental music, 1 act, A. Gual, prem 30-I-1899, Líric (Barcelona), unpub, location of MS score unknown.

La cieguecita de Betania (El portalico de Belén), chamber op, 1 act, G. Miró, private home (Vallcarca, Spain), 1914, unpub, MS, nd, Cdm.

Follet, op, 3 acts, A. Mestres, prem 4-IV-1903, Liceu (Barcelona), unpub, MS, vs, orch score, parts, nd, Cdm, MS, inc vs, Pml.

Gaziel, drama líric, 1 act, A. Mestres, prem 27-X-1906, Principal (Barcelona), unpub, MS, nd, Es.

Goyescas, op, 1 act, F. Periquet, prem 28-I-1916, Metropolitan Opera, New York, vs, GS, 1915, unpub orch score, MS lost, facs MS, Gs, MS, vs, nd, Hsa.

Liliana, poema escénica, 1 act, A. Mestres, prem 9-VII-1911, Palau de Belles Arts (Barcelona), unpub, MS, nd, Es, MS, orch sections only, Cdm.

María del Carmen, op, 3 acts, J. Feliu y Codina, prem 12-XI-1898, Parish (Madrid), 3 nos. ("Canción de la zagalica," "Malagueña murciana," "Canción cartagenera") pub Madrid, Pablo Martín, 1899, MS, orch score, inc, Ns, MS, orch score possibly revised by Eduardo Granados and F. Montserrat i Ayarbe, parts and vs in Sgae, copyist copy of inc vs, Lcw, MS, short score, Bn (revision pub Madrid, ICCMU, 2003).

Miel de la Alcarria, op. 54, incidental music, 3 acts, J. Feliu y Codina, prem 1895, unpub, MS, nd, Es, MS, orch parts only, Cdm.

Ovillejos o La gallina ciega, sainete lírico, 2 acts, inc, J. Feliu y Codina, 1897–8, MSS, Cdm, MS ("La gallina ciega"), 9-I-1914, Mm.

Petrarca, op, 1 act, inc, A. Mestres, 1899, unperf, unpub, MS, nd, Es.

Picarol, drama líric, 1 act, A. Mestres, prem 23-II-1901, Tívoli (Barcelona), unpub, MS, nd, Es.

Torrijos, incidental music, ICCMU, 2006, MS, nd, Ra.

ORCHESTRAL

Dante, op. 21 (1. L'entrada a l'infern, 2. Paolo e Francesa), 2. with mez sop, prem Palau de la Música Catalana (Barcelona), VI-1908, GS, 1915, ICCMU, 2006.

Danza gitana, cham orch, full orch, ICCMU (both versions), 2006, MS (cham orch), nd, Biblioteca March Servera de Palma de Mallorca, MS (full orch), orch parts only, Cdm.

Elisenda (1. El jardí d'Elisenda, 2. Trova, 3. Elisenda, 4. La tornada o Final), voice, pf, harp, str qnt, fl, ob, cl, text A. Mestres, prem 7-VII-1912, Sala Granados (Barcelona), ICCMU, 2006, MS, orch (mvmts 1,2), 1910, MS, orch (mvmts 1, 2, 3), 1912, Cdm, MSS, inc pf score, Oc, Mm, Cdm.

Intermezzo, from op *Goyescas*, prem 28-I-1916, Metropolitan, New York, GS, 1916, ICCMU, 2006, MSS, nd, Sa, Am.

Marcha de los vencidos, prem 31-X-1899, Barcelona, ICCMU, 2006, MS, nd, Cdm.

Navidad, cham orch (dbl qnt of winds, strings, pf) (from *La cieguecita de Betania*), prem 31-V-1916, Sociedad Nacional de Música (Madrid), unpub, MS, nd, Cdm.

La nit del mort (Poema desolación), ICCMU, 2006, MSS, nd, Cdm, Mm.

Suite árabe u oriental, inc, ICCMU, 2006, MS, nd, Cdm.

Suite sobre cantos gallegos, prem 31-X-1899, Barcelona, UME, nd, ICCMU, 2006.

Danza de los ojos verdes, prem 10-II-1916, Maxine Elliot Theater (New York), ICCMU, 2006, MS, nd, Cdm.

CHAMBER

Canto (Melodía), vc, included in *Álbum, París, 1888*, unpub, MS, Mm.

Danza española, No. 10, arr vln, pf, unpub, MS, vln part only, nd, Mm, MS score location unknown.

Danza gallega, from 2d mvmt of orch *Suite sobre cantos gallegos*, arr vc, pf, UME, 1971, MS ("*Danza No. XIII, de las escenas Gallegas*"), nd, Mm.

Escena religiosa, vln, org, pf, tim, unpub, MS, nd, Cdm.

Intermedios, Misa de boda de Dionisio Conde (1. Marcha, 2. Meditación), str qt, harp, org, unpub, MS, nd, Cdm.

Madrigal, vc, pf, prem 2-V-1915, Sala Granados (Barcelona), UME, nd, MS, nd, Mm.

Melodía, vln, pf, prem 21-VI-1903, Eldorado (Barcelona), unpub, MS lost.

Pequeña romanza, str qt, UME, 1975, MS, Ag.

Piano Quintet in G Minor, op. 49 (1. Allegro, 2. Allegretto cuasi andantino, 3. Molto presto), str qt, pf, prem 15-II-1895, Madrid, UME, 1973, EB, 2004, MS, str parts, nd, Cdm, MS, nd, Mm.

Piano Trio, op. 50 (1. Poco allegro con expresione, 2. Scherzetto (Vivace molto), 3. Duetto (Andante con molta espresione), 4. Finale (Allegro molto)), vln, vc, pf, prem 15-II-1895, Salón Romero (Madrid), UME, 1976, MS, 2-I-1894, Mm.

Romanza, vln, pf, UME, 1971, MS, nd, Mm.

Serenata, 2 vlns, pf, prem 4-IV-1914, Salle Pleyel (Paris), unpub, MS, inc (final page lost), nd, Mm.

Sonata, vln, pf, UME, 1971, MS, nd, Ag, also MS sketches for 3 more mvmts: *Scherzo, Intermedio, Final*, nd, Mm.

Tres Preludios (1. La góndola, 2. El toque de guerra, 3. Elevación), vln, pf, UME, 1971, MS, nd, Mm.

Trio, 2 vlns, vla, MS, parts only, nd, Cdm.

Trova, vc, pf (arr of 2d mvmt of *Elisenda*), prem 2-V-1915, Barcelona, unpub, MS, nd, Oc.

PIANO

A la antigua (Bourrée) [for the "Piano-pedalier Caetura"], JA, nd. DLR III:19

A la pradera, op. 35, UME, 1966, MS, nd, Mm. DLR III:24

A la cubana, op. 36 (1. Allegretto, 2. Un poco vivo), GS, 1914, MS, nd, Lcw. DLR V:14

Álbum: París, 1888 (1–4. 4 Melodías (1. Andantino, 2. Allegretto, 3. Mireya, 4. Cant del marino), 5–7. 3 Melodías (5. Kind im Einschlummern, 6. Parlant, 7. A Sara), 8–13. 6 Melodías (8. Pregant, 9. Enyorança, 10. Conte, 11. ¡¡Morta!!, 12. ¡. . .! (En el abanico de María de Alba), 13. Glückes genug), 14. 2ª Parte, 15. Passats, 16. Primavera (Romanza sin palabras), 17. ¿Beethoven?, 18. Coral (Cuatro voces), 19. Wagner (Melodrama), 20. Allegro vivace, 21. ¡Chopin. . .! (Mazurka), 22. Cuatro notas (Vals), 23. ¡Oh. . .!, 24. Andante (C Major), 25–27. Cantos orientales (25. La odalisca, 26. La esclava, 27. La esclava muerta), 28. En un álbum, 29. Preludio (F Major), 30. ¡En la playa!, 31. ¡Lejos de ti!, 32. Mazurka (F Major), 33. Mazurka (G Minor), 34. Mazurka (E-flat Major), 35. A Mercurio—A Baco, 36. Lección), *Mazurka* (E-flat Major)*, Keyboard Classics,* I-1985, MS, Mm. DLR III:1

Allegro appassionato, MS, nd, Mm. DLR IV:6

Allegro de concierto, prem IV-1904, Unión Musical (Madrid), UME, 1906, GS, 1916. DLR V:8

Andalucía (Petenera), MS, nd, Mm. DLR III:6

Andantino espressivo, UME, 1973, as *Estudio (andantino espressivo)*, MS ("Obras fáciles para educación del sentimiento"), nd, Mm. DLR IV:11

Aparición [for the "Piano-pedalier Caetura"], LM, nd. DLR III:18

Apariciones (1. Presto, 2. Vals mélodico [pub as No. 1 of the *Valses poéticos*], 3. ***** (Cadencioso), 4. Vals elegante [pub as No. 2 of the *Valses poéticos*], 5. ?. . ., 6. Ecos, 7. Fantasmas, 8. Sensitiva, 9. Pastoral, 10. ¡Fuera tristeza!, 11. Vals vienés, 12. Vals dramático, 13. Vals brillante [pub as No. 5 of the *Valses poéticos*], 14. Vals sentimental [pub as No. 6 of the *Valses poéticos*], 15. Andantino quasi allegretto), MS, nd, Mm. DLR VII:5

Arabesca, prem Líric (Barcelona), 20-IV-1890, *La ilustración musical hispano-americana* (Barcelona), c. 1890. DLR III:16

Balada, prem 15-II-1895, Salón Romero (Madrid), unpub, MS lost.

Barcarola, op. 45, UME, 1966, MS (not holograph), nd, Mm. DLR V:4

La berceuse, MS, nd, Mm. DLR III:9

Bocetos: Colección de obras fáciles (1. Despertar del cazador, 2. El hada y el niño, 3. Vals muy lento, 4. La campana de la tarde), prem 23-III-1913, Barcelona, UME (nos. 1–2), nd, 1918, CD (nos. 3–4), nd, MS, inc, nd, Mm. DLR IV:10

Canción árabe, UME, nd, pub with *Moresque*. DLR III:14

Canción morisca, *La ilustración moderna* (Barcelona), c. 1890. DLR III:15

Canto del pescador, MS, nd, Mm. DLR III:8

Capricho español, op. 39, JBP, nd, UME, 191? DLR V:1

Carezza, op. 38, JBP, nd. DLR VII:3

Cartas de amor (Valses íntimos), op. 44 (1. Cadencioso, 2. Suspirante, 3. Dolente, 4. Appassionato), *La ilustración musical hispano-americana* (Barcelona), nd, UME, nd, MS, nd, Mm, MS, inc, Yale University, Frederick R. Koch Collection. DLR VII:6

Clotilde (Mazurka), MS, nd, Am. DLR III:3

Crepúsculo (Goyescas), MS, nd, Mm. DLR II:2

Cuentos de la juventud, op. 1 (1. Dedicatoria, 2. La mendiga, 3. Canción de mayo, 4. Cuento viejo, 5. Viniendo de la fuente, 6. *****, 7. Recuerdos de la infancia, 8. El fantasma, 9. La huerfana, 10. Marcha), *Musical Emporium* (Barcelona), nd, UME, 1977, MS, nd, Mm. DLR IV:2

Dans le bois, MS, 1-VI-1888, Cdm, MS ("Ensayo"), nd, Ra. DLR III:11

Danza característica, UME, 1973, MS, nd, Mm. DLR I:1

Danza lenta, op. 37, prem 8-V-1915, Barcelona, GS, 1914, UME, 1966, MS, nd, Am. DLR I:6

Danzas españolas (1. Galante, 2. Oriental, 3. Fandango, 4. Villanesca, 5. Andaluza (Playera), 6. Rondalla aragonesa, 7. Valenciana, 8. Sardana, 9. Rómantica, 10. Melancólia, 11. Arabesca, 12. Bolero), prem Líric (Barcelona), 20-IV-1890, CD, c. 1890, UME, nd. DLR I:2

Dolora en La menor, prem 27-XI-1984, Madrid, CEM, 1982, MS, nd, Mm. DLR III:7

Dos impromptus (1. Vivo e appassinato, 2. Impromptu de la codorniz), UME, 1912. DLR V:6.1−2

Elvira (Mazurka), RG, nd. DLR III:2

Escenas infantiles (Miniaturas), op. 38 (1. Recitando, 2. Pidiendo perdón, 3. El niño duerme, 4. Niño que llora, 5. 7ª melodía), MS, nd, Mm. DLR IV:1

Escenas poéticas [1st series] (1. Berceuse, 2. Eva y Walter [sic], 3. Danza de la rosa), UME, 1912. DLR V:10

Escenas poéticas [2d series] (1. Recuerdo de países lejanos, 2. El ángel de los claustros, 3. Canción de Margarita, 4. Sueños del poeta), UME, 1923. DLR V:10

Escenas rómanticas (1. Mazurka, 2. Berceuse, 3. **** [Lento con estasi], 4. Allegretto (Mazurka), 5. Allegro appassionato, 6. Epílogo), prem 20-XI-1904, Unión Musical (Madrid), UME, 1930. DLR V:7

Estudio (Andantino expressivo), see *Andantino espressivo*.

Exquise…! (Vals tzigane), pub in unknown periodical, c. 1900, transcribed by M. Oltra from a performance by A. de Larrocha. DLR VII:7

Fantasía (Cheherazada), op. 34, inc, MS, 28-XII-1912, Mm. DLR V:11

La góndola (Escena poética) [for the "Piano-pedalier Caetura"], JA, nd, MS, nd, Liceu Conservatory. DLR III:25

Goyescas (Los majos enamorados) (Book I: 1. Los requiebros, 2. Coloquio en la reja, 3. El fandango de candil, 4. Quejas o La maja y el ruiseñor; Book II: 5. El amor y la muerte (Balada), 6. Epílogo (Serenata del espectro)), prem 11-III-1911, Palau de la Música Catalana (Barcelona), 2-IV-1914, Salle Pleyel (Paris), UME, 1912−14, MS, facs, Book I, Oc, 1911; Los requiebros, MS, inc, Am; Epílogo (Serenata del espectro), MS, 28-XII-1911, Oc, MS, inc, Mm. DLR II:4

L'himne dels morts, MS facs, *Revista musical catalana*, n150 (June 1916) (Barcelona). DLR V:5

Impromptu (Allegro assai), op. 39, GS, 1914, MS, nd, Am. DLR V:6.3

Intermezzo (from op *Goyescas*), arr pf, GS, 1916. DLR II:6

Jácara (Danza para cantar y bailar), op. 14, UME, 1973. DLR II:1

El jardí d'Elisenda, arr pf, 1st mvmt of suite of same title, UME, CD, 1913, MSS, inc, Oc, Cdm. DLR VI:2

Jota de Miel de la Alcarria, Hereu (Barcelona), 1897. DLR I:3

Libro de horas (1. En el jardín, 2. En invierno (La muerte del ruiseñor), 3. Al suplicio), prem 23-III-1913, Barcelona, UME, nd, MS, inc, nd, Mm. DLR V:12

Marcha real, MS, Xavier Turull Archive, Barcelona. DLR III:22

Marche militaire, op. 38, prem 31-X-1915, Barcelona, GS, 1914, MS, nd, Cdm. DLR III:23.1

Marchas militares (2), MS, nd, Cdm. DLR III:23.2–3

Mazurka (A Minor), op. 20, MS, nd, Mm. DLR III:5

Mazurka (alla polacca), *La ilustración moderna* (Barcelona), c. 1890. DLR III:4

Mazurka (alla polacca), op. 2, UME, 1973.

1ª Melodía (Jeunesse), MS, nd, Mm. DLR III:10.1

Melodía (Para el abanico de Laura González), MS, nd, Mm. DLR III:10.4

Melodía (Para el abanico de Lola González), MS, nd, Mm. DLR III:10.3

Melodía (2ª Melodía), MS, nd, Mm. DLR III:10.2

Minuetto [for the "Piano-pedalier Cateura"], LM, nd. DLR III:17

Moresque, UME, nd, pub with *Canción árabe*. DLR III:13

Oriental (Canción variada, Intermedio y Final), VLB, nd, UME, 1973. DLR I:5

Paisaje, op. 35, CD, nd, MS, nd, Oc. DLR V:13

Países soñados (El palacio encantado en el mar), UME, nd, pub with *Bocetos*, MS, inc, nd, Mm. DLR V:9

Parranda-Murcia, inc, MS, nd, Mm. DLR I:4

Pastoral, *Mundial musical* (Valencia), 191? DLR III:12

El pelele (Escena goyesca), prem Escola Choral (Terassa, Spain), 29-III-1914, GS, 1915, MS, nd, Mm. DLR II:5

Preludio (D Major), op. 30, MS, nd, Mm. DLR IV:12

Rapsodía aragonesa, VLB, 1901. DLR V:3

Reverie-Improvisation, Clavier (Evanston, Illinois), 1967, transcribed by H. Levine and S. Randlett from an improvisation recorded by Granados for the Aeolian Company, New York, 1916. DLR II:7

Sardana, op. 37, GS, 1914. DLR I:7

Seis estudios expresivos en forma de piezas fáciles (1. Tema, Variaciones y Finale, 2. Allegro moderato, 3. El caminante, 4. Pastoral, 5. La última pavana, 6. María (Romanza sin palabras)), UME, nd, MS (no. 6), nd. Am. DLR IV:5

Seis piezas sobre cantos populares españolas (Preludio, 1. Añoranza, 2. Ecos de la parranda, 3. Vascongada, 4. Marcha oriental, 5. Zambra, 6. Zapateado), UME, 1930, MS (no. 1), nd, Mm. DLR V:2

Serenata Amparo, MS, 20-V-1893, Mm. DLR III:20

Serenata española, prem Líric (Barcelona), 20-IV-1890, unpub, MS location unknown.

Serenata goyesca, MS, nd, Mm. DLR II:3

Siete estudios (1. A Major, 2. F-sharp Minor, 3. E Major, 4. D-flat Major, 5. G Major, 6. C-sharp Major, 7. B-flat Major), MS, nd, Mm. DLR IV:4

La sirena (Vals Mignone), *La ilustración moderna* (Barcelona), c. 1890, also pub *Keyboard Classics* (Katonah, New York), 12-XI-1989. DLR VII:2

Los soldados de cartón (Marcha), *La ilustración moderna* (Barcelona), c. 1890, UME, 1973, MS, nd, Mm. DLR III:21

Valse de concert, op. 35, GS, 1914. DLR VII:9

Valses poéticos (Introducción: Vivace molto, 1. Vals melódico, 2. Vals apasionado, 3. Vals lento, 4. Vals humorístico, 5. Vals brillante, 6. Vals sentimental, 7. Vals mariposa, 8. Vals ideal), prem Salón Romero (Madrid), 15-II-1895, UME, nd, MS, nd, Mm. DLR VII:8

Valses sentimentales (1. "Mis lloros y añoranzas eran cantos tristes," 2. Andante, 3. "Nos habíamos apasionado mutuamente," 4. "¡No había ya más que tristeza donde faltara ella!" 5. Allegro appassionato, 6. Andantina amoroso, 7. Allegro pastoral en forma de vals, 8. Sentimentale, 9. Dolente, 10. Allego final), MS, nd, Mm. DLR VII:4

PIANO ENSEMBLE

Dos marchas militares, UME, nd. DLR VIII:2
En la aldea (1. Salida del sol, 2. Maitines, 3. El cortejo (Marcha nupcial), 4. La oración, 5. Regreso (Marcha nupcial), 6. Canto recitado, 7. La siesta, 8. Danza pastoril, 9. Final, 10. La puesta del sol), prem Conservatorio Municipal de Música (Barcelona), 3-IV-1984, inc in *Álbum: París, 1888*, MS, Mm. DLR VIII:1

VOICE AND PIANO

Balada, unpub, MS, inc, nd, Mm.
La boira, prem Sala Chaissaigne (Barcelona), 13-II-1902, GM, MS, 1-II-1900, Mm.
Canción, GM, MS, inc, nd, Mm.
Canción del postillón, GS, 1916.
Canciones amatorias (1.Mira que soy niña, 2. Mañanica era, 3. Serranas de Cuenca [text L. de Góngora], 4. Gracia mía (En vuestros verdes ojuelos nos mostráis vuestro valor), 5. Descúbrase el pensamiento, 6. Lloraba la niña (¡Llorad, corazón, que tenéis razón!) [text L. de Góngora], 7.No lloréis, ojuelos [text L. de Vega]), prem Sala Granados (Barcelona), 5-IV-1915, UME, 1962, GM. Mira que soy nina, MS (marked "Romancero general—anónimo"), 24-III-1915, Am, another MS of same, 11-X-1914, Ag; Gracia mía, MS, by copyist with holograph annotations and corrections, nd, Mm; Descúbrase el pensamiento, MS, 21-III-1915, Am; Lloraba la niña, MS, nd, Mm.
Canço d'amor (from *Boires baixes*), text J. M. Roviralta, CD, 1902, GM.
Cançó de Gener, inc, Catalan text, GM, MS, nd, Mm.
Cançoneta (Dorm nineta), op. 51, text A. Mestres, GM, MS, nd, Mm.
Cantar I, GM. Same as *Día y noche Diego ronda*.
Canto gitano, UME, nd, GM.
El cavaller s'en va a la guerra, text A. Mestres, unpub, MS, lost.
Día y noche Diego ronda (also pub as *Madrigal*, vc, pf), unpub, MS, nd, Ag.
Elegía eterna, text A. Mestres, prem 10-VI-1914, Barcelona, UME, 1962, GM.
L'ocell profeta (Canço del poeta; Lieders), text Comtessa de Castellà, prem 22-VI-1911, Barcelona, UME, 1972, GM, MS (not holograph), nd, Cdm.
Mignon, French text, unpub, MS, nd, Mm.
Por una mirada, un mundo, text G. A. Bécquer, GM, MS (not holograph), nd, Mm.
El rey y'l juglar, inc, text A. Mestres, MS, nd, Ag.
Serenata, GM.
Si al Retiro me llevas (Tonadilla), text "autor desconocido del siglo XVIII," UME, 1971, GM.
Tonadillas (en estilo antiguo) (1. Amor y odio, 2. Callejeo, 3. El majo discreto, 4. El majo olvidado, 5. El majo tímido, 6. El mirar de la maja, 7. El tralalá y el punteado, 8. La maja de Goya, 9-10-11. La maja dolorosa (Nos.1-3), 12. Las currutacas modestas), text F. Periquet, prem Palau de la Música Catalana (Barcelona), 10-VI-1914, UME,

1912, GM. El majo tímido, MS, nd, Oc; El tralalá y el punteado, MS (not holograph), nd, Mm; La maja de Goya, MS ("La maja desnuda," signed by Granados and Periquet), nd, Bc; La maja dolorosa, No. 2, MS, nd, Oc.
Yo no tengo quien me llore, GM.

CHORAL

Cant de les estrelles, chor, pf, org, prem Palau de la Música Catalana (Barcelona), 11-III-1911, EB, 2006, MS (chor, org), nd, Oc, MS (pf), nd, Ra.

L'herba de amor (Pregaría en estil gregoriá), chor, org, Catalan text, UME, 1971, MS, 27-II-1914, Montserrat Monastery Archive.

Salve regina, op. 1, no. 1, chor, org, Latin text, unpub, MS, 13-III-1896, Ag.

PEDAGOGICAL

Breves consideraciones sobre el ligado, MS, nd, Am. DLR IV:14

Dificultades especiales del piano (1. Dificultad del cuarto y cinco dedo, 2. Escalas y arpeggios con cambio del primero y cinco dedo, 3. Elasticidad del cuarto y cinco dedo), MS, nd, Mm. DLR IV:7

Ejercicios de terceras, MS, nd, Mm. DLR IV:9

Método, teórico-práctico, para el uso de los pedales del piano, VLB, 1905, UME, 1954. DLR IV:15

Ornamentos, MS, nd, Am. DLR IV:8

El piano, MS, nd, Mm. DLR IV:3

Reglas para el uso de los pedales del piano, unpub printer's proof, Barcelona, IX-1913, Mm, MS, nd, Mm. DLR IV:16

Sobre la 1ª y 2ª Conferencia del Maestro Granados (1913), MS (notes on the lectures, but not by Granados), nd, Am. DLR IV:13

ARRANGEMENTS, TRANSCRIPTIONS, AND EDITIONS

Azulejos (I. Albéniz), completed by Granados, prem Palau de la Música Catalana (Barcelona), 11-III-1911, EM, 1911, UME, 1947, MS, 25-V-1910, Cdm. DLR VI:3

Chorale (J. S. Bach), arr cham orch, unpub, MS, nd, Cdm.

Concerto, op. 21 (Chopin), re-orch of 1st mvmt, prem Sociedad de Conciertos Clásicos (Barcelona), 11-XI-1900, MS, inc, nd, Ag.

Fugue in C-sharp Minor (J. S. Bach), str, fl, ob, cl, bsn, trpt, tromb, prem Líric (Barcelona), 15-V-1900, unpub, MS, nd, Cdm.

Jota aragonesa (A. Noguéra y Balaguer), arr pf, orch, prem 3-V-1904, Barcelona, unpub, MS, nd, Cdm.

Momento musical (Schubert), edition, unpub, MS, nd, Ag.

Triana (I. Albéniz), arr 2 pf, EB, 1990, MS, nd, Am. DLR VIII:3

26 Sonatas (D. Scarlatti) (K. 520, 521, 522, 518, 541, 540, 102, 546, 190, 110, 534, 535, 553, 555, 554, 547, 109, 211, 552, 537, 528, 139, 48, 536; two not by Scarlatti: No. 10 in A Major

by Francisco Courcelle, and No. 13 in E Major by anon.), arr pf, prem Principal
(Barcelona), 1-III-1906, VLB, 1905, UME, 1967, MS, inc, nd, Mm. DLR VI:1

Sonatinas, op. 36, Nos. 1–4 (Clementi), arr str trio, unpub, MS, 3-IV-1891, Cdm.

Vuelos de la romería, from *Suite vasca* (Padre Menesio Otaño), arr, pf, unpub, MS, nd,
Cdm.

FRAGMENTS

Álbum: París 1888, pf (1. Vivo, 2. Marcha oriental, 3. Para el abanico de la Srta X), Mm.

El amor de la Virgen, pf, MS, nd, Ag.

El amor del majo, voice, pf, MS ("Apuntes y temas para mis obras"), nd, Mm.

Andante, vln, pf, MS, nd, Ag.

Boires baixes, sym poem after Roviralta, MS, c. 1901, Am.

Chanson pastorale, pf, MS, nd, Ag.

Concerto, pf, orch, MSS, nd, Cdm, Mm.

Concerto (Allegro serio), vc, orch, MS, nd, Mm.

Contemplación, pf, MS, nd, Ag.

Epílogo (from *Goyescas*), arr vc, pf, MS, nd, Ag.

Galicia (Gallegada), MS, nd, Ag.

Impresiones de viaje (Hacia París: Ante la tumba de Napoleón), pf, MS, VII-1912, Ag.

Llegenda de la fada, orch, vocal soloists, MS, nd, Cdm.

Malagueña muriciana, pf, MS, nd, Ag.

Marcha fúnebra, pf, MS, nd, Ag.

Melopea, stage work, Catalan text, MS, nd, Am.

Minuetto de la felicidad, MS, nd, Ag.

Recuerdo a la memoria de mi padre, MS, nd, Ag.

Romeo y Julieta, 2 pf, MS ("Poema"), nd, Am.

Rosamor, stage work, MS, nd, Am.

Seguidillas manchegas, pf, MS, nd, Ag.

Sinfonia (E Minor), MS, nd, Cdm, MS, pf score (2 mvmts), 17-VIII-1912, Ag.

Sonata, vc, pf, MS, nd, Ag.

SPURIOUS

Dos Gavotas (Gavottes from J. S. Bach, *English Suite*, BWV 811, in D Minor), UME, 1971.

NOTES

PRELUDIO

1. Cayetano Luca de Tena, "Pequeña historia del año 1891," *Blanco y Negro* 79 (November 1, 1969): 63. It is true that this sentiment reflects the pro-bourgeois ideology of the Franco era during which the article was written, but that does not invalidate the observation. Dahlhaus makes the crucial point that aristocrats continued to play a major role in music during the 1800s. In particular, they sponsored private concerts featuring leading musicians such as Beethoven, Chopin, and Liszt. Bavarian King Ludwig II's patronage of Wagner was of decisive importance. See Carl Dahlhaus, *Nineteenth-Century Music*, trans. J. Bradford Robinson (Berkeley: University of California Press, 1989), 49.

2. Robert Hughes, *The Shock of the New* (New York: Alfred A. Knopf, 1996), 373.

3. See the exhibition catalogue by Juan J. Luna and Priscilla E. Muller, *De Goya a Zuloaga: la pintura española de los siglos XIX y XX en The Hispanic Society of America* (Madrid: BBVA, 2000).

4. There were more newspapers in Madrid than in London, but they tended to be much smaller. Salvador de Madariaga attributed this to "the individualism of the Spaniard, which, by preventing amalgamation and stimulating individual initiative, leads to a large number of small newspapers." See his *Spain: A Modern History* (New York: Frederick A. Praeger, 1958), 96–97.

5. See Walter Aaron Clark, *Isaac Albéniz: Portrait of a Romantic* (Oxford: Oxford University Press, 1999; paperback, 2002).

6. E. Inman Fox notes that in the late nineteenth century, Spain was still in "transition between a proto-industrial economic structure and industrialization." The educational system was antiquated, and over 50 percent of the population was illiterate. See his "Spain as Castile: Nationalism and National Identity," in *The Cambridge Companion to Modern Spanish Culture*, ed. David T. Gies (Cambridge: Cambridge University Press, 1999), 21.

7. As Benedict Anderson points out, the mid-nineteenth century in Europe witnessed a dramatic increase in the size and budgets of state bureaucracies, both civil and military, "despite the absence of any major local wars." The increase in Spain was 25 percent. See his *Imagined Communities: Reflections on the Origin and Spread of Nationalism*, rev. ed. (London: Verso, 1991), 76.

8. Guillermo de Boladeres Ibern, *Enrique Granados: Recuerdos de su vida y estudio crítico de su obra por su antiguo discípulo* (Barcelona: Editorial Arte y Letras, 1921), 37–38.

9. Lionel Salter, "Spain: A Nation in Turbulence," in *The Late Romantic Era: From the Mid-19th Century to World War I*, ed. Jim Samson (Englewood Cliffs, NJ: Prentice Hall, 1991), 151–52, provides a capable summary of this history. His description of Sorolla and Zuloaga as "only minor figures," however, is incorrect. An excellent overview of Spanish history and culture dur-

ing the nineteenth century is available in Mary Vincent and R. A. Stradling, *Cultural Atlas of Spain and Portugal* (Abingdon: Andromeda Oxford, 1995), 121–46.

10. See Gerald Brenan, *The Spanish Labyrinth: The Social and Political Background of the Spanish Civil War* (Cambridge: Cambridge University Press, 1943/reprint 2001), xviii. As Brenan points out (p. xvi): "The main political problem has therefore always been how to strike a balance between an effective central government and the needs of the local autonomy."

11. See Albert Balcells, *Cataluña contemporánea, 1900–1936* (Madrid: Siglo XXI de España Editores, 1974), 10–11, for a summary of the conflict in the context of Catalan politics, with relevant historical documentation (pp. 77–83).

12. Such interventions did not begin with Prim. During the reign of Fernando VII, army officers under the leadership of General Rafael del Riego y Núñez (1785–1823) rose up in 1820 against their monarch in defense of the Constitution of 1812, which Fernando detested. Liberalism prevailed for three years, until the French invasion of 1823 restored Fernando's power and cost the general his life. See Raymond Carr, *Spain 1808–1975*, 2d ed. (Oxford: Clarendon Press, 1982), 129–46. After Fernando's death, the Spanish army continued to intervene periodically in the country's political life.

13. Ann Livermore, "Granados and the Nineteenth Century in Spain," *Musical Review* 7 (1946): 81.

14. For a useful overview of the Spanish economy in the 1800s, see Gabriel Tortella, *The Development of Modern Spain: An Economic History of the Nineteenth and Twentieth Centuries* (Cambridge, Mass.: Harvard University Press, 2000), 1–21. Tortella points out that the other "Euro-Latin" countries of Portugal and Italy experienced similar difficulties.

15. Industrialization was confined to a few urban centers in Catalonia and the Basque region. Most of the country remained underdeveloped, and its "backward economy [continued to be] dominated by an undynamic agrarian sector employing roughly two-thirds of the labour force." The 1898 war nearly bankrupted the treasury and greatly impeded development, though in the long run it relieved Spain of costly colonial burdens. See Joseph Harrison, "Introduction: The Historical Background to the Crisis of 1898," in *Spain's 1898 Crisis: Regenerationism, Modernism, Post-colonialism*, ed. Joseph Harrison and Alan Hoyle (Manchester: Manchester University Press, 2000), 1–3.

16. The Universal Exposition of 1888 was a deliberate attempt on the city's part to present itself to the world as "an independent, prosperous and industrially strong urban centre with its eyes on the future." See Marilyn McCully's Introduction to *Homage to Barcelona: The City and Its Art, 1888–1936* (London: Arts Council of Great Britain, 1985), 16.

17. See Xosé Aviñoa, "Barcelona, del wagnerismo a la generación de la República," in *España en la música de Occidente: Actas del Congreso Internacional celebrado en Salamanca 29 de octubre – 5 de noviembre de 1985*, Vol. 2 (Madrid: Ministerio de Cultura, 1987), 324–34.

18. Francesc Bonastre, "Barcelona," *DME*, 230.

19. A detailed study of musical periodicals in Spain during this period is available in Jacinto Torres, *Las publicaciones periódicas musicales en España (1812–1990): Estudio crítico-bibliográfico* (Madrid: Instituto de Bibliografía Musical, 1991).

20. According to Pierre Vilar, *Spain: A Brief History*, trans. J. B. Tate (Oxford: Oxford University Press, 1967), 76, "The Castilian [saw] only the abrupt, money-grubbing, petty-minded Catalan; the Catalan on the other hand the proud and lazy Castilian. . . . leading to unbridgeable mistrust, in which language was the rallying point and history an arsenal of arguments." Mark Larrad, "The Catalan Theatre Works of Enrique Granados" (Ph.D. diss., University of Liverpool, 1992), 67, aptly remarks that "the Catalan feeling of economic superiority to the rest of Spain fostered an acute sense of social and cultural superiority."

21. See the entry on Verdaguer in the *Gran enciclopèdia catalana* (Barcelona: Gran Enciclopèdia Catalana, 1986), as well as the essay by Ricard Torrents, "Verdaguer, culmainació i con-

tradicció de la Renaixença," in *La Renaixenca, cicle de conferencies fet a la Institució cultural del CIC de Terrassa, curs 1982/83* (Barcelona: Publicaciones de l'Abadia de Montserrat, 1986), 39–50. Verdaguer's major poem was *L'Atlantida*, later the basis for a work by Manuel de Falla.

22. From a letter cited in Pablo Vila San-Juan, *Papeles íntimos de Enrique Granados* (Barcelona: Amigos de Granados, 1966), 78.

23. Quoted in Antonio Fernández-Cid, program notes for *Ciclo La obra pianística de Enrique Granados, octubre/noviembre 1991* (Albacete: Junta de Comunidades de Castilla-La Mancha, 1991), 17. "[F]iel a sí mismo."

24. José Ortega y Gasset, *Papeles sobre Velázquez y Goya*, 2d ed., rev., ed. Paulino Garagorri (Madrid: Alianza Editorial, 1987), 328. He made this observation in relation to Goya's artistic personality, but it applies equally well to Goya's admirer Granados.

25. Felipe Pedrell, "La personalidad artística de Granados," in his series *Quincenas musicales*, *La vanguardia*, probably 1916 [undated clipping in the Am]. "[P]oeta que podía decir, como Rubén Darío, que su poesia era 'suya en él', y sostener la primera condición de su existir porque vivió en un intenso amor á lo absoluto de la belleza."

26. Francisco Márquez Villanueva, "Literary Background of Enrique Granados," paper read at the "Granados and *Goyescas*" Symposium, Harvard University, January 23, 1982.

27. Hélène Reibold, "Enrique Granados," *La vie musicale* 7 (May 1914): 133, remarks that "the Catalans call Granados 'our poet of the piano'" ("les Catalans appellent Granados 'nuestro poeta del piano'").

28. Conchita Badia, "Granados: A Personal Portrait," *Recorded Sound*, n77 (January 1980): 57–58.

29. Lluís Millet, "Granados," *Revista musical catalana* 13 (1916): 187. "[U]n poètic sentiment elegiac."

30. Felip Pedrell, "La personalitat artística d'En Granados," *Revista musical catalana* 13 (1916): 173. "[A]nima genial i poètica."

31. J. Ma. Corredor, *Conversations with Casals*, trans. André Mangeot (New York: E. P. Dutton, 1956), 165.

32. Boladeres Ibern, *Granados*, 27–28; 173.

33. From "De mi cartera," in Betty Jean Craige, trans., *Selected Poems of Antonio Machado* (Baton Rouge: Louisiana State University Press, 1978), 99.

1. A BORN PIANIST

1. Lérida in Castilian. See the entry on Lleida in the *Gran enciclopèdia catalana* (1986 ed.).

2. The records of his military service survive in the Agm, legajo G-3864.

3. This is according to his 1829 petition requesting that Calixto be admitted, at age 5, to the corps of cadets, which he finally joined in 1830. The records of Manuel's military service survive in the Agm, legajo G-3878.

4. According to Natalia Granados, the composer's daughter, in an interview with Del Arco, "Mano a mano: Natalia Granados," *La vanguardia española*, January 22, 1957, 14, Calixto's ancestors came from nearby Asturias. As yet we have no documentation of this. A *granado* is also a pomegranate tree.

5. See Alberto y Arturo García Carraffa, *Diccionario heráldico y genealógico de apellidos españoles y americanos*, Vol. 39: *Gorriz–Guil* (Salamanca: Imprenta Comercial Salamanca, 1931).

6. The information about Calixto's ancestry and that of his wife comes from the records of his military service.

7. This was published on the front page of the Lleida newspaper *La mañana* in 1956 (clipping in the Mm, fons Granados), on the occasion of a festival marking both the 40th anniversary of his death and then continuing into the following year to celebrate the 90th anniversary

of his birth. The headlines fairly blared the news: "Granados was a Leridan. Here is irrefutable proof: the baptismal certificate." ("Granados, Leridano. He aquí la prueba irrebatible: la certificación de bautismo.") Even though there had never been any doubt about it, given the suppression of Catalan culture by the Franco regime, this was not an insignificant detail to local residents, and it merited repetition. The certificate was found by one Blas Mola Pinto in the archive of the Vicariato General Castrense in Madrid. Granados maintained a close relationship with Lleida throughout his life.

8. In an interview with a certain J.C., "Memòria d'Enric Granados," *Revista musical catalana* 4/33–34 (July–August 1987), 11, Granados's son-in-law, Antoni Carreras i Verdaguer, said that Granados used Catalan in Barcelona but "most often spoke Castilian."

9. This policy is located among his papers in the Mm, fons Granados.

10. This letter is in the Bc, Epistolario Albéniz, sig. M. 986.

11. We learn the names of Enrique's siblings from the death certificate for the elder Calixto, dated June 24, 1882, and located in the Registro Civil in Barcelona (on p. 83 of the register for that year in the Concepción parish). This also gives the age of his wife at that time (46).

12. The records of the younger Calixto's military service are in the Agm, legajo G-3865. They indicate that he was highly rated in character and knowledge of military science. He also spoke French and could translate English. In 1876 he was awarded the Medal of Alfonso XII, and two years later, the White Cross (first class). Most of his career was spent in northeastern Spain.

13. Antonio Fernández-Cid, *Granados* (Madrid: Samarán Ediciones, 1956), 170, 173.

14. See Vila San-Juan, *Papeles íntimos*, 49. The diary was not originally part of the family archive. In an interview that appeared in *Diario de Barcelona*, January 29, 1957, by "Sempronio," Natalia Granados said, "These are his memoirs, just given to me by an old student. I confess I did not know of their existence." Several pages were obviously ripped from it, and their contents are unknown. The diary itself is now missing, and no one seems to know where it is—or more exactly, whoever does know is not telling.

15. Vila San-Juan, *Papeles íntimos*, 50–51. In this same discussion Granados digresses to express his opinion of Barcelona's most recent architecture. He refers to the many buildings he does not approve of as "a palpable demonstration of the epidemic of architects from which we suffer. In our city architecture has suffered many setbacks. . . . The creation of neo-styles has been a plague." Was this a reference to the buildings of Gaudí and Domènech i Montaner? Such observations would seem to speak to Granados's deeply conservative nature.

16. Vila San-Juan, *Papeles íntimos*, 53. Commentators such as A. L. Mason and Ann Livermore have speculated about the ethnic origins of Granados's mother and the possible influence of her lullabies and folk songs on the composer's style, especially in his manner of ornamentation and elaborated repetition of themes. As we know, she was from Santander and not Galicia, as the aforementioned authors thought. But in the diary we can get some clarity regarding this issue. Nowhere does he mention his mother's singing, yet the songs Rosa sang to him made an impression somewhere between the grotesque and ludicrous. As for ornamentation and elaboration, there is little in his works with a folkloric character that could not just as easily have come from Chopin and Liszt.

17. Vila San-Juan, *Papeles íntimos*, 55.

18. According to Francisco Baldello, *La vanguardia española*, September 20, 1966, this was a religious institution founded in the eighteenth century. He asserts that Granados's early training there "exerted a positive influence on his moral formation." This may be claiming too much, but such a notion was consistent with the journalistic tenor of the Franco years.

19. This appears in a review of his 1890 concert at the Líric, in L.M., "Enrique Granados y Campiña," *Ilustración musical* 3/59 (1890): 282–83. It seems credible because it is close in time to the events it relates, and the information probably came straight from Granados, who was not prone to dissimulation about himself.

20. Vila San-Juan, *Papeles íntimos*, 55.

21. Ibid., 56.

22. This discussion of Pujol is indebted to Mònica Pagès i Santacana, *Acadèmia Granados-Marshall: 100 anys d'escola pianística a Barcelona*, in Catalan, Spanish, and English (Barcelona: Acadèmia Marshall, 2000), 145.

23. Mark R. Hansen, "The Pedagogical Methods of Enrique Granados and Frank Marshall: An Illumination of Relevance to Performance Practice and Interpretation in Granados's *Escenas románticas*" (DMA lecture-recital, University of North Texas, 1988), 1.

24. Quoted in Albert McGrigor, "The Catalan Piano School," liner notes for *The Catalan Piano Tradition*, Catalog No. IPA 109 (International Piano Archives. New York: Desmar, 1970).

25. Vila San-Juan, *Papeles íntimos*, 56.

26. The following year Granados performed Gottschalk's *Bamboula!* at the competition for the ceremony during which prizes were awarded. He was not a contestant.

27. Corredor, *Conversations with Casals*, 164. Casals qualified this encomium somewhat: "He made me think of Chopin. Chopin as I imagined he was: nervy, delicate, listless, ailing, not a great worker but a born pianist. He could tackle any of the big works written for piano, and would improvise passages to avoid working at them."

28. To be sure, Calixto, Jr.'s records suggest an earlier date for this Olot assignment, from 1879 to late 1880; thereafter, he was assigned to Vilafranca del Panedés. In 1882 the younger Calixto got married. There are two possible explanations for this. One is that Granados's recollection that his father died only two months after the family's return from Olot was mistaken. The other is that Calixto, Jr., was in Olot in 1882 on a temporary basis.

29. All this information is provided in the death certificate at the Registro Civil cited earlier. Until now, the exact date of his death was unknown.

30. Vila San-Juan, *Papeles íntimos*, 55, 66.

31. His funeral arrangements are listed in the Registro de Defunciones, 1882, 24:131, no. 5047, housed at the Serveis Funeraris in Barcelona. Calixto was buried in niche 2 of island C3, a space owned by one Patricia Mesanza. The Granados family rented this space from Mesanza, and when they could no longer make the payments, the remains were removed. Today the niche is unmarked and, apparently, empty. The only living beings that visit it now are the resident pigeons and cats, along with the occasional stray musicologist.

32. A copy of this play is in the Mm, fons Granados. Granados may well have had it in mind as a possible basis for a stage work, but nothing ever came of this.

33. See the "Café" entry in the *Gran enciclopèdia catalana* (1986 ed.).

34. Vila San-Juan, *Papeles íntimos*, 67.

35. Ibid., 65–66.

36. Ibid., 66.

37. Granados's account of these jobs is in ibid., 66.

38. Reviewed in an untitled article in *Diario de Barcelona*, April 10, 1886, 4202.

39. See Boladeres Ibern, *Granados*, 30.

40. Amadeu Vives, "N'Enric Granados i l'edat d'or: Evocació," *Revista musical catalana* 13 (1916): 175–76.

41. Boladeres Ibern, *Granados*, 19.

42. By coincidence, Bériot died in the same year as Granados. His impact on the Catalan piano tradition had been great, and F. Lliurat wrote an admiring memorial to him in "Necrología," *Revista musical catalana* 13 (1916): 139–40.

43. See his account of the illness and recovery in Vila San-Juan, *Papeles íntimos*, 69–70.

44. Oddly, the works of Granados rarely appeared on his programs, perhaps because he was drawn to the avant-garde and found his friend's works too conservative. However, he did introduce Parisians to the *Danzas españolas* at a concert of the Société Nationale on June 9, 1904.

And he performed selections from *Goyescas* in San Sebastián (1916) and Milan (1919); "El fandango de candil" bears a dedication to him. See Montserrat Bergadà, Màrius Bernadó, and Nina Gubisch-Viñes, *Ricart Viñes i Roda (1875–1943): testimoni d'un temps* (Lleida: Col·lecció La Banqueta, 1996), 48, and Elaine Brody, "Viñes in Paris: New Light on Twentieth-Century Performance Practice," in *A Musical Offering: Essays in Honor of Martin Bernstein*, ed. Edward H. Clinkscale and Claire Brook (New York: Pendragon Press, 1977), 59.

45. Ricardo Viñes, "Granados íntimo: recuerdos de su estancia en Paris," *Revista musical hispano-americana* (1916): 2–6. The diary was in the possession of the late musicologist Elaine Brody, but its present whereabouts are unknown.

46. See Brody, "Viñes in Paris," 47.

47. Viñes, "Recuerdos," 3. "Todos los días despertaba yo a Granados, que era algo tardío en levantarse y pasaba buena parte de la mañana bostezando y desperezandose antes de deciderse a saltar de la cama, pero que una vez á su trabajo, trabajaba muy de versa y con ardorosísimo afán."

48. Viñes, "Recuerdos," 5. "[C]onstituyeron, meses y meses, nuestro cotidiano espiritual alimento. Los recitábamos de coro a todas horas, y Granados, inspirándose en algunos de ellos, puso felizmente en música . . . aquella tan sencilla, pero vehemente cuarteta: Por una mirada un mundo; / Por una sonrísa un cielo; / Por un beso . . . ¡yo no sé / Qué te diera por un beso!" Granados's setting is in Enrique Granados, *Integral de l'obra per a veu i piano,* ed. Manuel García Morante (Barcelona: Trító, 1996).

49. Viñes, "Recuerdos," 6. "'¿Recuerdas aquellos años?'—nos dimos al fin casi a un tiempo. Y fué todo."

50. Reprinted in *Ilustración musical hispano americana* on September 22, 1889, 144.

51. L.M., "Enrique Granados y Campiña," 283. "Granados será de los buenos artistas que buscarán siempre el aplauso en el arte puro, sin relumbrones ni concesiones culpables."

52. C. Cuspinera, "Enrique Granados," *Diario de Barcelona,* April 22, 1890, 5075–76. "Como pianista es el tipo de la elegancia y del sentimiento. Sin esfuerzos gimnásticos de esos que adoptan á menudo algunos concertistas para singularizarse, arranca del piano los sonidos que convienen a su antojo, sirviendose de un mecanismo que se lo permite todo."

53. Granados did not have to contend at all with a hostile public or press, but he did have to struggle with a horrible instrument, "a piece of junk [verdadero cascajo]," as reported in *Diario de Barcelona,* April 12, 1892, 5500.

54. Vila San-Juan, *Papeles íntimos,* 80.

55. Ibid., 81.

56. This document is in the Archivo del Obispado in Barcelona. We learn from it that Granados had been living in the parish of Santa María de Jesús de Gracia since May and that before that he had resided for fifteen years in the Concepción parish.

57. Registro de Matrimonios, 1892, no. 1913, in the Arxiu Administratiu de la Ciutat in Barcelona.

58. In the interview that appeared in *Diario de Barcelona,* January 29, 1957, by "Sempronio." "Padre de seis hijos, tuvo la fortuna de verse asistido por una esposa fuerte, amorosa, perfecta ama de casa y entusiasta compañera del artista, . . . los discípulos, que le veneraban, formaban como una prolongación de la familia."

59. Fernández-Cid, *Granados,* 70.

60. Mary Nash, *Defying Male Civilization: Women in the Spanish Civil War* (Denver: Arden Press, 1995), 10–11. Ian Gibson provides the reason for this diminished status: "Etched deep into the Spanish unconscious, male and female, is the belief that women are inferior to men, second-rate citizens." See his *Fire in the Blood: The New Spain* (London: Faber and Faber, 1992), 85.

61. Cited in Luca de Tena, "Pequeña historia," 59.

62. These letters are in the Am, and I leave them unedited for punctuation (Granados ignored accents, but otherwise his writing was always precise and correct). It is not clear where

or under what circumstances they were written, though it is likely he wrote them from Madrid during late 1894 and early 1895, as he makes a reference to completing the Piano Trio he premiered at that time. The second is dated simply "Dia 2" but does make reference to his having just jotted down two popular songs. There is also a reference to an "establecimiento de aguas minero-medicinales." Possibly he was at a spa "taking the waters" for some ailment. "Cielo querido de mi alma: T'adoro con toda mi alma vida de mi vida . . . ¡Te quiero tanto! ¡Te acuerdas de mi todos momentos como yo lo hago? Piensas mucho en tu Enrique? Le quieres mucho? Pienso mucho en mi cielo, pienso que te quiero mas que a mi vida. Que rico es tener el carino de una Titin." "Estoy esperando la alegria de recibir una carta tuya, amor! La devorare con los ojos y con el corazon. . . . Todavia me doy ahora mas cuenta de lo feliz que soy a tu lado."

63. Cited in Fernández-Cid, *Granados*, 78.

64. According to his diary entry in Vila San-Juan, *Papeles íntimos*, 73.

65. Cited in Andrés Ruiz Tarazona, *Enrique Granados: El último romántico* (Madrid: Real Musical, 1975), 23.

66. In a letter to Pedrell from this period (Bc, Epistolario Pedrell, M. 964), he reports meeting Albéniz in Madrid and describes a trip to the Escorial, which impressed him with its "grandeza." He also mentions the rehearsals of the Quintet. Although the letter is undated, it must have been written around the time of the Romero performance in early 1895.

67. Cited in Fernández-Cid, *Granados*, 216–17.

68. Vila San-Juan, *Papeles íntimos*, 74.

69. Miquel Saperas, *El mestre Enric Morera* (Andorra la Vella: Editorial Andorra, 1969), 23.

70. Enthusiastically reviewed by J. Borrás de Palua in "Los conciertos á dos pianos, en Novedades," *La música ilustrada hispano-americana* 2/13 (June 25, 1899): 3–4.

71. Cited and translated in "Poet & Piano," *MD: Medical Newsmagazine* 11/12 (December 1967): 187.

72. Antonio Rodrigo, "Conchita Badia entre Granados y Pau Casals," *Historia y vida* 10/117 (December 1977): 88.

73. Rosendo Llates, "Granados: Señor de la música," *Señor* 11/42 (February 1966): 56–57.

74. Ibid., 57.

75. Boladeres Ibern, *Granados*, 135.

76. For instance, see Juan Llongueras, "De como conocí al maestro Enrique Granados," in *Evocaciones y recuerdos de mi primera vida musical en Barcelona* (Barcelona: Libreria Dalmau, 1944), 117.

77. Boladeres Ibern, *Granados*, 135.

78. Ibid. This revelation first appeared in Apeles Mestres, *Volves musicals* (Barcelona: Salvador Bonvía, 1927), 6. "Si en una sala hay mil espectadores, y me consta que novecientos noventa y nueve son devotos admiradores mios; pero que hay uno que sé que no he de convencer, tocaré mal, porque, para mí, no habrá en la sala sino aquél, que ya sé que ha de encontrar malo todo cuanto yo haga."

79. Llongueras, "Como conocí," 111.

80. Mestres, *Volves musicals*, 6. "La nerviositat d'En Granados fou sempre la nota dominant del seu caràcter: una nerviositat excessiva, indomable, así en l'entusiasme com en la depressió, en l'alegría com en la tristesa, en la broma com en els actes mes seriosos de la seva vida. Aquest és, al meu entendre, el secret de l'extrema vibració de la seva música. "

81. Boladeres Ibern, *Granados*, 22.

82. Llongueras, "Como conocí," 113. "[Granados] era infantil y enamoradizo, tímido y soñador, aristócrata y desordenado, pero por encima de todo era un artista; un artista apasionado, un artista sincero, un artista personalísimo."

83. *Le guide musical*, Paris, March 1905. "[L]a force et la délicatesse dans la sonorité, la rectitude de la mesure, la fermeté et la largeur du style et cette possession de soi-même qui donne

tant d'assurance á son jeu et de sécurité a l'audieteur." This and the following press excerpts are from a booklet entitled *Enrique Granados: Algunas opiniones de la prensa sobre sus conciertos* (Barcelona: Musicografía Wagner, n.d.). A copy is in the Am.

84. Paul de Stoeklin, "MM. Granados et Jacques Thibaud," *Le courrier musical*, Paris, June 1909. "Granados est un admirable pianiste qui ne tape pas, qui joue avec sobriété discrétions, sans mauvais goût, sans tours de forces inutiles demeurant toujours musicals."

85. Jean Huré, "Concert Granados-Crickboom," *Le monde musical*, 1905. "hardie, élégante, toujours impeccable, parfois endiablée."

86. *Gaceta del Norte*, Bilbao, 1906. "En la sonata 53 (No. 21) de Beethoven, estuvo Granados COLOSAL. Como artista de corazón, sondea y penetra los arcanos y profundidades del romántico maestro, ignotas aún para muchos entendidos."

87. *El liberal*, Madrid, 1906. "El joven pianista español interpretó a Beethoven de una manera magistral con una pasión y una riqueza emotiva verdaderamente portentosa."

88. *En el Conservatorio*, Valencia, 1909. "Es el poeta del piano. Sus manos pulsan el teclado con una delicadeza, con un espiritualismo, de extraordinaria singularidad; ... Le veíamos embebecido, transportado, electrizado ante el piano cuyos acentos vibraban elocuentes y emocionantes con las inspiraciones del autor y del intérprete, fundidas en un todo de grandeza subyugadora."

89. Boladeres Ibern, *Granados*, 50. Toward the end of his life, Granados the "artist" dispensed with technical practice altogether. As he put it, "The more I practice, the worse I play." Ibid., 120.

2. THE EMERGING COMPOSER

1. Related by Eduardo L. Chavarrí, "Enrique Granados: El hombre, El artista," *Revista musical hispano-americana* 3 (April 30, 1916): 13–14. "Pues, ese jardín, esas flores, ese cielo azul y naranjo, esta paz de jazmines."

2. Amadeu Vives, "Evocació," 180. Cited in English translation in Pagès, *100 anys*, 144. It is not clear from Vives's article exactly when this occurred, as he simply gives the date of July 15. However, from the context, it is obvious this event took place in the late 1880s, before Granados was married.

3. Cited in Alicia de Larrocha, "Granados, the Composer," trans. Joan Kerlow, *Clavier* 6/7 (October 1967): 22.

4. Conchita Badia, "Personal Portrait," 59.

5. Henri Collet, *Albéniz et Granados* (Paris: Éditions Le Bon Plaisir, 1948), 188.

6. Quoted in Fernández-Cid, *Ciclo La obra pianística de Enrique Granados*, 18. "Con un lápiz y un papel blanco, ya tengo asegurada la vida."

7. Fernández-Cid, *Granados*, 141–42.

8. Ibid.

9. Fernández-Cid, *Ciclo La obra pianística de Enrique Granados*, 18. "[E]scribía con espontaneidad, sin preocuparse por rigores en la proporción; elástico, flexible, barroco, musical."

10. Boladeres Ibern, *Granados*, 143.

11. Douglas Riva, Program Notes, *Ciclo Granados*, Fundación Juan March, Madrid, February–March 1996, 5. "Su música tiene más que ver con la tendencia de la poesia española de volver y volver sobre las mismas ideas. . . . añadiendo a cada repetición una decoración distinta y cada vez más luminosa y suntuosa."

12. In an interview with Orpheus, "El mestre Pedrell i el seu deixeble Granados," *El teatre català* 5/216 (April 15, 1916): 137, Pedrell claimed that Granados began to study with him at age 18, shortly after winning the Pujol competition. Of course, he won that in 1883, when he was

16 years old. Pedrell himself was on the jury, so it is not clear whether he recalled the year of the competition or Granados's age incorrectly. Riva, "Granados," *DME*, 852, writes that he studied with Pedrell on a regular basis from 1884 to 1891, excepting, of course, the two years he was in Paris (1887–89). The date of 1884 is confirmed by other sources, including "Enrique Granados," *Música* 2/31 (April 5, 1916): 53–54.

13. See my entry on Pedrell in *NGD* (2d). Both Albéniz and Granados adopted Pedrell's pan-Hispanic aesthetic and rejected Catalan nationalism in music. In fact, Granados rarely used Catalan folk songs in his works. His indifference to making arrangements of Catalan folk songs diminished his credibility among those who were dedicated to the cause.

14. As Roger Aliér points out, by 1888, Pedrell's position was "already becoming obsolete, for he had a traditional . . . view of Spanish music as a whole, without quite grasping that Catalan music had sources of its own; these could not be reconciled with his own music." See his "Musical Life in Barcelona, 1888–1936," in *Homage to Barcelona: The City and Its Art, 1888–1936*, 277.

15. A useful summary of Pedrell's relation to Spanish nationalism is found in Francesc Bonastre, "La personalitat musical de Catalunya: Felip Pedrell i el nacionalisme a Catalunya," *Revista musical catalana* 1/2 (December 1984): 33–34. Bonastre reminds us that, though Pedrell was influenced by the eighteenth-century theorist Padre Antonio Eximeno, the famous saying attributed by Pedrell to Eximeno, "Every people should construct its musical system on the basis of national song" ("Sobre la base del canto nacional debería contruir cada pueblo su sistema"), was spurious. But that Eximeno never said that hardly matters after all. Pedrell believed it, and he imparted that belief to a generation of composers who made that belief a reality.

16. Riva, "Granados" [MS English version of his entry in *DME*, containing material that was deleted in the Spanish publication]. The Clementi MS is in the Cdm.

17. This and other letters to Pedrell are in the Bc, Epistolario Pedrell, sig. M. 964. As was so often the case with his manuscripts and letters, Granados did not date this item, except to write "Miercoles" (Wednesday).

18. Dated simply "Lunes" (Monday). "[P]refiero una palabra de mi maestro a todos los triunfos . . . que pueda tener. La mayor parte de mi revelación artística, se le debo a Vd; a Vd pues le doy yo la enhorabuena de mi triunfo."

19. Orpheus, "El mestre Pedrell," 137.

20. Pedrell, "La personalidad artística de Granados." "[Granados] poseía . . . una facultad de asimilación tan portentosa que no tenía necesidad de solidarla abriendo y estudiando libros, ni tratados, ni fijarse en corrientes de sistemas ó tendencias. Bastaba ponerle ante los ojos de un documento musical cualquiera para asimilarselo con aquella su facultad extraordinaria, y asi nacieron aquellas florescencias musicales que brotaban de repente del ambiente de una región española, fuese lo que fuese; aquellas *Murcianas*, aquellas *Valencianas*, aquellos *Valses poéticos*, aquellos *Valses sentimentales*, que más que asimilaciones diriase que eran trozos autobiográficos arrancados del corazón."

21. Douglas Riva discovered the notebook among some papers in the family archive in 1981 and discussed them in his article "Master Class: A Newly Discovered Mazurka by Granados," *Keyboard Classics: The Magazine You Can Play* (January/February 1985): 20–22, 38–39. He premiered eleven of the solo pieces from the manuscript on April 3, 1984, at the Barcelona Conservatory. He presented them at Carnegie Hall on March 15, 1985 and has recently recorded them on a Naxos CD (8.557141, 2004). They are published in DLR 5.

22. Riva, "Granados" [English version], 34.

23. See Riva, "Granados," *DME*, 853. Later works making use of this song were "Quejas o La maja y el ruiseñor" from *Goyescas*, "En invierno (La muerte del ruiseñor)," from *Libro de horas*, "El poeta y el ruiseñor," *Escenas románticas*, and the opera *Follet*. Albéniz wrote a piece with a similar title, *Fiesta de aldea*, and apparently this was a joint effort with Granados; the

two may have been inspired by an excursion of some kind. Albéniz's effort later did double duty as the Prelude to his English operetta *The Magic Opal.*

24. This was shortly before his return to Barcelona in July 1889. The concerto appeared on his program at the Navas home in September of that year.

25. Vila San-Juan, *Papeles íntimos,* 70.

26. Granados's claim in his memoirs that he began them in 1883 is hardly credible and may be due to scholars' mistaking an "8" for a "3" in his handwriting. See Riva, "Granados" [English version], 34, and DLR 2, 19.

27. Quoted in Fernández Cid, *Ciclo La obra pianística de Enrique Granados,* 20. Also found (translated into Catalan from the original French) in Joan Salvat, "Enric Granados: Notes biogrà-fiques," *Revista musical catalana* 13 (1916): 199. There were at least two letters from Cui, dedicatee of book 3, dated July 13, 1892, and September 16, 1894. These are reproduced in Antonio Iglesias, *Enrique Granados: su obra para piano,* 2 vols. (Madrid: Editorial Alpuerto, 1985), 1:167–68.

28. Alfonso Albéniz, "Albéniz y Granados," *Revista musical hispano-americana* 3 (April 30, 1916), 7.

29. Pedrell's commentary appeared in *Diario de Barcelona* and was cited in Salvat, "Notes biogràfiques," 200. He claimed that they were of "transcendental significance" for Spanish music, but that is hyperbole.

30. Georges Jean-Aubry, "Enrique Granados," *The Musical Times* 57 (December 1, 1916): 536.

31. Bryce Morrison, "Granados: The Complete Piano Music of Granados Recorded for CRD by Thomas Rajna," *Musical Opinion* 99 (1976): 204.

32. The bolero interpretation of these opening two bars comes from Vincent A. Craig, "Traditional Spanish Folk Dance Rhythms in the Piano Music of Isaac Albéniz and Enrique Granados" (DMA lecture-recital paper, Peabody Conservatory, 2002), 45.

33. An insightful analysis of these various markers and their deployment in French music is available in Ralph P. Locke, "Cutthroats and Casbah Dancers," in *The Exotic in Western Music,* ed. Jonathan Bellman (Boston: Northeastern University Press, 1998), 116–17. Granados was certainly exposed to the similarly clichéd *espagnolade* in Paris, but its impact on his personal style was minimal. Another subtitle for No. 2 is "Arabe." See DLR 2, 97.

34. From editor Christopher Maurer's introduction to *Federico García Lorca: Collected Poems,* rev. bilingual ed. (New York: Farrar, Straus and Giroux, 2002), xv.

35. Mary M. V. Samulski-Parekh, "A Comprehensive Study of the Piano Suite 'Goyescas' by Enrique Granados" (DMA thesis, University of Missouri, Kansas City, 1988), 36.

36. Vila San-Juan, *Papeles íntimos,* 78.

37. Alicia de Larrocha, "Granados, the Composer," 22, says that this is especially true of *Spanish Dance No. 7,* "[w]here not only the details of phrase and musical punctuation in the theme are at variance, but where the two versions have completely different finales."

38. DLR 2 includes both the published and recorded versions (the recorded one having been transcribed).

39. The play premiered at the Teatro de la Comedia in Madrid on February 14, 1896. Granados saw a production of it during one of his trips to the Spanish capital and was deeply impressed.

40. See the entry on Feliu y Codina in *Enciclopedia universal ilustrada europeo-americana* (1958 ed.).

41. Márquez Villanueva, "Literary Background," 4. In this sense, the drama is reminiscent of Mascagni's opera *Cavalleria rusticana* (Rustic Chivalry), a veristic drama about jealousy and violent death in the impoverished Sicilian countryside.

42. Fernández-Cid, *Granados,* 244.

43. In an interview with Herbert F. Peyser, "Granados Here for Production of *Goyescas,*" *Musical America* 23 (December 25, 1915): 3, Granados referred to a work (unnamed) he had begun in 1898 under the inspiration of Goya, which he intended to portray the "life and character" of

his country. He also claimed that he had recycled some of this "failed" work into *Goyescas*. He was clearly referring to *Los Ovillejos*.

44. See Douglas Riva, "El Llibre d'Apunts d'Enric Granados," *Revista de Catalunya*, n28 (January 1989): 93, and Larrad, "Catalan Theatre Works," 20. Riva is convinced the work is not complete, while Larrad believes that it is.

45. The manuscripts for *Los Ovillejos* are now located in the Cdm. In addition to the hand-written libretto, there are actually four scores: (1) a draft of the first scene, (2) what appears to be a full score for the zarzuela in one act (unbound), (3) a copy of this in a copyist's hand (titled "Avillejos"), and (4) a full score, bound, for a two-act version. This has gotten wet, however, and the second act has faded in places (it can still be read). None of these versions agree completely. The copyist's version is scored for 2 flutes, 2 oboes, 2 clarinets, 2 bassoons, 2 horns, 2 trumpets in B-flat, 3 trombones, tuba, timpani, assorted percussion, and strings. There are no parts and no vocal score. None of these scores is complete, and even the bound volume has the finale of act 1 barely sketched in. So, none of these could be used for a reconstruction, edition, or performance, unless one wanted to fill in the blanks.

46. "El fandango de candil" from book 1 of *Goyescas* and "La calesa" from the opera of the same title were all originally conceived for *Los Ovillejos*.

47. Antonio Fernández-Cid, *Cien años de teatro musical en España (1875–1975)* (Madrid: Real Musical, 1975), 368.

48. The only copy of this is in the Centre de Documentació i Museu de les Arts Escèniques de L'Institut del Teatre in Barcelona. See the *Epílogo* for more information about the revision, its sources, and its recent revival.

49. Collet, *Albéniz et Granados*, 209–11. In fact, Collet took his plot summary and musical commentary straight from the entry on *María del Carmen* in Albert Torrellas, *Diccionario enciclopédico de la música ilustrado* (Barcelona: Central Catalana de Publicaciones, 1927–29), ii, 719–20, without citing his source.

50. The three musical examples that appear here are from these numbers, published in vocal score in Madrid: Pablo Martín, n.d.

51. Albéniz's *Pepita Jiménez* (1896) is a similar happy-ending *verismo*-style opera. Albéniz thought *verismo* operas "horrifying." See Clark, *Portrait*, 136–73, for a discussion of *Pepita Jiménez* and p. 182 for his low opinion of Italian opera.

52. Antonio Guerra y Alarcón, "La ópera nueva, María del Carmen," *Heraldo de Madrid*, November 10, 1898, 3.

53. Collet, *Albéniz et Granados*, 209.

54. "Para mirarte, mis ojos; / Para quererte, mi alma; / Para dormirte, mis brazos; / Para guardarte, mi hierro."

55. Larrad, "Catalan Theatre Works," 32.

56. Fernández-Cid, *Granados*, 246.

57. There is a contract between the authors of *María del Carmen* in the Mm, fons Granados. It indicates that Granados was staying at San Geronimo, 13, in Madrid.

58. His family received in his stead the Cortina prize for 4,000 pesetas from the Academia de la Lengua; the previous year he had received the Piquer prize from the Real Academia Española for the play. Rubén Darío had high praise for the play as well, citing the author as a "great talent" and a "delicious musician of verse." See his *España contemporánea* (Madrid: Biblioteca Rubén Darío, n.d.), 197.

59. "Revista de Madrid," *Diario de Barcelona*, November 20, 1898, 12618. In fact, it was *El liberal* that said the public had wanted more traditional numbers, especially in the second act. "Los hombres del oficio creen que el asunto de la obra es poco musical, echan de menos algun duo y alguna romanza de la antigua escuela y opinan que el Señor Granados ha abusado de los diálogos cantados, que son la especialidad de Wagner."

60. Morphy was writing in the first issue of *La música ilustrada*, which appeared on December 25, 1898.

61. Reported in Eduardo Muñoz, "Teatro de Parish: *María del Carmen*," *El imparcial*, November 13, 1898, 2. "¡Esto es wagneriano y deben llevarlo al Real!" In "La música de Wagner. Las cortes," *La ilustración artística* n897 (March 6, 1899) (repr. *La vida contemporánea (1896–1915)* (Madrid: Editorial Magisterio Español, 1972), 54), Emilia Pardo Bazán expressed her admiration for Wagner as pre-imperial Germany's "last genius," one who united "technique and inspiration" to a greater degree than any other artist.

62. A., "Teatro de Parish," *El correo*, November 13, 1898, 2. "[O]tros maestros de reputación europea."

63. R. Blasco, *La correspondencia de España*, November 13, 1898, 3. "le dan brillante color local." However, an anonymous critic at the Barcelona production the following year and writing in *Lo teatre català*, June 30, 1899, 2, found a shocking lack of originality in Granados's manner of utilizing folklore: "[T]he 'Parranda' which Señor Granados has put in his work . . . is the exact same which appears in Ynzenga's collection of popular songs of Murcia, page 19. Yet, not only has Granados copied the melodic part but he uses the actual accompaniment composed by Don Julian Calvó." [La 'Parranda' que'l Sr. Granados ha posat en sa obra y que tant rembombori entre'ls profanes ha mogut està exacta en lo tomo de *Cansóns populars* de Murcia, pàgina 19, de la obra de Ynzenga. Y no sols ha copiat la part melodica, sino que ho ha fet de l'acompanyament degut a D. Julian Calvó.]

64. "Teatro de Parish: *María del Carmen*," *La época*, November 13, 1898, 1. "debe responder siempre a 'sentimientos que sean de los que canten,' como decía Rossini."

65. The suggestion that Feliu y Codina had been rather careless in his transformation of the play into a libretto appears in the same article that details their journey to Murcia, that is, Muñoz, "Teatro de Parish," 2.

66. J. Arimón, "Teatro Circo de Parish," *El liberal*, November 13, 1898, 3. "La ópera es el último refugio del romanticismo, y, por tanto, requiere por regla general la elección de un asunto verdaderamente poético y levantado, al que sean ajenas las prosáicas familiaridades de la vida común."

67. He actually wrote two reviews, both in *El heraldo de Madrid*. The first one appeared on November 10 (p. 3), in anticipation of the premiere, and the second on the 13th, this time on the front page, beneath a drawing of the set for act 2. The placement of the review right next to important news from the Philippines suggests that *madrileños* took their *ópera española* rather seriously.

68. "[L]as soluciones de continuidad de la ópera italiana. . . . La melodía, en efecto, corre abundante por la partitura . . . melodía a la moderna, dividida en porciones, que sigue a la creación dramática y va y viene y se repite en diferentes formas, ahondando la psicología del personaje o comentando la acción."

69. José Subirá, "En memoria de Enrique Granados," *Música* 1/5 (May–June 1938): 17–20. Subirá had the letter in his private collection.

70. María Cristina of Habsburg was the daughter of Archduke Charles of Austria and married Alfonso XII in November 1879. Her husband died November 6, 1885, at the early age of 26, while she was still pregnant with the future monarch, who was born on May 17, 1886. She served as regent until her son, Alfonso XIII, attained his majority and ascended to the throne in May 1902. There were high hopes that he could restore Spain to some measure of greatness, but those hopes went largely unfulfilled. See Carr, *Spain*, 524–32, for insights into the disillusionment of Spanish intellectuals with his reign.

71. Rodrigo, "Conchita Badia," 85.

72. Edgar Allison Peers, *Catalonia Infelix* (Westport, Conn.: Greenwood Press, 1970), 143, reminds us that if the separatists were unsuccessful in freeing themselves from Madrid, it was because "the main characteristic of these years was disunity among the Catalonians. Numerous as were their grievances, they seemed quite unable to achieve any kind of solidarity."

73. See the entry on Barcelona in the *Gran enciclopèdia catalana* (1986 ed.).

74. Boladeres Ibern, *Granados*, 28–30.

75. As Joseph Harrison memorably puts it, "the motley assortment of parasites who dominated Restoration society: corrupt politicians, sterile bureaucrats, pious bishops, pedantic academics and incompetent generals [who were] responsible for the nation's decline." See his "Tackling National Decadence: Economic Regenerationism in Spain after the Colonial Débâcle," in *Spain's 1898 Crisis*, 56.

76. Cited in Brenan, *Spanish Labyrinth*, 6.

77. Ibid., 8.

78. See Larrad, "Catalan Theatre Works," 33.

79. Fernández-Cid, *Granados*, 84.

80. It is important to bear in mind Xosé Aviñoa's observation, in *La música i el modernisme* (Barcelona: Curial, 1985), 350, about the Catalan critics (and clearly those in Madrid as well), that though they pretended to be impartial, they were always partisans of one sort or another.

81. This is reported in M.J.B., "Teatro del Tívoli: 'María del Carmen,'" *La vanguardia*, June 1, 1899, 5.

82. M.J.B., "Teatro del Tívoli," 5. The author published a shorter review two days later (p. 3) with correction of some errata in his first piece and a commentary on the performance. "Granados nos lleva á la huerta de Murcia, nos presenta la frescura del paisaje, lo sano del aire y el carácter de los moradores, sin engañarnos."

83. "Estreno de Sarsuelas," *Lo teatro català* 10/415 (June 31, 1899): 1–2.

84. Joan Borrás de Palau, "Enrique Granados," *La música ilustrada hispano-americana* 2/12 (June 10, 1899): 4. ". . . *María del Carmen*, cuyo éxito en el teatro del Tívoli es un argumento fuerte para defender la ópera española contra el desaliento o el excepticismo de los que no consideran posible consolidar tan importante institución nacional."

85. Joaquím Malats, "María del Carmen," *La música ilustrada hispano-americana* 2/13 (June 25, 1899): 5.

86. Melcior Rodríguez, "Teatro Tívoli," *La Renaixensa—Diari de Catalunya*, June 2, 1899, 3468–69. ". . . 'ls homes se portaren molt millor que las donas."

87. F. Suárez Bravo, "Teatro del Tívoli," *Diario de Barcelona*, June 2, 1899, 6137–39.

88. Subirá, "En memoria de Enrique Granados," 17–20, alludes to this production, without providing specifics. Jacques Pillois, "Un entretien avec Granados," *S.I.M. Revue musicale* 10, suppl. 3 (1914): 7, claims that the play was done by the Odeon in Paris under the title *Jardins de Murcie*. Collet, *Albéniz et Granados*, 178, confirms that *María del Carmen* is an opera "on the subject of *Jardins de Murcie*, so popular in France."

89. "Teatros," *El correo español*, November 14, 1898, 3. "en la galería de artistas de reconocido valimiento."

3. WORKS FOR PIANO IN A CENTRAL EUROPEAN STYLE

1. From Unamuno's *Una visita al viejo poeta* (1899, 2:745–51) and cited in Frances Wyers, *Miguel de Unamuno: The Contrary Self* (London: Tamesis Books, 1976), 9.

2. See DLR 16, 19. Although none are dated, several manuscripts for this work survive in the Mm, fons Granados, and are discussed in this same source.

3. For instance, in 1813 Lord Byron published a poem entitled *The Waltz: An Apostrophic Hymn*, expressing "his initial shock at the waltz and [referring] to 'hands which may freely range in public sight where ne'er before.'" Cited in Andrew Lamb's entry on the waltz in *NGD* (2d), 73.

4. The *Cartas de amor* are similarly labeled "Cadencioso," "Suspirante," "Dolente," and "Appassionato."

5. See Annemarie Schuessler, "An Introduction to the Three Stylistic Periods in the Piano Works of Enrique Granados y Campiña" (DM lecture-recital, Northwestern University, 1985), 11–12.

6. Incomplete works include two solo sonatas, one for violin and the other for cello. He did finish a small-scale string quartet. A serenade for two violins and piano was performed by Granados on April 4, 1914, at the Salle Pleyel in Paris. See Fernández-Cid, *Granados*, 216, 218.

7. Luis Carlos Gago, liner notes for "Beaux Arts Trio Play Turina and Granados," Menahem Pressler, piano; Ida Kavafian, violin; Peter Wiley, cello (Philips CD, 446684–2, 1996).

8. These details of the competition are found in a typewritten document entitled "Mis recuerdos sobre Granados" by Julio Gómez of the Real Academia de Bellas Artes de San Fernando, dated Barcelona, May 1966. This is now in the Mm, fons Granados. Bretón informed Granados of the jury's decision in a letter of January 30, 1904, which is cited in Fernández-Cid, *Granados*, 185. The most detailed and reliable account of the competition, based on actual documentation in the archive of the Real Conservatorio, is by Jacinto Torres, "Cien años del Concurso de Piano del Conservatorio: Los *Allegro de Concierto* de Granados y Falla," *Música. Revista del Real Conservatorio Superior de Música de Madrid*, n10 (2003): 277–86. There is no basis for stating that the results of the jury's deliberations were unanimous, as nothing in the records refers to a vote. Bretón was trying not only to promote native composition but also improve the standards of the Conservatorio, bringing them into line with those of other such institutions in Europe by sponsoring a competition. However, this initiative proved to be both the first and last of its kind at the Conservatorio.

9. Samulski-Parekh, "Goyescas," 35.

10. Ibid., 36.

11. Ibid., 11–15. She makes the observation that though the secondary dominant of V appears repeatedly in mm. 7–10, the dominant chord itself does not arrive until m. 11. Such avoidance of the dominant is not typical of Chopin.

12. See ibid., 26–43, for a discussion of this movement. She cites Schumann's "Eintritt" from *Waldszenen*, op. 82, as a prototype for the opening.

13. Ibid., 44, considers this an example of ABA form.

14. According to Natalia Granados in an interview with Del Arco, "Mano a mano," 14.

15. See DLR 8, 21. The MS is entitled "Recuerdo," from an *Album variado*, op. 48. This MS also contains an incomplete "Marcha fúnebre," dedicated to "mí." Considering the attention the angel of death had devoted to his family, this "me" is not as enigmatic as it might at first seem. Perhaps he was in a morbid mood when he began it.

16. J. Barrie Jones, "Enrique Granados: A Few Reflections on a Seventieth Anniversary," *Music Review* 47/1 (February 1986/7): 20. Wagner's opera was first produced in Barcelona in 1905, but there is no reason to believe this work was composed that early. It does seem that the collection was composed not very long before its publication in 1912. See DLR 12, 20.

17. Márquez Villanueva, "Literary Background," 3, finds a modernist flavor in the very title *Libro de horas*.

18. Indeed, the melody in mm. 27–35 of this work is identical to mm. 190–98 in "El amor y la muerte" from *Goyescas*. See DLR 12, 20.

19. This provides another example of self-borrowing, as mm. 13–14 derive from both mm. 80–81 of "Coloquio en la reja" and mm. 1–2 of "El amor y la muerte," from *Goyescas*. See ibid.

20. John Milton has researched the Tiana home of Godó, where Granados was often a guest. His description of the garden is in *The Fallen Nightingale* (Edina, Minn.: Swan Books, 2004), 233–34, 241–43.

21. En el jardín de los cipreses y las rosas, / apoyado en el pedestal de mármol blanco, / esperando su hora, / se durmió el poeta … / A su lado y acariciando su frente, / vela la musa.

4. TEACHER, CONDUCTOR, ORGANIZER

1. Boladeres Ibern, *Granados*, 15–17.

2. Vila San-Juan, *Papeles íntimos*, 57.

3. In J.C., "Memòria d'Enric Granados," 11, the composer's son-in-law Antoni Carreras i Verdaguer said, "The whole Barcelona aristocracy took its children to the Academy."

4. According to Aviñoa, *Música i modernisme*, 117, Serracant was the chapelmaster at Sant Pere de les Puel·les beginning in 1892. We recall that Enrique and Amparo Granados were married in that church in December of that year. Perhaps that is where they made his acquaintance.

5. See Llates, "Granados: Señor de la música," 56.

6. Information on the faculty, courses, and tuition of the Academy in its sixth year, while still at Fontanella, 14, comes from a brochure published October 1, 1906, in the Am.

7. This appeared in the very first issue, published in 1916. A copy of it is in the Am.

8. Milton, *The Fallen Nightingale*, 304.

9. Reported in "Una nova sala de concerts," *Revista musical catalana* 9 (1912): 24.

10. See the entry on him in the *Gran enciclopèdia catalana* (1986 ed.).

11. Fernández-Cid, *Granados*, 44. John Milton, *The Fallen Nightingale*, 49–60, devotes considerable attention to fleshing out Granados's relationship with Carmen and Salvador, and his numerous trips to Puigcerdà, a locale of considerable natural beauty and relative tranquility that the composer found an attractive antidote to his stressful life at home and at work. It was probably there that he composed the *Valses poéticos*.

12. Published Barcelona: Vidal Llimona y Boceta, 1905; reprinted 1954 by Unión Musical Española and now available in DLR 9. In emphasizing the pedal, Granados broke with a traditional emphasis on the fingers to produce sound. He also taught flexibility of movement rather than rigidity of the hand and exaggerated independence of the fingers. Although other teachers outside of Spain were advancing these ideas as well, especially Ludwig Deppe (1828–1890) in Germany, Tobias Matthay (1895–1945) in England, and Theodore Leschetizsky (1830–1915) in Austria, Granados was working in relative isolation in Barcelona and arrived at these innovations on his own. See Carol A. Hess, "Enrique Granados and Modern Piano Technique," *Performance Practice Review* 6/1 (Spring 1993): 92–94.

13. From a conversation between Mark Hansen and Alicia de Larrocha of April 14, 1983, quoted in Hansen, "The Pedagogical Methods," 13. Hansen goes on to point out that "Deviation from this primary training comes when the student has demonstrated mastery of the principle involved, and the readiness to exercise freedom" (p. 34).

14. In the Mm. the Am has several other manuscripts of pedagogical interest: four pages of exercises for developing use of the pedal with various rhythms and subdivisions of notes; another manuscript of exercises designed to strengthen the little finger; and a small music notebook entitled *Piano = Ornamentos de Mtro Granados* (Document Number 1474). The text is typewritten and interspersed with handwritten musical examples. It covers various types of mordents and how to play them. None of these are dated. The *Ornamentos* has been published in DLR 9 along with several other pedagogical works previously available only in manuscript.

15. These have now been published, for the first time, in DLR 9, 60–71. As this edition points out, these are not actual scripts from which Granados read but rather summations of his remarks written down and illustrated after the fact by someone else, perhaps his student Simone Saulnier. See DLR 9, 20–21. The translations that follow here are my own.

16. "Siempre que en una melodia, dos notas esten a una distancia (intervalo) en tiempo mayor que la correspondiente a dos tiempos de un andante, la segunda nota deberemos atacarla con una intensidad aproximadamente igual a la que queda de la nota primera."

17. "La interpretación de las obras musicales está en paralelo con la vida del artista; si éste ha vivido en la sociedad y el medio ambiente que son causa de la producciones musicales, si conoce los sentimientos humanos, la expresión fluirá intuitivamente sin que tal vez se de cuenta el mismo artista; pero si éste no los conoce, no es probable que sin preparación lleve a cabo con éxito una tarea tan difícil."

18. Vila San-Juan, *Papeles íntimos*, 62–63.

19. The entire interpretation is in Vila San-Juan, *Papeles íntimos*, 116–17.

20. Boladeres Ibern, *Granados*, 79.

21. In an undated letter to Pedrell (Bc, Epistolario Pedrell, M. 964), Granados states this as the purpose of his recently published *Seis estudios espresivos en forma de pequeños poemas musicales.* "[E]ducar a mis jovenes discípulos dentro del sentimiento poético que debe respirar casi toda obra musical." In this letter, he goes on to explain the essence of each movement.

22. For more detail about this initiation into the Granados program, see Boladeres Ibern, *Granados*, 45–55.

23. Ibid., 59.

24. Ibid., 77.

25. Ibid.

26. The student posing the question was none other than Boladeres Ibern, *Granados*, 86.

27. Ibid., 102–3.

28. Pagès, *100 anys*, 145.

29. Badia, "Personal Portrait," 58.

30. Boladeres Ibern, *Granados*, 61.

31. Llates, "Granados: Señor de la música," 57.

32. Fernández-Cid, *Granados*, 101.

33. This dimension of his life is discussed in some detail by his student Paquita Madriguera, "Enrique Granados," *Clave: Voz de la juventud musical Uruguaya* 43 (1961): 16–20. John Milton's research suggests that the symptoms of which Granados complained regarding his digestion are consistent with a diagnosis of Crohn's disease, that is, chronic inflammation of the intestines.

34. A. L. Mason, "Enrique Granados," *Music and Letters* 14 (July 1933): 236.

35. Boladeres Ibern, *Granados*, 44.

36. Ibid., 38–39.

37. Llates, "Granados: Señor de la música," 56.

38. Badia, "Personal Portrait," 58.

39. Conference given by Víctor Granados, no date. From Archives of the History of Art, The Getty Center for the History of Art and the Humanities, Los Angeles.

40. Cited in Fernández-Cid, *Granados*, 58.

41. Madriguera presents this episode in some detail in her memoir *Visto y oído: La estrella del alba* (Buenos Aires: Editorial Nova, 1947), 17–19.

42. Ibid., 14. John Milton fleshes out this affair in *The Fallen Nightingale*. He conducted interviews with Clotilde's descendants, who confirmed the relationship. Clotilde married again in 1920, but that marriage was also a failure. The great love of her life was apparently Granados.

43. Madriguera, *Visto y oído*, 22. Paquita's mother confronted Granados in New York about this, and he poured out his heart to her, without winning any sympathy.

44. Madriguera, "Granados," 17.

45. See Vila San-Juan, *Papeles íntimos*, 35–37. The priest, Father Garriga, wrote about this incident in a letter to Natalia Granados dated December 1, 1965. The letter is in the Ag.

46. Saperas, *Enric Morera*, 17.

47. Vila San-Juan, *Papeles íntimos*, 78.

48. Saperas, *Enric Morera*, 38–39. Morera founded the Catalunya Nova choral organization in 1885, and its artistic agenda was unabashedly Catalanist. For instance, it sang the *Marseillaise*

in Catalan, along with arrangements of Catalan songs such as *Els segadors* (The Reapers), which became the hymn of the movement. See Enrich Jardí Casany, *Historia de Els Quatre Gats* (Barcelona: Editorial Aedos, 1972), 157.

49. F. Suárez Bravo, "Teatro Lírico: Primer concierto clásico," *Diario de Barcelona*, May 16, 1900, 5896–97. "[O]ir 'clásico' es lo mismo que decir aburrido: una cosa grave, correcta, pero fria e pesada." Another review, "Notas artísticas," appeared in *Catalunya artística* 1 (1900): 246. Granados stated his intentions for the ensemble in a circular sent out to those he hoped would help found and support the group. This circular is in the Arxiu Històric de la Ciutat and is cited in Aviñoa, *Perfil histórico-biográfico*, DLR 18, 27–28.

50. Suárez Bravo, "Primer concierto," 5897. "Significa que de su repertorio queda excluido todo lo que sea vulgar, ramplón, antiestético: todo lo que no se ajuste á las leyes del arte."

51. "P" [Joaquím Pena?] laments its passing and speculates on its fate in "Crónica musical: varias," *Joventut* 2 (1900): 53.

52. Mentioned by Eduardo López Chavarrí, *Guide musical*, 383. (Cited in Partridge, "Enrique Granados," 67.)

53. Reported in "Noves," *Revista musical catalana* 7 (1910): 109.

54. See "La qüestió de la Banda Municipal," *Revista musical catalana* 7 (1910): 227–33.

55. Mention of the competition and jury is found in "Festa de la Música Catalana, Any IV: Veredicte," *Revista musical catalana* 4 (1907): 144–45. See also Aviñoa, *Música i modernisme*, 238, for a summary of the judges and winners in this and other years. Arranging Catalan folk songs demonstrated a composer's dedication to Catalanism, and Granados never cared for it.

56. The Concours Diémer began in 1903. One sometimes reads that Granados won it during his studies in Paris (1887–89), but that is impossible. This appointment was announced in "Noves," *Revista musical catalana* 6 (1909): 120. For the composition of the committee, see Rény Fasolt, "Le jury du Concours Diémer de 1909," *Musica* 81 (June 1909): 93. Granados was invited to be on the committee again in 1912, and Fauré's letter of invitation (dated March 1, 1912) is reproduced in Vila San-Juan, *Papeles íntimos*, 20.

57. The event was reported in "Homenatge al Mestre Granados," *Revista musical catalana* 8 (1911): 54–55.

5. *MODERNISME CATALAN*

1. "L.A. Phil's Force of Nature Presses for a Sea Change," *Los Angeles Times*, August 26, 2003, E5. Michael White interviewed the conductor for this piece.

2. Miroslav Hroch, "From National Movement to the Fully-formed Nation: The Nation-building Process in Europe," in *Mapping the Nation*, ed. Gopal Balakrishnan (London: Verso, 1996), 84.

3. In fact, the games continued on an informal, private basis from 1940 to 1970. The tradition spread to many parts of the Hispanic world, however, among the Catalan diaspora, which had participated in colonization or had fled the Civil War. See the entry on the *Jocs Florals* in the *Gran enciclopèdia catalana* (1986 ed.).

4. Robert Hughes, *Barcelona* (New York: Alfred A. Knopf, 1992), 454.

5. Riva, "Granados" [English version], speculates that this love of curving lines "might be akin to the sinuous melodic curves in Granados's mature music (i.e., the two-violin *Serenata*, or the suite *Elisenda*)."

6. Gaudí was a conservative Catholic who did not approve of the Catalan-modernist political agenda, especially insofar as the movement had been condemned by the Church. Hence, he fits somewhat awkwardly into the *moderniste* category, not unlike Granados himself. See Ignasi de Solà-Morales, "Modernista Architecture," in *Homage to Barcelona: The City and Its Art*, 124.

7. Alexandre Cirici Pellicer, "Wagnerisme i modernisme," in *Wagner i Catalunya* (Barcelona: Edicions del Cotal, 1983), 172.

8. Ibid.

9. Hughes, *Barcelona*, 455.

10. See José María Jover Zamora, "La época de la Restauración: panorama político-social, 1875–1902," in *Historia de España: Revolución burguesa oligarquía y constitucionalismo (1834–1923)*, ed. Manuel Tuñón de Lara (Madrid: Editorial Labor, 1981), 323.

11. The connection between cityscape and Catalan modernism is made in Rodolfo Cardona, "Granados' Spain," paper presented at the "Granados and *Goyescas*" Symposium, Harvard University, Cambridge, Mass., January 23, 1982, 6.

12. Barcelona got its first taste of Wagner, however, in 1862 with a performance of the Pilgrims' Chorus from *Tannhäuser*, conducted by Josep Anselm Clavé.

13. For the occasion, the lighting of the theater was arranged to simulate that at Bayreuth, with the stage fully lit and the hall in darkness. Bayreuth became for Catalan Wagnerites the mecca it was for devotees of the master elsewhere in Europe. See Casany, *Historia de Els Quatre Gats*, 156.

14. This summary appears in Aviñoa, "Barcelona," 324. The curtain rose one hour before midnight, when Bayreuth's exclusive rights would expire. See Aviñoa, *Perfil histórico-biográfico*, DLR 18, 13.

15. Aviñoa, "Barcelona," 331.

16. Pena was a critic for *Joventut*. The Associació was also the result of pro-Wagner agitation in the writings of authors like Joaquím Marsillach (1859–83), who penned the influential essay *Ricardo Wagner: Ensayo biográfico crítico* (1878). The founding took place at one of the most important cultural institutions of the modernist epoch: Els Quatre Gats, which means, literally, "The Four Cats" but is also Catalan slang for any gathering of friends. It was inspired by the famous cabaret Le Chat Noir in Paris. The beer hall-cabaret-casino did not have a long life, keeping its doors open only from 1897 to 1903. During those six years, however, it presented numerous performances by leading musicians (including Granados), poetry readings, and art exhibitions featuring paintings by Regoyos and Picasso.

17. The Associació Wagneriana is still in existence and celebrated its centenary in 2001. An earlier but short-lived such group in Barcelona was the Sociedad Wagner, founded in 1881.

18. Aviñoa, *Música i modernisme*, 353.

19. In philosophy and literature, Nietzsche exerted a comparable impact, especially on Maragall.

20. Pellicer, "Wagnerisme i modernisme," 175.

21. The Palau de la Música Catalana features other sculptural décor of interest, all of which tells us something about the musical tastes of that time. In addition to one of Wagner, there are busts of Palestrina, Bach, and Beethoven.

22. Enrique Granados, "Parcival," *El teatre català* 2/65 (May 24, 1913 [Wagner issue]): 351. "*Parcival!* Com un ser ideal, creat a semblança de lo diví! Estudiem-lo, sentim-lo fervorosament. Perfeccionem els nostres esperits. *Parcival* els faci oblidar les ofenses dels humans i perfeccioni la nostra ànima! Musicalment, no puc . . . no dec. No deu dir-se res d'una obra que deixa d'esser música per a arribar a quelcom més gran que la música mateixa."

23. Rafael Moragas recalls this gathering in "Records d'Enric Granados," *Mirador*, December 5, 1935, 8. The pieces included the newly composed *Goyescas*, book 1.

24. See Ramon Planes, *El modernisme a Sitges* (Barcelona: Editorial Selecta, 1969), 17.

25. Maragall is cited in E. Inman Fox, *La invención de España* (Madrid: Catedra, 1997), 87. Fox writes that "the thesis of the Catalan nationalists was that Spain's troubles were the result of Castilian dominance" (p. 65).

26. Brenan, *Spanish Labyrinth*, xvi.

27. Xosé Aviñoa, "El fracàs del Teatre Líric Català a la Barcelona finisecular," *Revista musical catalana* 6/54 (April 1989): 20.

28. There were other venues, however. Of special significance were the *Festes Modernistes* (Modernist Festivals) celebrated in Sitges, just south of Barcelona, from 1893 to 1897. Music played an important part in these festivals, and Morera's opera *La fada* (The Fairy) was featured at the final Festival. Sitges was also the location of Santiago Rusiñol's home, the Cau Ferrat ("Iron Shed"), which became a mecca for Catalan modernists, including Granados. It is now a museum featuring Rusiñol's art collection.

29. Miquel Utrillo i Morlius (1862–1934) was an artist and promoter who was also involved in founding the café Els Quatre Gats.

30. See Larrad, "Catalan Theatre Works," 127.

31. Cited in Francesc Curet, *Teatre català* (Barcelona: Editorial Aedos, 1967), 408.

32. See Christopher Webber, *The Zarzuela Companion* (Lanham, Md.: Scarecrow Press, 2002), 3–5, for a brief but illumining history of the zarzuela during this period.

33. Luca de Tena, "Pequeña historia," 107.

34. The works were usually done in pairs, and in the fashion of modern movies, these would be repeated several times during an evening, starting at 5 P.M. or so and continuing on occasion past midnight.

35. See the entry on Gual in *Gran enciclopèdia catalana* (1986 ed.).

36. These recollections about the investors and first production are found in an article entitled "La primera zarzuela que musicó Enrique Granados," by T. Caballé y Clos himself. The clipping, without periodical title or date, is in the Am.

37. For this production, Miquel Utrillo designed sets with grand gardens and classical architecture, all of it reminiscent of Puvis de Chavannes. See Adrià Gual, *Mitja vida de teatre: Memòries* (Barcelona: Editorial Aedos, 1957), 96.

38. See Casany, *Historia de Els Quatre Gats*, 86.

39. Llongueras, "Como conocí," 114.

40. Gual, *Mitja vida de teatre*, 102, recalls that Albéniz was first offered the opportunity to compose for *Blancaflor* but turned it down, perhaps because he was absorbed in his own Arthurian operatic trilogy. Hence, Granados was called in at the last minute.

41. The original is found in Aurelio Campany, *Cançoner popular* (Barcelona, 1901–13), and reproduced in Larrad, "Catalan Theatre Works," 108.

42. "Barcelona," *Diario de Barcelona*, January 31, 1899, 1250.

43. E. Senyol, "La música de 'Blancafor [*sic*],'" *La veu de Catalunya*, February 1, 1899, 1.

44. "Teatro Lírico," *La vanguardia*, January 31, 1899, 6. "Nos hemos de limitar, pues, á decir que una gran parte del público no *vió* ni *sintió* por completo ni una ni otra de las dos obras representadas. . . . Sigan adelante en su noble empresa, . . . quizás otro día alcanzarán la victoria, que anoche no lograron."

45. Gual, *Mitja vida de teatre*, 103.

46. And neither shall it return, at least with Granados's music. All we retain are the parts for the first and second violins and the violas. Certainly wind parts once existed, as members of the Banda Municipal were engaged for the performance. Granados wrote another work possibly intended for the Teatre Íntim at this time. Entitled *Llegenda de la fada* (The Legend of the Fairy), it has traditionally been listed in catalogs of Granados's works as a symphonic piece, largely because what have come down to us are professionally copied instrumental parts for it (there is no score). Although we know nothing of its genesis and there is no record of its ever having been performed, it may have been a dramatic and not purely symphonic work because it is divided into three acts, and fragments of vocal parts exist (these sources are at the Cdm).

It is discussed in some detail in Larrad, "Catalan Theatre Works," 199–202. We have no idea who might have authored the text, which does not survive, but the work's title suggests the influence of Morera's *La fada*.

47. Gual, *Mitja vida de teatre*, 179, recalls that the premiere took place on July 14, but this was a fully staged version. It was followed by a restaging of *Picarol* by Granados and Mestres, a work discussed in the next chapter.

48. This account appears in Apeles Mestres, "Enric Granados: Notes íntimes," *El teatre català* 5/216 (April 15, 1916), 137. Mestres does not specify when the meeting took place. It may have been in the period 1882–87, after the death of Granados's father and before the young pianist's departure for Paris.

49. Mestres would make up the melodies and have professional musicians devise piano accompaniments for them. See the entry on Mestres in the *Gran enciclopèdia catalana* (1986 ed.). Mestres competed three times in the *Jocs Florals*, in 1883, 1884, and 1908. He won prizes on all three occasions, the last time receiving the contest's highest honor, "Mestre en Gai Saber," for his poem *Els pins*.

50. Not all critics regard him highly. Márquez Villanueva, "Literary Background," 5, has this unflattering assessment to offer: "[H]e was prone to indulge into [*sic*] extremes of both stale Romanticism and a tart, biting humor. Personally, I find him rather vapid, an immense talent smothered by its own facility and a lack of serious intellectual purpose."

51. Curet, *Teatre català*, 445.

52. Larrad, "Catalan Theatre Works," 283.

6. CATALAN WORKS WITH TEXTS BY APELES MESTRES

1. The manuscripts of all of these except for *Follet* are in the Sa, where Larrad examined them. This chapter is indebted to his work.

2. Edita Mas-López, "Apeles Mestres: Poetic Lyricist," *Opera Journal* 13–14 (1980–81): 25.

3. Larrad, "Catalan Theatre Works," 91.

4. Borrás de Palau, "Enrique Granados," 4.

5. The Am has a manuscript containing the first few pages of *Petrarca*, an orchestral score with the piano part below. Like all the other manuscripts, it is undated. Its importance lies in what it tells us about his method of composition, as the piano part continues for ten bars after the orchestral parts end (after m. 22), demonstrating that he first wrote out the piano below and orchestrated from it.

6. Larrad, "Catalan Theatre Works," 221–23.

7. Mas-López, "Apeles Mestres," 33.

8. See Larrad, "Catalan Theatre Works," 228–42, for detailed treatment of the score.

9. Larrad, "Catalan Theatre Works," 134, speculates that insofar as "Sadurní was one of the musical directors of the Teatre Líric Català, the Sitges performance took place during the late spring or summer of 1901."

10. One does not find the spoken dialogue in either of the extant scores but rather in the published drama itself (1901).

11. N.N.N., "Teatros" [review of *Picarol*], *La Esquella de la Torratxa* 23/1155 (March 1, 1901): 169. "Granados ha sapigut embellirla, ab un esclat de música inspiradísima." "[U]na nova proba del seu talent pel cultiu de la escena lírica."

12. "Barcelona" [review of *Picarol*], *Diario de Barcelona*, February 26, 1901, 2594. "[E]l sello de distinción y de elegancia melódica."

13. Emili Tintorer, "Teatres: Liric-Catala" [review of *Picarol*], *Joventut* 2/52 (February 7, 1901): 165.

14. Joaquím Pena, "Teatres: Liric-Catala" [review of *Picarol*], *Joventut* 2/52 (February 7, 1901): 166–67.

15. *Catalunya artística*, October 17, 1901, 522, reported that it was going to be done the following spring. See Clark, *Portrait*, 205–6, for a discussion of this venture.

16. Reported by J. Roca y Roca, "La semana en Barcelona" [review of *Follet*], *La vanguardia*, April 12, 1903, 4.

17. *Pèl & Ploma* 4 (1903): 148–51, published act 2, however. The manuscripts for *Follet* are in the Cdm. A fragment of the vocal score, dated Ripollet and Barcelona, October and November 1901, is in the Pierpont Morgan Library in New York (Cary Catalogue no. 117). See J. Rigbie Turner, "Nineteenth-century Autograph Music Manuscripts in the Pierpont Morgan Library: A Check List," *19th-Century Music* 4 (1980–81): 49–76.

18. F. Suárez Bravo, "'Follet': Drama lírico de A. Mestres y E. Granados," *Diario de Barcelona*, April 6, 1903, 4267. "Una tarde se presentó en su jardín Enrique Granados, pidiéndole de buenas á primeras el libreto para una ópera; un drama lírico, 'de pocos personajes, sin acción apenas . . . un idilio . . . un duo, todo pasión, todo naturaleza!'"

19. Cited in Larrad, "Catalan Theatre Works," 256, and in the possession of the Granados family.

20. "Que denota la honda tristeza de Follet por no creerse ser merecedor de Nadala."

21. "Este tema indica el desfallacimiento por tener que abandonar la dicha; tristeza que le causa a Nadala abandonar a su amado."

22. Cited in Larrad, "Catalan Theatre Works," 260.

23. Ibid., 266.

24. "Noves" [review of *Follet*], *Joventut* 4/165 (April 9, 1903): 256.

25. *La vanguardia*, April 7, 1903, 3, reported that the prelude to act 3 was based on a popular Catalan song but failed to cite the title. *La Esquella de la Torratxa* 25/1266 (April 10, 1903): 233, also referred to his use of a "large number" of folk melodies, but the reviewer, "N.N.N.," likewise did not name them.

26. Suárez Bravo, "Follet," 4268. "Grandes compositores han tenido que esperar muchos mas años que él antes de dar pruebas de una personalidad independiente."

27. Rafael Moragas, "Música i musiqueta," *Pèl & Ploma* 4 (1903): 142. "[N]o es més qu'un delicat idili dramátic, impregnat de tendra poesía, . . . un dels pilars ahont te qu'apoyarse l'edifici de l'ópera catalan."

28. Roca y Roca, "La semana en Barcelona." "Nuestro público, y en especial el que suele asistir al Gran Teatro, no está acostumbrado á esta clase de pruebas, en las cuales un obra deja siempre mucho por adivinar. Puesta sin aparato escénico, ni movimiento de los personajes, á manera de concierto; confiadas las partes, no á cantantes de cartel, sino a inexpertos alumnos, nada más ocasionado á un fracaso o siquiera á que la obra no sea debidamente comprendida y apreciada." "Cualquier *pasticcio* impuesto por el mercantilismo de las casas editoriales Italianas . . . mientras á nuestros compositors se les cierra á piedra y lodo todas las puertas, haciéndoles víctimas de desconfianzas y desdenes."

29. For instance, X., "Gazeta Musical" [review of *Follet*], *La veu de Catalunya*, April 5, 1903, 4, thought that the young baritone Sr. Segura possessed a beautiful voice. The tenor, Sr. Arcada, sustained his part with much determination, despite the small volume of his voice.

30. Reported in "Teatre del Bosch," *Revista musical catalana* 3 (1906): 170. No reason for this was given, except to say that the management had decided to substitute two other operas (*Salieri* and *Redhya*, by Costa Nogueras and Bosch) instead.

31. Curet, *Teatre català*, 412. The libretto of *Gaziel* was based on Mestres's dramatic poem of the same title, published in 1891. As Larrad, "Catalan Theatre Works," 84, points out, this "was the first work in which he adopted the orthographical changes which had been pioneered by Pompeu Fabra in the Catalan journal *L'Avenç*."

32. For a good summary of Graner's career as an impresario, see Curet, *Teatre català*, 411–15.

33. Ibid., 340.

34. See Larrad, "Catalan Theatre Works," 139.

35. Fans of *Star Trek: The Next Generation* will recognize something of the character Q in Gaziel.

36. There is one autograph score extant, though Granados's copyist, J. Calduch, rendered the piano part. The numerous cuts and revisions indicate that the work was altered during rehearsals, under some pressure. See Larrad, "Catalan Theatre Works," 162–63.

37. See Larrad, "Catalan Theatre Works," 169, for further discussion of the parallels between Mestres's *Gaziel* and Goethe's *Faust*.

38. Ibid., 170.

39. Ibid., 180.

40. On the other hand, according to M., "Gazeta de teatres" [review of *Gaziel*], *La veu de Catalunya*, October 29, 1906, the *brindisi* had to be repeated at the audience's insistence. This review contains a good plot summary.

41. F., "Teatres y Concerts" [review of *Gaziel*], *El poble català*, October 28, 1906, 3.

42. "Teatre Principal" [review of *Gaziel*], *Revista musical catalana* 3 (1906): 192.

43. J.B. de P., "Espectáculos" [review of *Gaziel*], *El correo catalán*, October 30, 1906. "[D]elicada y de intensa poesia que satisface las exigencies del buen gusto." "[I]dentificado con el poema, penetrando sus finezas una á una."

44. "Barcelona" [review of *Gaziel*], *Diario de Barcelona*, October 29, 1906, 12341.

45. "Teatros y artistas" [review of *Gaziel*], *Noticiero universal*, October 29, 1906, 2.

46. "Teatro Principal" [review of *Gaziel*], *La vanguardia*, October 28, 1906, 9.

47. Federico Urrecha, "Crónicas menudas" [review of *Gaziel*], *El diluvio*, November 1, 1906, 14.

48. J.B. de P., "Espectáculos."

49. Curet, *Teatre català*, 448.

50. Cited in Larrad, "Catalan Theatre Works," 186. "Eren menuts de cos, camacurts y barbuts; lleugers com esquirols, intrepits com musteles, prudents com gats-mesquers y com fúines astuts. . . . Propensos per instint a viure al aguait sempre, cercaren llur refuig, y'n feren llurs palaus, en els caus conillers, en els cataus de fures y en les mines sens fi de rapbufos y taus."

51. Ibid., 193. This comes from a letter that Granados wrote, probably to Georges Jean-Aubry, on October 22, 1911, providing an analysis of the work, complete with musical examples.

52. Alexandre Plana (L'espectacle) and A.B.C. (La música), "'Liliana' a Belles Arts," *El poble català*, July 12, 1911, 1. "Aquest panteisme líric dels poetes alemanys romántics—de Tieck, Uhland, Heine,—que fa animada la natura y vives les plantes y humanisades les bestioles, . . . que les tradicions germaniques mantenen vius en la imaginació del poble, ha trobat entre nosaltres a un poeta, l'Apeles Mestres, que les redueix a imatge amb el vers y amb el liapis."

53. Larrad, "Catalan Theatre Works," 188, informs us that in addition to the autograph, we retain a professionally copied prompter's score, the only such score to survive among the Catalan theater pieces. This gives us important insights into how the work was actually performed.

54. This number was such a hit that Pahissa was compelled to repeat it at the conclusion of the performance.

55. "Revista de Espectáculos" [review of *Liliana*], *Diario de Barcelona*, July 10, 1911, 9346. "El cortejo de silfos, mariposas de alas relucientes e insectos de relumbrantes caparazones, es de lo más vistoso que cabe en la escena."

56. "Liliana," *El poble català*, July 9, 1911, 2. A brief piece on the opera appeared the following day, again on p. 2. It reported that a large audience was very enthusiastic about the work.

57. I.F., "Palau de Belles Arts" [review of *Liliana*], *Revista musical catalana* 8 (1911): 220–21.

58. "Palacio de Bellas Artes" [review of *Liliana*], *La vanguardia*, July 10, 1911, 4.

59. Xarau, "Glosari" [review of *Liliana*], *L'Esquella de la Torratxa* 33/1698 (July 14, 1911): 442.

60. See Larrad, "Catalan Theatre Works," 190. The suite comprised nos. 1, 2, 3, and 6 from the stage version.

61. "Teatros y conciertos: Barcelona," *Musical Emporium* 6/51 (January 1913): 5.

62. Untitled clipping, Mm, fons Granados.

63. See García Morante, *Integral*, 20–21, 32–34.

64. Ibid., 32.

65. The insight on Catalan composers is found in the *Daily Telegraph*, June 22, 1914. Press coverage of the Orfeó's tour was summarized in "Londres," *Revista musical catalana* 11 (1914): 256–65, translated into Catalan.

66. Márquez Villanueva, "Literary Background," 5.

67. Ibid., 6.

7. *LA MAJA DE GOYA*

1. Márquez Villanueva, "Literary Background," 10.

2. Cited in ibid., 11.

3. Aviñoa, *Música i modernisme*, 357.

4. Trans. and cited in Amy A. Oliver, "The Construction of a Philosophy of History and Life in the Major Essays of Miguel de Unamuno and Leopoldo Zea" (Ph.D. diss., University of Massachusetts, 1987), 106. Unamuno turned away from Europeanization after 1897, a year of personal crisis that altered his philosophy. Thereafter he promoted the idea of *hispanidad*, the distinctive traits that united people of the Hispanic world, in contradistinction to the rest of Europe, and that resulted in their marginalization. This rejection of Europe was accompanied by an increasingly interiorized spirituality.

5. Gayana Jurkevich, *In Pursuit of the Natural Sign: Azorín and the Poetics of Ekphrasis* (London: Associated University Presses, 1999), 42.

6. Azorín thought Granados's fellow Catalan Amadeu Vives was the composer whose music most closely embodied the views of the Generation of '98, though others would claim those laurels for Granados himself. See José Martínez Ruiz, *Madrid*, intro., notes, and biblio. José Payá Bernabé (Madrid: Biblioteca Nueva, 1995), 174.

7. José Martínez Ruiz (Azorín), *Castilla*, 7th ed. (Buenos Aires: Editorial Losada, 1969), 123. See also English trans. by Michael Vande Berg (New York: Peter Lang, 1996).

8. Martínez Ruiz, *Madrid*, 159.

9. Other authors preoccupied with Castile included '98 poet Antonio Machado, for example, his *Campos de Castilla* (Castilian Fields), and philosopher Ortega y Gasset. See Fox, "Spain as Castile," 32.

10. Jurkevich, *In Pursuit of the Natural Sign*, 32.

11. Ibid.

12. Generation of '98 literary criticism focused on the *Siglo de Oro*, particularly Cervantes, Calderón, and Lope de Vega. See Francisco Florit Durán, "La recepción de la literatura del Siglo de Oro en algunos ensayos del 98," in *La independencia de las últimas colonias españolas y su impacto nacional e internacional*, ed. José María Ruano de la Haza, series: Ottawa Hispanic Studies 24 (Ottawa: Dovehouse Editions, 2001), 279–96.

13. Oliver, "The Construction of a Philosophy," 102.

14. See Joseph R. Jones, "Recreating Eighteenth-century Musical Theater: The Collaborations of the Composer Enrique Granados (1867–1916) and the Librettist Fernando Periquet y Zuaznábar (1873–1940)," *Dieciocho* 24/1 (Spring 2001): 143. The Conde championed repatriation of Goya's remains from Bordeaux to Spain, which finally took place, with great fanfare, in 1900.

15. Ibid., 2.

16. Miguel Salvador, "The Piano Suite *Goyescas* by Enrique Granados: An Analytical Study" (DMA essay, University of Miami, 1988), 11.

17. Deborah J. Douglas-Brown, "Nationalism in the Song Sets of Manuel de Falla and Enrique Granados" (DMA document, University of Alabama, Tuscaloosa, 1993), 75. See also Janis A. Tomlinson, *Francisco Goya: The Tapestry Cartoons and Early Career at the Court of Madrid* (Cambridge: Cambridge University Press, 1989), 32–33.

18. A *tonadilla* with this same title with music by José Palomino premiered at the Teatro Príncipe in 1774.

19. See Nigel Glendinning, *Goya and His Critics* (New Haven: Yale University Press, 1977), 19. The event was reviewed in *Blanco y negro* on April 7, 1900.

20. When the Prado opened in 1819, there had been but two on view. The sixty-three "cartoons" that Goya created for the Santa Bárbara Tapestry Factory (1775–92) were not discarded after use but rather rolled up and stored, many in the basement of the royal palace. Discovered there in 1868 by art historians, they helped fuel the Goya revival that blossomed in the 1890s, in tandem with the sesquicentenary of Goya's birth. See Glendinning, *Goya*, 11.

21. These had been purchased by a wealthy German banker, Emile Erlanger, in 1873. He donated them to the Prado in 1881, but only five were exhibited. The rest were kept in storage or hung in offices. See Samulski-Parekh, "Goyescas," 89.

22. In fact, the model for those memorable images was probably Pepita Tudó, the mistress of Prime Minister Manuel de Godoy, who himself was rumored to be the queen's lover. See Robert Hughes, *Goya* (New York: Alfred A. Knopf, 2003), 241–42. Hughes very much doubts that Goya ever had a sexual liaison with the Duchess of Alba, but the notion remains enshrined in the popular imagination.

23. The word *sainete* comes from *saín*, fatty parts of a kill given to hunting dogs. Thus, *sainete* means literally a kind of treat or delicacy (in cooking, it means seasoning or sauce).

24. Ortega y Gasset, *Papeles sobre Velázquez y Goya*, 300.

25. Azorín set forth these views in "Exhortación a las majas," *ABC*, June 1, 1917, 1. "La nación es toda una e indivisible."

26. This letter is in the archive of the Am. Also in the archive is a report in *El Punt* of January 15, 1998, and *La vanguardia*, January 15, 1998, of the discovery of a short serenade for voice and piano by Granados dated Madrid, October 28, 1894, and dedicated "A mi queridísimo Isaac." Joan Gay found this in the archive of the Museu d'Art de Girona. The text is: "Girl that I love / Listen to the sad song that says I adore you / Girl that I love ("Niña de mis amores / oye la triste canción del que te adora / niña de mis amores."). Since the premiere did not go well, this was his way of consoling Albéniz. It is only 12 measures long. For more about Albéniz's zarzuela, see Clark, *Portrait*, 113–21. In a letter cited in Fernández-Cid, *Granados*, 210, Granados says that he himself "suffered horribly" at the premiere because of the failure of Albéniz's work. He and other friends of the composer did their best to sustain applause and gain him curtain calls, but the "fiasco" could not be redeemed.

27. Derived from Luis Iglesias de Souza, *Teatro lírico español*, 4 vols. (Coruña: Excma. Diputación Provincial de la Coruña, 1994). There were several other such works produced after 1920. Many more *sainetes* than all of these, however, were composed around 1800 in celebration of the exploits of *majos* and *majas*.

28. One other musical influence of the eighteenth century was J. S. Bach. Granados knew Bach's music intimately and was in the front rank of those promoting it in Barcelona, programming several of Bach's works on his own recitals. See Francesc Bonastre, "La labor de Enric Granados en el proceso de la recepción de la música de Bach en Barcelona," *Anuario musical*, n56 (2001): 173–83.

29. See W. Dean Sutcliffe, *The Keyboard Sonatas of Domenico Scarlatti and Eighteenth-century Musical Style* (Cambridge: Cambridge University Press, 2003), for a thorough study of

these pieces. On pp. 119–20, Sutcliffe makes the common mistake of conflating Andalusian flamenco with Spanish folk music in general. Scarlatti knew little of flamenco as we understand it, for that did not yet exist. The fandangos and *seguidillas* popular in Madrid were not absorbed into flamenco until the nineteenth century, when it became a commercial form of entertainment and its audience and repertoire expanded. During Scarlatti's Spanish tenure, it remained the domain of Andalusian Gypsies who performed it largely for themselves in their own *barrios*.

30. The manuscript was thought lost after Granados made his edition, but in the 1980s it resurfaced at the Bc and has been studied by Maria Ester-Sala. Her initial findings were published in "Un manuscript scarlattià retrobat," *Revista musical catalana* 5/43 (May 1988): 13. A later, more detailed study by her is "D. Scarlatti—E. Granados: Noticia sobre la localización de un manuscrito de tecla extraviado," in *Livro de Homenagem a Macario Santiago Kastner*, ed. Maria Fernanda Cidrais Rodrigues, Manuel Morais, and Rui Vieira Nery (Lisbon: Fundação Calouste Gulbenkian, 1992), 231–52. The manuscript, in the Bc, sig. M. 1964, contains keyboard works by other composers, not just Scarlatti, though his are by far the most numerous.

31. These appear as numbers 31 and 34 in the manuscript, and X and XIII in the Granados edition. They are in DLR 13–14, with all the other transcriptions. One is a Sonata in A Major by Francisco Courcelle, and the other is by an unknown composer.

32. Reported in "Noves," *Revista musical catalana* 2 (1905): 88.

33. In an open letter translated into Catalan and published in "Una carta d'en Risler a n'en Granados," *Revista musical catalana* 2 (1905): 109. "Per fi, un *artista*, després de tants *cabotins* y de tantas nulitats!"

34. The critic D. Bonet y Cembrano, "Concerts Granados," *Joventut* 7/317 (March 8, 1906): 154–55, wrote that Granados would be taking his program on tour throughout Spain, to Valencia, Madrid, Bilbao, San Sebastián, Pamplona, and Zaragoza. As yet, we know little else about this tour, or whether it even took place.

35. F. Suárez Bravo, "Teatro Principal: Primer concierto Granados," *Diario de Barcelona*, March 2, 1906, 2668–69.

36. The *Tonadillas* are now available in García Morante, *Integral*. The exceprts here come from that source.

37. See Mariano Perez Gutiérrez, "The Interaction between Iberian and European Music in the Nineteenth Century," in *Welttheater: Die Künste im 19. Jahrhundert*, ed. Peter Andraschke and Edelgard Spaude (Freiburg: Rombach Verlag, 1992), 36. See also José Subirá, *La tonadilla escénica: sus obras y sus autores* (Barcelona: Editoríal Labor, 1933).

38. Márquez Villanueva, "Literary Background," 7.

39. Periquet once declared, "Goya is for me the King of Spanish painters, and I feel myself king among his admirers." In Fernando Periquet, "'Goyescas,' How the Opera Was Conceived," trans. S. de la Selva, *The Opera News* 7/12 (January 29, 1916): 4.

40. Cited by Rogelio Villar in "Granados," *La revista de música* 3/4 (October 1929): 227–29. This article appeared in conjunction with the production of *Goyescas* in Buenos Aires that year. In fact, Periquet claimed in his article "La ópera española moderna: 'Goyesca,'" *The World's Work: La revista del mundo* (April 1916): 180, that he had met Granados "twenty-five years earlier" (i.e., in 1891) in Albéniz's room at the Hotel París in Madrid. This seems unlikely, as Albéniz was living in London at that time.

41. Fernando Periquet, "Apuntes para la historia de la tonadilla y de las tonadilleras de antaño," paper read at the Ateneo in Madrid, May 26, 1913, n.p. [copy in the Oc], 3, in conjunction with the performance there.

42. Ibid., 5. "[P]erseguido el españolismo neto por lo garra opresora del gusto extranjero, refugióse el sentimiento patriótico en las clases populares, y en ellas cual perfume concentrado, según frase de Feliu y Codina, esperó á que el tiempo aireará nuestra tierra, para difundirse con más intensidad que nunca por la nación entera."

43. Quoted in an anonymous article, "Goyescas o los majos enamorados," *ABC* (2d ed.), February 1, 1916, 12–13. "Además, la palabra Goya, para todo español culto poeta, no es solo un apellido, sino también una época. Goya época significa amores y pasiones, en punto a sentimientos; y socialmente, una mezcla extraña de todas las clases, algo así como un albor de democracia que ponia los toreros junto a las duquesas, y a los principes cerca de las tonadilleras."

44. Samulski-Parekh, "Goyescas," 92, observes, "[Spain] was attempting to reconstruct her political and social systems, hoping to create a greater sense of democracy. This, along with Spain's awakening pride in her national character, . . . fueled the growing interest in Goya and his times."

45. Periquet, "La ópera española," 178.

46. Ramón Barce, "Las 'tonadillas' de Granados y el folklore ciudadano," *Tercer programa* 1 (April 1966): 169.

47. Two *Tonadillas* were dedicated to the baritone Emilio de Gogorza as an expression of gratitude for his assistance arranging a Paris premiere of the opera *Goyescas*: "El majo olvidado" and "Día y noche Diego ronda." The latter piece was not published during the composer's lifetime (now available in García Morante, *Integral*). Granados instead arranged it for cello and piano with the title *Madrigal* and premiered it with Gaspar Cassadó on May 2, 1915, in Barcelona.

48. For an excellent overview of this sort of writing, see Linton E. Powell, Jr., "Guitar Effects in Spanish Piano Music," *Piano and Keyboard*, n180 (May–June 1996): 33–37. Similar evocations in Scarlatti's Sonatas exerted a powerful influence on Spanish nationalists over a century later.

49. These sketches are in his notebook *Apuntes y temas para mis obras*, now in the Pierpont Morgan Library. More will be said of it in chapter 8.

50. Riva, "Granados" [English version], 53. Badia's historic and previously unreleased recordings of several of the *Tonadillas* (accompanying herself on the piano) are on a CD produced by the city council of Sant Pol de Mar in 1995, entitled *Conxita Badia: Veu*.

51. *Granados: Integral de l'obra per a veu i piano*, Maria Lluïsa Muntada, soprano, and Josep Surinyac, piano (La Mà de Guido 2024, 1998).

52. See Jones, "Recreating Eighteenth-century Musical Theater" (Spring 2001): 122. Granados regarded her as a mere epigone capitalizing on the *Goyesca* trend his piano suite had set in motion. As we know, that trend had been in motion for some time before.

53. For instance, see Barce, "Tonadillas," 172. He finds Granados's tonal schemes and use of the piano reminiscent of Schubert, Brahms, and Mahler.

54. Juan José Mantecón, "Un recuerdo: Granados en el Ateneo," *Revista musical hispano-americana* 3 (April 30, 1916): 15. "El recuerdo de aquella noche en que Granados nos hizo conocer sus canciones, nos decía que la actividad nuestra no estaba muerta, que el polen fecundador de nuestro sentir patrio, resurgía en el alma de artista."

8. *GOYESCAS*

1. This letter is in the Mm, fons Granados. "Y he escrito este verano una colección de *Goyescas*, obras de gran vuelo y dificultad."

2. The most readily available source of information on this now is DLR 3–4.

3. No MS exists for this short work (pub. Unión Musical Española, 1973); see DLR 3.

4. These two works were never published in Granados's lifetime and appeared for the first time in print in DLR 3.

5. This was first transcribed by Henry Levine and Samuel Randlett and published in Gregor Benko, "'Reverie-Improvisation' by Enrique Granados," *Clavier* 6/7 (October 1967): 27. It is now available in DLR 3.

6. A detailed study of the contents of this book is available in Riva, "El Llibre d'Apunts d'Enric Granados," 89–106. The book came into the possession of the soprano Amelita Galli-

Curci, who performed in Barcelona during 1913–15. In 1963 she gave it to her friend William Seward, who sold it to the Pierpont Morgan Library in 1985, where it remains today. The book is not large, measuring only 11 x 17 cm.

7. "Estas *Tonadillas* originales no son las conocidas anteriormente y armonizadas. He querido crear la colección que me sirve de documento para la obra *Goyescas*. Y ha de saberse que, a excepción de *Los requiebros* y *Las quejas*, en ninguna otra de mis *Goyescas* se encuentra temas populares. Hecho en modo popular, sí, pero originales."

8. This letter is in the Bc, Epistolario Albéniz, sig. M. 986. "Adios querido . . . para ti nada, paciencia y tiempo para que veas cuanto te admiro y quiero."

9. From Collet, "Albéniz et Granados," 230, cited and trans. in Jean Rogers Longland, "Granados and the Opera *Goyescas*," *Notes Hispanic* 5 (1945): 97–98.

10. Cited in Antonio Fernández-Cid, "Goya, 'Goyescas,' Granados, Alicia de Larrocha," *Academia: Boletín de la Real Academia de Bellas Artes de San Fernando*, n75 (Second Semester 1992): 106.

11. Letter dated December 11, 1910 (Mm, fons Granados, 10.034). "En 'Goyescas' he concentrado toda mi personalidad: me enamoré de la psicología de Goya y de su paleta; por lo tanto, de su maja, señora; de su majo aristocrático; de él y de la Duquesa de Alba, de sus pendencias, de sus amores, de sus requiebros; aquel blanco rosa de las mejillas, contrastando con las blondas y terciopelo negro con alamares; aquellos cuerpos de cinturas cimbreantes, manos de nácar y carmín, posadas sobre azabaches, me han trastornado."

12. Ernest Newman, "The Granados of the *Goyescas*," *Musical Times* 58 (August 1, 1917): 343.

13. Salvador, "*Goyescas*," 47, finds the suggestion of acciacaturas, a particular kind of dissonant ornament associated with Scarlatti, in "El fandango de candil," m. 105.

14. Schuessler, "An Introduction to the Three Stylistic Periods," 16, draws the following intriguing comparison between Granados and Goya in regard to eighteenth-century Italian artists and musicians working in Spain: "Just as Granados learned a sense of concentrated expressiveness from . . . Scarlatti, Goya's study of the etchings of . . . Giovanni Battista Tiepolo (1727–1804) bore fruit in a highly refined sense of detail and contrast, but with the addition of his own, almost modernistic, element of caricature."

15. Linton E. Powell, Jr., *A History of Spanish Piano Music* (Bloomington: Indiana University Press, 1980), 88. As Tomás Marco points out, *Goyescas* deals with history, evoking an idealized vision of Spain in the late 1700s, whereas *Iberia* is preoccupied with a sense of place and offers a "spiritual transformation of the landscape." See his *Spanish Music in the Twentieth Century*, trans. Cola Franzen (Cambridge, Mass.: Harvard University Press, 1993), 8.

16. Indeed, as Ernest Newman points out in "Granados," 347, one could never say of this work what Wagner said of Chopin's music, that it is "music for the right hand." As Newman observed, "[M]any pages . . . of the 'Goyescas' look at first like arrangements for two hands of an organ or orchestral work."

17. For example, in *Goyescas*: con garbo y donaire, con gallardía, con sentimiento amoroso, caprichoso y con alma, expresivo, a piacere, meno allegro, teneramente calmato, con molta gallardía e ben marcato, appassionato, calmato e amoroso, lento e ritmico, grandioso, con dolore e appassionato, largamente, con molta fantasía, tres capricieux, avec sourdine, bien chanté. This aspect of the score was not the result of premeditation or affection but simply, as one might expect, spontaneous feeling.

18. Riva, "Granados" [English version], 42.

19. Salvador, "*Goyescas*," 63. This author aptly points out that many of the drawings in Goya's "Sanlúcar diary" contain scenes of flirtation. For a discussion of this etching, see Hughes, *Goya*, 187–88, who views the vignette as an encounter between a prostitute and a potential client. Goya noted on his preliminary drawing for this work (now in the Prado) that "The old women laugh themselves sick because they know he hasn't a penny."

20. Salvador, "*Goyescas*," 63.

21. Riva, "El Llibre d'Apunts d'Enric Granados," 103.

22. Interestingly, it was also the basis for Pedro Albéniz's *Rondo brillante sobre la canción del Trípili*, op. 26. Pedro (1795–1855), unrelated to Isaac, played an important role in the development of Spanish pianism.

23. The melody and text of the original are quoted in full in Powell, *Spanish Piano Music*, 85.

24. Douglas Riva, "The *Goyescas* for Piano by Enrique Granados: A Critical Edition" (Ph.D. diss., New York University, 1982), 17.

25. A theme from "Coloquio en la reja" (containing the quintuplet turn) even appears outside the suite, in the "Sueños del poeta" (mm. 80–81) from *Escenas poéticas*, possibly of 1912. See Xosé Aviñoa and Douglas Riva, "Introducción a Goyescas," DLR 1, 22. These authors also see a thematic connection between "El amor y la muerte" and "Al suplicio" from *Libro de horas*, also ca. 1912.

26. See Samulski-Parekh, "Goyescas," 117–20.

27. In addition, mm. 29–32 are clearly derived from "La maja dolorosa," mm. 7–12.

28. See Iglesias, *Granados*, 2:342–43 (n. 44) for more on Mesonero Romanos's work.

29. This is cited in Salvador, "*Goyescas*," 84, who raises the issue of the title's correct interpretation.

30. Samulski-Parekh, "Goyescas," 74.

31. Salvador, "Goyescas," 89. It is crucial to understand that the fandango was not integrated into the flamenco repertoire until the nineteenth century. Granados's understanding of the fandango may have been influenced by "flamencoized" varieties of it ca. 1900, but in the context of this work, the fandango is an example of regional folklore, not flamenco per se.

32. Larrocha, "Granados, the Composer," 23.

33. See Gilbert Chase, *Music of Spain* (New York: W. W. Norton, 1941), 231, for this observation about the *pasacalle*. This may be a bit of a stretch, as there is no other connection between this work and the Castilian *pasacalle*, based as it is on a Valencian song. Then again, Granados himself may have been combining elements of both styles.

34. See Wendy Pfeffer, *The Change of Philomel: The Nightingale in Medieval Literature* (New York: Peter Lang, 1985), 29.

35. Enrique Granados, "Notas," program notes for a performance of *Goyescas*, Academia Granados, May 30, 1915 (Am).

36. Granados, "Notas."

37. Aviñoa and Riva, "Introducción a *Goyescas*," DLR 1, 23.

38. Cited in Riva, Program Notes, 14. "Tres grandes sentimientos aparecen en esta obra: el dolor intenso, el amor añorado y la tragedia final—la muerte."

39. Salvador, "*Goyescas*," 32.

40. See Aviñoa and Riva, "Introducción a *Goyescas*," DLR 1, 21. Specifically, compare mm. 54–60 of *Jácara* with mm. 245–49 of "Epílogo."

41. Salvador, "*Goyescas*," 58.

42. "Le spectre disparait pinçant les cordes de sa guitare."

43. Boladeres Ibern, *Granados*, 198.

44. Riva, "*Goyescas* for Piano," 7.

45. "He tenido la dicha por fin de encontrar algo grande—Las Goyescas." From the composer's personal diary (formerly in the possession of Natalia Granados) and cited in Riva, "*Goyescas* for Piano," 1.

46. "Goyescas es el pago de mis esfuerzos para llegar; dicen que he llegado." In a letter to Joaquím Malats, December 11, 1910, and cited in ibid., 1.

47. Fernández-Cid, *Granados*, 205.

48. The cartoon dates from the early 1790s, when Goya was at the end of his tenure at the Royal Tapestry Factory. Granados premiered his piece at a benefit for the French Red Cross at

the Palau de la Música Catalana on March 5, 1915, though he introduced an "improvisation" on this subject at a performance on March 29, 1914, at the Escola Choral in Tarrasa. Moreover, Granados recorded a "Pelele" improvisation, though its relationship to the Tarrasa version remains unclear. See Iglesias, *Granados*, 1:283.

49. Larrocha, "Granados, the Composer," 23.

50. Wyers, *Miguel de Unamuno*, 3.

51. See Anthony D. Smith, *Nationalism: Theory, Ideology, History* (Cambridge: Polity Press, 2001), 49–51.

52. Gabriel Alomar, "Las Goyescas," *El poble català*, September 25, 1910. "Nadie como el me ha hecho sentir el alma musical de España. [*Goyescas* es] como una mezcla de las tres artes, pintura, música, poesía, delante de un mismo modelo: España, la 'Maja' eterna."

53. Luis Villalba, *Enrique Granados: Semblanza y biografía* (Madrid: Imprenta Helénica, 1917), 33. "Y sobre el tejido de melodías y armonías, flota una súplica como de canción bien castiza, donde á la sexualidad en fiesta y á los amores del color con la música, se junta la negrura de ojos de la Maja-Nación, negrura de clérigos en callejuelas sin sol, y de tribunales secretos, y autos de fe en plazas sombreadas por conventos, y procesiones de Semana Santa y manicomios convulsivos y brujas nocturnas."

54. A copy of this program is in the Mm, fons Granados.

55. The manuscript is in the Cdm; published in DLR 14. See Clark, *Portrait*, 265, for an account of the circumstances under which Albéniz's soon-to-be widow gave Granados the manuscript to complete. *Azulejos* was originally intended to be another suite, but Albéniz had only completed much of the first number, "Preludio," when he died. F. Suárez Bravo, "Concierto Granados," *Diario de Barcelona*, March 13, 1911, 3398–99, claimed that "With *Iberia*, Albéniz opened up an unknown horizon to Spanish composers" ("Albéniz abrió con su última obra [*Iberia*] un horizonte desconocido a los compositores españoles"). He saw *Azulejos* as an extension of *Iberia* in its revelation of "Spanish music dressed in modernity" ("una música española . . . vestida a la modernidad").

56. The Pleyel piano on which he played *Goyescas* in Paris is now at the Cdm.

57. Pillois, "Un entretien avec Granados," 3. "Goya est le génie représentatif de l'Espagne. Dans le vestibule du musée du Prado, à Madrid, sa statue s'impose au regard, la première. J'y vois un enseignement: nous devons, à l'exemple de cette belle figure, tenter de contribuer à la grandeur de notre pays. Les chefs-d'oeuvre de Goya l'immortalisent en exaltant notre vie nationale. Je subordonne mon inspiration à celle de l'homme qui sut traduire aussi parfaitement les actes et les moments caractéristiques du peuple d'Espagne."

58. Press reaction to the concert is summarized (in Catalan translation) in "L'Enric Granados a París," *Revista musical catalana* 11 (1914): 140–42. This quote is from a review in *Paris-Midi* by Le Colleur d'Affiches. "Asturies, Galicia, el país basc i Catalunya reben corrents estètiques diferents, vingudes generalment de l'exterior; Andalusía, Murcia i Valencia estàn impregnades de tradicions hispano-moresques; solament el cor d'Espanya, Castella i Aragó, viu sostreta de tota intervenció estrangera. Es d'aquesta Espanya que l'art d'en Granados ha sortit; es aquest esperit nacional, en tota sa puresa i sa integritat, que anima la seva obra i li dóna aquest color inimitable, aquest color especial."

59. As Carol Hess points out, Spanish composers themselves considered "Castile the center of Spain and suggestive of universalism rather than 'local color.'" See *Manuel de Falla and Modernism in Spain, 1898–1936* (Chicago: University of Chicago Press, 2001), 3.

60. See Fox, "Spain as Castile," 29. The impact of Arabic on Castilian is one obvious example of "foreign intervention."

61. "L'Enric Granados a París," in *Excelsior* by E. Montoriol-Tarrés. "Es el cantaire de l'ànima de la nostra raça, és la veu de la nostra terra." Of the 1913 New York premiere of *Goyescas* by Schelling, a reviewer for the *New York Times* thought the work gave evidence of Granados's

individuality, and that the Spain "embodied in his music is authentic." Authentic compared to what? Evidently to Albéniz, who "saw Spain through the veil of the modern Frenchman." Given the immense influence of Schumann, Chopin, and Liszt on Granados's late Romantic idiom, was his *españolismo* necessarily more "authentic" than Albéniz's? In any case, these sentiments reflect those of Pedrell, who also found French influence "corrupting." And as Carl Dahlhaus reminds us, "The discovery (or the construction, as the case may be) of a national musical character, which was felt to distinguish a nation from the pan-European tradition, was itself a pan-European phenemenon." See his *Between Romanticism and Modernism: Four Studies in the Music of the Later Nineteenth Century,* trans. Mary Whittall (Berkeley: University of California Press, 1980), 90.

62. Lily Litvak, *España 1900: Modernismo, anarquismo y fin de siglo* (Barcelona: Anthropos, 1990), 246.

63. One is reminded of Christopher Hitchens's view of this sort of thing: "The unspooling of the skein of the genome has effectively abolished racism and creationism. . . . But how much more addictive is the familiar old garbage about tribe and nation and faith." See his *Letters to a Young Contrarian* (Cambridge, Mass.: Basic Books, 2001), 108.

64. Fox, *La invención de España,* 16.

65. Consult Gary Tinterow and Geneviève Lacambre, *Manet/Velázquez: The French Taste for Spanish Painting* (New York: Metropolitan Museum of Art, 2003). Despite the catalogue's title, Goya figures prominently in this history, especially in Juliet Wilson-Bareau's essay "Goya and France," and Ilse Hempel Lipschutz's "Goya and the French Romantics." Goya's paintings and etchings prefigured and influenced several later movements, including Romanticism, Realism, Impressionism, and Expressionism. The mysterious world of Goya's *Caprichos* inspired French Romantic critics and poets such as Gide, Hugo, and Baudelaire. See Glendinning, *Goya and His Critics,* 242–45.

66. E. Montoriol-Tarrés, "Enric Granados," *Revista musical catalana* 13 (1916): 196. Montoriol-Tarrés was an accomplished pianist who, in fact, gave the first Parisian performance, in early 1914, weeks before Granados. See Carol A. Hess, *Enrique Granados: A Bib-Bibliography* (New York: Greenwood Press, 1991), 28 n. The award was reported in Maurice Bex, "Concerts et recitals," *La revue musical* (July–August 1914): 48.

67. An interview by José del Castillo with Schelling's widow appears in Vila San-Juan, *Papeles íntimos,* 89–91.

68. His various contracts with Schirmer are in the Mm, fons Granados. Granados was to receive 50 percent for orchestral works and 12.5 percent for all others, though this was changed to 10 percent the following year.

69. Unless otherwise noted, this and other letters to Schelling from Granados are in the Schelling Archive, now housed at the University of Maryland, College Park.

70. The opera was originally entitled *Goyesca,* singular, but the tendency of the press and public to conflate the opera's name with that of the piano suite was irresistible, and in the end the authors reconciled themselves to the plural, *Goyescas,* though they continued to use the singular even after the production.

71. Quoted in "Goyescas o los majos enamorados," *ABC,* February 1, 1916, 12. "Así escribió su encatadora partitura, sin palabras, en absoluta libertad, viendo en su mente toda una cabalgata de figures goyescas, majas, duquesas, guardias reales, brujas, aquelarres."

72. Ibid.

73. Granados makes mention of this in an undated note to Ernest Schelling. Cited in Riva, "*Goyescas* for Piano," 24. In fact, a little inconsistency might have made the "drama" less predictable.

74. Charles Wilson, "The Two Versions of 'Goyescas,'" *Monthly Musical Record* 81 (October 1951): 207.

75. Samulski-Parekh, "Goyescas," 200.

76. Longland, "Granados and the Opera *Goyescas*," 98. The complete title was rather wordy, and not very coherent: *Goyesca: Literas y calesas, o Los majos enamorados*.

77. Peyser, "Granados Here," 3.

78. Larrad, "Catalan Theatre Works," 53.

79. Susann Waldmann, *Goya and the Duchess of Alba* (Munich: Prestel, 1998), 37, makes this intriguing observation about the symbolism of the *pelele*: "Women dominated social life in the aristocratic circles of late eighteenth-century Spain, while men tended to play a subordinate role [a situation exemplified by Carlos IV and his domineering wife María Luisa, and by the Duke and Duchess of Alba themselves]. [The *pelele* is] an allusion to the helplessness of men subject to women's caprices in the perennial game of the sexes."

80. A letter from Rouché confirming the agreement is dated June 22, 1914, and reproduced in Fernández-Cid, *Granados*, 37.

81. He had planned to go there the year before, in the summer of 1913, but illness prevented him from doing so. Ignacy Paderewski was a neighbor of Schelling's, and Granados got to know him during his stay. Schelling approached the Chicago Grand Opera Co. about producing *Goyescas*; they were interested but noncommittal.

82. Vila San-Juan, *Papeles íntimos*, 83.

83. The correspondence between Granados and Rouché is excerpted in an article in *Le Temps* of July 7, 1915 (clipping is in the Mm, fons Granados). "Après la victoire de notre pays."

9. A WORLD OF IDEAS

1. Pi i Sunyer (1879–1965) was yet another of the renaissance men who contributed so much to the cultural and intellectual life of Barcelona in the early twentieth century. He served as president of the Associació de Música da Camera. See Montserrat Albet, "August Pi i Sunyer i la música," in *Centenari de la naixença d'August Pi i Sunyer* (Barcelona: n.p., 1979), 177–79.

2. It is also called *La navidad de los niños* (The Children's Christmas). This account is in Heliodoro Carpintero, "Tres grandes amigos" [newspaper unknown], February 18, 1965 (clipping in Mm, fons Granados). It can also be found in Albet, "Pi i Sunyer," 179. The incomplete MS for the little theater piece is in the Cdm. According to Albet, the text itself is lost.

3. Badia, "Personal Portrait," 60.

4. Miró also died relatively young, in 1929 at the age of 50. He penned a moving tribute to his friend Granados entitled "El dedo de Dios," which appeared in the *Revista musical catalana* 13 (1916): 184–85, shortly after Granados's death. It is reproduced in Vila San-Juan, *Papeles íntimos*, 38–40.

5. Márquez Villanueva, "Literary Background," 13. In 1915, at this same time, Granados was intrigued by the possibility of some sort of collaboration with another giant of Spanish letters, Vicente Blasco Ibañez. Granados and Casals wrote to the author, who expressed his openness to the idea in a letter of March 5, 1915, from Paris, reproduced in Vila San-Juan, *Papeles íntimos*, 30–31. In this letter, the famous author stated his "enormous admiration" for Granados. Another leading author who approached him to collaborate was Gregorio Martínez Sierra, best known for his work with Manuel de Falla. See ibid., 40–42. Nothing came of either of these prospects.

6. The MS, now in the Mm, fons Granados, is dated March 13, 1896, and is most certainly not his first opus. Granados wrote an undated letter to Pedrell (Bc, Epistolario Pedrell, sig. M. 964) making reference to this work: "El tema es 'Nadie es Viejo en el saber'" (The theme is: No one is old in knowledge).

7. Once, when one of his children was sick while he was away from home, he entered a church and prayed to a figure of Christ illuminated by a single candle. Upon learning in a letter from Amparo that his child was "out of danger," he enthusiastically wrote back, "I sincerely believe that God heard my pleas the other night." See Fernández-Cid, *Granados*, 83–84.

8. He was also persuaded to give an informal concert there. The event is reported in *Revista montserratina* 8/3 (March 1914): 129.

9. The MS for this work is in the Cdm. "El Angel: Ven alma, mi Dios te llama para premiar tu martirio. / El Alma: Voy a vivir en el seno del Señor y rogar por los mios."

10. See Rodrigo, "Badia," 88.

11. Riva, "Granados" [English version], 54.

12. See García Morante, *Integral*, 20, for a discussion of textual and editorial matters.

13. Felix Borowski wrote detailed program notes for the occasion, "Fourth Program of the Twenty-fifth Season (1915–16) of the Chicago Symphony Orchestra" (Chicago: Orchestral Association, 1915), 44–49, which were reused for the 1924 concert (197–200).

14. Quoted in "Teatre del Bosch," *Revista musical catalana* 3 (1906): 170. "Pera aixó m'inspiro en el cèlebre quadro d'en G. Rossetti sobre 'l mateix motiu. La meva idea a l'escriure Dante no ha sigut seguir pas a pas la *Divina Comedia*, sinó donar la meva impressió sobre una vida y una obra: Dante–Beatriu y la *Divina Comedia* són pera mi una mateixa cosa; més encara: desitjo enriquir la meva obra amb quelcom de la *Vita Nuova*. No poden condensarse totes en una sola? Per al 'l quadro patètic de la mort de Beatriu sento un color molt especial de l'orquesta. En alguns passatges desitjo produir sonoritats que s'apropin més al color que als sons: vull pintar amb l'orquesta. Aquelles tintes violàcies, carmí y verd del quadro d'en Rossetti han impressionat tant intensament els meus ulls, que'l meu oit no vol ser menys: vull sentir música d'aquell color. Vull trobar aquell bés que li dóna Dante a Beatriu per medi de l'àngel de l'amor."

15. In his entry on Granados in *NGD* (2d), Mark Larrad describes the chromaticism as "pedantic" and points to the work's overall "formal incoherence." Considering the new ground Granados was breaking in the context of Spanish music, this assessment may be too severe.

16. Riva, "Granados" [English version], 54.

17. Borowski, "Fourth Program of the Twenty-fifth Season (1915–16)," 47.

18. Granados would have had ample opportunity to hear Strauss's works in Barcelona, where the German composer was hugely popular. Strauss traveled to Barcelona in 1897 to conduct his *Don Juan* and *Tod und Verklärung*. The critics gave these works a rapturous reception. See Aviñoa, *Música i modernisme*, 77.

19. F. Suárez Bravo, "Orquesta Sinfónica de Madrid," *Diario de Barcelona*, May 27, 1915, 6667–69. "Francesca es un rayo de luz que ilumina aquellos antros." "[E]s una composición de gran vuelo; el maestro se ha mostrado ambicioso, pero es porque podia serlo."

20. "Sinfónica de Madrid," *Revista musical catalana* 12 (1915): 179.

21. Manuel Valls, "Granados, encara una sorpresa," *Guia musical*, n12 (April 15, 1982): 2.

22. For a useful summary of Granados's connection to and activities in Lleida, along with a list of all the Granados events sponsored by the city up to 1967, see Juan Riera, *Enrique Granados (Estudio)* (Lerida: Instituto de Estudios Llerdenses, 1967), 95–104.

23. La Argentina, so named because she was born in Buenos Aires, made her New York debut at Maxine Elliott's Theatre on February 10, 1916, and the *New York Herald* reported ("Sprightly Spanish Dancer Sings as She Snaps Castanets") on the following day (p. 12) that "[h]er dancing is not brazen, suggestive or sensuous. Instead she has a winning smile, pretty eyes, very nimble feet and heels and sensitive hands." Ignacio Zuloaga designed her costumes. On this occasion she performed a work written for her debut by Granados, *The Dance of the Green Eyes* (*Danza de los ojos verdes*), and the composer was on hand to offer his approbation.

24. Particularly in its issues on December 30, 1915, January 6, 13, 27, and February 3, 10, 17, 24, 1916.

25. In a curious historical irony, it was another Spaniard, Manuel García, who introduced Spanish opera (his own, albeit in Italian) to New York, in 1825. We recall that García was the maternal grandfather of Charles de Bériot, Granados's piano teacher in Paris.

26. See Janet Sturman, *Zarzuela: Spanish Operetta, American Stage* (Urbana: University of Illinois Press, 2000), 59–66.

27. A fascinating essay on this phenomenon is found in Carleton Sprague Smith's preface to *Granados and Goyescas: Catalogue of an Exhibition Honoring Enrique Granados and the American Premiere of Goyescas*, the Spanish Institute, May 27–July 9, 1982 (New York: Spanish Institute, 1982). Prescott, of course, wrote a celebrated history of the Spanish conquest. Irving's evocation of the Alhambra, based on his tenure in Spain as American ambassador in the 1840s, is a classic, while Longfellow also spent many months in Spain and translated classics of Spanish literature into English. Velásquez, El Greco, and other Spanish masters profoundly influenced American painters, and Sargent was actually a pupil of the Spanish-oriented Carolus Duran. Sargent's *Jaleo* is one of the most arresting images of flamenco performance ever committed to canvas. Whistler's 1884 portrait of Pablo de Sarasate (*Arrangement in Black*), who toured the United States in 1867 and 1889, is likewise a monument to the close connection between the United States and Spain.

28. See James D. Fernández, "Latin America and Spain in U.S. Hispanism," in *Spain in America: The Origins of Hispanism in the United States*, ed. Richard L. Kagan (Urbana and Champaign: University of Illinois Press, 2002), 124–25. Educators demanded increased emphasis on Spanish because they felt the nation's future lay more with the Hispanic realm than with the warring European countries.

29. On a voyage to Mallorca years earlier, Granados suffered from seasickness and, counting the hours and minutes, longed for the trip to end. Upon his return, he half-jokingly suggested to his students at the Academy that a railroad bridge should be built out to the island. Related in Boladeres Ibern, *Granados*, 46.

30. Mestres, *Volves musicals*, 61.

31. According to Antoni Carreras i Verdaguer in J.C., "Memòria d'Enric Granados," 11. The letter is in the Ag.

32. Llongueras, "Como conocí," 117.

33. This is according to José Lassalle, "Granados héroe," *Revista musical hispano-americana* 3 (April 30, 1916), 12. Lassalle had boarded the *Montevideo* during a stop in Cádiz and soon became privy to Granados's misgivings. Apparently Granados had already been contemplating bolting the ship and returning to Barcelona by train from Cádiz.

34. The boarding incidents were reported by Periquet in an article, "Desde Nueva York," which appeared in the Madrid daily *El liberal* on February 1, 1916. Periquet goes on to give his impressions of New York, which amazed him with its "monstrous" skyscrapers, obsession with business, and ubiquitous cabarets catering to New Yorkers' other obsession, dancing.

35. In a typewritten letter now in the Mm, fons Granados. "Desde que salimos de Cádiz, que solo deben emplearse 10 días hasta New York, hemos empleado 15—solo tuvimos unas cuantas horas de reposo, y lo demás un temporal deshecho. Creíamos Mamá y yo no volveros a ver. . . . Ha sido terrible." Juan Ramón Jiménez, the Spanish Nobel-winning writer, spent time with Granados in New York and described him as perpetually nervous: "Enrique Granados was afraid, horrified, and one saw this in his spirit and his body. Horrified of what? Of everything—always the sea, of abstract New York, of the hotel, the theater, the people." See his *Españoles de tres mundos* (Madrid: Alianza, 1987), 72.

36. Periquet reported this in an article entitled "Un concierto en el mar," which appeared in the May 1, 1916, issue of *Lira española* in Madrid. The concert took place on the evening of December 13, 1915, two days before their arrival in New York. In a curious historical irony, the concert was a benefit for victims of shipwreck.

37. "Poet & Piano," 187.

38. J.L., "El próximo concierto del Maestro Granados," *Las novedades*, February 17, 1916, 12.

39. From Ernest Hutcheson, *The Literature of the Piano*, 3d ed. (London, 1974), 362; quoted in Barrie Jones, "Enrique Granados," 17.

40. For Albéniz's encounters with the "languish or stab" stereotype of Spaniards, see Clark, *Portrait*, 80.

41. Richard Aldrich, "Granados in His Own Music," *New York Times*, January 24, 1916.

42. "Granados in New York: Soul of Spanish Composer Is Not for Sale," *Kansas City Times*, n.d.

43. From J. B. Trend, *Manuel de Falla and Spanish Music* (New York: Alfred A. Knopf, 1929), 33.

44. Richard H. Walthew, "Enrique Granados: 1867–1916," *Musical Observer* 19/3 (1920): 14.

45. Grenville Vernon, "New York Hears Its First Spanish Opera," *The Opera News* 7/13 (February 5, 1916): 2, shed light on the homeland of *Goyescas*: "Spain is before us—not the Spain of Philip II, but the Spain of the toreador, and perhaps of the philosophical anarchist"!

46. Periquet related his story of the opera's genesis in "'Goyescas': How the Opera was Conceived." Laying it on thickly, with a trowel, Periquet concluded with this invocation: "May all redound in honor of Goya, the most Spanish of painters, the most gallant of *majos*, the bravest of men and the most ardent lover of those valiant, lovely, dreamy, passionate, gay, and honest *majas*, mothers of our mothers." For the record, *Granados's* grandmothers were not *majas*.

47. "El estreno de *Goyescas* en Nueva York," *Musical Emporium* 9/76 (January–February 1916): 4–5. "Granados, como lo hizo antes Albéniz, ha llevado al extranjero, para popularizarlos y glorificarlos, los aires característicos de España, fuente de inagotable inspiración." "Un pasado de grandeza, con grandeza perdido, y con grandeza recobrado."

48. Red and yellow are the colors of the Spanish flag; *plus ultra*, "ever farther," is the motto on the flag.

49. This is a partial quote, partial paraphrase of the Alfonso de Castilla article, "España Aquí," *Las novedades*, January 27, 1916, 6. "Porque así es, se enorgullece Nueva York de abrir sus brazos a España, que llega, fraternal, envuelta en resplandores augustos."

50. Many Spaniards blamed their own government for stumbling into the debacle, and the army and navy for losing the war. As Donald M. Goldstein et al. point out in *The Spanish-American War: The Story and Photographs* (Washington: Brassey's, 1998), 166, "Spaniards in general seemed to bear no malice toward the Americans and appeared relieved that the war had ended and Spain had been freed from the crushing financial and personnel cost of maintaining reluctant colonies."

51. Peyser, "Granados Here," 4.

52. Carmen has been an irritant to many Spanish artists. Teresa Berganza wrote notes in the program for a 1977 production of the opera at the Edinburgh Festival, in which she sang the lead. Her anguished commentary reveals the same misgivings Granados had: "My greatest wish . . . is to . . . erase for good from the public's mind and imagination the false idea of Carmen. . . . I shall . . . do my best to present to the public the image of a real Spain." Cited in James Parakilas, "How Spain Got a Soul," in *The Exotic in Western Music*, ed. Jonathan Bellman (Boston: Northeastern University Press, 1998), 163.

53. Actually, newspaper accounts differ as to his exact words, though not his general meaning. He would have spoken through an interpreter, and this permitted multiple translations. For instance, an undated clipping (gotten through the Internet reproduction service ProQuest) from an unidentified New York newspaper, entitled simply "Enrique Granados Arrives," put these words in his mouth: "[Foreign artists] have given the impression to the American people that Spanish songs are jingly and that the dances are performed in a jumpy manner of the twanging of a guitar." This certainly took the onus off audiences in the United States, who were helpless victims of foreign "misinterpretation" of Spanish culture, by performers who "do not understand the language or the people."

54. "Poet & Piano,"187.

55. "Rehearsal of *Goyescas*," *New York Herald*, January 27, 1916, 13. This short piece lists some of the grandees in attendance.

56. Longland, "Granados and the Opera *Goyescas*," 107, provides a detailed description of this manuscript and notes that there is "surprisingly little variation" between it and the published version. Granados autographed it on May 28, 1914, and Periquet a few weeks later, on July 14. It bears an affectionate dedication to Ernest Schelling's first wife, Lucie. Shortly after Granados's arrival in New York, Schirmer published the vocal score of the opera in a bilingual edition. The distinguished African American author James Weldon Johnson did the English translation. The Castilian libretto was published separately in 1916 by R. Velasco in Madrid.

57. According to H. L. Kirk, *Pablo Casals, A Biography* (New York: Holt, Rinehart & Winston, 1974), 308, Granados requested Casals's assistance because of errors in the score and a paucity of expression marks, all of which complicated preparations. This same author tells us (p. 310) that the morning after Granados had composed his Intermezzo, Casals found him "depressed and close to tears," because he had been forced to capitulate to "unreasonable demands."

58. Corredor, *Conversations with Casals*, 165.

59. Goya was born in Fuendetodos and grew up in Zaragoza. A piano reduction of the famous Intermezzo is in DLR 3.

60. See Samulski-Parekh, "Goyescas," 212, for a discussion of the seven vocal scores in the Met archive that were used for the production and the cuts they contain.

61. Granados visited doctors in New York and a dentist in Washington, D.C., for treatment, receiving various prescriptions and a list of dietary guidelines (now in the Ra).

62. Milton, *The Fallen Nightingale*, 455–57, is of the opinion that La Argentina was elbowed out of the production by Bonafiglio, whose mistress and future second wife was Galli. La Argentina had traveled from Argentina to New York before learning this news, however, and had to be consoled with another performance. This was a source of embarrassment to Granados.

63. Riva, "Granados" [English version], 20.

64. The much-maligned Periquet must be given his due in this regard. He devoted meticulous and devoted study to getting this aspect of the production right. The materials he collected are in the library of the Hispanic Society of America. Contained in a volume entitled "Decorado. Vestuario. Accesorios." and dated Madrid, June 1914, they include typewritten indications for sets in each scene as well as photos of San Antonio de la Florida and other locales, postcards of Goya's paintings (*El pelele*, *La maja vestida*, *La maja y los embozados*), shots of mannequins in period dress from the National Archeological Museum in Madrid, as well as examples of *literas* and *calesas*.

65. "He caido de pie aquí. Hay una atmosfera magnífica." This letter is in the Archivo Familia Gabriel Miró.

66. "'Goyescas,' Spanish Opera, Has World Premiere Here," *New York Herald*, January 29, 1916, 12.

67. Corredor, *Conversations with Casals*, 165.

68. Henry T. Finck, *Musical Progress* (Philadelphia: Theodore Presser, 1923), 73.

69. Cited in Riva, "Granados" [English], 21.

70. Jones, "Recreating Eighteenth-century Musical Theater" (Spring 2001): 145.

71. "New Grenados [*sic*] Opera; Mme. Barrientos' Debut Here," *New York Herald*, January 30, 1916, 11.

72. Vernon, "New York Hears Its First Spanish Opera," 2. On p. 5 of this article, we learn that "a most disagreeable claque" disrupted the premiere, though the audience "gave every evidence of pleasure, and called the artists, the composer," et al. for repeated curtain calls.

73. In the *World* of January 29, 1916.

74. "'Goyescas' in World Premiere: A Fair Success," clipping without periodical title or date in the New York Public Library's file on Granados and *Goyescas* in New York.

75. Cited in Riva, "Granados" [English version], 20.

76. Herbert Weinstock, "America," *Opera* 20 (1969): 497–98. He reviewed a production by the Opera Theater of the Manhattan School of Music.

77. Harold C. Schonberg, "Colorful World of Old Spain," *New York Times*, March 15, 1969. This was a performance by the Little Orchestra Society.

78. Ellen Pfeifer, "Boston Concert Opera: Granados's *Goyescas*," *High Fidelity/Musical America* 32 (1982): 32.

79. Harvey E. Phillips, "Reports: New York," *Opera News* 33 (May 17, 1969): 24. This is a review of the same Manhattan School of Music production that Weinstock stoically endured.

80. R.V., "La ópera 'Goyescas,'" *La esfera* 3/117 (March 25, 1916): n.p. "Los críticos mas autorizados . . . consagran artículos encomiásticos á la obra de Granados en los que reconocen las cualidades salientes de la música de *Goyescas*." "[E]l triunfo de Granados en Nueva York es de una importancia capital para la música española."

81. See, for instance, the Niagara Falls of American encomiums that roars over the pages of Lively [*sic*], "Les *Goyescas* a Nova York," *Revista musical catalana* 13 (March 1916): 78–83.

82. Vila San-Juan, *Papeles íntimos*, 87.

83. Adolfo Salazar, "'Goyescas' y el 'color local,'" *Revista musical hispano-americana* 3 (April 30, 1916): 9. "[E]l criterio extranjero del *españolismo* es algo inseparable de un *andalucismo* chirle."

84. Ibid., 10. "[I]ncapacidad de percibir suficientemente en ellas las gradaciones del 'color local.'" "[E]ncima de banales convenciones, demasiado cómodas para una crítica superficial o un gusto fácil."

85. Rogelio Villar, "El estreno de Goyescas," *La esfera* 3/108 (January 22, 1916): n.p. "Los compositors españoles, cuando se proponen hacer arte nacional, sienten y se expresan . . . en un andaluz convencional o en un arabismo u orientalismo falso. Granados . . . no necesita recurrir a la música andaluza, aunque algunas veces emplee sus giros y ritmos." "[A]ctualmente el compositor español más original."

86. Boladeres Ibern, *Granados*, 140.

87. Cited in Albert McGrigor, "The Catalan Piano School."

88. José Subirá, *Enrique Granados: Su producción musical, su madrileñismo, su personalidad artística* (Madrid: Zoila Ascasíbar, 1926), 21.

89. Cited in Riva, "Granados" [English], 17.

90. Cited in ibid., 20.

91. "Friends of Music Applaud Mr. Granados, Composer-Pianist," *New York Herald*, January 24, 1916, 13.

92. "Granados, Pianist, in American Debut," *Toledo Times*, February 6, 1916. Richard Aldrich, "Granados in His Own Music," shared this view, saying they "grazed closely the line of salon music, and sometimes broke through it."

93. J.L., "El próximo concierto," 12. "[C]onozco los puntos flacos de mi música: pero en tanto que la generalidad se deleita con ella . . . los críticos muchas veces se complacen en apuntar los trazos débiles."

94. Interview in an untitled clipping dated January 6, 1916, in the NYPL file on Granados and *Goyescas*.

95. "Aeolian Hall: Concierto del Maestro Granados," *Las novedades*, February 24, 1916, 5.

96. "Granados Plays His Own Works: Spanish Composer-Pianist Heard by New Yorkers. Anna Fitziu Sings His Songs," *Musical America*, March 1916.

97. This account of his visit comes from Fernández-Cid, *Granados*, 36. Granados had experienced more than a little homesickness during his time in the United States. He told Casals that he missed familiar little things, like his own furniture and, of course, his own piano.

98. An account of the evening appeared in "Wilsons Give Musicale: Distinguished Assembly Includes about 300 Guests," *Washington Post*, March 8, 1916, 4. The invitation to Granados was

extended by Henry Junge, the official who was in charge of organizing such events at the White House.

99. Vives, "Evocació," 182. "Per fi he vist els meus somnis realizats. Es veritat que tinc el cap ple de cabells blancs i que es pot dir que ara començo la meva obra, mes estic ple de confiança i d'entusiasme per treballar més i més. . . . Soc un supervivent de la lluita estèril a que ens sotmet la ignorancia i la indiferencia de la nostra patria. Tota la meva alegría actual, és més per lo que ha de venir, que per lo fet fins ara. Somnio amb París, i tinc un món de projectes."

100. According Mestres himself in "Enric Granados: Notes íntimes," 137.

101. Riva, "Granados" [English version], 21.

102. This is according to José María Pi y Sunyer in an article in *Labor Lérida*, n169 (1957): 9. The clipping is in the Mm, fons Granados.

103. "Poet & Piano," 188.

104. This was related by Bliss to Malvina Hoffman. Hoffman's correspondence is now in the Getty Center for the History of Art and the Humanities. While in New York, Granados practiced on Hoffman's piano, which had belonged to her late father, Richard, a concert pianist.

105. The bronze life mask is now on display at the Hispanic Society of America, in New York.

106. However, Wilder G. Penfield was a passenger who reported that during the voyage, the *Sussex* "passed through clumps of bales and an occasional raft. The rumor went about that two merchant vessels had been sunk there not very long before." His account is in "Some Personal Experiences in the *Sussex* Disaster," *Princeton Alumni Weekly* 16/29 (1918): 680.

107. According to a Mrs. Clarence Handyside, who was with the Granadoses at the time. An account of Granados's last pianistic essay appears in Pablo Vila San-Juan, "Los cuatro pianos de Enrique Granados," *La vanguardia española*, March 24, 1966, 48. This article places the piano in the dining room, but John Milton's research suggests that any piano on the *Sussex* would have had to be in the smoking room, as no other area was large enough to accommodate it.

108. "El 'Sussex,'" *Diario de Barcelona*, March 27, 1916, 4062. This article informs us that the *Sussex* was built at Dumbarton in 1896 and displaced 1,353 tons. It was not a large ship.

109. Longland, "Granados and the Opera *Goyescas*," 110, reports that a "week earlier Mr. and Mrs. Reginald De Koven had traveled on [the *Sussex*] and had with difficulty obtained two antiquated life belts for three persons." However, Edward Marshall, an American journalist on the *Sussex* who survived the attack, reported to *The Times* the following day that "Fifty per cent of those who were thrown into the sea by the accident or jumped in were not wearing lifebelts, although I saw plenty of lifebelts on the ship." There may have been plenty of them, but they were not in good condition. The ship was actually owned by the French national railway and was flying the French tricolor when it left port.

110. This account is found in Chapter 12: The *Sussex* Affair, in James Mark Baldwin's *Between Two Wars: 1861–1921*, vol. 1 (Boston: Stratford Co., 1926), 214–15. Baldwin (1861–1924) was a psychologist who wrote books and established programs at leading universities.

111. For his biography and a photo, see www.peoplehelp.com.au/stories/harry.html. He was born in 1889.

112. This was reported in the *Oregonian*, June 14, 1923, in an article entitled "Sinker of *Sussex* Dead," upon the arrest and testimony of a German admiral then in French custody. The ship was widened astern to accommodate troops at the beginning of the war, and then it was returned to civilian service when it was sold to the French railway.

113. Baldwin, *Between Two Wars*, 216.

114. Then again, maybe Pustkuchen was just following orders to torpedo all Allied shipping and was made the fall guy when the sinking erupted in an international scandal and propaganda coup for the Allies. This is the view of David Walton, "Two Last Journeys: Enrique Granados and the 'Sussex,'" *Newsletter of the Iberian and Latin American Music Society*, n18 (Autumn 2004): 5–6 . He believes that there is no way a submarine captain could have mis-

taken the *Sussex* for anything other than what it was. In any case, Pustkuchen and his ship paid the ultimate price. He remained in command of UB-29 until November 2, 1916, then took charge of UC-66, which was sunk on June 12, 1917, by the British trawler *Sea King*. The UB-29 had already been sunk by depth charges, on December 13, 1916. His first command had been UC-5, which was sunk in April 1916.

115. According to Compton Mackenzie, *Greek Memories* (Frederick, Md.: University Publications of America, 1987), 146, "In the forward saloon . . . several of the members of an Italian theatrical company died of terror, and their corpses propped up against the tables kept in death their last grimaces. . . . The crew had started to cut off the fingers of the dead passengers in order to steal their rings," until a British naval officer drove them off.

116. Mrs. Robert Woods Bliss, who traveled with the Granadoses over the Atlantic but took the shorter route across the Channel, later heard from *Sussex* survivors that "They were seen clinging, one to a raft, the other to a chair. . . . when Mr. Granados saw his wife clinging to the raft, he tried to reach her, and in so doing threw away the chair. They could not hold on to the raft and they both went down together." This is in a letter of March 20, 1916, from Bliss to Malvina Hoffman. Other accounts claim that (1) both were in a raft, and when she accidentally fell out, he jumped in to save her, or (2) he was rescued by a raft but returned to the water after hearing her cries for help. Whatever the case, the outcome was the same.

117. From an interview with Mario Serra entitled "Cómo murió Granados (Relato de un superviviente)," periodical and date unknown [clipping in the Mm, fons Granados]. Riva, "Granados" [English version], 22, has another theory. He believes that when the explosion occurred, the Granadoses were "almost certainly in the first-class salon and died instantaneously." This would not explain why others saw them struggling in the water.

118. *La vanguardia*, March 30, 1916, 10 [clipping in the Mm, fons Granados]. "¿Quién pudo sospechar un fin trágico para tan gloriosa carrera?"

119. Natalia Granados and her siblings were present at the concert. During the program, Rafael Moragas received news of the attack and the disappearance of Enrique and Amparo, but kept it from the children until after the concert was over. This is according to Natalia herself, in a short essay she contributed to *Rubinstein y España* (Madrid: Fundación Isaac Albéniz, 1987), 133.

120. *New York Times*, April 23, 1916, 2.

121. Hess broached this subject in her bio-bibliography (p. 33), but no definitive conclusion is possible. See H. C. Peterson, *Propaganda for War: The Campaign for American Neutrality, 1914–1917* (1936; reprint, Port Washington, N.Y.: Kennikat Press, 1968), 222, and Samuel Flagg Bemis, *A Diplomatic History of the United States* (New York: Holt, Rinehart and Winston, 1936), 616.

122. This is reported on p. 183 of the unpublished memoirs of Samuel F. Bemis (in the Flagg Archive, Yale University Library), an American history professor also on the *Sussex*. Bemis recalled seeing Granados before the attack "walking about the ship in his coat and cap of Astrakhan fur."

123. Jean-Aubry, "Enrique Granados," 535.

124. "Les manes de l'auteur de Lakmé saluent la memoire de Granados en ce jour de réparation pour le crime du *Sussex*."

125. A copy of this program is in the archive of the Am. Mme. Paderewski, along with Mme. Casals and Mme. Kreisler, sold the items at various exits from the theater.

126. Natalia Granados, "*Goyescas* and Enrique Granados," in *Granados and Goyescas: Catalogue of an Exhibition Honoring Enrique Granados and the American Premiere of Goyescas*, Boston Athenaeum Gallery, January 18–30, 1982, 10.

127. See "Teatros y conciertos: Madrid," *Musical Emporium* 9/77 (March–April 1916): 3. The latter concert was reviewed in the following number (May–June) on p. 3. *Navidad* was the *Suite llamada de Navidad* for double quintet of flute, oboe, clarinet, horn, bassoon and two violins, viola, cello bass, derived from *Navidad de los niños*, the other title of *La cieguecita de Betania*.

128. Recounted in "Homenatge al Mestre Granados," *Ilustració catalana/Feminal* 14 (1916): n.p.

129. A formal and detailed ledger listing both income and expenses during the fund-raising campaign is located in the Mm, fons Granados. As of January 22, 1917, a whopping total of 129,309.83 pesetas had been collected. The king of Spain, Alfonso XIII, donated the less-than-stunning sum of 1,000 (after all, the Associació de Música da Camera of Barcelona contributed as much), and the French president, Poincaré, added 500. The Allied Red Cross came up with 2,000. Benefits performed by the Orfeó Català and Sinfónica de Madrid raised 3,569.20. The Met benefit made available an impressive 57,725 pesetas. Two subscriptions launched by the Spanish ambassador in the United States brought in almost half as much (22,334.24 and 6,160.59, respectively).

130. The *actas* of the Consejo are in the Mm, fons Granados, and go from 1917 to 1927.

131. These excerpts appear in an undated clipping from a Spanish newspaper (Mm, fons Granados).

132. All of these eulogies appeared in *Revista musical hispano-americana* 3 (April 30, 1916): passim.

133. Clipping entitled "El caso Granados" (Mm, fons Granados).

134. E. González Fiol, "Las prácticas de la guerra y el derecho de los neutrales," *La esfera* 3/119 (April 8, 1916): 25–27.

135. Joaquín Nin, "Evocaciones sobre Enrique Granados," *Revista musical hispano-americana* 3 (May 31, 1916): 2. "A los sobresaltos de angustia y contracciones de dolor de nuestros hermanos latinos, los franceses, mezclábamos, instintivamente, la secreta esperanza de conservar intactas las fuerzas vivas de nuestra raza y de nuestro intelecto para una resurreción futura, necesaria, próxima é indudable."

136. Ibid., 4. See also Hess, *Manuel de Falla and Modernism in Spain*, 65–78, for a detailed treatment of race, politics, and aesthetics in Spain during the Great War.

137. However, *España*, n63 (April 6, 1916), featured on its cover a drawing of Wagner and Beethoven receiving Granados into heaven, asking not to be blamed for sufferings that they themselves had also endured at the hands of their own people.

138. Untitled review of May 27, 1916, in the NYPL file on Granados and *Goyescas* in New York Public Library.

139. That these military figures were there appears in a clipping entitled "Aux Écoutes" from an unidentified French periodical (Mm, fons Granados). Granados had performed for Poincaré during the president's visit to Spain six years earlier. He played Saint-Saëns's Fifth Piano Concerto at the Teatro Real on October 8, 1913, in a concert given in honor of Poincaré. The performance received a favorable review in "Teatros y conciertos: Madrid," *Musical Emporium* 6/58 (October 1913): 3. He had performed this concerto before, at the Liceu on April 2, 1908, with the composer in attendance. On this same program, he and the French master performed Saint-Saëns's arrangement for four hands of the Chopin Sonata Op. 35. Glowing reviews appeared in "Associació Musical de Barcelona," *Revista musical catalana* 5 (1908): 47, and [untitled], *Diario de Barcelona*, April 3, 1908, 4157–58.

140. From a clipping (newspaper unknown) entitled "'Goyescas' en Paris, Gran Triunfo de una Ópera Española," dated "Paris 17 (1,53 t.)," in the Mm, fons Granados. "En fin, el éxito de la noche ha sido para la Reina, para Amalia Molina, para Zuloaga y para el hijo de Granados."

141. Henry Bidou, "Goyescas—Tarass Boulba—Anna Pavlova," *L'Opinion*, 1919, 639; Henri Collet, "Théatre et Musique," *Pittoresque*, 1919 (undated clippings in the Mm, fons Granados).

142. Granados signed a contract with the Teatro Colón while he was in New York, and this is now in the Mm, fons Granados. This contract was worth 50,000 pesetas. The correspondence between Periquet and Eduardo concerning *Goyescas* in Buenos Aires is also in that collection. Part of the reason Periquet was so upset was that the Colón had already paid several hundred dollars for the score and parts. Eduardo had the orchestral score but would not release

it until a copy was made. This delayed matters hopelessly. Apparently, he stopped answering Periquet's telegrams and letters, and that did not help matters either.

143. In the Mm, fons Granados, is a February 23, 1916, telegram to Granados and Periquet from Florencio Constantino asking what the Met would charge for sets and costumes to bring *Goyescas* to Los Angeles and "under what conditions yourself would agree to come. Old Spanish Californians enthusiastic to greet eminent author." Their manager, Antonia Sawyer, wired on February 29 that the Met would charge $600 and Granados, $5,000. Constantino wired back on March 1 wanting to know the cost of six performances guaranteed in May. For many reasons, this never happened.

144. This poem first appeared in *Revista musical catalana* 13 (1916): 186. It was later reproduced, with slight editorial changes, in Enric Palau, "La tràgica mort d'Enric Granados," *La nau*, March 24, 1928, 5. The version here is the original, translated for the first time into English (by Ruth Cabré Chacón and myself). "En la mort de l'Enric Granados." Per guardar tot ensemps amb tes despulles, ta inspiració, tos ideals, ta gloria, calía una gran tomba; y aqueixa tomba, el monstre de la Guerra—justicier malgrat ell—te l'ha donada. Dorm en pau allí al fons, allà ont no torban les lluites homicides la santa pau dels morts. La tomba és fonda y és ampla i és sagrada; l'onada alsantse és el fossar que l'obra, la llosa que la clou, un'altra onada. Quan de nit les estrelles eixint del mar com notes lluminoses se desgranin pel cel y magnifiquin l'immensitat del firmament, llavores ens semblaràn excelses melodíes, sepultades ab tu, qu'al cel envíes. I per demunt del passatger estrèpit d'aqueix gran crim qu'anomenan "la guerra" tes derreres cansons, fetes estrelles, ressonaràn eternament més belles, en el concert de la bellesa eterna.

EPÍLOGO

1. Granados wrote versions of *Danza gitana* for chamber orchestra and for full orchestra. Only the MS for the chamber version survives, however. It is undated. In addition, he penned a piano reduction, which has been published in DLR 2. Valencia, whose costumes were designed by Ignacio Zuloaga, also choreographed *Spanish Dance No. 5*. Douglas Riva has edited Granados's orchestral works for publication by the Instituto Complutense de Ciencias Musicales (Madrid) in 2006.

2. Aviñoa, *Música i modernisme*, 339.

3. Ibid., 340.

4. Xavier Montsalvatge, "Una importante obra de Enrique Granados, inédita," *Destino*, April 16, 1955, 33–34. Dating the MS is difficult, though it is probably from the period 1904–10.

5. They are for two pianos, with marginalia indicating the orchestration. One should note that Granados's manuscripts are generally legible but not always easy to decipher. Because he usually did not date them, establishing a chronology of his works is very difficult. In the sketches, he was often working on different pieces at the same time, and excerpts from them are mixed up. He was careless with accidentals, not necessarily indicating them in all octaves and clefs within a measure but rather indicating the alteration of one note only. This tendency was exacerbated by his sometimes dispensing with key signatures altogether, preferring to write out each accidental. He also had a curious way of proceeding, starting first with pencil and then writing over this in ink, creating an effect that is not always easy to read. See the section Research of Material and Sources for the Edition in Aviñoa and Riva, "Perfil histórico-biográfico," DLR 18, 76–77.

6. Boladeres Ibern, *Granados*, 127.

7. Granados also began but never finished a cello concerto and one for piano.

8. Clark, *Portrait*, 284.

9. Joaquín Turina, "Sobre Granados," *Revista musical hispano-americana* 3 (April 30, 1916): 7. "Granados comprendió que había llegado su hora y se lanzó por aquel camino, pero adaptándolo a su temperamento de soñador para lo cual se colocó en los comienzos del siglo XIX."

10. Pedrell, "La personalidad artística de Granados." "[N]o experimentó jamás ninguna veleidad de asimilación exótica; ni la tentadora, pero corruptora, francesa, que ha inutilizado a tantos."

11. Georges Jean-Aubry, *La musique et les nations* (Paris: Les Éditions de la Siréne, 1922), 123.

12. William W. Austin, *Music in the 20th Century from Debussy through Stravinsky* (New York: W. W. Norton, 1966), 1.

13. Celsa Alonso, "Nazionalismo spagnolo e avanguardia: la presunta praticabilità dell'Impressionismo," *Musica/Realtà* 15/44 (August 1994): 82.

14. Nin, "Evocaciones," 5. "La obra le interesó prodigiosamente. 'Tinc el cap plé de ritme,' me dijo, en catalán."

15. Pillois, "Un entretien avec Granados," 4.

16. However, it falls well short of modern standards. As Anatole Leikin points out, this technology reproduced rhythm and tempo accurately, but it was still "devoid of the wealth of tonal and dynamic colors, as well any pedaling refinement," which is why these "piano-roll recordings sound 'dead' to many serious music lovers." See "Piano-roll Recordings of Enrique Granados: A Study of a Transcription of the Composer's Performance," *Journal of Musicological Research* 21/1–2 (January–June 2002): 5–6.

17. See Aviñoa and Riva, "Perfil histórico-biográfico," DLR 18, 65, for a chart listing the works recorded by Granados for each company. This also lists vinyl and CD reissues of these early recordings.

18. See Lionel Salter, "Granados as Pianist," *Pianola Journal*, n10 (1998): 57, 60. Leikin, "Piano-roll Recordings," 7–13, makes a similar point in his revealing comparison of Granados's own rendition of the *Spanish Dance No. 5* and the published score. This poses the question as to whether any version of his piano works, published or recorded, can be considered definitive.

19. This question is posed by Benko, " 'Reverie-Improvisation' by Enrique Granados," 27.

20. See the section on Granados and the Technology of Musical Reproduction in Aviñoa and Riva, "Perfil histórico-biográfico," DLR 18, 56–57.

21. Eduardo made the beginnings of a brilliant career in music, having moved to Madrid after his parents' death. He had first studied with his father and later worked with Amadeu Vives and Conrado del Campo. He was a composer in his own right and a conductor. None of the Granados children showed his musical promise. Enrique, perhaps determined not to become the next drowning victim in the family, became a champion swimmer instead of a musician.

22. Riva, "Granados" [English version], 23. They were brought to light and studied by Mark Larrad in his seminal research of the late 1980s and early 1990s, but they have yet to be published and revived. I am currently preparing an edition of *Follet*, the only Mestres opera not sold to Salabert.

23. After his death, his son Antoni took on the responsibility. He also published a brief biography of his grandfather (for Litoclub's *Gent Nostra* series, in 1988). Already in 1984 Dr. Carreras and Natalia had given some materials to the Museu de la Música in Barcelona, and between 1991 and 1993 Antoni donated almost all the remaining archive, retaining only a small portion for the family. The fons Granados is at this writing undergoing recataloging but was made available to me in its entirety for consultation. Although there has been some dispersal of the Granados archive among various collections, it all remains in Barcelona. Eduardo's own archive remains with his descendants in Madrid. See Valentina Granados Simón, "Los archivos de Enrique Granados Campiña y Eduardo Granados Gal: dos soluciones distintas para casos diferentes," in *El patrimonio musical: los archivos familiares (1898–1936)* (Cáseres: Fundación Xavier de Salas, 1997), 81–87.

24. Arturo Llopis, "El recuerdo de Enrique Granados. Un aniversario: 24 de marzo de 1966," *La vanguardia española*, March 24, 1966, 37.

25. See Gerard Dapena, "Spanish Film Scores in Early Francoist Cinema (1940–1950)," *Music in Art* 27/1–2 (Spring–Fall 2002): 149–50, for an intriguing analysis of the political overtones of this film in the context of Franco's recent ascent to absolute power in Spain. The chief characteristic of the movie is a juxtaposition of high and low culture, of passages from Granados's scores with popular music of the eighteenth century. The overall effect is "an aristocratic's daydream of popular life as an endless succession of revelry and pleasure, far removed in its aestheticism and idealization from the image of abject, violent proletarians that circulated among Spain's Right during and after the war. The haunting tone of Granados's [*Spanish Dance No. 5*] underlies the wistful nature of this utopian vision of the populace."

26. Jones, in "Recreating Eighteenth-century Musical Theater" (Spring 2001): 146, cites the case of an earlier movie entitled *Goyescas* that was (according to Longland) produced in 1927. After an exhaustive search, he was only able to uncover a screenplay (*guión*) by Periquet for the silent picture (now in the Bn), but not the actual film itself.

27. "Es nuestro propósito hacer una gran película con todo cariño y entusiasmo. Le agradecería mucho su apoyo, colaboración y ayuda para que esta película pueda desarrollarse de una manera elevada." A letter from Pemán himself, in Cádiz on August 19, 1953, assured Antonio that the part of the script he did not like would be deleted. This correspondence is in the Mm, fons Granados.

28. According to the *New York World Telegram*, September 10, 1938. Clipping in the files on Granados in the library of the Hsa.

29. In a contract dated January 22, 1940, Víctor acknowledged his receipt of $300 from Shilkret. In a letter from New York dated November 30, 1939 (Mm, fons Granados), Víctor explained to Antonio the reasons for his actions. In truth, there were no good reasons, only poor excuses. By his own admission, Víctor was mentally unstable. For a biography of Shilkret, see Nathanial Shilkret, *Nathanial Shilkret: Sixty Years in the Music Business*, ed. Niel Shell and Barbara Shilkret (Lanham, Md.: Scarecrow Press, 2005).

30. Letter from Nathaniel Shilkret to Malvina Hoffman, March 25, 1943. Shilkret expressed a desire to "give the splendid Granados music to the world."

31. The piano provides a lengthy introduction (the voices are tacet for the first 145 mm., and the organ for the first 82).

32. According to the score, the text was "inspiré d´une poesie de H. Haine [*sic*]." The work was never published, and the rest of the MS is in the Oc. My search of the complete poems of Heine yielded no obvious candidate as the inspiration. Granados could not read German, so either he read the poem in translation or got the assistance of one of his German-speaking Catalan associates, perhaps Maragall or Mestres.

33. Translation by John Milton. "Feblesa porten al cor. / Debades repos cerque! / Volem coneixer nous mort! / Encisos d'amor trenquem / No podem rompr'els grillons / Inmensitat eternitat! / Ah!"

34. "Concert Granados," *Revista musical catalana* 8 (1911): 90. The following day at the Palau, Juan Lamote de Grignon conducted his orchestrations of three of the *Danzas españolas* ("Oriental," "Andaluza," and "Rondalla aragonesa") at a Lenten concert of the Orfeo.

35. Pangloss, untitled review, *La publicidad*, March 15, 1911, 4.

36. The attribution of revisions to Eduardo Granados and F. Montserrat i Ayarbe appears in Mark Larrad's entry on Granados in *The New Grove Dictionary of Opera*, ed. Stanley Sadie (London: Macmillan, 1992). The MSS include full and vocal scores as well as parts. There is also a short score in the Bn. I first examined the materials at the SGAE in 1990 but sadly concluded that they did not constitute the original version I had hoped to find. Much more recent consultations of the MS full score, by me and by Douglas Riva, have led again to the conclu-

sion that it is at best a hybrid and not the original. However, conductor Max Bragado Darman believes that, though many changes and additions were made, most of the extant score is in the composer's own hand and that the parts are a reliable guide to his original intentions. He has published an edition of the opera on the basis of these sources (Madrid: Instituto Complutense de Ciencias Musicales, 2003).

37. On the Marco Polo label (8.225292–93, 2003), featuring Max Bragado, conductor, and Diana Veronese in the title role. There was almost another version. In a letter of May 11, 1964 (Mm, fons Granados), Federico Moreno Torroba and Jesús María de Arozamena (in Madrid) proposed to Dr. Carreras reviving *María del Carmen* by converting it into a zarzuela, presumably by changing the recitative to spoken dialogue. They were requesting authorization to do this for the next season at the Teatro de la Zarzuela, though to the best of our knowledge, this was never done.

38. Even with its dramatic liabilities, the work would be performed more frequently if it were not for its diminutive size coupled with the relatively large number of costumes and sets it requires, along with a sizable chorus. In a longer work, such expense would be normal, but in a one-act opera, it can be prohibitive.

39. Two letters, dated April 19 and 21, are in the Mm, fons Granados.

40. R.G., "'María del Carmen,' de Granados," *Mirador*, December 5, 1935, 8. Conxita Badia appeared in the title role, and Juan Lamote de Grignon conducted.

41. See Rafael Moragas, "*María del Carmen* del compositor Enrique Granados," *El día gráfico*, November 30, 1938, 6, and "Los crimenes de la Alemania del Kaiser los repite ahora la Alemania de Hitler," *El día gráfico*, March 24, 1938, 8.

42. The Franco episode in the opera's career is treated in Carol Hess, "Enrique Granados and Spanish Musical Criticism *al fin de siglo*," unpublished paper delivered at the annual meeting of the American Musicological Society, Pittsburgh, November 4, 1992, 19. A review of the production is found in "Gran Teatro del Liceo," *La vanguardia española*, December 10, 1939, 5. The anonymous reviewer invoked the "providential destiny" of the "glorious Caudillo" (Franco). Periquet was a fervent supporter of Franco, and even joined the Nationalist army at age 67; he was wounded in combat. See Jones, "Recreating Eighteenth-century Musical Theater" (Spring 2001): 140.

43. "Las *Goyescas* de Granados en Berlin," *Destino*, October 26, 1940, 12. "[T]eniendo en cuenta la simpatía con que son recibidas nuestras manifestaciones artísticas." "Si bien interpretada por bailarines no españoles, la música de Granados infundirá a los mismos el fuego de nuestro espiritu racial latente en cada nota de la partitura de *Goyescas*."

44. This report appears in Vila San-Juan, "Los cuatro pianos." Of course, this choice of chapel held symbolic significance, as Lepanto was a famous Spanish naval victory against the Turks in 1571.

45. On the bright side, one goal set forth at the meeting has been realized, if only partially. There now exists a critical edition of his piano works (DLR), however, the "opera omnia" dreamed of in 1957 will have to wait. See "Brillante epílogo de los homenajes de Granados," *La vanguardia española*, February 9, 1957, 17.

46. Treated in Clark, *Portrait*, 286–88.

47. See the edition by Francisco Fernández Turienzo (Madrid: Ediciones Alcalá, 1971), 105. Unamuno was, in fact, indifferent to music, as was the rest of the Generation of '98, and they paid scant attention to Spanish composers in their writings. See Federico Sopeña Ibañez, *Historia de la música española contemporánea* (Madrid: Rialp, 1958), 73–80. In Sopeña's view, the relationship of the Generation of '98 to music could be summed up in one word: "nada" (nothing).

48. Robert Boas, "Lille," *Opera* 37 (1986): 71–73.

49. Jean-Aubry, "Enrique Granados," 535.

50. This incident is related by Badia herself in an interview conducted by one Agustí that

appeared in the magazine *Labor Lérida,* n168, special edition for the 1956–57 commemoration (clipping is in the Mm, fons Granados). The same anecdote appears in Fernández-Cid, *Granados,* 224–25.

51. Badia, "Personal Portrait," 60–61. For whatever reason, Marshall did not invite Natalia and Dr. Carreras to this occasion. The selection of these three pieces gives us a clue as to how Falla in particular may have viewed Granados's *Goyescas,* which appears to form a link between the classicism of Beethoven's early piano sonatas and the neoclassicism of Falla's puppet-theater opera. He may well have viewed Granados's Goya-inspired works as important precursors to his own neoclassical compositions of the years between Granados's death and this ceremony.

BIBLIOGRAPHY

A. "Teatro de Parish." *El correo*, November 13, 1898, 2.

A.B.C. "'Liliana' a Belles Arts (La música)." *El poble català*, July 12, 1911, 1.

"Aeolian Hall: Concierto del Maestro Granados." *Las novedades*, February 24, 1916, 5–6.

Albéniz, Alfonso. "Albéniz y Granados." *Revista musical hispano-americana* 3 (April 30, 1916): 7.

Albet, Montserrat. "August Pi i Sunyer i la música." In *Centenari de la naixença d'August Pi i Sunyer*. Barcelona: n.p., 1979.

Aldrich, Richard. "Granados in His Own Music." *New York Times*, January 24, 1916.

Aliér, Roger. "Musical Life in Barcelona, 1888–1936." In *Homage to Barcelona: The City and Its Art, 1888–1936*, 277–86. London: Arts Council of Great Britain, 1985.

Alomar, Gabriel. "Las Goyescas." *El poble català*, September 25, 1910.

Alonso, Celsa. "Nazionalismo spagnolo e avanguardia: la presunta praticabilità dell'Impressionismo." *Musica/Realtà* 15/44 (August 1994): 81–106.

"Al Palau de Belles Arts" [review of *Liliana*]. *El poble català*, July 10, 1911, 2.

Álvarez Pallàs, Josep M. "Síntesi biogràfica dels grans músics lleidatans Granados-Viñes-Pujol." In *Tríptic Musical (Granados-Viñes-Pujol): Himne a Lleida*, ed. Teresina Jordà i Cervera, 14–20. Lleida: Artis Estudis Gràfics, 1977.

Anderson, Benedict. *Imagined Communities: Reflections on the Origin and Spread of Nationalism*. Rev. ed. London: Verso, 1991.

Arimón, J. "Teatro Circo de Parish" [review of *María del Carmen*]. *El liberal*, November 13, 1898, 3.

"Associació Musical de Barcelona." *Revista musical catalana* 5 (1908): 47.

Austin, William W. *Music in the 20th Century from Debussy through Stravinsky*. New York: W. W. Norton, 1966.

Aviñoa, Xosé. "Barcelona, del wagnerismo a la generación de la República." In *España en la música de Occidente: Actas del Congreso Internacional celebrado en Salamanca 29 de octubre – 5 de noviembre de 1985*. Vol. 2, 323–40. Madrid: Instituto Nacional de las Artes Escénicas y de la Música, 1987.

———. "El fracàs del Teatre Líric Català a la Barcelona finisecular." *Revista musical catalana* 6/54 (April 1989): 19–21.

———. *La música i el modernisme*. Barcelona: Curial, 1985.

Aviñoa, Xosé, and Douglas Riva. "Introducción a Goyescas." *Integral para piano de E. Granados*. Vol. 1. Barcelona: Editorial Boileau, 2002.

———. "Perfil histórico-biográfico. Estudio crítico." *Integral para piano Enrique Granados*. Vol. 18. Barcelona: Editorial Boileau, 2002.

Badia, Conchita. "Granados: A Personal Portrait." *Recorded Sound*, n77 (January 1980): 57–61.

Balcells, Albert. *Cataluña contemporánea, 1900–1936*. Madrid: Siglo XXI de España Editores, 1974.

Baldwin, James Mark. *Between Two Wars: 1861–1921*. 2 vols. Boston: Stratford Co., 1926.

Barce, Ramón. "La ópera y la zarzuela en el siglo XIX." In *España en la música de Occidente: Actas del Congreso Internacional celebrado en Salamanca 29 de octubre – 5 de noviembre de 1985*. Vol. 2, 145–53. Madrid: Instituto Nacional de las Artes Escénicas y de la Música, 1987.

———. "Las 'tonadillas' de Granados y el folklore ciudadano." *Tercer programa* 1 (April 1966): 165–73.

"Barcelona" [review of *Blancaflor*]. *Diario de Barcelona*, January 31, 1899, 1250.

"Barcelona" [review of *Picarol*]. *Diario de Barcelona*, February 26, 1901, 2594.

"Barcelona" [review of *Gaziel*]. *Diario de Barcelona*, October 29, 1906, 12341.

Barrie Jones, J. "Enrique Granados: A Few Reflections on a Seventieth Anniversary." *Music Review* 47/1 (February 1986/7): 16–23.

Bemis, Samuel Flagg. *A Diplomatic History of the United States*. New York: Holt, Rinehart and Winston, 1936.

Benko, Gregor. "'Reverie-Improvisation' by Enrique Granados." *Clavier* 6/7 (October 1967): 27.

Bergadà, Montserrat, Màrius Bernadó, and Nina Gubisch-Viñes. *Ricart Viñes i Roda (1875– 1943): testimoni d'un temps*. Lleida: Col·lecció La Banqueta, 1996.

Bex, Maurice. "Concerts et recitals." *La revue musical* (July–August 1914): 48.

Bidou, Henry. "Goyescas—Tarass Boulba—Anna Pavlova." *L'Opinion*, 1919, 639 [undated clipping in Mm, fons Granados].

Blasco, R. "Parish" [review of *María del Carmen*]. *La correspondencia de España*, November 13, 1898, 3.

Bly, Robert, trans. *Times Alone: Selected Poems of Antonio Machado*. Middletown, Conn.: Wesleyan University Press, 1983.

Boas, Robert. "Lille" [review of *Goyescas*]. *Opera* 37 (1986): 71–73.

Boladeres Ibern, Guillermo de. *Enrique Granados: Recuerdos de su vida y estudio crítico de su obra por su antiguo discípulo*. Barcelona: Editorial Arte y Letras, 1921.

Bonastre, Francesc. "Barcelona." In *Diccionario de la música española e hispanoamericana*, ed. Emilio Casares. Madrid: Sociedad General de Autores y Editores, 2000.

———. "La labor de Enric Granados en el proceso de la recepción de la música de Bach en Barcelona." *Anuario musical* n56 (2001): 173–83.

———. "La personalitat musical de Catalunya: Felip Pedrell i el nacionalisme a Catalunya." *Revista musical catalana* 1/2 (December 1984): 33–34.

Bonet y Cembrano, D. "Concerts Granados." *Joventut* 7/317 (March 8, 1906): 154–55.

Borowski, Felix. "Fourth Program of the Twenty-fifth Season (1915–16) of the Chicago Symphony Orchestra." Chicago: Orchestral Association, 1915, 44–49. (Reprinted in program notes for 1923–24 season, 197–200.)

Borrás de Palau, Joan. "Enrique Granados." *La música ilustrada hispano-americana* 2/12 (June 10, 1899): 4.

———. "Los conciertos á dos pianos, en Novedades." *La música ilustrada hispano-americana* 2/13 (June 25, 1899): 3–4.

———. "María del Carmen." *El correo catalán*, June 2, 1899, 6–7.

Brenan, Gerald. *The Spanish Labyrinth: The Social and Political Background of the Spanish Civil War*. Cambridge: Cambridge University Press, 1943/reprint 2001.

Bretón, Tomás. "Un recuerdo de Granados." *Revista musical hispano-americana* 3 (April 30, 1916): 6.

"Brillante epílogo de los homenajes de Granados." *La vanguardia española*, February 9, 1957, 17.

Brody, Elaine. "Viñes in Paris: New Light on Twentieth-Century Performance Practice." In *A Musical Offering: Essays in Honor of Martin Bernstein*, ed. Edward H. Clinkscale and Claire Brook, 45–62. New York: Pendragon Press, 1977.

Cardona, Rodolfo. "Granados' Spain." Paper presented at the "Granados and *Goyescas*" Symposium, Harvard University, Cambridge, Mass., January 23, 1982.

Carr, Raymond. *Spain 1808–1975*. 2d ed. Oxford: Clarendon Press, 1982.

Carreras i Granados, Antoni. *Granados*. Series: Gent nostra. Barcelona: Litoclub, 1988.

Casanovas, Josep. "El Teatre Líric Català." *Revista musical catalana* 6/54 (April 1989): 23–25.

Casany, Enrich Jardí. *Historia de Els Quatre Gats*. Barcelona: Editorial Aedos, 1972.

Castilla, Alfonso de. "España Aquí." *Las novedades*, January 27, 1916, 6.

Chase, Gilbert. *The Music of Spain*. New York: W. W. Norton, 1941.

Chavarrí, Eduardo L. "Enrique Granados: El hombre, el artista." *Revista musical hispano-americana* 3 (April 30, 1916): 13–14.

Clark, Walter Aaron. *Isaac Albéniz: Portrait of a Romantic*. Oxford: Oxford University Press, 1999/2002.

Collet, Henri. *Albéniz et Granados*. Paris: Éditions Le Bon Plaisir, 1948.

———. "Théâtre et Musique." Pittoresque, 1919 [undated clipping in the Mm, fons Granados].

Comte de Carlet. "Enric Granados." *El teatre català* 5/216 (April 15, 1916), 136.

"Concert Granados." *Revista musical catalana* 8 (1911): 89–90.

Conchita Badia 1897–1975: Canción del arte. Exposición del Archivo Manuel de Falla, Granada, March 21 – May 24, 1997. Granada: Archivo Manuel de Falla, 1997.

Condesa del Castellá. "La última jornada." *Revista musical hispano-americana* 3 (April 30, 1916): 8–9.

Corredor, J. Ma. *Conversations with Casals*. Trans. André Mangeot. New York: E. P. Dutton, 1956.

"Correo de espectáculos" [review of *María del Carmen*]. *El resumen*, November 14, 1898, 1.

Craig, Vincent A. "Traditional Spanish Folk Dance Rhythms in the Piano Music of Isaac Albéniz and Enrique Granados." DMA lecture-recital paper, Peabody Conservatory, 2002.

Craige, Betty Jean, trans. *Selected Poems of Antonio Machado*. Baton Rouge: Louisiana State University Press, 1978.

Curet, Francesc. *Teatre català*. Barcelona: Editorial Aedos, 1967.

Cuspinera, C. "Enrique Granados." *Diario de Barcelona*, April 22, 1890, 5075–76.

Dahlhaus, Carl. *Between Romanticism and Modernism: Four Studies in the Music of the Later Nineteenth Century*. Trans. Mary Whittall. Berkeley: University of California Press, 1980.

———. *Nineteenth-Century Music*. Trans. J. Bradford Robinson. Berkeley: University of California Press, 1989.

Dapena, Gerard. "Spanish Film Scores in Early Francoist Cinema (1940–1950)." *Music in Art* 27/1–2 (Spring–Fall 2002): 141–51.

Darío, Rubén. *España contemporánea*. Madrid: Biblioteca Rubén Darío, n.d.

Debussy, Claude. "Carta de M. Debussy." *Revista musical hispano-americana* 3 (April 30, 1916): 2.

Del Arco. "Mano a mano: Natalia Granados." *La vanguardia española*, January 22, 1957, 14.

D'Indy, Vincent. "Carta de M. d'Indy." *Revista musical hispano-americana* 3 (April 30, 1916): 4–5.

D'Ors, Eugení. "Boires-Baixes." *Pèl & Ploma* 3 (1902): 260–74.

Douglas-Brown, Deborah J. "Nationalism in the Song Sets of Manuel de Falla and Enrique Granados." DMA document, University of Alabama, Tuscaloosa, 1993.

E. "Teatres" [review of *Gaziel*]. *Ilustració catalana* 4/179 (November 4, 1906): 702.

"El estreno de *Goyescas* en Nueva York." *Musical Emporium* 9/76 (January–February 1916): 4–5.

"El mestre Enrich Granados y la seva esposa." *Ilustració catalana/Feminal* 14/109 (April 30, 1916): 240–42.

"Enrique Granados." *Música* 2/31 (April 5, 1916): 53–54.

Enrique Granados: Algunas opiniones de la prensa sobre sus conciertos. Barcelona: Musicografía Wagner, n.d.

"Enrique Granados y Campiña." *La ilustración musical hispano-americana* 3/59 (June 30, 1890): 282–83.

Enrique Granados y su tiempo: Contrapunto filatélico al centenario del nacimiento de un gran músico. Barcelona: Amigos de Granados, 1969.

Esplá, Oscar. "Impresiones sobre la obra de Granados." *Revista musical hispano-americana* 3 (April 30, 1916): 6.

Esteban, Julio. "Master Lesson on a Granados Dance." *Clavier* 6/7 (October 1967): 39.

Ester-Sala, Maria. "D. Scarlatti—E. Granados: Noticia sobre la localización de un manuscrito de tecla extraviado." In *Livro de Homenagem a Macario Santiago Kastner,* ed. Maria Fernanda Cidrais Rodrigues, Manuel Morais, and Rui Vieira Nery, 231–52. Lisbon: Fundação Calouste Gulbenkian, 1992.

———. "Un manuscript scarlattià retrobat." *Revista musical catalana* 5/43 (May 1988): 13.

"Estreno de Sarsuelas" [review of *María del Carmen*]. *Lo teatro català* 10/415 (June 31, 1899): 1–2.

F. "Teatres y Concerts" [review of *Gaziel*]. *El poble català,* October 28, 1906, 3.

Falla, Manuel de. "Enrique Granados: Evocación de su obra." *Revista musical hispano-americana* 3 (April 30, 1916): 5.

Fasolt, Rény. "Le jury du Concours Diémer de 1909." *Musica* 81 (June 1909): 93.

Fauré, Gabriel. "Carta de M. Fauré." *Revista musical hispano-americana* 3 (April 30, 1916): 5.

Fernández, James D. "Latin America and Spain in U.S. Hispanism." In *Spain in America: The Origins of Hispanism in the United States,* ed. Richard L. Kagan, 122–41. Urbana: University of Illinois Press, 2002.

Fernández-Cid, Antonio. *Cien años de teatro musical en España (1875–1975).* Madrid: Real Musical, 1975.

———. "Goya, 'Goyescas,' Granados, Alicia de Larrocha." *Academia: Boletín de la Real Academia de Bellas Artes de San Fernando,* n75 (Second Semester 1992): 103–10.

———. *Granados.* Madrid: Samarán Ediciones, 1956.

———. Program notes for *Ciclo La obra pianística de Enrique Granados, octubre/noviembre 1991.* Albacete: Junta de Comunidades de Castilla-La Mancha, 1991.

"Festa de la Música Catalana, Any IV: Veredicte." *Revista musical catalana* 4 (1907): 144–45.

Finck, Henry T. *Musical Progress.* Philadelphia: Theodore Presser, 1923.

Florit Durán, Francisco. "La recepción de la literatura del Siglo de Oro en algunos ensayos del 98." In *La independencia de las últimas colonias españolas y su impacto nacional e internacional,* ed. José María Ruano de la Haza, 279–96. Series: Ottawa Hispanic Studies 24. Ottawa: Dovehouse Editions, 2001.

Fox, E. Inman. *La invención de España.* Madrid: Catedra, 1997.

———. "Spain as Castile: Nationalism and National Identity." In *The Cambridge Companion to Modern Spanish Culture,* ed. David T. Gies, 21–36. Cambridge: Cambridge University Press, 1999.

"Friends of Music Applaud Mr. Granados, Composer-Pianist." *New York Herald,* January 24, 1916, 13.

Fuenmayor, Diego de. "A los treinta y nueve años de ser torpedeado el 'Sussex." *Diario de Barcelona,* June 15, 1955, 4.

Gago, Luis Carlos. Liner notes for "Beaux Arts Trio Play Turina and Granados." Menahem Pressler, piano; Ida Kavafian, violin; Peter Wiley, cello. Philips CD, 446684–2, 1996.

Gandara, Francisco. "Noted Spanish Composer Here to See his Opera." *New York Times Magazine,* December 19, 1915, 7.

García Carraffa, Alberto y Arturo. *Diccionario heráldico y genealógico de apellidos españoles y americanos.* Vol. 39, *Gorriz–Guil.* Salamanca: Imprenta Comercial Salamanca, 1931.

Gibson, Ian. *Fire in the Blood: The New Spain.* London: Faber and Faber, 1992.

Glendinning, Nigel. *Goya and His Critics.* New Haven: Yale University Press, 1977.

Goldstein, Donald M., et al. *The Spanish-American War: The Story and Photographs.* Washington, D.C.: Brassey's, 1998.

Gomà, Enrique. "Las 'Danzas españolas de Enrique Granados." *Revista musical hispano-americana* 3 (April 30, 1916): 15–16.

Gómez Amat, Carlos. *Historia de la música española.* Vol. 5, *Siglo XIX.* Madrid: Alianza, 1984.

González Fiol, E. "Las prácticas de la guerra y el derecho de los neutrales." *La esfera* 3/119 (April 8, 1916): 25.

"Goyescas." *Las novedades,* January 27, 1916, 9–10.

"Goyescas o los majos enamorados." *ABC* (2d ed.), February 1, 1916, 12–13.

"'Goyescas,' Spanish Opera, Has World Premiere Here." *New York Herald,* January 29, 1916, 12.

Granados and Goyescas. Catalogue of an Exhibition Honoring Enrique Granados and the American Premiere of Goyescas. Boston Athenaeum Gallery, January 18–30, 1982. Boston: Boston Athenaeum, 1982.

Granados, Enrique. *Integral de l'obra per a veu i piano* [Complete Works for Voice and Piano]. Ed. Manuel García Morante. Barcelona: Tritó, 1996.

———. *Integral para piano* [Complete Works for Piano]. 18 vols. Ed. Alicia de Larrocha and Douglas Riva. Barcelona: Editorial Boileau, 2002.

———. "La ópera española moderna: 'Goyesca.'" *The World's Work: La revista del mundo* (April 1916): 177.

———. "Parcival." *El teatre català* 2/65 (May 24, 1913 [Wagner issue]): 351.

"Granados in His Own Music." *New York Times,* January 24, 1916.

"Granados in New York: Soul of Spanish Composer Is Not for Sale." *Kansas City Times,* n.d.

Granados, Natalia. "Goyescas and Enrique Granados." In *Granados and Goyescas: Catalogue of an Exhibition Honoring Enrique Granados and the American Premiere of Goyescas.* Boston Athenaeum Gallery, January 18–30, 1982, 8–10. Boston: Boston Athenaeum, 1982.

"Granados, Pianist, in American Debut." *Toledo Times,* February 6, 1916.

"Granados Plays His Own Works: Spanish Composer-Pianist Heard by New Yorkers. Anna Fitziu Sings His Songs." *Musical America,* March 1916.

Granados Simón, Valentina. "Los archivos de Enrique Granados Campiña y Eduardo Granados Gal: dos soluciones distintas para casos diferentes." In *El patrimonio musical: los archivos familiares (1898–1936),* 81–87. Cáseres: Fundación Xavier de Salas, 1997.

Gran enciclopèdia catalana. Barcelona: Gran Enciclopèdia Catalana, 1986. S.v. "Andreu i Grau, Salvador," "Café," "Casas, Ramon," "Cau Ferrat," "Gual i Queralt, Adrià," "Jocs Florals," "Lleida," "Maragall, Joan," "Maricel," "Mestres i Oñós, Apel·les," "Modernisme," "Pi i Sunyer, August," "Pla, Josep," "Els Quatre Gats," "Renaixença," "Romeu, Pere," "Rusiñol i Prats, Santiago," "Sitges," "Utrillo, Miquel," "Verdaguer, Jacint."

"Gran Teatro del Liceo" [review of *Goyescas*]. *La vanguardia española,* December 10, 1939, 5.

Gual, Adrià. *Mitja vida de teatre: Memòries.* Barcelona: Editorial Aedos, 1957.

Guerra y Alarcón, Antonio. "La ópera nueva: María del Carmen." *Heraldo de Madrid,* November 10, 1898.

———. "Los estrenos: María del Carmen." *Heraldo de Madrid,* November 13, 1898.

Guillemot, Jules. Untitled review of concert by Granados and Thibaut. *Revista musical catalana* 6 (1909): 198–99.

Halperson, M. "Spanien's Musik und Granados' 'Goyescas.'" *Sonntagsblatt der New-Yorker Staats-Zeitung,* January 23, 1916.

Hansen, Mark R. "The Pedagogical Methods of Enrique Granados and Frank Marshall: An Illumination of Relevance to Performance Practice and Interpretation in Granados's *Escenas románticas.*" DMA lecture-recital, University of North Texas, 1988.

Harrison, Joseph. "Introduction: The Historical Background to the Crisis of 1898." In *Spain's 1898 Crisis: Regenerationism, Modernism, Post-colonialism*, ed. Joseph Harrison and Alan Hoyle, 1–8. Manchester: Manchester University Press, 2000.

———. "Tackling National Decadence: Economic Regenerationism in Spain after the Colonial Débâcle." In *Spain's 1898 Crisis: Regenerationism, Modernism, Post-colonialism*, ed. Joseph Harrison and Alan Hoyle, 55–67. Manchester: University Press, 2000.

Hess, Carol A. "Enric Granados i la vida musical barcelonina entre 1891–1916." In *Actes del Sisè Col·loqui d'Estudis Catalans a Nord Amèrica (Vancouver, 1990)*, ed. Arseni Pacheco and Karl Kobbervig, 469–81. Montserrat: Publicacions de l'Abadia de Montserrat, 1992.

———. *Enrique Granados: A Bib-Bibliography.* New York: Greenwood Press, 1991.

———. "Enrique Granados and Modern Piano Technique." *Performance Practice Review* 6/1 (Spring 1993): 89–94.

———. "Enrique Granados and Spanish Musical Criticism *al fin de siglo.*" Paper delivered at the annual meeting of the American Musicological Society, Pittsburgh, November 4, 1992.

———. *Manuel de Falla and Modernism in Spain, 1898–1936.* Chicago: University of Chicago Press, 2001.

———. *Sacred Passions: The Life and Music of Manuel de Falla.* New York: Oxford University Press, 2005.

"Homenatge al Mestre Granados." *Ilustració catalana/Feminal* 14 (1916): n.p.

"Homenatge al Mestre Granados." *Revista musical catalana* 8 (1911): 54–55.

Hroch, Miroslav. "From National Movement to the Fully-formed Nation: The Nation-building Process in Europe." In *Mapping the Nation*, ed. Gopal Balakrishnan, 78–97. London: Verso, 1996.

Hughes, Robert. *Barcelona.* New York: Alfred A. Knopf, 1992.

———. *Goya.* New York: Alfred A. Knopf, 2003.

———. *The Shock of the New.* New York: Alfred A. Knopf, 1996.

I.F. "Palau de Belles Arts" [review of *Liliana*]. *Revista musical catalana* 8 (1911): 220–21.

Iglesias, Antonio. *Enrique Granados: su obra para piano.* 2 vols. Madrid: Editorial Alpuerto, 1985.

———. "Granados, un continuador del Romanticismo." *Enciclopedia Salvat de los grandes compositores.* Vol. 4. Pamplona: Salvat, 1981.

Iglesias de Souza, Luis. *Teatro lírico español.* 4 vols. Coruña: Excma. Diputación Provincial de la Coruña, 1994.

Isern, Jordi. "El legado de Granados, su técnica pianística." *Monsalvat*, n194 (June 1991): 12–13.

J.B. de P. "Espectáculos [review of *Gaziel*]." *El correo catalán*, October 30, 1906.

J.C. "Memòria d'Enric Granados." *Revista musical catalana* 4/33–34 (July–August 1987): 10–12.

J.L., "El próximo concierto del Maestro Granados," *Las novedades*, February 17, 1916, 12.

Jean-Aubry, Georges. "Enrique Granados." *The Musical Times* 57 (December 1, 1916): 536–37.

———. *La musique et les nations.* Paris: Les Éditions de la Sirène, 1922.

Jiménez, Juan Ramón. *Españoles de tres mundos.* Madrid: Alianza, 1987.

Jones, Joseph. "Recreating Eighteenth-century Musical Theater: The Collaborations of the Composer Enrique Granados (1867–1916) and the Librettist Fernando Periquet y Zuaznábar (1873–1940)." *Dieciocho* 23/2 and 24/1 (Fall 2000 and Spring 2001): 183–212 and 121–46.

Jover Zamora, José María. "La época de la Restauración: panorama político-social, 1875–1902." In *Historia de España: Revolución burguesa oligarquía y constitucionalismo (1834–1923)*, ed. Manuel Tuñón de Lara, 271–408. Madrid: Editorial Labor, 1981.

Jurkevich, Gayana. *In Pursuit of the Natural Sign: Azorín and the Poetics of Ekphrasis.* London: Associated University Presses, 1999.

Kamen, Henry. *Empire: How Spain Became a World Power, 1492–1763.* New York: Harper-Collins, 2003.

Kirk, H. L. *Pablo Casals, a Biography.* New York: Holt, Rinehart & Winston, 1974.

Kuehl, Olga Llano. "Three Stylistic Periods in the Piano Compositions of Enrique Granados." DMA thesis, University of Cincinnati, 1979.

L.M. "Enrique Granados y Campiña." *Ilustración musical* 3/59 (1890): 282–83.

Lamote de Grignon, Joan. "Enric Granados." *El teatre català* 5/216 (April 15, 1916): 136.

"La qüestió de la Banda Municipal." *Revista musical catalana* 7 (1910): 227–33.

Larrad, Mark. "The Catalan Theatre Works of Enrique Granados." Ph.D. diss., University of Liverpool, 1992.

———. "Granados, Enrique." *The New Grove Dictionary of Music* and Musicians. 2d ed. Ed. Stanley Sadie. London: Macmillan, 2001.

———. "Granados, Enrique." *The New Grove Dictionary of Opera.* Ed. Stanley Sadie. London: Macmillan, 1992.

Larrocha, Alicia de. "Granados, the Composer." Trans. Joan Kerlow. *Clavier* 6/7 (October 1967): 21–23.

Lassalle, José. "Granados héroe." *Revista musical hispano-americana* 3 (April 30, 1916): 12.

"Las *Goyescas* de Granados en Berlin." *Destino*, October 26, 1940, 12.

Laspeyres, Isabelle. "Enrique Granados à Paris." *Revue internationale de musique française*, n26 (June 1988): 37–52.

Leiken, Anatole. "Piano-roll Recordings of Enrique Granados: A Study of a Transcription of the Composer's Performance." *Journal of Musicological Research* 21/1–2 (January–June 2002): 3–19.

"L'Enric Granados a París." *Revista musical catalana* 11 (1914): 140–42.

"Liliana." *El poble català*, July 9, 1911, 2.

Litvak, Lily. *España 1900: Modernismo, anarquismo y fin de siglo.* Barcelona: Anthropos, 1990.

Lively [*sic*]. "Les *Goyescas* a Nova York." *Revista musical catalana* 13 (March 1916): 78–83.

Livermore, Ann. "Granados and the Nineteenth Century in Spain." *Musical Review* 7 (1946): 80–87.

———. *A Short History of Spanish Music.* New York: Vienna House, 1972.

Llates, Rosendo. "Granados: Señor de la música." *Señor* 11/42 (February 1966): 56–64.

Lliurat, F. "El nacionalismo de Enrique Granados." *Revista musical hispano-americana* 3 (April 30, 1916): 17–18.

———. "Necrología." *Revista musical catalana* 13 (1916): 139–40.

Llongueras, Juan. "De como conocí al maestro Enrique Granados." In *Evocaciones y recuerdos de mi primera vida musical en Barcelona*, 108–18. Barcelona: Libreria Dalmau, 1944.

Llopis, Arturo. "El recuerdo de Enrique Granados. Un aniversario: 24 de marzo de 1966." *La vanguardia española*, March 24, 1966, 37.

———. "Muerte y recuerdo de Enrique Granados." 1957 [clipping from unknown newspaper, in Mm, fons Granados], 20.

Locke, Ralph P. "Cutthroats and Casbah Dancers." In *The Exotic in Western Music*, ed. Jonathan Bellman, 104–36. Boston: Northeastern University Press, 1998.

"Londres." *Revista musical catalana* 11 (1914): 256–65.

Longland, Jean Rogers. "Granados and the Opera *Goyescas*." *Notes Hispanic* 5 (1945): 94–112.

Lopez, Rosa Angelica. "Granados' *Escenas Románticas*: Its Romantic Sources and Progressive Features." DMA diss., University of Texas, Austin, 1982.

Luca de Tena, Cayetano. "Pequeña historia del año 1891." *Blanco y Negro* 79 (November 1, 1969): 35–130.

Luna, Juan J., and Priscilla E. Muller. *De Goya a Zuloaga: la pintura española de los siglos XIX y XX en The Hispanic Society of America*. Madrid: BBVA, 2000.

M. "Gazeta de teatres" [review of *Gaziel*]. *La veu de Catalunya*, October 29, 1906, 2.

M.J.B. "Teatro del Tívoli: 'María del Carmen.'" *La vanguardia*, June 1, 1899, 5.

Mackenzie, Compton. *Greek Memories*. Frederick, Md.: University Publications of America, 1987.

Madariaga, Salvador de. *Spain: A Modern History*. New York: Frederick A. Praeger, 1958.

Madriguera, Paquita. "Enrique Granados." *Clave: Voz de la juventud musical Uruguaya* 43 (1961): 16–20.

———. "Teatro del Tívoli: La interpretación de *María del Carmen*." *La vanguardia*, June 3, 1899, 3.

———. *Visto y oído: La estrella del alba*. Buenos Aires: Editorial Nova, 1947.

Malats, Joaquím. "María del Carmen." *La música ilustrada hispano-americana* 2/13 (June 25, 1899): 5.

Manén, Juan. "Tres impresiones: Manén, Millet, Salvat." *Revista musical hispano-americana* 3 (April 30, 1916): 18.

Mantecón, Juan José. "Un recuerdo: Granados en el Ateneo." *Revista musical hispano-americana* 3 (April 30, 1916): 14–15.

Marco, Tomás. *Spanish Music in the Twentieth Century*. Trans. Cola Franzen. Cambridge, Mass.: Harvard University Press, 1993.

Márquez Villanueva, Francisco. "Literary Background of Enrique Granados." Paper read at the "Granados and *Goyescas*" Symposium, Harvard University, January 23, 1982.

Martínez Ruiz, José (Azorín). *Castilla*. 7th ed. Buenos Aires: Editorial Losada, 1969.

———. *Madrid*. Intro., notes, and biblio. José Payá Bernabé. Madrid: Biblioteca Nueva, 1995.

Martinotti, Sergio. "Note critiche su Granados." *Chiagana* 34 (1967): 131–41.

Mas-López, Edita. "Apeles Mestres: Poetic Lyricist." *Opera Journal* 13–14 (1980–81): 24–33.

Mason, A. L. "Enrique Granados." *Music and Letters* 14 (July 1933): 231–38.

Maurer, Christopher, ed. *Federico García Lorca: Collected Poems*. Rev. bilingual ed. New York: Farrar, Straus and Giroux, 2002.

McCully, Marilyn. Introduction to *Homage to Barcelona: The City and Its Art, 1888–1936*, 15–78. London: Arts Council of Great Britain, 1985.

McGrigor, Albert. "The Catalan Piano School." Liner notes for *The Catalan Piano Tradition*. Catalog No. IPA 109. International Piano Archives. New York: Desmar, 1970.

Mestres, Apeles. "En la mort de l'Enric Granados." *Revista musical catalana* 13 (1916): 186.

———. "Enric Granados: Notes íntimes." *El teatre català* 5/216 (April 15, 1916): 137–39.

———. *Volves musicals*. Barcelona: Salvador Bonvía, 1927.

Millet, Lluís. "Enric Granados: Notes íntimes." *El teatre català* 5/216 (April 15, 1916): 139.

———. "Granados." *Revista musical catalana* 13 (1916): 187.

———. "Tres impresiones: Manén, Millet, Salvat." *Revista musical hispano-americana* 3 (April 30, 1916): 18.

Milton, John. *The Fallen Nightingale*. Edina, Minn.: Swan Books, 2004.

Miró, Gabriel. "El dedo de Dios." *Revista musical catalana* 13 (1916): 184.

———. "Los huérfanos de Granados." *La esfera* 3/131 (July 1, 1916): 15–16.

Montoliu, Manuel de. "A la memoria de Enrique Granados." *Diario de Barcelona*, February 13, 1957, 3.

Montoriol-Tarrés, E. "Enric Granados." *Revista musical catalana* 13 (1916): 196.

Montsalvatge, Xavier. "Enrique Granados (1867–1916): un aspecto del modernismo en Cataluña." *Revista del occidente* 20 (1968): 95–105.

———. "En silueta: Enrique Granados." *La vanguardia española*, November 15, 1961, 32.

———. "Una importante obra de Enrique Granados, inédita." *Destino*, April 16, 1955, 33–34.

Moragas, Rafael. "Los crimenes de la Alemania del Kaiser los repite ahora la Alemania de Hitler." *El día gráfico*, March 24, 1938, 8.

———. "*María del Carmen* del compositor Enrique Granados," part 1, *El día gráfico*, November 30, 1938, 6; part 2, December 1, 1938, 6.

———. "Música i musiqueta" [review of *Follet*]. *Pèl & Ploma* 4 (1903): 142–44.

———. "Records d'Enric Granados." *Mirador*, December 5, 1935, 8.

Morrison, Bryce. "Granados: The Complete Piano Music of Granados Recorded for CRD by Thomas Rajna." *Musical Opinion* 99 (1976): 203–4.

Muñoz, Eduardo. "Teatro de Parish: *María del Carmen*." *El imparcial*, November 13, 1898, 2.

N.N.N. "Teatros" [review of *Picarol*]. *La Esquella de la Torratxa* 23/1155 (March 1, 1901): 169.

———. "Teatros" [review of *Follet*]. *La Esquella de la Torratxa* 25/1266 (April 10, 1903): 233.

———. "Teatros" [review of *Gaziel*]. *La Esquella de la Torratxa* 28/1453 (November 2, 1906): 732.

Nash, Mary. *Defying Male Civilization: Women in the Spanish Civil War*. Denver: Arden Press, 1995.

"Necrología." *Revista musical catalana* 13 (1916): 139–40.

"New Grenados [*sic*] Opera; Mme. Barrientos' Debut Here." *New York Herald*, January 30, 1916, 11.

Newman, Ernest. "The Granados of *Goyescas*." *Musical Times* 58 (August 1, 1917): 343–47.

Nin, Joaquín. "Evocaciones sobre Enrique Granados." *Revista musical hispano-americana* 3 (May 31, 1916): 2–5.

"Notas artísticas." *Catalunya artística* 1 (1900): 246.

"Noves" [review of *Follet*]. *Joventut* 4/165 (April 9, 1903): 256.

"Noves." *Revista musical catalana* 2 (1905): 88.

"Noves." *Revista musical catalana* 6 (1909): 120.

"Noves." *Revista musical catalana* 7 (1910): 109.

Oliver, Amy A. "The Construction of a Philosophy of History and Life in the Major Essays of Miguel de Unamuno and Leopoldo Zea." Ph.D. diss., University of Massachusetts, 1987.

"Opera in Spanish, First Sung Here, Fails to Impress." *World*, January 29, 1916.

"Orfeó Català: Concerts de Quaresma." *Revista musical catalana* 7 (1910): 55.

Orpheus. "El mestre Pedrell i el seu deixeble Granados." *El teatre català* 5/216 (April 15, 1916): 136–7.

Ortega y Gasset, José. *Papeles sobre Velázquez y Goya*. 2d ed., rev. Ed. Paulino Garagorri. Madrid: Alianza Editorial, 1987.

P [Joaquím Pena?]. "Crónica musical: varias." *Joventut* 2 (1900): 53.

P del O. "Crónica" [review of *María del Carmen*]. *La Esquella de la Torratxa* 21/1065 (June 9, 1899): 362–63.

Packard, Dorothy Ream. "Searching Spain for Background Color." *Clavier* 6/7 (October 1967): 24–26.

Pagès i Santacana, Mònica. *Acadèmia Granados-Marshall: 100 anys d'escola pianística a Barcelona*. In Catalan, Spanish, and English. Barcelona: Acadèmia Marshall, 2000.

Pahissa, Jaume. "Enric Granados: Notes biogràfiques." *El teatre català* 5/216 (April 15, 1916): 140–41.

"Palacio de Bellas Artes" [review of *Liliana*]. *La vanguardia*, July 10, 1911, 4.

Palau, Enric. "La tràgica mort d'Enric Granados." *La nau*, March 24, 1928, 5.

Pangloss. Untitled review. *La publicidad*, March 15, 1911, 4.

Parakilas, James. "How Spain Got a Soul." In *The Exotic in Western Music*, ed. Jonathan Bellman, 137–93. Boston: Northeastern University Press, 1998.

Pardo Bazán, Emilia. *La vida contemporánea (1896–1915)*. Madrid: Editorial Magisterio Español, 1972.

Partridge, Roland Edward. "Enrique Granados." Master's thesis, Boston University, 1930.

Pedrell, Felipe. "La personalidad artística de Granados." In his series *Quincenas musicales. La vanguardia*, probably 1916 [undated clipping in the Am]. Revision of an earlier article with the same title that appeared in *Revista musical catalana* 13 (1916): 173–74.

Peers, Edgar Allison. *Catalonia Infelix*. Westport, Conn.: Greenwood Press, 1970.

Pellicer, Alexandre Cirici. "Wagnerisme i modernisme." In *Wagner i Catalunya. Antologia de textos i gràfics sobre la influència wagneriana a la nostra cultura*, 171–75. Barcelona: Edicions del Cotal, 1983.

Pena, Joaquím. "Musichs que fugen." *Joventut* 3/121 (June 5, 1902): 383–85.

———. "Teatres: Liric-Catala" [review of *Picarol*]. *Joventut* 2/52 (February 7, 1901): 166–67.

Penfield, Wilder G. "Some Personal Experiences in the Sussex Disaster." *Princeton Alumni Weekly* 16/29 (1918): 680.

Pérez Gutiérrez, Mariano. "The Interaction between Iberian and European Music in the Nineteenth Century." In *Welttheater: Die Künste im 19. Jahrhundert*. Ed. Peter Andraschke and Edelgard Spaude, 35–48. Freiburg: Rombach Verlag, 1992.

Periquet, Fernando. "Apuntes para la historia de la tonadilla y de las tonadilleras de antaño." Paper read at the Ateneo in Madrid, May 26, 1913. N.p. Copy in Oc.

———. "'Goyescas': How the Opera was Conceived." Trans. S. de la Selva. *The Opera News* 7/12 (January 29, 1916): 4.

———. *Goyescas o Los majos enamorados*. Madrid: R. Velasco, 1916.

———. "La ópera española moderna: 'Goyesca.'" *The World's Work: La revista del mundo* (April 1916): 178–82.

———. "Un concierto en el mar." *Lira española*, May 1, 1916.

Persia, Jorge de. *En torno a lo español en la musica del siglo XX*. Granada: Diputación de Granada, 2003.

Peterson, H. C. *Propaganda for War: The Campaign for American Neutrality, 1914–1917.* 1936; reprint, Port Washington, N.Y.: Kennikat Press, 1968.

Peyser, Herbert F. "Granados Here for Production of *Goyescas*." *Musical America* 23 (December 25, 1915): 3–4.

Pfeffer, Wendy. *The Change of Philomel: The Nightingale in Medieval Literature*. New York: Peter Lang, 1985.

Pfeifer, Ellen. "Boston Concert Opera: Granados's *Goyescas*." *High Fidelity/Musical America* 32 (1982): 32.

Phillips, Harvey E. "Reports: New York" [review of *Goyescas*]. *Opera News* 33 (May 17, 1969): 24.

Pillois, Jacques. "Un entretien avec Granados." *S.I.M. Revue musicale* 10, suppl. 1–4 (1914): 1–4.

Plana, Alexandre. "'Liliana' a Belles Arts (L'espectacle)." *El poble català*, July 12, 1911, 1.

Planes, Ramon. *El mestre Morera i el seu món*. Barcelona: Editorial Pòrtic, 1972.

———. *El modernisme a Sitges*. Barcelona: Editorial Selecta, 1969.

"Poet & Piano." *MD: Medical Newsmagazine* 11/12 (December 1967): 185–93.

Powell, Linton E., Jr. "Guitar Effects in Spanish Piano Music." *Piano and Keyboard*, n180 (May–June 1996): 33–37.

———. *A History of Spanish Piano Music*. Bloomington: Indiana University Press, 1980.

R.G. "'María del Carmen', de Granados." *Mirador*, December 5, 1935, 8.

R.R.M.C. "Obres liriques de Granados sobre textos d'Apel·les Mestres." *Revista musical catalana* 6/54 (April 1989): 28.

R.V. "La ópera 'Goyescas.'" *La esfera* 3/117 (March 25, 1916): n.p.

"Rehearsal of *Goyescas*." *New York Herald*, January 27, 1916, 13.

Reibold, Hélène. "Enrique Granados." *La vie musicale* 7 (May 1914): 128–34.

"Revista de Espectáculos" [review of *Liliana*]. *Diario de Barcelona*, July 10, 1911, 9345–46.

"Revista de Madrid" [review of *María del Carmen*]. *Diario de Barcelona*, November 20, 1898, 12618.

Riera, Juan. *Enrique Granados (Estudio)*. Lérida: Instituto de Estudios Llerdenses, 1967.

Risler, Edouard. "Una carta d'en Risler a n'en Granados." *Revista musical catalana* 2 (1905): 109.

Riva, Douglas. "El Llibre d'Apunts d'Enric Granados." *Revista de Catalunya*, n28 (January 1989): 89–106.

———. "The *Goyescas* for Piano by Enrique Granados: A Critical Edition." Ph.D. diss., New York University, 1982.

———. "Granados, Enrique." *Diccionario de la música española i hispanoamericana*. Ed. Emilio Casares. Madrid: Sociedad General de Autores y Editores, 1999–2002.

———. "Master Class: A Newly Discovered Mazurka by Granados." *Keyboard Classics: The Magazine You Can Play* (January/February 1985): 20–22, 38–39.

———. Program Notes. *Ciclo Granados*, Fundación Juan March, Madrid, February–March 1996.

Roca y Roca, J. "La semana en Barcelona" [review of *Follet*]. *La vanguardia*, April 12, 1903, 4.

Rodrigo, Antonio. "Conchita Badia entre Granados y Pau Casals." *Historia y vida* 10/117 (December 1977): 84–93.

Rodríguez, Melcior. "Teatro Tívoli." *La Renaixensa—Diari de Catalunya*, June 2, 1899, 3468–69.

Roe, Susan. "The Opera *Goyescas* by Enrique Granados: An Investigation of Stylistic Influences and Performance Practice with Concentration on Tableau III." DMA diss., University of California, Los Angeles, 2004.

Rómulo. "María del Carmen." *Las noticias*, June 2, 1899, 1.

Rostand, Claude. "Une grande première: *Goyescas* de Granados." *Disques* 58 (1953): 438–39.

Rubinstein y España. Madrid: Fundación Isaac Albéniz, 1987.

Ruiz Tarazona, Andrés. *Enrique Granados: El último romántico*. Madrid: Real Musical, 1975.

Saint-Saëns, Camille. "Carta de M. Saint-Saëns." *Revista musical hispano-americana* 3 (April 30, 1916): 4.

"Sala Granados" [review of *Elisenda*]. *Revista musical catalana* 9 (1912): 195–96.

Salazar, Adolfo. "'Goyescas' y el 'color local.'" *Revista musical hispano-americana* 3 (April 30, 1916): 9–10.

Salter, Lionel. "Granados as Pianist." *Pianola Journal*, n10 (1998): 54–60.

———. "Spain: A Nation in Turbulence." In *The Late Romantic Era: From the Mid-19th Century to World War I*, ed. Jim Samson, 151–66. Englewood Cliffs, NJ: Prentice Hall, 1991.

Salvador, Miguel. "Granados." *Revista musical hispano-americana* 3 (April 30, 1916): 2, 22–23.

Salvador, Miguel. "The Piano Suite *Goyescas* by Enrique Granados: An Analytical Study." DMA essay, University of Miami, 1988.

Salvat, Joan. "Enric Granados: Notes biogràfiques." *Revista musical catalana* 13 (1916): 197–207.

———. "Tres impresiones: Manén, Millet, Salvat." *Revista musical hispano-americana* 3 (April 30, 1916): 18.

Samulski-Parekh, Mary M. V. "A Comprehensive Study of the Piano Suite 'Goyescas' by Enrique Granados." DMA thesis, University of Missouri, Kansas City, 1988.

Saperas, Miquel. *El mestre Enric Morera*. Andorra la Vella: Editorial Andorra, 1969.

Schonberg, Harold C. "Colorful World of Old Spain." *New York Times*, March 15, 1969.

———. "Goya Captured in Music." *New York Times*, November 26, 1967.

Schuessler, Annemarie. "An Introduction to the Three Stylistic Periods in the Piano Works of Enrique Granados y Campiña." DM lecture-recital, Northwestern University, 1985.

Sempronio. "La cosas, como son: Granados, recordado por su hija." *Diario de Barcelona*, January 19, 1957, 4.

Senyol, E. "La música de 'Blancafor [sic].'" *La veu de Catalunya*, February 1, 1899, 1.

Shilkret, Nathanial. *Nathanial Shilkret: Sixty Years in the Music Business*. Ed. Niel Shell and Barbara Shilkret. Lanham, Md.: Scarecrow Press, 2005.

"Sinfónica de Madrid." *Revista musical catalana* 12 (1915): 179.

Smith, Anthony. *Nationalism: Theory, Ideology, History.* Cambridge: Polity Press, 2001.

Smith, Carleton Sprague. Preface to *Granados and Goyescas: Catalogue of an Exhibition Honoring Enrique Granados and the American Premiere of Goyescas.* The Spanish Institute, May 27–July 9, 1982. New York: Spanish Institute, 1982.

Solà-Morales, Ignasi de. "Modernista Architecture." In *Homage to Barcelona: The City and Its Art, 1888–1936,* 115–32. London: The Arts Council of Great Britain, 1985.

Sopeña Ibáñez, Federico. *Historia de la música española contemporánea.* Madrid: Rialp, 1958.

Sturman, Janet. *Zarzuela: Spanish Operetta, American Stage.* Urbana: University of Illinois Press, 2000.

Suárez Bravo, F. "Concierto Granados." *Diario de Barcelona,* March 13, 1911, 3398–99.

———. "'Follet': Drama lírico de A. Mestres y E. Granados." *Diario de Barcelona,* April 6, 1903, 4267–69.

———. "Orquesta Sinfónica de Madrid." *Diario de Barcelona,* May 27, 1915, 6667–69.

———. "Teatro del Tívoli." *Diario de Barcelona,* June 2, 1899, 6137–39.

———. "Teatro Lírico: Primer concierto clásico." *Diario de Barcelona,* May 16, 1900, 5896–97.

———. "Teatro Principal: Primer concierto Granados." *Diario de Barcelona,* March 2, 1906, 2668–69.

Subirá, José. "El compositor Enrique Granados en Madrid." *Diario de Barcelona,* February 15, 1957, 3.

———. "En memoria de Enrique Granados." *Música* 1/5 (May–June 1938): 5–37.

———. *Enrique Granados: Su producción musical, su madrileñismo, su personalidad artística.* Madrid: Zoila Ascasíbar, 1926.

———. "Granados tonadillero." *Revista musical hispano-americana* 3 (April 30, 1916): 16–17.

———. *La tonadilla escénica, sus obras y sus autores.* Barcelona: Editorial Labor, 1933.

Sutcliffe, W. Dean. *The Keyboard Sonatas of Domenico Scarlatti and Eighteenth-Century Musical Style.* Cambridge: Cambridge University Press, 2003.

"Tasques d'hivern." *Revista musical catalana* 5 (1908): 169–70.

Taylor, Robin. "Enrique Granados: Goyescas." Master's thesis, San Jose State University, 1976.

"Teatre del Bosch." *Revista musical catalana* 3 (1906): 170.

"Teatre Principal" [review of *Gaziel*]. *Revista musical catalana* 3 (1906): 192.

"Teatres y Concerts" [review of *Gaziel*]. *El poble català,* October 28, 1906, 3.

"Teatro de Parish: *María del Carmen.*" *La época,* November 13, 1898, 1.

"Teatro Lírico" [review of *Blancaflor*]. *La vanguardia,* January 31, 1899, 6.

"Teatro Principal" [review of *Gaziel*]. *La vanguardia,* October 28, 1906, 9.

"Teatros" [review of *María del Carmen*]. *El correo español,* November 14, 1898, 3.

"Teatros y artistas" [review of *Gaziel*]. *Noticiero universal,* October 29, 1906, 2.

"Teatros y conciertos: Barcelona." *Musical Emporium* 6/51 (January 1913): 5.

"Teatros y conciertos: Madrid." *Musical Emporium* 6/58 (October 1913): 3.

"Teatros y conciertos: Madrid." *Musical Emporium* 9/77 (March–April 1916): 3.

"Teatros y conciertos: Madrid." *Musical Emporium* 9/78 (May–June 1916): 3.

Tinterow, Gary, and Geneviève Lacambre. *Manet/Velázquez: The French Taste for Spanish Painting.* New York: Metropolitan Museum of Art, 2003.

Tintorer, Emili. "Teatres: Liric-Catala" [review of *Picarol*]. *Joventut* 2/52 (February 7, 1901): 165–66.

Tomlinson, Janis A. *Francisco Goya: The Tapestry Cartoons and Early Career at the Court of Madrid.* Cambridge: Cambridge University Press, 1989.

Torrents, Ricard. "Verdaguer, culmainació i contradicció de la Renaixença." In *La Renaixenca, cicle de conferencies fet a la Institució cultural del CIC de Terrassa, curs 1982/83,* 39–50. Barcelona: Publicaciones de l'Abadia de Montserrat, 1986.

Torres, Jacinto. "Cien años del Concurso de Piano del Conservatorio: Los *Allegro de Concierto* de Granados y Falla." *Música: Revista del Real Conservatorio Superior de Música de Madrid,* n10 (2003): 277–86.

———. *Las publicaciones periódicas musicales en España (1812–1990): Estudio crítico-bibliográfico.* Madrid: Instituto de Bibliografía Musical, 1991.

Torrellas, Albert. *Diccionario enciclopédico de la música ilustrado.* 2 vols. Barcelona: Central Catalana de Publicaciones, 1927–29.

Tortella, Gabriel. *The Development of Modern Spain: An Economic History of the Nineteenth and Twentieth Centuries.* Cambridge, Mass.: Harvard University Press, 2000.

Trend, J. B. *Manuel de Falla and Spanish Music.* New York: Knopf, 1929.

Turina, Joaquín. "Sobre Granados." *Revista musical hispano-americana* 3 (April 30, 1916): 7–8.

Turner, J. Rigbie. "Nineteenth-Century Autograph Music Manuscripts in the Pierpont Morgan Library: A Check List," *19th-Century Music* 4 (1980–81): 49–76.

Unamuno, Miguel de. *En torno al casticismo.* Ed. Francisco Fernández Turienzo. Madrid: Ediciones Alcalá, 1971.

"Una nova sala de concerts." *Revista musical catalana* 9 (1912): 24.

"Una producció notable" [review of *Dante*]. *Revista musical catalana* 5 (1908): 119.

[Untitled]. *Diario de Barcelona,* April 10, 1886, 4202.

[Untitled]. *Diario de Barcelona,* November 2, 1899, 12065.

[Untitled]. *Diario de Barcelona,* December 6, 1899, 13498.

[Untitled]. *Diario de Barcelona,* April 3, 1908, 4157–58.

Urrecha, Federico. "Crónicas menudas" [review of *Gaziel*]. *El diluvio,* November 1, 1906, 14.

Valls, Manuel. "Granados, encara una sorpresa." *Guia musical,* n12 (April 15, 1982): 2.

Vernon, Grenville. "New York Hears Its First Spanish Opera." *The Opera News* 7/13 (February 5, 1916): 2–3, 5.

Vila San-Juan, Pablo. "Los cuatro pianos de Enrique Granados." *La vanguardia española,* March 24, 1966, 48.

———. *Papeles íntimos de Enrique Granados.* Barcelona: Amigos de Granados, 1966.

Vilar, Pierre. *Spain: A Brief History.* Trans. J. B. Tate. Oxford: Oxford University Press, 1967.

Villalba, Luis. *Enrique Granados: Semblanza y biografía.* Madrid: Imprenta Helénica, 1917.

———. "Una impresión sobre Granados." *Revista musical hispano-americana* 3 (April 30, 1916): 11–12.

Villar, Rogelio. "El estreno de Goyescas." *La esfera* 3/108 (January 22, 1916): n.p.

———. "Granados." *La revista de música* 3/4 (October 1929): 227–29.

———. "Granados pianista." *Revista musical hispano-americana* 3 (April 30, 1916): 10–11.

Vincent, Mary, and R. A. Stradling. *Cultural Atlas of Spain and Portugal.* Abingdon: Andromeda Oxford, 1995.

Viñes, Ricardo. "Granados íntimo: recuerdos de su estancia en Paris." *Revista musical hispano-americana* (1916): 2–6.

Vives, Amadeu. "N'Enric Granados i l'edat d'or: Evocació." *Revista musical catalana* 13 (1916): 175–83.

———. "Palabras de Vives [open letter to Rogelio Villar]." *Revista musical hispano-americana* 3 (April 30, 1916): 18–22, 23.

Waldmann, Susann. *Goya and the Duchess of Alba.* Munich: Prestel, 1998.

Walthew, Richard H. "Enrique Granados: 1867–1916." *Musical Observer* 19/3 (1920): 14–15.

Walton, David. "Two Last Journeys: Enrique Granados and the 'Sussex.'" *Newsletter of the Iberian and Latin American Music Society,* n18 (Autumn 2004): 5–6.

Webber, Christopher. *The Zarzuela Companion.* Lanham, Md.: Scarecrow Press, 2002.

Weinstock, Herbert. "America." *Opera* 20 (1969): 497–98.

Wilson, Charles. "The Two Versions of 'Goyescas.'" *Monthly Musical Record* 81 (October 1951): 203–7.

"Wilsons Give Musicale: Distinguished Assembly Includes about 300 Guests." *Washington Post*, March 8, 1916, 4.

Wolfe-Ralph, Carol Anne. "The Passion of Spain: The Music of Twentieth-Century Spanish Composers with Special Emphasis on the Music of Enrique Granados." DMA diss., University of Maryland, 1995.

Wyers, Frances. *Miguel de Unamuno: The Contrary Self.* London: Tamesis Books, 1976.

X. "Gazeta Musical" [review of *Follet*]. *La veu de Catalunya*, April 5, 1903, 2.

X. "Sala Granados." *Revista musical catalana* 9 (1912): 51.

X. "Una nova sala de concerts." *Revista musical catalana* 9 (1912): 24.

Xarau [Santiago Rusiñol]. "Glosari" [review of *Liliana*]. *L'Esquella de la Torratxa* 33/1698 (July 14, 1911): 442 (pictures of costumes on p. 435 of this issue).

Z. "Sala Granados." *Revista musical catalana* 12 (1915): 184.

WORKS INDEX

GENERAL INDEX